CATHOLIC SOCIAL TEACHING

CATHOLIC SOCIAL TEACHING

LEARNING & LIVING JUSTICE

MICHAEL PENNOCK

ave maria press · notre dame, indiana

The Ad Hoc Committee to Oversee the Use of the Catechism, National Conference of Catholic Bishops, has found this catechetical text, copyright 2007, to be in conformity with the *Catechism of the Catholic Church*.

Nihil Obstat: The Reverend Michael Heintz
                    Censor Liborum

Imprimatur: The Most Reverend John M. D'Arcy
                    Bishop of the Diocese of Fort Wayne–South Bend
Given at Fort Wayne, IN, on 14 February 2006.

The *Nihil Obstat* and *Imprimatur* are official declarations that a book or pamphlet is free of doctrinal or moral error. No implication is contained therein that those who have granted the Nihil Obstat and Imprimatur agree with its contents, opinions, or statements expressed.

Scripture texts in this work are taken from the *New American Bible with Revised New Testament and Revised Psalms* © 1991, 1986, 1970 Confraternity of Christian Doctrine, Washington, D.C., and are used by permission of the copyright owner. All rights reserved. No part of the *New American Bible* may be reproduced without permission of the copyright owner.

English translation of the *Catechism of the Catholic Church* for the United States of America copyright © 1994, United States Catholic Conference, Inc.—Libreria Editrice Vaticana. Used with permission.

Theological Consultant:
William M. Lies, C.S.C.
Director, Center for Social Concerns
Professor of Political Science
University of Notre Dame, Notre Dame, IN

Other references cited as Notes with each chapter.

Founded in 1865, Ave Maria Press is a ministry of the Indiana Province of Holy Cross.

www.avemariapress.com

ISBN-10: 1-59471-102-X   ISBN-13: 978-1-59471-102-2

Project Editor: Catherine M. Odell

Cover design by John Carson

Interior text design by Brian C. Conley

Photography: **Associated Press**: Page 45, 113, 127, 128, 156, 178, 183, 185, 187, 188, 192, 193, 2239, 205, 222 © *Associated Press* / **Brian Atkinson/Global Aware**: Page 62 © *Brian Atkinson* / **Corbis**: Page 10, 11, 21, 38, 40, 46, 54, 57, 58, 65, 78, 86, 91, 103, 109, 123, 139, 149, 152, 177, 181, 191, 211, 241 © *Corbis* / **Design Pics**: Page 60, 61, 67 / **The Image Works**: Page 102, 174 © *The Image Works Archives* / **Skjold Photographs**: Page 47 © *Skjold Photography* / **Thomas Merton Center**: Page 190. *Photograph of Thomas Merton by John Lyons. Used with permission of the Merton Legacy Trust and the Thomas Merton Center at Bellarmine University.* / **Picturequest**: Page 9, 31, 48, 53, 63, 75, 83, 150, 173, 186, 195 / **Veer**: Page 23

Printed and bound in the United States of America.

I DEDICATE THIS BOOK TO FOUR MEN WHOSE LIVES HAVE INSPIRED ME. ALL OF THEM WERE CALLED FRANCIS. IT IS THEIR NAME I PROUDLY BEAR FOR MY MIDDLE NAME.

TO SAINT FRANCIS OF ASSISI, THE PATRON SAINT OF CATHOLIC ACTION AND ECOLOGISTS, FOR HIS SIMPLICITY OF LIFE AND AUTHENTIC, PEACEFUL LIVING OF THE GOSPEL IN HARMONY WITH GOD'S BEAUTIFUL CREATION;

TO SAINT FRANCIS XAVIER, THE PATRON SAINT FOR MISSIONARIES, FOR HIS ZEAL IN PREACHING THE GOSPEL AGAINST TERRIFIC OBSTACLES AND HIS WILLINGNESS TO OFFER HIS LIFE FOR HIS LORD;

TO SAINT FRANCIS DE SALES, THE GENTLEMANLY PATRON SAINT OF WRITERS, FOR HIS PASTORAL CARE OF SOULS AND HIS BELIEF THAT THE PEN WINS CONVERTS THROUGH GENTLE PERSUASION;

TO FRANCIS ARTHUR PENNOCK, MY FATHER, WHO DIED SHORTLY BEFORE I BEGAN WORK ON THIS BOOK. HIS DEEP DEVOTION TO MY MOTHER, HIS LOVE FOR HIS CHILDREN, HIS FIDELITY TO HIS JOB AND HIS CHURCH, HIS SIMPLE AND UNPRETENTIOUS WAYS, HIS LOVE OF THE BLESSED MOTHER—ALL THESE HAVE INSPIRED ME TO CONTINUE TO WORK AT MY VOCATIONS OF HUSBAND, FATHER, GRANDFATHER, AND RELIGIOUS EDUCATOR.

ENGAGING MINDS, HEARTS, AND HANDS

An education that is complete is one in which the hands and heart are engaged as much as the mind. We want to let our students try their learning in the world and so make prayers of their education.

FR. BASIL MOREAU,
FOUNDER OF THE CONGREGATION OF HOLY CROSS

IN THIS TEXT, YOU WILL FIND:

a wealth of up-to-date information on moral and ethical issues facing society today

prayerful reflections and references to contemporary and classical Catholic Social Teaching

hands-on applications that encourage you to make a difference in the world

CONTENTS

1   CATHOLIC SOCIAL JUSTICE: AN OVERVIEW   9

2   JUSTICE AND VIRTUES   29

3   JUSTICE AND SOCIETY   53

4   JUSTICE AND THE RIGHT TO LIFE   75

5   JUSTICE AND PREJUDICE   101

6   JUSTICE AND RACISM   123

7   JUSTICE AND POVERTY   145

8   JUSTICE AND PEACE   173

9   JUSTICE AND WORK   203

10   JUSTICE AND THE ENVIRONMENT   229

APPENDIX   CATHOLIC HANDBOOK FOR FAITH   250

GLOSSARY   273

INDEX   275

SCRIPTURE INDEX   279

CATECHISM OF THE CATHOLIC CHURCH INDEX   281

CHAPTER OVERVIEW

Your Catholic Faith and Social Justice
Catholic social teaching is a body of doctrine that the Church has developed with the Holy Spirit's guidance to apply the gospel to our life together as one human family.

Principles of Catholic Social Teaching
The main principles of Catholic social teaching are rooted in the "life and dignity of the human person."

How Christians View the Human Person
Christians look to Jesus as the source and knowledge of what it means to be human.

Our Rights as Humans
There are some rights that are universal, inviolable, and inalienable. The flip side of rights is responsibilities.

More On Human Rights
Examine the issue of pornography in light of the fundamental dignity afforded the human person and personal freedom associated with many rights.

Blessed Mother Teresa of Calcutta
Mother Teresa had the utmost respect for the basic human dignity of each person.

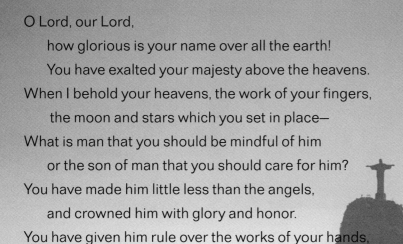

O Lord, our Lord,

how glorious is your name over all the earth!

You have exalted your majesty above the heavens.

When I behold your heavens, the work of your fingers,

the moon and stars which you set in place—

What is man that you should be mindful of him

or the son of man that you should care for him?

You have made him little less than the angels,

and crowned him with glory and honor.

You have given him rule over the works of your hands,

putting all things under his feet.

—Psalm 8:2; 4–7

1

CATHOLIC SOCIAL JUSTICE: AN OVERVIEW

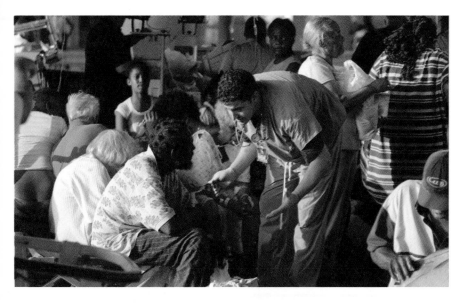

YOUR CATHOLIC FAITH AND SOCIAL JUSTICE

Have you ever been cheated, lied to, or treated unfairly?

Have you ever wondered what kind of person would willfully start a forest fire that results in the loss of human and animal life and millions of acres of land?

What do you think when you see on television the results of a mindless terrorist car bombing that killed scores of innocent people, including children, and maimed dozens of others?

What thoughts go through your mind when you read accounts of how people are denied their basic human rights simply because of the color of their skin?

If any of these questions touch you, then you instinctively have a strong sense of justice, of basic fairness, of fundamental human rights, of the dignity of people.

You belong to a faith community, the Catholic Church, that has a profound message of good news for people and how they should treat one another. We believe in, and share with our world, the gospel of Jesus Christ. This gospel proclaims that human beings are made in

God's image and likeness, conformed to Christ Jesus who is "the image of the invisible God." Because God makes us in the divine image, we are beings of incomparable worth, endowed with a human soul with its two great powers—intellect and **free will**. Humans are the only beings that God created for our own sakes, destining us from our very conceptions for eternal happiness.

Human intellect enables us to recognize and understand God's command to do good and avoid evil. Free will enables us to choose good with the guidance of our conscience and to obey God's law of love. As we seek truth and goodness, we find our perfection and happiness. In a perfect world our intellects and wills would wholly be attuned to God's will.

However, as you know, our world is hardly perfect. **Original sin** has weakened us, inclining us to commit evil by making bad judgments and choosing lesser goods. It is for this reason that many injustices exist in today's world.

Consider these disturbing facts:

- Malnutrition, defined as the lack of some or all the nutritional elements necessary for human health, is responsible for the death of over five million children per year. Yet, the world produces enough food to feed everyone enough calories to sustain health and life.[1]

- Violence against women and girls is the most pervasive violation of human rights in the world today. For example, the vast majority of the more than one million children forced into prostitution each year are female, most of them from Asia.[2]

- Half the world—nearly three billion people—live on less than two dollars a day.[3]

- Over 46 million babies have been aborted in the United States of America since *Roe v. Wade* legalized abortion in 1973.[4]

free will—"The power, rooted in reason and will, . . . to perform deliberate actions on one's own responsibility" [CCC, 1731].

original sin—The state or condition of sin into which all generations of people are born since the time of Adam and Eve's turning away from God.

Despite statistics like these, and hundreds of others like them, we do not give up hope. As Catholics we proclaim that Jesus Christ has freed us from Satan and sin, giving us new life in the Holy Spirit. Baptism, and the other sacraments of initiation—Confirmation and the Eucharist—make us children of God. This adoption into God's family imparts in us the life of Christ and enables us to live morally. The life of Christ in us by the power of the Holy Spirit enables each of us to be agents of God's justice in the world. We are called by Jesus Christ to be part of the solution to a world that hungers for justice.

Consider the oft-told story of a sophisticated office worker who ran into an ill-clothed, hungry, and shivering child on a downtown street corner one cold February morning. The man became angry with this scene and said to God, "Why do you allow this to happen? Why don't you do something about it?"

Later in the day, while the man was still musing over that scene, God did reply, quite clearly: "In fact I did do something. I made you."

In *Catholic Social Teaching: Learning and Living Justice*, you will be called to recognize and name some of the injustice in our midst. You will also discover, in light of our Catholic faith and tradition, how to analyze some causes of injustice. Finally, you will learn how we, both as individuals and as a community of faith, should respond to injustice. In brief, this text is a primer on Catholic social justice, an essential and central part of our Catholic faith and life.

What do we mean by Catholic social justice teaching? Simply, the social justice teaching of the Church deals with that body of Church doctrine (teaching) that comes from what God reveals to us about the truth of human dignity, human solidarity, and the moral principles of justice and peace. This doctrine attempts to understand how societies work and then makes moral judgments about economic and social matters in light of revealed truth and the demands of peace and justice. Modern Catholic social teaching comes to us from a strong tradition of the writings of popes, especially since Pope Leo XIII (1878–1903). It also comes from council documents and the rich and varied statements of national conferences of Catholic bishops.

Catholic social justice finds its roots in the teachings of the Hebrew prophets who proclaimed God's special love for the poor and called God's Chosen People to be just, loving, and peace-filled. However, Catholic social justice flows primarily from the life and words of Jesus Christ, who came to proclaim the good news to the poor and to teach his followers how to recognize and respond to the least in our midst. The Lord is also bound to us in the Paschal Mystery—his life, death, and resurrection—and in the holy Eucharist.

Finally, Catholic social justice comes from reflecting on what God

POPE LEO XIII

11

CHRIST HAS NO BODY NOW ON
EARTH BUT YOURS,
NO HANDS BUT YOURS, NO FEET
BUT YOURS;
YOURS ARE THE EYES THROUGH
WHICH CHRIST'S COMPASSION
LOOKS OUT ON THE WORLD,
YOURS ARE THE FEET WITH WHICH
HE IS TO GO ABOUT DOING GOOD
AND YOURS ARE THE HANDS WITH
WHICH HE IS TO BLESS US NOW.
—SAINT TERESA OF AVILA (1515–1582)

dignity—The quality or state of being worthy, honored, or esteemed. Humans possess dignity because we are made in God's image and likeness, endowed with a spiritual soul. Therefore, we are valuable, worthy of honor and esteem, simply because we are so precious in God's eyes.

social justice doctrine—The body of Church doctrine that applies Jesus' gospel to our life together, that is, to society, its institutions, and its economic and political structures.

himself has revealed to us. Our God is a Trinity of persons. Therefore, God revealed that he has a communal and social nature. God the Father gives us his Son, Jesus Christ, and bestows on us the Holy Spirit, a gift of love. God is love. Love is relational. Made in God's image, we are to reflect God's love. We, and everyone else God created, have incomparable worth and dignity. We are God's family who live in community. We are to be other Christs in the world, reaching out to others—our brothers and sisters—to build a loving and just world.

Simply put, the teachings of the Church known as Catholic social justice doctrine are a body of doctrine that the Church has developed, with the Holy Spirit's guidance, to apply the gospel of Jesus Christ to our life together as members of one human family. It has three aspects:
1. It gives us principles for reflection.
2. It provides criteria for judgment.
3. It gives guidelines for action (CCC, 2423).

Why is it important for you to learn these principles, criteria, and guidelines of Catholic social justice? Because you are the Lord's presence in the world today—his loving hands, compassionate eyes, and voice that speaks out for the weak. He needs you and your wisdom and your youthful idealism to help him establish a just world. At Confirmation, you are called to be a "witness to all the world." Learning and living the Church's social teaching is a specific way you can witness to the Christian faith.

Make this prayer your own as you prepare to study the profound teaching of Catholic social justice:

May the Lord Jesus and his Holy Spirit burn within my heart. May I have the eyes to notice those in need. May I develop a keen mind to help understand how to respond to them. And may I have a courageous and compassionate heart to act on their behalf. Amen.

WHAT DO YOU THINK?

We all know that life can be complex. For example, life is not always fair. For no apparent reason, some of us have it better than others. The following statements consider this observation in more detail. Check the column that best reflects your own view: **SA=strongly agree; A=agree; DK=I don't know what to think; D=disagree; SD=strongly disagree.**

Some Statements to Think About	SA	A	DK	D	SD
1. People with physical disabilities should be given special treatment in schools, stores, lines, parking lots, and the like.					
2. It is wrong for American corporations to outsource jobs to foreign countries to avoid paying high wages and health benefits to their American workers.					
3. Economically poor students who have received a substandard education should be given special consideration when they begin college.					
4. There are winners and losers. Winning is the only thing that counts.					
5. Society is still so tipped in favor of males that women must work much harder than men to get ahead in the professional world.					
6. People can get good, meaningful jobs if they put their minds to it.					
7. There is no reason ever to justify denying a person his or her God-given, "inalienable" rights.					

- Which of these statements are based on fact? Which are mere opinions?
- How are the statements in number 4 generally accepted by society?
- Give an example to support your response to statement 7.

PRINCIPLES OF CATHOLIC SOCIAL TEACHING

In their 1998 document, *Sharing Catholic Social Teaching: Challenges and Directions—Reflections of the U.S. Catholic Bishops*,[5] the American bishops highlighted seven principles that serve as the foundation of the Church's social teaching. Knowing and adopting these principles for our own lives can motivate us to action, help us to make correct choices, and ultimately lead us to be "principled" people in the area of social justice.

The purpose of the *Sharing Catholic Social Teaching* document is to alert Catholics to the fact that the Church's teaching on social justice—sometimes ignored—is an *essential* part of our Catholic faith. We must teach social justice. We must learn about social justice. We must put the principles of social justice into action if we are to be "good" Catholics and faithful followers of Jesus Christ.

To aid memory, the diagram below presents the principles of Catholic social justice in the form of an image—the wheel of justice. Think of the wheel as taking us on a journey. Our ultimate destination is God's kingdom. Along the way, there are obstacles. These include evils like poverty, prejudice, abortion, war, hunger, and so forth. The wheel of justice comes into play by rolling over these barriers leading us to God's kingdom. The principles on the wheel need to be applied to smooth out the road, to help us on our common task of working to bring about God's kingdom.

Sharing Catholic Social Teaching listed seven principles. Our wheel image divides the bishops' first principle—"life and dignity of the human person"—into two

principles: *dignity of the human person* and *respect for life*. The reason for this is to emphasize the inherent dignity of the human person as the foundational principle that leads first and foremost to the respect for human life, but to all the other principles as well. In other words, the hub of the wheel is human dignity—from it all other principles flow. We have dignity because we are made in God's image and likeness (the triangle in the hub represents the Triune God in whose image we are made). Human dignity means we have worth and value. This is why all the other principles that follow are true.

Our wheel also includes the principle of the *common good*, another principle that flows from and to the dignity of each person.

A brief introduction to each principle follows.

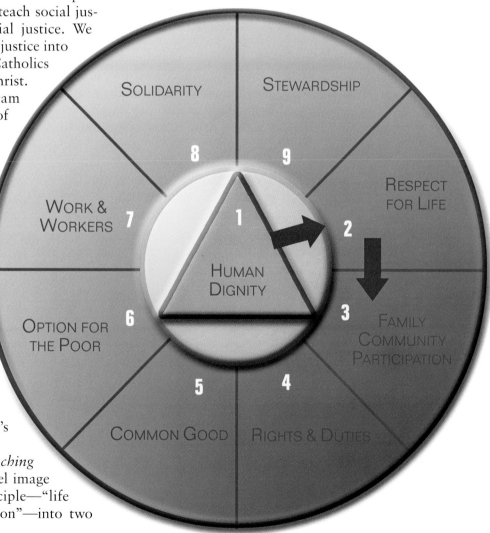

WHEEL OF JUSTICE: CATHOLIC SOCIAL JUSTICE THEMES

Dignity is defined as "the quality of being worthy of respect or esteem; inherent worth." Write a portrait of the person for whom you have the most respect. Share reasons why you especially esteem this person.

rights—Claims we can make on each other and on society to guarantee attaining certain basic minimum conditions to live a truly human life.

THE PRINCIPLE OF THE DIGNITY OF THE HUMAN PERSON

This foundational principle holds that every person—regardless of gender, race, age, nationality, religion, or economic status—deserves respect. Our dignity does not come from what we have or what we do; it comes from being God's special creation. As the document puts it, "Every human being is created in the image of God and redeemed by Jesus Christ, and therefore is invaluable and worthy of respect as a member of the human family" (*Sharing Catholic Social Teaching*, p. 1).

THE PRINCIPLE OF RESPECT FOR HUMAN LIFE

Every stage of a human's life—womb to tomb—is precious and worthy of our respect and protection. Unless human life is treated as sacred and respected as such, we simply cannot have a just society. According to the document: "Every person, from the moment of conception to natural death, has inherent dignity and a right to life consistent with that dignity" (*Sharing*, pp. 1–2).

THE PRINCIPLE OF THE CALL TO FAMILY, COMMUNITY, AND PARTICIPATION

The document lays out this principle: "In a global culture driven by excessive individualism, our tradition proclaims that the person is not only sacred but social. . . . The family is the central social institution that must be supported and strengthened, not undermined. . . . We believe people have a right and duty to participate in society, seeking together the common good and well-being of all" (*Sharing*, pp. 4–5).

Related to this principle, governments must guarantee and protect human life and dignity and promote the common good and the well-being of all citizens, especially the poor and weak among us.

THE PRINCIPLE OF RIGHTS AND RESPONSIBILITIES

The essential, fundamental right is the right to life—the right that makes all other **rights** possible. Every person also has a right to the necessities that make for human decency—faith and family life, food and shelter, education and a job, and health care. Rights have corresponding responsibilities to each other, to our families, and to the larger society. "The Catholic tradition teaches that human dignity can be protected and a healthy community can be achieved only if human rights are protected and responsibilities are met" (*Sharing*, p. 5).

THE PRINCIPLE OF THE COMMON GOOD

The common good includes the social conditions that permit people to reach their full human potential and to realize their human dignity. Three essential elements of the common good are respect for the person, the social well-being and development of the group, and peace and security. In our interdependent world, there is also a universal common good that requires international structures that can promote universal human development (see the Task Force "Summary" in *Sharing*, p. 25).

THE PRINCIPLE OF THE PREFERENTIAL OPTION AND LOVE FOR THE POOR AND VULNERABLE

The most basic human test answers this question: "How are our most vulnerable members doing?" Jesus taught in the story of the Last Judgment (Mt 25) that we must put the needs of the poor and vulnerable first. Why? Our response to our vocation in Christ and the common good requires that the powerless and the poor must be protected or society will fragment and all will suffer. The poor and vulnerable are our brothers and sisters. They deserve respect, the protection of their rights, the ability to participate and to share in God's good creation. In other words, they deserve justice.

THE PRINCIPLE OF THE DIGNITY OF WORK AND THE RIGHTS OF WORKERS

The economy must serve the people, not the other way around. Work helps us to make a living and to participate in God's creation. The dignity of work is safeguarded when workers' rights are respected. These rights include productive work, decent and fair wages, union participation, private property, and economic initiative. "Respecting these rights promotes an economy that protects human life, defends human rights, and advances the well-being of all" (*Sharing*, p. 5).

THE PRINCIPLE OF SOLIDARITY

We are members of the same human family. Therefore, the principle of solidarity reminds us "that we are our brothers' and sisters' keepers, wherever they live. . . . 'Loving our neighbor' has global dimensions in an interdependent world" (*Sharing*, p. 5). Catholic teaching requires us to commit ourselves to the common good—the good of each and every person. Why? As Pope John Paul II wrote, "Because we are all really responsible for all" (*On Social Concern*, §38). Above all, the virtue of solidarity requires us to work for peace and justice in the world marked by violence and war.

THE PRINCIPLE OF STEWARDSHIP

As the document puts it, "We are called to protect people and the planet, living our faith in relationship with all of God's creation" (*Sharing*, p. 6). In short, we respect our loving Creator by being good stewards of the earth.

In addition to these nine principles, two others appear frequently in Catholic social justice documents. First, the principle of equality holds that although people have different talents, we are essentially equal because of our fundamental dignity as God's children made in his image and likeness. Therefore, any form of discrimination or prejudice that contradicts the rights that flow from this equality is unjust.

Second, the principle of subsidiarity deals with "the responsibilities and limits of government, and the essential roles of voluntary organizations" (*Sharing*, p. 6). It teaches that the lowest level of an organization should handle a function if it is capable of doing so without the higher level intruding. The idea is that individuals or groups are closer to problems that affect them and should be given the first opportunity to solve them without higher levels (e.g., the government) intruding.

In whatever way we organize and name the fundamental principles of Catholic social justice, it is important always to keep in mind the relationship of each principle to human dignity. As the bishops point out:

These principles build on the foundation of Catholic social teaching: the dignity of human life. This central Catholic principle requires that we measure every policy, every institution, and every action by whether it protects human life and enhances human dignity, especially for the poor and vulnerable (Sharing, *p. 6*).

HOW CHRISTIANS VIEW THE HUMAN PERSON

Abba—An Aramaic term of endearment that means "papa" or "dada." Jesus taught us that God is a loving and compassionate Father (Abba) whom we can and should approach with faith and trust.

Write your own definition of what it means to be human.

There are many definitions of what it means to be human. Here is a sampling:

Man, when perfected, is the best of animals, but, when separated from law and justice, he is the worst of all.
—ARISTOTLE

How beauteous mankind is!
O brave new world
That has such people in't!
—WILLIAM SHAKESPEARE

You have created us for Yourself, and our heart is not quiet until it rests in You.
—SAINT AUGUSTINE OF HIPPO

Every man has a wild beast within him.
—FREDERICK THE GREAT

Man's the bad child of the universe.
—JAMES OPPENHEIM

Man is Heaven's masterpiece.
—FRANCIS QUARLES

Man is an exception, whatever else he is. If he is not the image of God, then he is a disease of the dust.
—G. K. CHESTERTON

Our view of how humans should act depends on how we see ourselves. If we see ourselves as the "bad child of the universe," then perhaps we won't be too concerned about acting maturely and responsibly. On the other hand, if we see ourselves as created in the image of God, then we know we are called to reflect all the marvelous qualities of the Creator.

Christians look to Jesus Christ as the source of true knowledge of who we truly are and who we are called to be. Jesus has revealed us to be magnificent creatures of a loving **Abba**, a Father who created us out of love for love. This loving Father has proved our worth by sending his Son, the Lord Jesus, to live among us as a friend, instruct us on the meaning of life and love, save us from our sins, and win for us eternal life through his death and resurrection.

This passage from the first creation story reveals several important traits of what it means to be human:

Then God said: "Let us make man in our image, after our likeness. Let them have dominion over the fish of the sea, the birds of the air, and the cattle, and over all the wild animals and all the creatures that crawl on the ground."
God created man in his image;
in the divine image he created him;
male and female he created them.
God blessed them, saying: "Be fertile and multiply; fill the earth and subdue it" (Gn 1:26–28).

IN GOD'S IMAGE AND LIKENESS
(CCC, 1700–1715; 1929–1938; 1943–1945)

The Genesis creation account reveals the spectacular truth that each of us is made in God's image. This bedrock truth is the foundation of Catholic social teaching. It has many implications, including those that follow.

Each human being has tremendous dignity. God's image is reflected in each person. This fact makes us worthy of profound respect from the very first moment of our existence.

Each human being is a child of God. If God is our Father, then we are brothers and sisters to one another.

We are special in God's eyes. As the saying goes, "God does not make junk." Each of us reflects God's glory, his goodness, his love. Each of us is fundamentally good and worthwhile. Each of us has special talents and a unique way of reflecting God's image.

We have rights and responsibilities. A right is a claim we can make on each other and on society for certain basic minimum conditions. The most basic right from which all others flow is the right to life. It is God who gives this right and all others. For every right there is a corresponding responsibility.

We have a spiritual nature. We possess a spiritual and immortal soul that has two powers: an intellect (that allows us to think) and free will (that allows us to choose and to love). This spiritual nature makes us unique among all of God's creations. Our intellect and free will give us the ability to do right, to discover and choose God's will for our lives.

God made us for himself. Because God shared his life with us by endowing us with a spiritual soul, he calls us to himself. He wants us to be one with him forever, a life of blissful joy with the Blessed Trinity. We look to Jesus Christ, God's only Son and our Savior, as the model on how to live loving, holy lives of serving others on our journey to God.

We possess freedom; we must use it responsibly. Free will, "the power, rooted in reason and will. . . . to perform deliberate actions on one's own responsibility" (CCC, 1731), is a wonderful gift. But this freedom is not absolute. It must be used for good and just causes, otherwise we sin. Also, our free will cannot be exercised in isolation. It must be acted on in relationship with others. With every free choice is a corresponding responsibility.

We are social beings. God did not intend for man or woman to live alone (Gn 2:18). God made us with and for others. God's very nature is community. God is a Trinity of Persons—a holy family of relationships—Father, Son, and Holy Spirit.

We image God best when we love one another. We grow as humans in a community that loves. In a special way, we must look out for and respond to the needs of our weakest members, we must have a "preferential love for the poor."

God made us co-creators with him. We find meaning, develop our potential, and glorify God when we cooperate with his plan of creation.

We are not God. The Genesis account makes it clear that God is God and we are not. We are his creatures. We are not the Creator. When humanity forgets this truth, it sins.

We are wounded by sin and inclined to evil and error. Genesis 2:15–3:24 reports the unhappy consequence of Adam and Eve's original sin of disobedience. Both as individuals and as societies, we often fail to do the good that we intend to do. We are weak and inclined to commit sin. As individuals we commit sin. And our sins sometimes develop into structures of sin that create unjust societies, ones that especially hurt the weak and defenseless. We need a savior to help show us the way to be the children of God we are meant to be.

GOD'S ATTRIBUTES

List five qualities that you have learned are essential characteristics or attributes of God. Some examples would be: loving, compassionate, creative, just, beautiful, intelligent, understanding, and so forth. Then write an example from your own life of how you "image" each of these divine qualities.

FROM THE DOCUMENTS:

THE DIGNITY OF THE PERSON IS MANIFESTED IN ALL ITS RADIANCE WHEN THE PERSON'S ORIGIN AND DESTINY ARE CONSIDERED: CREATED BY GOD IN HIS IMAGE AND LIKENESS AS WELL AS REDEEMED BY THE MOST PRECIOUS BLOOD OF CHRIST, THE PERSON IS CALLED TO BE A "CHILD IN THE SON" AND A LIVING TEMPLE OF THE SPIRIT, DESTINED FOR ETERNAL LIFE OF BLESSED COMMUNION WITH GOD. FOR THIS VERY REASON EVERY VIOLATION OF THE PERSONAL DIGNITY OF THE HUMAN BEING CRIES OUT IN VENGEANCE TO GOD AND IS AN OFFENSE AGAINST THE CREATOR OF THE INDIVIDUAL.

—POPE JOHN PAUL II, *CHRISTIFIDELES LAICI*, 5[6]

WHAT JESUS REVEALS ABOUT BEING HUMAN

In the life of man, God's image shines forth anew and is again revealed in all its fullness at the coming of the Son of God in human flesh. "Christ is the image of the invisible God" (Col 1:15), he "reflects the glory of God and bears the very stamp of his nature" (Heb 1:3). He is the perfect image of the Father. —The Gospel of Life, §36

For Christians, no picture of the human person is adequate without looking to Jesus Christ. He has much to reveal about who we are and how we should treat each other. Jesus reveals our true identity as God's children. Among the other truths Jesus taught are the following:

We are saved sinners. God so loves us that he sent his Son to live with us, to teach us, to guide us, to show us how to live, how to be just, how to love (see Jn 3:16). Jesus Christ freely gave up his life so we can have eternal life. His passion, death, and resurrection have liberated us from sin, delivered us from the power of Satan, and bestowed on us a new life in the Holy Spirit. God's grace given at Baptism makes us adopted members of the divine family. The Father and the Son give us the gift of the Holy Spirit who dwells within us. The Holy Spirit guides us to live loving and just lives as God intends. The Lord continues to show his love by coming to us in the Eucharist. We are not alone in our quest to do God's will for us. God himself is with us.

We are called to be compassionate as Jesus was compassionate. Jesus' mission in life was to reveal God's compassion (see Lk 4:18-19). Jesus revealed in his own words and deeds that God is a compassionate God, a God who cares for, gives life to, tenderly embraces, and warmly accepts everyone. In short, our vocation is to be like Jesus, our Savior.

We are friends of the Lord. Consider the good news of Jesus calling us his friends. What tremendous worth we have. What great value Jesus sees in us. He relates to us as a special friend by revealing his Father to us. He invites us to call God Abba, papa, and to trust in Abba's love and mercy. God's love is unconditional and always faithful. The Lord Jesus is the one friend who will never let us down. He is the friend who gave up his life for us so that we might live forever.

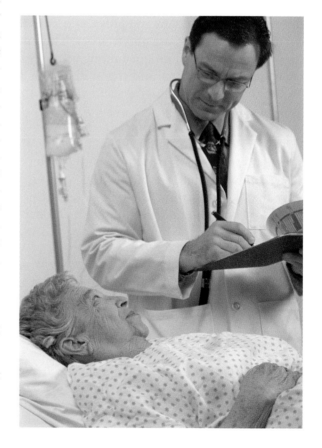

The Lord asks for one thing in return—that we love. Love is the heart of Christian morality. When we love, we are most human. Love guarantees that we are always just to our brothers and sisters: We treat them with respect. We honor their rights. We see that they get what they deserve as God's children. Love also means treating the neighbor as another self, even to the point of sacrificing the way Jesus did for us. And love means especially that we respond to those with whom Jesus so strongly identified: the weak in our midst. The friend of Jesus takes very seriously Jesus' teaching about his standard for judging whether we are worthy to join him in heaven or not:

And the king will say to them in reply, "Amen, I say to you, whatever you did for one of these least brothers of mine, you did for me" (Mt 25:40).

"THE GLORY OF GOD IS A HUMAN PERSON FULLY ALIVE."

—SAINT IRENAEUS (ca.125–202)

Find a picture in a magazine of a person who seems to you to be fully alive. Be prepared to explain to a classmate what quality this "fully alive" person possesses that glorifies God.

SCRIPTURE LINK

The Old Testament reveals many attributes of God. Read about these attributes in the passages indicated. Then, answer each question.

Read Genesis 17:1–9: A God of covenant
1. What does God promise to Abraham?
2. What does he promise to the people?

Read Exodus 3:7–14: A compassionate God
3. What injustice is God responding to?
4. How does he propose to respond to it?
5. What does he reveal about his name?

Read Exodus 22:20–26: A lover of justice
6. List three unjust practices forbidden by God.

Read Isaiah 1:1–20: A just God
7. Describe the mood of the prophet.
8. Why won't God hear the prayers of the Israelites?
9. What is the remedy to this hapless situation?

Read Isaiah 61:1–11: A God of justice and peace
10. List three things Yahweh's agent will accomplish.

PRAYING THE PSALMS

The Psalms, called the masterwork of prayer in the Old Testament (CCC, 2596), are also essential to the prayer life of Christians. They include hymns or prayers of thanksgiving, lamentation, and praise. They express the heartfelt emotions of the psalmist including expressions of grief, fear, repentance, confidence, and humility. They often speak of God's marvelous deeds in human history.

Prayerfully read Psalm 103, a psalm of praise of God's goodness. This psalm also reveals that God is a God of justice.

After your prayer, write a verse in the style of Psalm 103 that praises God for some marvelous deed he has accomplished in your life.

OUR RIGHTS AS HUMANS *(CCC, 1944–1947)*

Read 1 Corinthians 12:4–31. Summarize the meaning of this passage.

encyclical–A pastoral papal letter sent to the whole Church, and sometimes to all people, on some important aspect of Church teaching.

Peace on Earth (Pacem in Terris)–An important social justice encyclical written by Pope John XXIII in 1963 that lists important human rights.

Related to the principle of human dignity is the principle of rights and responsibilities. A right is a claim we can make on other people and on society so we can live a full, human life. We do not have to earn rights. They are due us because we are made in God's image and likeness.

There are some rights that are universal, inviolable, and inalienable. *Universal* means that the rights are for every human being. *Inviolable* means that these rights are untouchable because they come from God. *Inalienable* means that these rights are inherent and beyond challenge. No one has authority to take them away because they are due us as children of God.

The flip side of rights is responsibilities. For every right we have, we have the duty to exercise it responsibly. We also have the duty to respect other peoples' rights.

In the **encyclical Peace on Earth** (1963), Pope John XXIII enumerated some of the fundamental human rights:

Right to Life "We see that every man has the right to life, to bodily integrity, and to the means which are suitable for the proper development of life; these are primarily food, clothing, shelter, rest, medical care, and finally the necessary social services. Therefore a human being also has the right to security in cases of sickness, inability to work, widowhood, old age, unemployment, or in any other case in which he is deprived of the means of subsistence through no fault of his own" (§11).

Moral and Cultural Rights "By the natural law every human being has the right to respect for his person, to his good reputation; the right to freedom in searching for truth and in expressing and communicating his opinions, and in pursuit of art, within the limits laid down by the moral order and the common good; and he has the right to be informed truthfully about public events (§12).

"The natural law also gives man the right to share in the benefits of culture, and therefore the right to a basic education" (§13).

Right to Worship God "This too must be listed among the rights of a human being, to honor God according to the sincere dictates of his own conscience, and therefore the right to practice his religion privately and publicly" (§14).

Right to Choose Freely One's State of Life "Human beings have the right to choose freely the state of life which they prefer, and therefore the right to set up a family, with equal rights and duties for man and woman, and also the right to follow a vocation to the priesthood or the religious life (§15).

"The family, grounded on marriage freely contracted, monogamous and indissoluble, is and must be considered the first and essential cell of human society. From this it follows that most careful provision must be made for the family both in economic and social matters as well as in those which are of a cultural and moral nature, all of which look to the strengthening of the family and helping it carry out its function (§16).

"Parents, however, have a prior right in the support and education of their children" (§17).

Economic Rights "If we turn our attention to the economic sphere it is clear that man has a right by the natural law not only to an opportunity to work, but also to go about his work without coercion (§18).

"The right to private property, even of productive goods, also derives from the nature of man" (§21).

The Right of Meeting and Association "From the fact that human beings are by nature social, there arises the right of assembly and association" (§23).

The Right to Emigrate and Immigrate "Every human being has the right to freedom of movement and of residence within the confines of his own country; and, when there are just reasons for it, the right to emigrate to other countries and take up residence there" (§25).

Political Rights "The dignity of the human person involves the right to take an active part in public affairs and to contribute one's part to the common good of the citizens" (§26).

As mentioned above, rights do not exist without corresponding responsibilities. For example, the right to life requires the duty to take care of and preserve one's own life. The right to a decent standard of living demands the right to a responsible lifestyle. The right to seek out the truth calls for the corresponding duty to search for truth. To claim one's rights while ignoring one's responsibilities diminishes the dignity of humans.

EXERCISE

Read Blessed Pope John XXIII's encyclical *Peace on Earth (Pacem in Terris)*. You can find it at the Vatican website (www.vatican.va) or other Catholic websites like the Office of Social Justice for the Diocese of St. Paul and Minneapolis (www.osjspm.org) or the Catholic Library at New Advent (www.newadvent.org).

Read sections 11–36 of this encyclical. List five rights discussed in this section of the encyclical. Then make a list of five responsibilities that correspond to each of these rights.

Right	Responsibility
1. _____	1. _____
2. _____	2. _____
3. _____	3. _____
4. _____	4. _____
5. _____	5. _____

With a classmate, compose a list of five student rights and their corresponding duties. Then, in a class discussion, share your lists and vote on what the class judges to be the five most important rights. Discuss these questions:
- How are these rights honored at your school?
- How do students routinely live up to their responsibility for each of their rights?
- If there are violations of rights, what can the school community do to remedy the situation?

MORE ON HUMAN RIGHTS

In his important encyclical on social justice, *On the Hundredth Anniversary of "Rerum Novarum"* (1991), commemorating one hundred years of papal social teaching, Pope John Paul II listed the following rights:

Among the most important of these rights, mention must be made of the right to life, an integral part of which is the right of the child to develop in the mother's womb from the moment of conception; the right to live in a united family and in a moral environment conducive to the growth of the child's personality; the right to develop one's intelligence and freedom in seeking and knowing the truth; the right to share in the work which makes wise use of the earth's material resources, and to derive from that work the means to support oneself and one's dependents; and the right freely to establish a family, to have and to rear children through the responsible exercise of one's sexuality. In a certain sense, the source and synthesis of these rights is religious freedom, understood as the right to live in the truth of one's faith and in conformity with one's transcendent dignity as a person (§47).

Compare this quote with the selections from Pope John XXIII above. Note two points Pope John Paul II stresses as key points of emphasis compared to the earlier document. Why do you think this is?

SHOULD PORNOGRAPHY BE ALLOWED? *(CCC, 2354)*

Two themes highlighted in this chapter are the fundamental dignity of the human person and personal freedom associated with many rights.

Examine the issue of the legalization of **pornography** related to these two themes.

Definition:

The original meaning of the word pornography is "writing about prostitutes." Today, we distinguish between "soft-core" and "hard-core" pornography. Soft-core pornography depicts nudity. Hard-core pornography engages in graphic sexual depictions of any kind. An important Church document entitled *Pornography and Violence in the Communications Media: A Pastoral Response*[7] describes pornography this way:

Pornography in the media is understood as a violation, through the use of audio-visual techniques, of the right to privacy of the human body in its male or female nature, a violation which reduces the human person and human body to an anonymous object of misuse for the purpose of gratifying lustful desires (§9).

Pros:

Those who support the legalization of pornography stress the right of humans to have freedom of expression in speaking, writing, publishing, painting, photography, film-making, on the Internet, and so forth. They fight any limitation on pornography because they fear it will limit artistic expression and access to truth. Further, they see efforts at censorship in this area as leading to the thwarting of unpopular views that need to be heard in a free society.

PORNOGRAPHY—THE depiction of sexual acts or nudity with the purpose of gratifying lustful desires. Pornography violates the privacy of the human body and debases human dignity by turning people into objects to be used rather than persons to be respected.

Cons:

Those who wish to ban pornography see it as a major threat to decency. They argue that words and images can be physically, psychologically, and spiritually harmful. They point to studies which demonstrate that viewing sexual material makes men more willing to be aggressive to women.[8] Also, they point out that pornography demeans its subjects—men and especially women. It disdains others as persons, treating them as objects for self-gratification. It undermines true sexual expression as a loving relationship between a husband and a wife. It encourages an unhealthy preoccupation in fantasy and behavior, stunting honest and mature relationships. It desensitizes people, making them morally numb by assaulting the dignity of all involved in its production, promotion, and consumption.

Further, opponents to pornography argue that the right to freedom of expression is not absolute. For example, no one has the right to yell "Fire" in a crowded theater when there is no fire.

Discuss and Debate:

* What would you define as "pornographic"? According to your definition, would anything on television or radio be considered pornographic?
* Take a side. Do you agree that pornography offends human dignity? Give examples to support your argument.

MAKING A DIFFERENCE

Activity 1

Internet pornography is a major social issue today and a gateway for sexual predators to seduce young people. A $57 billion industry worldwide ($12 billion in the United States), 12 percent of the websites on the Internet are pornographic. The average age for the first exposure to Internet pornography is eleven years old; the largest consumers of Internet porn are twelve- to seventeen-year-olds; and 90 percent of eight- to sixteen-year-olds have viewed porn online at one time or another, usually while doing homework.[9]

* Examine your school's policy on the use of the Internet. Identify what software is used to block undesirable websites. Note the penalties for abusing the school policy.
* Draw up a list of procedures you would use if you were parents who were responsible for monitoring the use of the Internet for your children, both pre-teens and teens.

Activity 2

In the pastoral *Reviewing the Mind of the Media*, the American bishops urge groups to develop a list of addresses, phone/fax numbers, and e-mail addresses of local media outlets in order to be able to protest offensive material and offer critique. As a class, or in several small groups, identify examples of how the media have offensively depicted the gift of human sexuality or promoted gratuitous violence. Then, contact the media outlet responsible and lodge a complaint.

Also, on a more positive note, identify some praiseworthy productions you have viewed recently and then contact the media outlet to express your gratitude.[10]

BLESSED MOTHER TERESA OF CALCUTTA (1910–1997)
EXEMPLAR OF LOVE

A compelling example of a person who recognized the basic dignity and goodness of each person was Mother Teresa of Calcutta. Such was her profound respect for others, that in her lifetime people of many faiths recognized her as a living saint.

Mother Teresa was born Agnes Gonxha Bonjaxhiu on August 26, 1910, in Albania. As a child she felt a desire to work for God. Her spiritual director assured her that she would know God was calling her if she felt joy with the idea of serving him in others. Agnes felt this joy and responded to the call by joining the Sisters of Our Lady of Loretto, a missionary order active in India. Agnes's training in religious life took place in Ireland where she took the name of Sister Teresa in memory of Saint Thérèse of Lisieux. When sent to India, Sister Teresa began her work by caring for the sick and starving and helpless mothers in a hospital run by her order. The endless misery she met in her first assignment greatly touched her.

Before long, Sister Teresa was sent to Calcutta to become a teacher. She became an effective and popular teacher and was eventually named principal of a high school for middle-class girls. However, close to this school was one of the great slums of Calcutta. Sister Teresa could not turn her eyes from the misery she found there. She continued to visit and minister to the poor in the slums and the hospitals, enlisting the help of her students in this precious work.

Eventually, Sister Teresa responded to a vocation within a vocation. God called her to minister to the poorest of the poor. She left her order, received some medical training, and began to work directly with the poor. Her good example drew others, including some of her former students, to help her in her work. By 1950 she had received permission to found a new religious order, the Missionaries of Charity. Besides taking the traditional religious vows of poverty, chastity, and obedience, the Missionaries take a fourth vow, service to the poorest of the poor. This marks their way to live and spread Christ's gospel— working for the salvation and sanctification of the poor.

Mother Teresa's unselfish work for the forgotten ones in society won her the Nobel Peace Prize in 1979. At the time of her death in 1997, the Gallup Poll reported that she was the most admired woman in the world. Her order had grown to serve the poor and suffering in many cities throughout the world: ministering to unwanted, abandoned babies; supporting unwed mothers; caring for dying AIDS patients; feeding the hungry; loving the unlovable. She was beatified on October 19, 2003.

Mother Teresa's motivation was simple. She taught by example that when we help and love a poor person we are helping and loving Jesus. God is not absent from our lives. He lives in our neighbor, most especially in those we tend to neglect and dislike.

The bottom line for Mother Teresa was that she had the utmost respect for the basic dignity of each person. In her many speeches around the world, she encouraged her listeners to do something beautiful for God. Every person, no matter how small, is a person of great dignity. Every person is Jesus-in-disguise.

Two quotes from Blessed Mother Teresa of Calcutta for busy teens to think about.

"Yesterday is gone. Tomorrow has not yet come. We have only today. Let us begin."

"There is a terrible hunger for love. We all experience that in our lives—the pain, the loneli-ness. We must have the courage to recognize it. The poor you may have right in your own family. Find them. Love them."

These quotes came from the Eternal Word Television Network website, where you can read more about this remarkable person.

- www.ewtn.com/motherteresa

Another good source for information about Mother Teresa is the official site for the cause of her canonization.

- www.motherteresacause.info

One of the most remarkable speeches ever addressed to officials of the United States government was delivered by Mother Teresa at the National Prayer Breakfast, February 3, 1994, sponsored by the United States Senate and House of Representatives. In this historic address, Mother Teresa spoke out for the dignity of all human life, but especially of the innocent lives of unborn babies. Read this speech at one of these websites:

- www.ewtn.com/New_library/breakfast.htm
- www.catholiceducation.org/articles/abortion/ab0039.html

Write in your journal the three most compelling lines that affected you the most. Compare your selections with those of a classmate.

CHAPTER SUMMARY

- Christian social teaching proceeds from the Church's faith in Christ and has been brought to life by charity. This body of teaching comes from reflecting on God's revelation of who we are and how we should act towards one another, especially in our social relationships. Guided by the Holy Spirit and passed on by the Church Magisterium, Catholic social teaching offers principles for reflection, criteria for judgment, and guidelines for action.

- Social justice is rooted in a correct, divinely revealed vision of the human person. This vision holds that we are made in God's image and likeness. Hence, we have tremendous dignity, are special in God's eyes, and are endowed with a spiritual nature that includes the powers to think and to choose. God made us for himself. He made us social beings, to be with and for other people, and co-creators with him in caring for the beautiful natural world. Because we are his children, we have fundamental rights that we do not have to earn, rights that we must use responsibly. Unfortunately, because of original sin, we are flawed creatures who can sin by misusing our freedom.

- Happily, Jesus has redeemed us from sin. He has given us the Holy Spirit, adopting us into the divine family. He calls us his friends and teaches by example how to be just and loving people. In short, the key to just Christian living is to be compassionate as Jesus and his Father are compassionate.

- No one but God bestows rights on us, that is, basic claims that we can make on others and society so we can live a human life. The fundamental right that must be respected is the right to life. Rights, however, must be exercised responsibly. And we have a duty to respect other people's rights as well.

Review Questions

1. What is the most pervasive violation of human rights worldwide today?
2. Where can we find Catholic social teaching?
3. What is Catholic social teaching? What are its three aspects?
4. List and briefly discuss nine principles of Catholic social teaching.
5. What does it mean to be made in God's image and likeness?
6. List two consequences of being made in God's image.
7. What powers does the human soul possess?
8. What does it mean to call humans "social beings"?
9. Explain how humans are flawed. Give three examples.
10. What does Jesus reveal about our true identity?
11. Explain what it means for you to be a friend of the Lord.
12. How does Jesus want us to manifest justice?
13. What is a right? Why are rights inalienable?
14. List ten human rights and a corresponding duty for each of the rights you list.
15. What is the fundamental human right? Why doesn't it have to be earned? Explain.
16. Does the media have the "right" to exhibit pornography without any limits? Why or why not?
17. Why does the Christian community consider Mother Teresa of Calcutta a model of justice?

RESEARCHING ON THE INTERNET

There is no doubt, however, that the document [Universal Declaration of Human Rights] represents an important step on the path towards the juridical political organization of all the peoples of the world. For in it, in most solemn form, the dignity of a human person is acknowledged to all human beings; and as a consequence there is proclaimed, as a fundamental right, the right of every man freely to investigate the truth and to follow the norms of moral good and justice, and also the right to life worthy of man's dignity, while other rights connected with those mentioned are likewise proclaimed.

— Pope John XXIII, Peace on Earth, §144

1. Search for and read the United Nations' Universal Declaration of Human Rights:
   - List five rights that you were not aware of before reading the Declaration.
2. Search and look up all of the following websites:
   United Nations High Commissioner for Human Rights (UNHCHR)
   United Nations High Commissioner for Refugees (UNHCR)
   UNICEF
   United Nations Development Program
   Amnesty International
   The International Committee of the Red Cross
   Human Rights Watch
   Based on information you find on these websites, do the following:
   What would you judge to be the most serious human rights crisis currently facing the world?

Gather five facts about this current crisis.

Locate a country where this crisis is taking place and note some basic facts about the demographics of this country.

3. Prepare a short report for your classmates. Locate the "World Service" pulldown from the BBC website (www.bbc.co.uk) and select one of the human rights issues from around the world discussed here. Write a research report on your findings.

PRAYER REFLECTION

Pray these words of Blessed Mother Teresa:

Dearest Lord, may I see you today and every day in the person of your sick, and, whilst nursing them, minister unto you.

Though you hide yourself behind the unattractive disguise of the irritable, the exacting, the unreasonable, may I still recognize you, and say, "Jesus, my patient, how sweet it is to serve you."

Sweetest Lord, make me appreciative of the dignity of my high vocation, and its many responsibilities. Never permit me to disgrace it by giving way to coldness, unkindness, or impatience. . . .[11]

NOTES

1. World Hunger Education Service, "World Hunger Facts 2004," <http://www.worldhunger.org/ articles/Learn/world%20hunger%20facts%202002.htm> (17 February 2005).
2. Charlotte Bunch, "The Intolerable Status Quo: Violence against Women and Girls," report found at UNICEF, "The Progress of Nations 1997."
3. Cited by Kofi Annan, the Secretary-General of the United Nations, in a speech given on the International Day for the Eradication of Poverty, 17 October 2000.
4. Statistics cited by National Right to Life.
5. National Conference of Catholic Bishops, *Sharing Catholic Social Teaching: Challenges and Directions—Reflections of the U.S. Catholic Bishops* (Washington, D.C.: United States Catholic Conference, 1998). The adaptation of the summary below was inspired by one of the consultants for the bishops in the writing of the document: William J. Byron, S.J. See his excellent article, "Building Blocks of Catholic Social Teaching," *America*, October 31, 1998, pp. 9–12.
6. *Christifideles Laici: On the Vocation and the Mission of the Lay Faithful in the Church and in the World.*
7. Pontifical Council for Social Communications, Vatican City, May 7, 1989, XXIII World Communications Day.
8. See Alice Leuchtag, "The Culture of Pornography," in *Taking Sides: Clashing Values in Crime and Criminology* (Guilford, CT: Dushkin Publishing Group/Brown & Benchmark Publishers, 1996), p. 135.
9. TopTen Reviews, Inc., "Internet Pornography Statistics."
10. Committee for Communications, United States Conference of Catholic Bishops, *Renewing the Mind of the Media* (Washington, D.C.: United States Catholic Conference, 1998).
11. Quoted in *The Book of Jesus*, edited by Calvin Miller (New York: Touchstone, 1998), p. 465.

CHAPTER OVERVIEW

You Can Make a Difference
A series of observations tells of the power of one.

Virtues
The Church distinguishes between two major categories of virtues: the theological virtues and the cardinal virtues.

Justice as a Virtue
The Catholic tradition defines four types of justice: commutative, distributive, legal, and social.

The Bible on Justice
The Old Testament and New Testament share the evolving story of God's justice for all people.

Catholic Social Teaching on Justice
Jesus' call to compassion is the root of the Church's modern teaching on justice.

Key Social Justice Documents: An Overview
Key Church social justice documents beginning with Rerum Novarum are chronicled.

Cesar Chavez
Cesar Chavez had unswerving devotion to justice issues related to his fellow farm workers.

You have been told, O man, what is good,
and what the Lord requires of you:
Only to do the right and to love goodness,
and to walk humbly with your God.

—Micah 6:8

2

JUSTICE AND VIRTUES

YOU CAN MAKE A DIFFERENCE

An anonymous author penned the following observations about the power of one:

One SONG *can spark a moment*
One FLOWER *can wake the dream*
One TREE *can start a forest*
One BIRD *can herald spring*
One SMILE *begins a friendship*
One HANDCLASP *lifts a soul*
One STAR *can guide a ship at sea*
One WORD *can frame the goal*
One VOTE *can change a nation*
One SUNBEAM *lights a room*
One CANDLE *wipes out darkness*
One LAUGH *will conquer gloom*
One STEP *must start each journey*

One WORD *must start a prayer*
One HOPE *will raise our spirits*
One TOUCH *can show you care*
One VOICE *can speak with wisdom*
One HEART *can know what is true*
One LIFE *can make a difference.*[1]

You can make a difference! And the prophet Micah tells us how: by doing good, that is, by exercising the virtues, especially the virtues of love and justice. Love is doing good for others, treating them as you would like to be treated. Justice is giving others their rights, being fair to them.

This chapter explores justice (and love) as a virtue related to the Church's social teaching, as well as the other cardinal and theological virtues.

WHAT DO YOU THINK?

Is this just or not? Benjamin Disraeli (1804–1881), a British writer and prime minister, once proclaimed, "I say that justice is truth in action." What do you think? Do the following practices ring true to you? Are they good examples of justice in action . . . or not? Check the column that best reflects your own personal view: **SA=strongly agree; A=agree; DK=I don't know what to think; D=disagree; SD=strongly disagree.**

Some Statements to Think About	SA	A	DK	D	SD
1. Citizens have the right to burn the American flag as an expression of free speech, for example, to protest what they believe is an unjust war.					
2. The children of undocumented workers should receive health-care benefits and free public education.					
3. Homosexual couples should have the right to adopt children.					
4. The social security system should reduce benefits by 20 percent to people over the age of sixty-five to help preserve the system for the generation of young people now in their teens.					
5. To save lives, states should continue to raise the driving age of teens and impose tougher requirements before they can obtain an unrestricted license.					
6. More tax credits in the form of family allowances should be awarded to people who earn wages at or below the minimum wage necessary to survive.					
7. Some type of national service should be required of every high-school graduate.					
8. People arrested as suspected terrorists should be subject to a more rigid justice system than ordinary criminals are.					

- How are all the items above social justice issues?
- Tell what makes a particular statement above either just or unjust.

VIRTUES (CCC, 1803-1845)

A **virtue** is a "habitual and firm disposition to do the good" (CCC, 1803). Under this definition, justice is a virtue.

Traditionally, the Church has distinguished between two major categories of virtues: the theological virtues and the **cardinal virtues**.

THE CARDINAL VIRTUES

Virtues make it possible for us to master ourselves so we can live good, moral lives more easily. The cardinal virtues are good habits that we can acquire by human effort. They help us cooperate with and respond to God's love for us. The four cardinal or "hinge" virtues are prudence, fortitude, temperance, and justice. Many other virtues derive from these four virtues. A brief description of the first three cardinal virtues follows.

Prudence is good common sense, human reason married to truth. Saint Thomas Aquinas called prudence "right reason in action" (CCC, 1806). Prudence helps us discover what is good in every situation and helps us choose the right ways of achieving it. A prudent person always seeks the most loving and just thing to do in a given circumstance.

Example: A young professional examines her buying habits to see if they make her a victim of consumerism and, therefore, less sensitive to the poor in our midst.

Fortitude gives us the firmness, strength, and courage to deal with temptations, difficulties, and dangers in doing what is right and true. Fortitude is spiritual "intestinal courage" to do what is right, helping us conquer fear, even of death, in defending a just cause (CCC, 1808).

Example: Even knowing you will be ridiculed, you decide to defend a person who is being badmouthed simply because the person looks or acts differently from the norm.

Temperance moderates the attraction of pleasures and provides balance in the use of created goods (CCC, 1809). God has given us many goods: for example, food, drink, sexual pleasure. Temperance is the virtue that enables us to control our appetites for these goods and use them in God-intended ways. We develop this virtue by acts of self-denial.

Example: A family decides to find more and better ways to recycle to help preserve the earth's goods for future generations.

List several ways you can exhibit each of these three cardinal virtues in your everyday life.

virtue—"Firm attitudes, stable dispositions, and habitual perfections of the intellect and will that govern our actions, order our passions, and guide our conduct according to reason and faith" (CCC, 1804).

cardinal virtues—"Hinge" virtues that enable us to live moral lives. Prudence is right reason in action, good common sense to discern the good and the ways to achieve it. Fortitude is the courage to persist in doing the good. Temperance regulates our sensual appetites. Justice enables us to render to God and each person what is their due.

theological virtues—God-given powers that direct us to our loving Triune God. Faith enables us to believe all that God has revealed, or his Church proposes for belief, because He is truth itself. Hope empowers us to trust in God's promises. Charity enables us to love God above all things and our neighbor as ourselves out of love of God.

commutative justice—Calls for fairness in exchanges between individuals and private groups.

distributive justice—Sees to the just distribution of the goods of creation that God intends for all to use and share.

legal justice—Regulates citizens' obligations to the larger society and government.

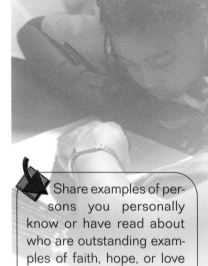

Share examples of persons you personally know or have read about who are outstanding examples of faith, hope, or love (charity).

THEOLOGICAL VIRTUES

The **theological virtues** are faith, hope, and charity. These three virtues are God-given, that is, they have as their origin, motive, and object God the Father, God the Son, and God the Holy Spirit. They relate directly to God and orient us to God. The cardinal and other virtues are rooted in these theological virtues, which are the very foundation of a Christian moral life. The theological virtues allow the Holy Spirit to live in and work through us. An explanation follows.

Faith empowers us to believe in God and all that God has said and revealed to us, including what the Church proposes for our belief, because God is truth itself (CCC, 1814). Faith is a gift from God that we must keep, live, profess, and spread.

Example: God reveals that all humans have profound dignity because we are made in his image. Therefore, all people are precious in God's eyes. You believe this truth because God has revealed it. Moreover, you decide to participate in a summer work camp week as a way to show your love and care for the poor.

Hope helps us desire heaven and eternal happiness, trusting firmly in Christ's promises and relying, not on our own efforts, but on the help and graces of the Holy Spirit (CCC, 1817). Hope gives us the strength to carry on as we help the Lord in his work of salvation.

Example: Despite never getting published, you continue to write pro-life letters to newspapers. You never give up trusting that the Lord Jesus is using you to help him to spread the good news of his kingdom—that God loves everyone, especially the most defenseless in our midst.

Charity or *love* enables us to love God above everything for his own sake and to love our neighbor as ourselves. Jesus makes charity his new commandment: "This I command you: love one another" (Jn 15:17). Out of love, Christ died for us. He told us to imitate his love, even to the point of loving our enemies and including everyone as our neighbor.

Charity is the most important virtue. Without it, Saint Paul tells us that we are nothing (see 1 Cor 13:2). It is the virtue that perfectly binds together all the virtues. We cannot work for justice without love. We cannot say we are just people if we are not first loving people.

Example: You have the talent and education to become very wealthy. Instead, you dedicate your life to teaching inner-city children to give them the opportunity to develop their talents and live fuller, happier lives.

JUSTICE AS A VIRTUE (CCC, 1928)

Injustice anywhere is a threat to justice everywhere.
—MARTIN LUTHER KING, JR.

Justice is the moral and cardinal virtue by which we give God and our neighbor what is their due by right. God made everything, including us, and out of love keeps us all in existence. For this reason it is only just to acknowledge God's goodness—to love God and worship him above everything.

Regarding our neighbors, justice "disposes one to respect the rights of each and to establish in human relationships the harmony that promotes equity with regard to persons and the common good" (CCC, 1807).

Our tradition distinguishes among four types of justice: commutative, distributive, legal, and social.

Commutative justice (CCC, 2411–2412) is the justice of exchange. It calls for fairness in agreements and exchanges between individuals or private social groups. It requires that we respect the equal human dignity of everyone in our economic transactions, contracts, or promises.

Put simply, commutative justice requires that you get what you pay for. It also obliges you to pay for what you get. For example, if a mother hires a babysitter to watch her toddler, then in justice the babysitter should do a good job of caring for the child and not spend the whole time on the phone talking to a friend. Similarly, the mother should pay the babysitter the agreed upon wage and not renege on her part of the agreement.

Commutative justice is based on *the principle of equality* between what is given and what is received. Out of common decency, it requires that we both respect the dignity of others and responsibly fulfill our obligations. Without commutative justice, a society could not function. It would be riddled with theft, fraud, and disregard for others and their property.

Distributive justice is justice that guarantees the common welfare. It involves sharing. Distributive justice sees to the just distribution of the goods of creation that God intends for us all to use and share.

The Second Vatican Council taught:

> God intended the earth with everything contained in it for the use of all human beings and peoples. . . . Thus, . . . attention must always be paid to this universal destination of earthly goods. . . . The right of having a share of earthly goods sufficient for oneself and one's family belongs to everyone. The Fathers and Doctors of the Church held this opinion, teaching that men are obliged to come to the relief of the poor and to do so not merely out of their superfluous goods (The Church in the Modern World, §69).

Basic human dignity requires that each person has a right to enough of the earth's goods to live a truly human life. Distributive justice guarantees that this right is recognized.

Because we belong to communities, we pass on to our governmental authorities the responsibility to make sure that everyone's basic needs are met. For example, a major reason we pay taxes is to guarantee that all citizens can get an education, have police and fire protection, have access to health care and disability compensation in times of forced unemployment, and the like. As social beings and members of God's family, we pay special attention to the weakest and poorest in our midst and make sure they are taken care of.

Legal justice is the flip side of distributive justice. Just as distributive justice concerns the obligations of the government to its citizens, legal justice relates to citizens' obligations toward the larger society and government. Legal justice requires that citizens obey the laws of society. Legal justice may also require that a citizen serve the government.

Social justice applies the gospel message of Jesus Christ to the structures, systems, and laws of society in

SURVEY OF OPINION ON PAYING TAXES

Interview three responsible, tax-paying Catholic adults. Let them know that you are learning about different types of justice, including distributive justice which requires citizens to share their wealth with others so that each person has enough for a decent human life. This is why governments tax their citizens, to guarantee certain basic rights for all people.

Ask them their opinions about the following:

- The fairness of the current federal graduated income tax.
- The fairness of the state and local tax systems.
- The morality of citizens protesting against the government by not paying their taxes.
- The morality of lying on tax returns.
- The kind of tax system they believe would be of most help to the poor (e.g., a national sales tax or a flat tax).

Summarize the opinions of your interviewees. Share your findings in a report to your classmates, offering your own opinion on what you would do in this situation.

In formulating your opinion on a fair tax structure, you might wish to research from the websites of the following organizations:

Citizens for Tax Justice

Center on Budget and Policy Priorities

United States Conference of Catholic Bishops (type "taxes" in search engine)

social justice—Applies the gospel of Jesus Christ to society's structures, systems, and laws so people's rights are guaranteed. Also known as contributive justice, it ensures that persons have a fair say in social, economic, and political institutions, thus fulfilling their duty to give back to the larger community.

• A high unemployment rate is the sign of an unjust society. Agree or disagree?

• What are the basic responsibilities of citizens in society?

order to guarantee the rights of individuals. Social justice is more than distributive justice. Social justice demands that everyone has a right to a fair say in the social, political, and economic institutions of society. Everyone, according to his or her ability, has the right to contribute to how society operates. Thus, social justice is also called *contributive justice.*

The American bishops in their pastoral letter on the economy, *Economic Justice for All,* put it this way:

Social justice implies that persons have an obligation to be active and productive participants in the life of society and that society has a duty to enable them to participate in this way. This form of justice can also be called "contributive," for it stresses the duty of all who are able to help create the goods, services, and other nonmaterial or spiritual values necessary for the whole community (§71).

In its most basic form, social justice recognizes that everyone has a right to be heard. Governments that do not allow people to participate according to their ability are unjust. Tyrannical governments that ignore or suppress their citizens' voices—especially their weakest members—are most unjust.

CHARITY AND JUSTICE COMPARED

Pope Pius XI taught that charity is the force that binds the minds and hearts of people. It is what promotes true peace and mutual help among men and women. However, charity must take justice into account. Pius XI wrote, "No vicarious charity can substitute for justice which is due as an obligation and is wrongfully denied" (*On Reconstructing the Social Order* [*Quadragesimo Anno*], §137).

The following chart indicates some differences between works of charity and the works of justice.[2]

Charity (Love) . . . . . Social Service Bible reference: Good Samaritan	**Justice . . . . . Social Change** Bible reference: Exodus story
This parable shows how the Samaritan gives temporary and prompt relief to the victim. It does not teach methods of coping with highway banditry.	Moses' message is "Let my people go." He challenges the very institution that oppresses the Chosen People. He does not look for temporary relief for the Jewish slave force.
Private, individual acts	Public, group actions
Responds to immediate needs	Addresses long-term needs
Provides direct service: food, shelter, clothing	Works to change institutions
Requires repeated actions	Resolves structural injustice
Directed at the symptoms of injustice	Directed at the root causes of injustice
Examples: homeless shelters, hunger kitchens, clothing drives, emergency relief	Examples: working to change laws, community organizing, changing the policies and practices of corporations

Read the following passages. In your journal, answer the questions that follow.

Read John 13:1–17

1. What is the basic meaning of this passage?
2. List three ways you can serve others.

Read Zechariah 7:9–14 and Isaiah 58:6–9

3. List four practices that just people will do.
4. What will happen if the people do not act in these ways?

Read Mark 2:1–12

5. How did Jesus cure the man's problem? How did Jesus cause the cure?

6. Is this an example of social change or social service?
7. List four sins in our world today that desperately need healing.

Read Matthew 14:13–22

8. What steps did Jesus take to solve the problem?
9. Is this an example of social change or social service as described above? Explain.
10. List three ways we can respond to the hungry in today's world.

THE BIBLE ON JUSTICE

To better understand the richness of justice, it is important to see how the Bible reveals its meaning.

The Bible has many profound ways to describe justice, for example that of a fast-moving stream rolling down the mountainside in Amos 5:24:

Let justice surge like water,
and goodness like an unfailing stream.

This mountain stream is meant to eradicate all injustice in its path—poverty, neglect of widows and orphans, discrimination against foreigners, and the like.

The Bible presents justice as a burning concern of God. Justice is not simply a balancing of the scales but a deep commitment to uphold a relationship. God made, formed, and loved his people. God revealed his justice by being faithful to them. Simply put, the biblical idea of justice involves fidelity to what relationships require. And God is always faithful.

The next sections point out some other images of justice found in the Bible.

JUSTICE IN THE OLD TESTAMENT

The Old Testament reveals that God formed a people from whom would come his own Son, the Messiah and our Savior. Yahweh-God entered into a **covenant** with Abraham, binding himself in an open-ended contract of love. God promised that he would be faithful to Abraham, blessing him with children, giving him a land, promising him descendants. For their part, God's people were to be faithful to the covenant, to obey God by living upright, just lives.

God proved himself just by blessing Abraham and the Chosen People and by keeping all his promises. Moreover, Yahweh defended his people by rescuing them from slavery in Egypt, freeing them from indignity and suffering. He sent the prophet Moses to lead his people to freedom:

But the LORD said, "I have witnessed the affliction of my people in Egypt and have heard their cry of complaint against their slave drivers, so I know well what they are suffering. Therefore I have come down to rescue them from the hands of the Egyptians and lead them out of that land into a good

American Images of Justice

Read and report on several images of justice described on this Supreme Court website:

www.supremecourtus.gov/about/figuresofjustice.pdf

COVENANT–An open-ended contract of love between God and his people. It involves promises and the duty to be faithful to the promises.

Read the Ten Commandments from Exodus 20:1–17. Note which commandments address:
- fidelity to God
- fidelity to neighbor
- fidelity to created goods

Read:
1. **Proverbs 21:13**
   Under what condition will God hear our prayers?
2. **Proverbs 31:8–9**
   What command is given here?
3. **Isaiah 10:1–2**
   What warning is given here?

and spacious land, a land flowing with milk and honey . . ." (Ex 3:7–8).

In return, the Israelites were to be faithful to God's covenant. Yahweh gave his people the Law, summarized in the Ten Commandments, which was a steady guide on how to live as God's people, a holy people. It spelled out the demands of a loving relationship with God, how to be faithful to a God who formed them and kept them in existence. In brief, the Commandments teach justice. And biblical justice is fidelity to God, neighbor, and to God's created goods.

However, the Old Testament reveals time and again how the Chosen People were unfaithful to God. They continually fell back into the worship of false gods. They continually acted selfishly toward foreigners, the weak in their midst, the poor.

Despite their infidelities, God did not abandon his Chosen People, although so many times they deserved to be punished. God sent prophets to hand out his justice. The prophet Isaiah said:

When you spread out your hands,
* I close my eyes to you;*
Though you pray the more,
* I will not listen.*
Your hands are full of blood!
* Wash yourselves clean!*
Put away your misdeeds from
* before my eyes;*
* cease doing evil; learn to do good.*
Make justice your aim: redress the
* wronged,*
* hear the orphan's plea, defend*
* the widow (Is 1:15–17).*

God's command to do justice is so eloquently repeated by the prophet Micah in this famous passage:

You have already been told what is right and what Yahweh wants of you.

Only this, to do what is right,
to love loyalty
and to walk humbly with your God (Mi 6:8, NJB).

JUSTICE IN THE NEW TESTAMENT

God never gave up on the Chosen People. God brought his covenant to fruition by sending his only Son, Jesus Christ. Jesus' life and death exemplify perfect fidelity. Jesus, God's new covenant with us, reveals justice-in-the-flesh.

In his words and in his actions, Jesus revealed God's true nature, one of love and compassion. Jesus preached the coming of the kingdom, one marked by justice. Quoting the prophet Isaiah, Jesus proclaims, "The Spirit of the Lord is upon me, because he has anointed me to bring glad tidings to the poor. He has sent me to proclaim liberty to captives and recovery of sight to the blind, to let the oppressed go free, and to proclaim a year acceptable to the Lord" (Lk 4:18–19).

Above all, Jesus' words and actions tell us that God's kingdom is marked by love, the most significant relationship of all. Jesus revealed the following:

Love for God and neighbor. New Testament justice is a command to love, to be like Jesus, even when it hurts. Jesus taught that love of God and love of neighbor as oneself are the Great Commandments (Mt 22:38–39):

"This is my commandment: love one another as I love you" (Jn 15:12).

The Beatitudes. Jesus taught that those who wish to embrace God's kingdom must live according to the Beatitudes he expressed at the Sermon on the Mount (Mt 5:1–12). For example, we must be poor in spirit, that is, humble people who put our trust in God and do not use possessions, prestige, prettiness, or power to act superior to others. We must be gentle people, ones who mourn for the sin and injustice in the world. We must hunger and thirst for righteousness (justice). We must show mercy, have a pure heart, work for peace, and accept suffering for the sake of God's kingdom. These attitudes of being Christ's disciples paint a wonderful portrait of a just person.

Respond to the least ones. In the parable of the goats and the sheep (Mt 25:31–46) we learn that our judgment is based on how we respond to the needs of the least in our midst: the hungry, thirsty, sick, and the like.

Embrace everyone. In the parable of the Good Samaritan (Lk 10:29–37), Jesus outlawed sexism, racism, nationalism, and any other "ism" that assaults a person's dignity. Jesus teaches that our neighbor is everyone.

Be compassionate. Jesus' parable of the day laborers (Mt 20:1–16) shows that God treats us in a way that differs from the world's standards. The laborers are paid not strictly according to their talents or what they produce but according to what they need. This seems illogical according to our notions of strict justice. But God's justice is theologic—God-logic. God values people, not what they produce.

Jesus' actions also show concretely how to be just, loving people. He exemplified God's compassion by seeking out the poor, the despised, those on the fringes. For example, he healed the sick. He associated with outcasts like sinners. He praised impoverished widows who gave all they had to God. He fed the hungry. He comforted the suffering. He forgave sinners ready to be stoned to death by the righteous.

Jesus' passion, death, and resurrection demonstrated in the most graphic way how God loves. With arms outstretched on a cross, dying next to two despised criminals, Jesus embraces everyone. He puts no conditions on his love because his heavenly Father loves, is compassionate towards, and desires the love of every single human being—"worthy" or not. Jesus' self-gift on the cross is a great act of justification; it saves us; it puts us in right relationship with God and with each other.

Throughout his ministry, Jesus formed a just community to carry on his work after his ascension into heaven. One criterion for membership into this community is that we must serve. Jesus reversed the human expectation of the first being first, and the last being last. He has given us strict orders:

"You know that those who are recognized as rulers over the Gentiles lord it over them, and their great ones make their authority over them felt. But it shall not be so among you. Rather, whoever wishes to be great among you will be your servant; whoever wishes to be first among you will be the slave of all" (Mk 10:42–44).

The key to working for justice is to serve as Jesus served. We who have been treated so well by God must imitate Jesus in our dealings with others on all levels:

- on the interpersonal level with family members and friends;
- in our dealings with those in groups to which we belong;

CHARITY IN ACTION

Read Saint Paul's great passage on love, 1 Corinthians 13. As Saint Paul writes, love (charity) is the greatest of all the virtues. When we practice it, we bring Jesus to others.

Make a plan to put Saint Paul's words into action. For the next week, do one or more of the following:

- Congratulate a classmate or teammate on a notable achievement.
- Help a younger brother or sister with their homework.
- Talk to your parents about your day. Ask them how their day went.
- Call up and chat with a grandparent.
- Eat lunch with a lonely classmate.
- Pray for a friend in need.
- Volunteer at a hunger center.
- Send a thank-you note.
- Run an errand for an elderly neighbor.
- Help out at a parish function, for example, as a teacher's aide in the parish school of religion.
- Take time to greet (and talk to) a school support staff member (for example, a secretary or custodian).
- Practice an act of courtesy (for example, holding a door open for someone; allowing another driver out of the parking lot before you; picking up trash around the school or neighborhood; etc.).

In your journal, jot some other ideas for how you can help someone this coming week. At the end of the week, write a reflection on how people reacted to your love and how you felt about putting your faith into action.

- in our participation in the various communities that count us as members (neighborhood, city, state, nation); and
- in our concern with people everywhere, even around the world.

As a wise person once remarked, "Service is the price we pay for the space we occupy." When we serve the cause of justice—of being faithful to our relationships—we are true disciples of Christ. Mother Teresa had it right in her famous statement, "God does not ask me to be successful, but to be faithful."

CATHOLIC SOCIAL TEACHING ON JUSTICE (CCC, 2419-2425)

The early Church took seriously Jesus' mandate to his followers to relate to others as brothers and sisters, taking special care to meet the needs of the poor and marginal. For example, the first Christians shared their property and goods (Acts 2:44–47), condemned selfishness (for example, 1 Cor 11:18–34), and encouraged generous sharing, especially when others were in need (2 Cor 8:1–15). Because of the Church's compassion, many were attracted to Christ and converted.

Down through the ages the Church has not ceased working for justice. It always had great saints and writers calling people back to the justice message of the gospel. For example, Saint Augustine of Hippo (354–430) wrote:

Do not grieve or complain that you were born in a time when you can no longer see God in the flesh. He did not in fact take this privilege from you. As he says, "Whatever you have done to the least of my brothers, you did to me."[3]

Or consider the observation of Church father, Saint Ambrose (340?–397):

You are not making a gift to the poor man from your possessions, but you are returning what is his. For what is common has been given for the use of all, you make exclusive use of it. The earth belongs to all, not to the rich.[4]

There were always great Christian heroes who dedicated their lives to the poor and needy. Saint Francis of Assisi (1182–1226), next to the Blessed Virgin the most popular Christian saint, stripped himself of his wealth to be free of its corrupting influence. He founded an order which dedicated itself to gospel simplicity and preached the gospel to the poor and ministered to their needs.

Other centuries brought other heroic examples of Christian love-in-action. For example, in seventeenth-century France, Saint Vincent de Paul (1581–1660) and Saint Louise de

SAINT VINCENT DE PAUL

Marillac (1591–1660) founded religious orders of women to serve the needs of the urban poor. In the early nineteenth century, Saint Elizabeth Ann Seton (1774–1821) and her Sisters of Charity began the Catholic school system in this country.

Despite the ebb and flow of history, the Church never neglected Jesus' call to compassion. As it became more organized, the Church established hospitals, homes for battered women, orphanages, a school system that educated the poor, homes for the aged and dying, and countless other institutions that address the needs of people. In fact, many of our contemporary human service agencies have their roots in the Church's mission to serve the needy. And this service continues today. For example, Catholic Charities is the largest private charitable organization in the United States. It raises countless millions of dollars to help meet people's basic needs so they might live in dignity.

SAINT LOUISE DE MARILLAC (1591–1660; FEAST DAY: MARCH 15)

Saint Louise was a trail-blazer in religious life when she founded in 1633, along with Saint Vincent de Paul, the first community of non-cloistered sisters, the Daughters of Charity.

Married to the secretary of the Queen of France, Louise socialized with the wealthy of France, but was also a servant to the poor when she took a leadership role in the Ladies of Charity, an organization of wealthy women who helped the poor. She had one son and devoted herself to his education during his childhood years.

After her husband died of a lengthy illness in 1625, her spiritual director, Saint Vincent de Paul, asked Louise to assist him with the Confraternities of Charity, which cared for destitute sick people in parishes throughout France. Through her association with these charities, Louise learned about the needs of the poor and developed the leadership skills that inspired her to train young women to help her serve the needy of her day. Thus, in 1633, she and Saint Vincent established the Daughters of Charity. This remarkable group of women, numbering 25,000 sisters, serve the needs of the Church and the poor to this day.

When Louise died on March 15, 1660 (a few months before the death of Saint Vincent de Paul), her community had established over forty hospitals, orphanages, and other institutions throughout France. She was proclaimed a saint in 1934, and Pope John XXIII named her the Patroness of all Social Workers in 1960. Her sacrificial life of serving others as a wife, mother, teacher, nurse, social worker, and foundress of a religious order provides a model of service to all Catholics and people of good will.

Saint Louise's words on serving poor people:

"As for your conduct toward the poor, may you never take the attitude of merely getting the task done. You must show them affection; serving them from the heart—inquiring of them what they need; speaking to them gently and compassionately; procuring necessary help for them without being too bothersome or too eager."[5]

Saint Vincent de Paul not only inspired Saint Louise to works of charity for the poor, but also Blessed Frédéric Ozanam, the founder of the Saint Vincent de Paul Society. Read about, and prepare a report on, the good works of this widely known organization. Search and use the websites of the Society of Saint Vincent de Paul and the International Council of the Saint Vincent de Paul Society.

MODERN TEACHING

More than a hundred years ago, the Church began to take a more vigorous approach in its official teaching to respond to social justice issues of the day. Historians trace the development of the Church's modern social teaching to Pope Leo XIII (1810–1903, pope from 1878–1903). Pope Leo XIII lived at a time when the ideas of Karl Marx (1818–1883) were gaining a strong following among the workers of the world. Marx was reacting to the abuses of *laissez-faire* capitalism, an unbridled economic system that so often exploited workers simply for profits. Industrial barons especially trampled on workers' rights. There was little or no social security system for retired workers. There was a lack of decent wages or working hours. Pensions, health insurance, collective bargaining opportunities, and so many other rights were unheard of. Marx preached revolt against these deplorable conditions. He claimed a workers' paradise, a utopia, would result from his ideas, labeled Marxism. In his view, the state would see to it that everyone would be treated equally.

Pope Leo XIII saw in *both* Marxism and unbridled capitalism tremendous dangers for the dignity of people. Marx's brand of socialism subordinated the individual to the state, thus destroying human dignity. Twentieth-century atheistic communism, a descendent of Marxism, took hold in the former Soviet Union and its satellite nations and proved the

pope's fears correct. In 1891, Pope Leo XIII wrote an encyclical entitled **Rerum Novarum** (*The Condition of Labor*) to condemn the abuses of both Marxist socialism and unbridled capitalism. This encyclical became a benchmark. Later popes used the anniversary of its publication to write their own encyclicals on social justice. Thus, Pope Pius XI wrote *Quadragesimo Anno* on the fortieth anniversary of *Rerum Novarum*, John XXIII wrote *Mater et Magistra* on the seventieth anniversary, Paul VI wrote *Octogesima Adveniens* on the eightieth anniversary, John Paul II wrote *Laborem Exercens* on the ninetieth and *Centesimus Annus* on the hundredth anniversary.

Since the publication of *The Condition of Labor* in 1891, popes in their encyclicals and speeches, synods of bishops in their statements, regional and national conferences of bishops and individual bishops in their pastoral letters have taught extensively on social justice themes. In addition, the Second Vatican Council had much to say about the dignity and rights of humans, especially in its important Pastoral Constitution, *The Church in the Modern World* (*Gaudium et Spes*). Rooted in the Bible and centuries of Christian living, these teachings help form the core of Catholic social teaching.

As both scholars and bishops have noted, however, so much of the Church's social teaching is our "best-kept secret." Perhaps this is so because of the difficult subject matter. Or perhaps it is because social teaching is controversial and challenging, especially to those who are well off. Facing this teaching might require a change of behavior and lifestyle. And many people resist change, so, in their minds, it is better to be ignorant.

KARL MARX

RERUM NOVARUM—THE SEMINAL SOCIAL JUSTICE ENCYCLICAL WRITTEN BY POPE LEO XIII IN 1891 TO ADDRESS ECONOMIC AND OTHER INJUSTICES PLAGUING THE LATE NINETEENTH-CENTURY WORLD. IT BEGAN THE CHURCH'S SOCIAL TEACHING IN THE MODERN ERA.

SOCIAL JUSTICE IS ESSENTIAL

Whatever the reason for a general lack of knowledge of the Church's teaching on social justice, it is extremely important and absolutely a central part of the gospel which the Church must proclaim. An important quote from the 1971 Synod of Bishops, *Justice in the World*, teaches:

Action on behalf of justice and participation in the transformation of the world fully appear to us as a constitutive dimension of the preaching of the Gospel, or, in other words, of the Church's mission for the redemption of the human race and its liberation from every oppressive situation (§6).

Simply put, the passage tells us that working for justice is an essential dimension of Christian living. It is not optional. For example, to treat a physically disabled person with less respect than any other person is sinful. To allow to go unchallenged corporate practices that put profits ahead of people is wrong. To ignore government policies that increase defense budgets while slashing aid programs for the needy is immoral. In short, to ignore social teaching is un-Christian and anti-human. Correcting such behavior requires a change of heart, repentance, and restitution where necessary.

Recalling a theme of Pope Paul VI, Pope John Paul II reminded us that the Church's social teaching is part of our Christ-given responsibility to preach the gospel. By doing justice, we are indeed witnessing to the gospel:

The teaching and spreading of her social doctrine are part of the Church's evangelizing mission. And since it is a doctrine aimed at guiding people's behavior, it consequently gives rise to a "commitment to justice," according to each individual's role, vocation, and circumstances (On Social Concern, §41).

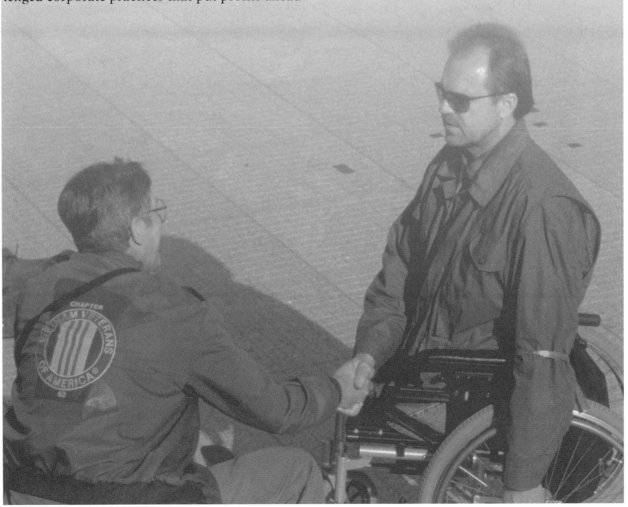

KEY SOCIAL JUSTICE DOCUMENTS: AN OVERVIEW

The following is a chronological list of some important social justice documents of the Catholic Church.

1891 Leo XIII—*The Condition of Labor (Rerum Novarum):* Emphasizes role of the state to pass laws to preserve rights of workers including right to work and unionize, to a just wage, and to own private property. Seminal document that begins more than a century of forward-looking social teaching.

1931 Pius XI—*The Reconstruction of the Social Order (Quadragesimo Anno):* Reaffirms *Rerum Novarum* on just wages and unions; critiques unbridled capitalism and communism; urges international economic cooperation; introduces idea of subsidiarity.

1961 John XXIII—*On Christianity and Social Progress (Mater et Magistra):* Criticizes disparities between rich nations and poor nations; urges global interdependence; encourages worker participation and collective bargaining for modern industrial workers.

1963 John XXIII—*Peace on Earth (Pacem in Terris):* Details basic human rights and corresponding responsibilities that flow from human dignity; decries arms race; stresses concept of the common good; addressed to Catholics and all people of good will.

1965 Vatican II—*The Church in the Modern World (Gaudium et Spes):* Analyzes the modern world in light of human dignity; looks at the relationship between the Church and the world; treats issues of the family, society, politics, economics, and world peace.

1967 Paul VI—*The Development of Peoples (Populorum Progressio):* Discusses relationship between development and peace; focuses on fair trade relationships to help underdeveloped nations; advocates a form of taxation of rich nations and international cooperation.

1971 Paul VI—*A Call to Action (Octogesima Adveniens):* Treats the problems caused by modern urbanization; discusses discrimination; encourages political action and involvement.

1971 Synod of Bishops—*Justice in the World:* Defines justice as an essential ingredient of the gospel and the Church's mission; cites modern injustices, especially against the poor and powerless for whom the Church should speak in a special way; encourages the Church itself to be an exemplar of justice in the way it treats its own members.

1981 John Paul II—*On Human Work (Laborem Exercens):* Develops a strong spirituality of work as it supports unions and workers' rights; reaffirms family life; criticizes both Marxism and capitalism.

1986 U.S. Bishops—*Economic Justice for All:* Applies the Christian vision of economic life to the American economy; issues a challenge to examine the inequalities in income, consumption, power, and privilege and their impact on the poor.

You can locate many of the Church's documents at various websites (for example, www.osjspm.org/cst/doclist.htm). Also, the Pontifical Council for Justice and Peace has also issued a compendium of quotes from the major documents entitled *The Social Agenda* at www.thesocialagenda.com

Obtain and read a copy of *Centesimus Annus*. It contains sixty-two sections. Report on individual sections. Prepare a short oral report on the contents of your particular reading. Write what you consider to be an important sentence from one section of reading. Read and explain the significance of the sentence in your oral report. You can find this encyclical at the Vatican website: www.vatican.va.

1987 John Paul II—*On Social Concern (Sollicitudo Rei Socialis):* Notes the obvious disparities in wealth between northern and southern hemispheres; critiques the West as succumbing to materialism and consumerism; critiques the moral bankruptcy of the East which ignores basic human rights; decries the arms race as an injustice to the poor; calls for refocusing of resources and cooperation for international development; highlights theme of preferential option for the poor.

1991 John Paul II—*On the One Hundredth Year of Rerum Novarum (Centesimus Annus):* Written in the wake of the collapse of communism; celebrates the centenary of *Rerum Novarum*; examines strengths and weaknesses of various forms of capitalism; reiterates themes of work, just wages, unemployment, profit, unions, atheism, family, etc.; explains how the Church offers a vision of human dignity rooted in Jesus who became one of us; underscores special option for the poor; critiques the abuses of consumerism as an excessive drain on the environment.

1995 John Paul II—*The Gospel of Life (Evangelium Vitae):* Defends the most fundamental right we have: the right to life. Discusses the sources of this right and its implications. Treats very well the topics of abortion, euthanasia, assisted suicide, capital punishment, and other modern-day threats to human life.

1998 John Paul II—*Faith and Reason (Fides Ratio):* Treats how faith and reason should work hand-in-hand in searching for truth. Shows how the search for knowledge is a search for God and that Christians find the ultimate meaning in life in the Paschal mystery of Christ. The Holy Father warns against some modern philosophies that lead to nihilism, which denies ultimate truth, and states firmly that humans have the ability to find the truth.

The above synopsis focuses on major social justice documents. However, we could also add the Christmas messages of Pope Pius XII, Vatican II's *Declaration on Religious Freedom*, Pope Paul VI's *Evangelization in the Modern World*, Pope John Paul II's *Redeemer of Mankind* and *Rich in Mercy*, the American Bishops' pastoral letter *The Challenge of Peace*, the Congregation of the Doctrine of Faith's *The Participation of Catholics in Political Life* (2002), statements from the Vatican's Peace and Justice Commission, key documents of other national and regional conferences of bishops, and the like.

Other links include:

- for papal encyclicals and the Documents of Vatican II: www.vatican.va

- for the statements of the United States Bishops: www.nccbuscc.org

Investigate these websites and write in three "notable quotes" on some aspect of the Church's social justice teaching that you found at these sites. Be sure to note the original source of the quote. Share these in class.

WHAT YOU CAN DO: WRITING A LETTER

As the saying goes, "The power of the pen is mightier than the sword."

WRITING LETTERS IS AN EFFECTIVE WAY FOR YOU TO:
- take a Christian stand by expressing your opinion on a social justice issue,
- seek more information on a particular topic,
- encourage those who are working for justice to continue their good work.

HERE ARE SOME TIPS ON HOW TO GO ABOUT EFFECTIVE LETTER WRITING:

WHAT TOPIC?

- Pick out some issue related to social justice that interests you. (For ideas, page through the rest of this text.)
- Learn enough about your topic that you will appear relatively informed when you write your letter.

TO WHOM?

- To governmental officials, for example, legislators.
- To newspapers expressing your opinion on a topic.
- To non-governmental organizations, for example, Amnesty International.
- To experts in the field to get more information.
- To social justice advocates, including Church workers, to encourage them in their work.

HOW?

- Address your letter properly. Find the correct address at your local library or off the Internet.
- Preferably type your letter. If you don't type it, write it legibly. Follow an accepted style manual for business letters. (Check your English grammar book.)
- Keep the letter short—one page is enough—using your own words.
- Be clear.
- Focus on one issue.
- If expressing your opinion, give reasons for it.
- Be constructive.
- Be specific when requesting information.
- Share some research findings if appropriate to your letter.
- It is quite appropriate to share Church teaching, for example, by quoting one of the relevant documents on social justice.
- Don't be afraid to ask questions and politely ask for a response to them.

SOME HINTS

- In the first paragraph, identify yourself and explain why you are writing.
- In the second paragraph, make your point or request information.
- In the closing paragraph, thank the reader for his/her kind consideration.
- If you get a response to your letter, be sure to write a thank-you note.

TO DO:
- Try your hand at writing a one-page letter on some social-justice issue in the news.
- Bring it to class and have at least three classmates critique it.
- Consider rewriting it and mailing it to the appropriate person or organization.

CESAR CHAVEZ (1927–1993)
JUSTICE FOR THE MIGRANT WORKER

It is possible to become discouraged about the injustice we see every-where. But God did not promise us that the world would be humane and just. He gives us the gift of life and allows us to choose the way we will use our limited time on earth. It is an awesome opportunity.
– *Cesar Chavez*[6]

Senator Robert F. Kennedy described Cesar E. Chavez as "one of the heroic figures of our time." When Chavez died in 1993, he was president of the United Farm Workers of America, AFL-CIO. He was only the second Mexican-American to receive the Presidential Medal of Freedom, conferred posthumously in 1994.

Born in 1927 on a small farm in Yuma, Arizona, Chavez left school after the eighth grade to help support his family. He labored as a migrant farm worker in the Southwest with thousands of other displaced families. As a young man, he served his country in the U.S. Navy. He married in 1948 and settled in a barrio in California nicknamed *Sal Si Puedes* ("get out if you can").

In the 1950s, he became an organizer with the Community Service Organization, helping with voter registration drives and fighting economic and racial discrimination against Chicanos in both California and Arizona. In 1962 he founded the National Farm Workers Association, which later affiliated with the AFL-CIO to become the United Farm Workers (UFW). This union fights for the rights of migrant farm workers, a greatly neglected segment of our society whose sacrifice helps put food on the tables of millions of Americans.

Through great personal sacrifice, Chavez helped mobilize workers to fight against unjust conditions like poor wages and benefits, unsafe and unhealthy working and living conditions, and various forms of discrimination. In 1965 he helped lead a five-year boycott against table and wine grape growers who were notorious in exploiting migrant workers. This effort was successful in bringing to the attention of the nation the rights of the invisible and powerless farm workers. It eventually convinced grape growers that it was wise policy to sign contracts with the UFW.

Cesar Chavez was a heroic figure because of his unswerving devotion to his fellow farm workers and his own personal sacrifice in working for justice. He did so in a spirit of peace and love for his opponents. From the beginning, the UFW pledged to use nonviolent means to achieve its goals of justice for its workers. Chavez even fasted for twenty-five days in 1968 to recommit himself and his union to the principles of nonviolence.

Chavez and the UFW's efforts resulted in farm workers receiving higher pay, family health and pension benefits, and other contract protections. Yet, Chavez remained ever vigilant because of lax efforts to enforce the laws that protected workers' rights. His message always remained the same: respect the dignity of the individual worker, appreciate the nobility of work, respond to the common good, and take responsibility to care for the earth.

Cesar Chavez lived out his years in a small town east of Bakersfield, California, with his wife Helen and eight children. His union wages at the subsistence level never exceeded $5,000 a year.

When he died at the age of sixty-six in 1993, more than 40,000 people attended his funeral. Cardinal Roger Mahony of Los Angeles was the principal celebrant of his funeral Mass.

Read and report on current activities of the United Farm Workers at their website: www.ufw.org.

You can also read more about, and watch a video of, Cesar Chavez at this same website.

Two other good sources for information about Cesar Chavez can be found at:

- Cesar E. Chavez Institute, headquartered at San Francisco State University: www.cesarechavezinstitute .org/home
- The Cesar E. Chavez Foundation: www.cesarechavezfoundation.org

CASE STUDY: THE IMMIGRATION ISSUE

A much-debated social justice issue concerns who should be let inside the United States' borders. Should the "nation of immigrants"—the United States—be generous in accepting new immigrants, for example, those escaping persecution in war-torn countries or those who want to come for better economic opportunities? And who should we accept? Only those who are highly trained specialists? Or anyone who desires a better life for whatever reason?

A pressing related issue to America's immigration policy is a major concern in an age of terrorism: What to do with immigrants who have entered without proper documentation? In analyzing the situation, we should note that the modern economic reality known as **globalization** has been a major factor feeding the rate of migration among the peoples of America. A key element involves how the economy of the United States requires unskilled workers in labor-intensive industries like agriculture, food processing, construction, and other services. On the one hand, American employers welcome migrants to work jobs, often poorly paid and dangerous, that few American citizens want to do. On the other hand, many migrants, for example from Mexico, leave their homeland and take up these jobs to provide a better life for their families.

However, once here, many migrants suffer from the effects of discrimination at their jobs and in the communities in which they live. They also fear the possibility of arrest and deportation and wonder if they and their children will have access to medical care, education, and other social services.

A recent survey found that today Americans have a more favorable opinion of immigrants than in recent years. However, the survey also showed that overall many non-immigrants feel that immigration is changing the country in a way that does not meet their approval. There are also more negative feelings toward illegal immigrants and a strong belief that the government should crack down and tighten the borders. In 2006 there were several large pro-immigration demonstrations in many U.S. cities highlighting the tensions around this issue.[7]

globalization–"The process whereby the world's goods, communications, and peoples are more fully integrated, accessible, and interdependent."[8]

Basic Questions for Debate:

- Should a rich and prosperous nation like the United States welcome with open arms those seeking religious or political asylum or wanting better economic opportunities to provide for their families?
- Do we see our country as a lifeboat that will capsize if we allow others to scramble aboard? Or do we see it a rich land flowing with "milk and honey," a country that has been blessed with much wealth and knowledge to help feed the hungry and give opportunity to the many?
- Do we welcome the stranger?
- Or do we give in to fear and even prejudice?
- Do we heed the words of Scripture: "You will not oppress the alien" (Ex 23:9)?

Cons:

Those who argue against accepting immigrants say that immigrants take jobs away from America's workers. They also claim that most come to the country illegally and overburden our social services by receiving health care, education, and welfare benefits for which they do not pay. Further, they argue that immigrants resist learning English and assimilation into our culture.

Pros:

Immigrants should be welcomed because we are a nation of immigrants. Our ancestors came to this country to escape ethnic, racial, or social conflict or to gain economic opportunity. Immigrants have helped build our nation. Fear, suspicion, hatred, and prejudice as motives to ban **refugees** and **immigrants** are contrary to the teaching of Jesus. Catholic teaching holds that people have a right to survive economically and to escape political persecution. Christians have a duty to share with others.

In their Pastoral Letter titled *Welcoming the Stranger Among Us: Unity in Diversity*, the Catholic bishops of the United States call Catholics to *conversion*, that is, to root out fear, prejudice, and a feeling of superiority towards other people. They also issue a call to *communion*, reminding Catholics to exercise the virtue of hospitality, to treat others with dignity, and to make efforts to learn about others' culture and customs. Finally, they issue a call to *solidarity*, the virtue of friendship and charity that shows special concern for "the least among us," most notably for **migrant** workers who are here either legally or illegally. This means that we must devote ourselves to recognize and respect the rights of immigrants and work hard to overcome all discrimination based on race, culture, or religion.[9]

- Most economists hold that immigration is a net benefit to the U.S. economy. Immigrants take jobs that U.S. citizens often reject. They help keep the U.S. economy competitive in the global economy. They stimulate job creation in depressed neighborhoods.
- Immigrants are generally efficient, productive, and reliable workers.
- Immigrants pay more in taxes than they receive in social services.
- Around three-fourths of the immigrants into our country arrive legally. Of the remainder, 50 percent enter legally on visas as students or tourists who stay beyond the expiration date.

The demand for English classes is great. Most immigrants want to be part of the dominant culture. Those who oppose immigration often have their facts wrong. For example:

Research and Debate:

- "We are a nation of immigrants." What do you know about the home countries of your mother's and father's people? Where did they come from? Why did they leave the homeland? When did they come over? Research this question by speaking with older family members. Also, check a history book to discover the attitudes of Americans toward immigrants at the time your ancestors arrived.
- The U.S. government has forecast a shortage of 20 million workers by 2026. Should the government enact more lenient immigration laws to meet the future demand for workers?
- The Pew Hispanic Center estimates that there are between 11.5 and 12 million illegal immigrants living in the United States; about 40 percent of them have lived there for less than five years. Three-fourths of the illegal immigrants come from Latin America, with the majority coming from Mexico.[10] The United States granted lawful permanent residence to 1,122,373 persons in the 2005 fiscal year. "Nearly three-fifths (58 percent) were granted permanent residence based on a family relationship with a U.S. citizen or legal permanent resident of the United States."[11] Research current governmental plans to extend citizenship to undocumented immigrants. What approaches seem most consistent with the virtues of hospitality and solidarity?
- "It is un-Christian to close our borders." Agree or disagree?
- "Laws prohibiting the granting of basic human services for 'illegal' immigrants are immoral." Agree or disagree? Do such laws violate basic human rights?

REFUGEE—A person who leaves his or her country and is unwilling to return because of fear of religious, racial, ethnic, political, or some other form of persecution.

IMMIGRANT—A person who leaves one country to take up permanent residence in another country. (An "undocumented" immigrant is in a country without the permission of that country's government.)

MIGRANT—One who moves within one's country or between nations, often in search of work.

In November 2002, the Catholic bishops of Mexico and the United States issued a pastoral letter on migration titled *Strangers No Longer: Together on the Journey of Hope*. In this letter, the bishops review five principles that underlie Church teachings on migration.

1. *Persons have the right to find opportunities in their homeland.* Meaningful work that provides a just, living wage is a basic human need.

2. *Persons have the right to migrate to support themselves and their families.* The goods of the earth belong to all people. When people cannot find jobs in their own country to support themselves and their families, they have a right to find work elsewhere—a right that nations should accommodate.

3. *Sovereign nations have the right to control their borders.* However, the Church rejects such control when it is exerted merely to gain additional wealth. Nations with a more powerful economy have a stronger obligation to help migrants.

4. *Refugees and asylum seekers should be afforded protection.*

5. *The human dignity and human rights of undocumented migrants should be respected.* Regardless of their legal status, all persons possess basic human dignity with rights. Therefore, governments should protect the rights of migrants and not subject them to harsh treatment.[12]

In light of these principles, answer these questions:

* Why do you think it is important for richer nations to help poorer nations to develop a strong economy?

* What does outsourcing jobs to other counties entail? Why is this done? Is it beneficial to the poorer nations or does it exploit workers there?

* What would be some benefits of legalizing the large number of undocumented workers in the United States? What would be any disadvantages?

CHAPTER SUMMARY

* Justice is a virtue. Virtues are good habits that enable us to do good with facility. There are two major categories of virtues: theological and cardinal. The theological virtues—faith, hope, and charity (love)—have their origin, motive, and object in our loving, Triune God. They help us to be just

persons. Faith empowers us to believe in God and his teachings and that of his Church. We are just when we make our faith an active faith. Hope helps us trust in God's promises of eternal life, working to achieve our goal with God's help and not relying solely on our own efforts. Christians working for justice trust that the Holy Spirit works through them and that their efforts are worthwhile because of God's presence. Charity is the queen of virtues, enabling us to love God above all and our neighbors as ourselves. Charity moves us to give people their due in all cases and to uproot injustice wherever we might find it.

- The cardinal virtues are the hinge virtues on which so many others depend. They are prudence, fortitude, temperance, and justice. Prudence helps us discover the good in every situation and choose the right methods for achieving it. Thus, it can help us recognize injustice and how to combat it. Fortitude is the spiritual courage to do what is right, even when we are fearful. It helps us work on behalf of others and for fairness, even in the face of personal sacrifice. Temperance regulates our appetites for created pleasures. It can motivate us to be just in how we use and develop the good creation that God gave to us.

- Justice is the cardinal virtue whereby we give God and neighbor what is their due by right. Commutative justice calls for fairness in our exchanges with others, respecting their dignity in transactions, contracts, and promises. Distributive justice, often administered by governmental agencies, shares the goods of creation, making sure that each person gets what is necessary to live a truly human life. Legal justice regulates the obligations citizens have to the larger society and to the government.

- Finally, social justice applies Jesus' gospel to society's structures, systems, and laws to protect people's rights and ensure a peaceful, loving society. It also sees to it that people have a fair say in the social, economic, and political institutions of society according to their ability. It is sometimes called contributive justice because we all have a duty to help create the goods, services, and other values necessary for living together in community.

- Charity cannot substitute for justice. Charity is more oriented to service and geared to private, individual acts, responding to immediate needs. Social justice is targeted to social change, working in the public arena to address long-term needs and to change unjust structures and institutions. We cannot say we are loving people if we are not just, if we refuse to give others what is their due by right.

- The Bible images justice as a mighty stream that washes away all injustice. Justice is a prime concern of God. The biblical view of justice is one of covenant, fidelity to relationships. We are just when we are faithful, that is, when we love God above all, love our neighbor as another self, and respect and wisely use God's good earth.

- Jesus came to do justice by ushering in God's kingdom. He taught that we must consider everyone our neighbor, a brother or sister of Abba. He told us to be Beatitude persons whose love embraces everyone without exception, especially the lowly, and even the enemy. Jesus told us that God is compassionate. He demonstrated in deed and in his loving sacrifice on the cross the meaning of compassion. His Father is compassionate. With the help of the Holy Spirit, he calls us to be compassionate, too, to suffer with others, to show them mercy, to do justice.

- Christians from the earliest days have taken to heart Jesus' call to be just by responding to the needy through the centuries. The Church's modern social teaching doctrine flows from the seminal papal encyclical of Pope Leo XIII, *Rerum Novarum* (1891), which responded to unjust economic realities of the day. This rich body of doctrine can be found in major papal encyclicals, papal speeches, documents of Vatican Council II, and pastoral letters of various synods and regional and national gatherings of the world's bishops.

- Catholics have a serious obligation to form their consciences in light of the social teaching of the Church. It forms an essential element in the proclamation of Christ's gospel.

REVIEW QUESTIONS

1. What is a virtue?
2. Describe how the cardinal virtues of prudence, fortitude, and temperance can help us be persons of justice.
3. What are the theological virtues? How can each help us in our task to be just persons?
4. Give a simple definition of justice.
5. Distinguish between and among:
    a. commutative justice
    b. distributive justice
    c. legal justice
    d. social justice
6. Why is social justice sometimes called contributive justice?
7. List three distinctions between justice and charity.
8. Contrast an American image of justice with a biblical image of justice.
9. "According to the Bible, justice is fidelity to relationship." Explain.
10. Cite four specific ways Jesus taught justice.
11. What does it mean to be compassionate?
12. Discuss several ways Christians have promoted justice through the ages.
13. Identify *Rerum Novarum*. Explain why it is so important for social justice doctrine.
14. Why can a Catholic not ignore the social teaching of the Church?
15. List five important social justice documents of the Church, who wrote them, and the year they were written.
16. Why do Christians admire Cesar Chavez as a model of justice?
17. Can Christians be against immigration? Explain.

RESEARCHING ON THE INTERNET

Christian love of neighbor and justice cannot be separated. For love implies an absolute demand for justice, namely a recognition of the dignity and rights of one's neighbor. Justice attains its inner fullness only in love. Because every person is truly a visible image of the invisible God and a sibling of Christ, the Christian finds in every person God himself and God's absolute demand for justice and love.

—*Synod of Bishops*, Justice in the World *(1971), §34.*

1. Do an Internet search to research and write a one-page summary of a relevant article on one of the following topics:
    * Cheating
    * Affirmative action
    * Immigration
    * Ethics and war
    * Corporate wrongdoing
2. The following websites will give you access to many important social justice documents on the Internet. Research and report on a current topic in the news that is of interest to you.
    * JusticeNet: www.justicenet.org
    * Salt of the Earth: http://salt.claretianpubs.org
    * Theology Library at Spring Hill College: www.shc.edu/theolibrary

PRAYER REFLECTION

To do justice consistently, cheerfully, and lovingly requires the virtue of generosity. Pray the "Prayer for Generosity" from Saint Ignatius of Loyola.

Teach us, Lord, to serve you as you deserve;
to give and not to count the cost;
to fight and not to heed the wounds;
to toil and not to seek for rest;
to labor and not to ask for any reward,
save that of knowing that we do your will,
Through Jesus Christ our Lord. Amen.

NOTES

1. Found at Inspiration Peak <http://www.inspirationpeak.com/lifepage2.html>.
2. Office for Social Justice of the Archdiocese of St. Paul and Minneapolis, "Charity and Justice" <http://www.osjspm.org/charjust.htm>.
3. Quoted in Jill Haak Adels, *The Wisdom of the Saints: An Anthology* (New York: Oxford University Press, 1987), p. 125.
4. Quoted in Pope Paul VI's *On the Development of Peoples*, §23.
5. Quote cited from *The Spiritual Writings of St. Louise* at the Vincentians' Eastern Province website.
6. Quotation found at <http://www.sfsu.edu/~cecipp/cesar_chavez/cesarquotes.htm>.
7. This poll was conducted by National Public Radio, the Kaiser Family Foundation, and Harvard's Kennedy School of Government and reported by NPR.org, "Immigration in America: Survey Overview," October 6, 2004.
8. Definition found in *Strangers No Longer: Together on the Journey of Hope: A Pastoral Letter Concerning Migration from the Catholic Bishops of Mexico and the United States* (Washington, D.C.: United States Conference of Catholic Bishops, 2003), p. 51.
9. U.S. Catholic Bishops, *Welcoming the Stranger Among Us* (Washington, D.C.: United States Conference of Catholic Bishops, 2000), pp. 23–54.
10. PBS Online, "Latinos Now: A National Conversation—Facts and Figures—Undocumented in the U.S." (26 June 2006).
11. U.S. Citizenship and Immigration Services, *2005 Yearbook of Immigration Statistics*.
12. *Strangers No Longer: Together on the Journey of Hope: A Pastoral Letter Concerning Migration from the Catholic Bishops of Mexico and the United States* (Washington, D.C.: United States Conference of Catholic Bishops, 2003), pp. 34–37.

CHAPTER OVERVIEW

We Belong to Each Other
We have obligations that flow from being a part of the human family.

Our Social Nature
Our social nature follows from being made in God's image and likeness, uniting with others as the three persons of the Holy Trinity.

Principle of Subsidiarity
The principle of subsidiarity teaches that justice and human welfare are best achieved at the most immediate level.

Principle of the Common Good
The common good concerns our life together, protecting the life of each individual who must in turn be concerned with the welfare of each other person.

The Human Family and Natural Law
The natural law is another source of the Church's social teaching. It can be discovered through human reason.

Responsibilities of Individuals and Society
A chart highlights the key responsibilities of both individuals and societies.

Centrality of the Family
The family is the "original cell of social life."

Saint Thérèse of Lisieux
Saint Thérèse modeled holiness through her "little way" of daily living and loving.

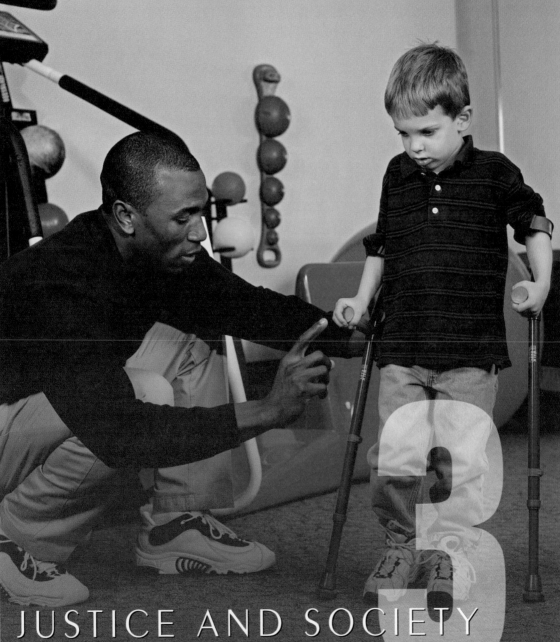

Love one another with mutual affection; anticipate one another in showing honor. Have the same regard for one another; do not be haughty but associate with the lowly; do not be wise in your own estimation.

—Romans 12:10, 16

JUSTICE AND SOCIETY

WE BELONG TO EACH OTHER

In 1923, nine of the richest men in the United States met at a famous hotel in Chicago to discuss their successes. They were on top of the world. Twenty-five years later their world had collapsed. Here is what happened to them:[1]

1923	1948
Charles Schwab, president of the largest steel company	Died bankrupt, living on borrowed money for five years before his death
Samuel Insull, president of the largest electric utility company	Died a fugitive from the law and penniless in a foreign country
Howard Hopson, president of the largest gas company	Diagnosed as insane
Arthur Cutten, great wheat speculator	Died abroad, insolvent
Richard Whitney, president of the New York Stock Exchange	Released from Sing Sing prison
Albert Fall, Secretary of the Interior in President Harding's cabinet	Pardoned from prison so he could die at home—broke
Leon Fraser, president of the Bank of International Settlements	Committed suicide
Jesse Livermore, greatest "bear" on Wall Street	Committed suicide
Ivar Krueger, headed world's largest monopoly	Committed suicide

All the wealth in the world did not protect these rugged individualists from a tragic end. They knew how to make money; they did not know how to live. Could it be they made money their god and ignored their fellow humans? Had they been more sensitive to others and developed a social conscience, recognizing that we all belong to each other, perhaps they would have died happy and fulfilled.

We cannot escape other people. We belong to the community of humankind. We find our true selves by associating with and caring for other people. This chapter will emphasize the important dimension of Catholic teaching on social justice, our social nature, and the obligations that flow from being made with and for others.

Charles Schwab

WHAT DO YOU THINK?

At the signing of the Declaration of Independence on July 4, 1776, Benjamin Franklin said, "We must all hang together, or assuredly we shall all hang separately." Going it alone is dangerous; "hanging together" makes sense because we are social beings. We depend on others, and they depend on us.

What do you think? Here are some statements related to this theme. Check the column that best reflects your own personal view: **A=strongly agree; A=agree; DK=I don't know what to think; D=disagree; SD=strongly disagree.**

Some Statements to Think About	SA	A	DK	D	SD
1. My neighbor is my brother or sister.					
2. I must not only be fair to others, I must love them. And love is a lot tougher than treating others fairly.					
3. People are basically evil; therefore, we should always be on guard lest they take advantage of us.					
4. The government should stay out of people's lives as long as they are not hurting anyone.					
5. Good old common sense is enough to tell us that we should respect each other.					
6. Cooperation is for the weak; competition is for the strong.					
7. It would be seriously wrong not to help someone financially who has a life-threatening need.					
8. Our national government does not do enough to support stable families. In fact, some of its policies undermine family life.					

- Share your responses to three of the statements above. Give a reason why you chose as you did.
- How would our society answer statement number 6? Give examples to support your response.
- What are some "life-threatening needs" referred to in number 7?

OUR SOCIAL NATURE (CCC, 1878–1896, 1943)

No man is an island.
— *John Donne*

The English poet John Donne knew quite well that we are not isolated beings who have no connection to each other. In the image of preacher and novelist Frederick Buechner, life is like a big spider web. We are all interconnected. Touch one strand and the whole web trembles. Who knows, for example, how your one act of kindness will reverberate out to others. Your one act might make another person behave the same way to another. A ripple effect of goodness might start because of your single act—a ripple effect that may touch the lives of countless people, even down through the ages. Similarly, think of the effect of one act of hostility. It will affect others and in turn may touch countless people. No man, no woman, no teen, no child is an island. We are made for each other.

From the beginning, God made us to be with and for each other. Recall the second creation account where God said it was not good for Adam to be alone, so he made Eve as a companion (Gn 2:18).

Note some actions you performed—both good and bad—that you discovered had a ripple effect on others.

RESPONDING TO OTHERS

Draw at least eight concentric circles. Place yourself in the center. As the circles radiate out, name various societies to which you belong, starting with the family.

Think of ways you can respond more openly to various people who are members of these groups. Resolve to do one or more of the following:

- Spend some quality time engaging in a favorite activity preferred by a younger sibling.
- Eat lunch with a teammate or a member of another extracurricular activity to which you belong with whom you do not usually associate.
- Greet in a friendly way five students you have never talked to before.
- Attend a Mass at your parish that you do not normally go to; make a point to talk to one parishioner you have never met before.
- Learn the name of the council person for your local city government; write him or her a letter of appreciation for the work he or she is doing to improve your neighborhood.
- Read about the economic situation of a poor country on another continent.

society—"A group of persons bound together organically by a principle of unity that goes beyond each one of them" (CCC, 1880).

Our social nature follows from being made in God's image and likeness. The three divine persons are bound in a community of love. God is one divine being, but a community of relationships—Father, Son, and Holy Spirit. God made us individuals but desires that we unite with others into communities that love and respect each other. This was the ardent prayer of Jesus:

I pray not only for them, but also for those who will believe in me through their word, so that they may all be one, as you, Father, are in me and I in you, that they also may be in us, that the world may believe that you sent me (Jn 17:20–21).

We cannot escape living in a society. It is part of our very nature.

MEANINGS OF SOCIETY

The *Catechism of the Catholic Church* defines **society** as "a group of persons bound together organically by a principle of unity that goes beyond each one of them" (1880). Societies are living realities that have both visible and spiritual dimensions that last through time. They connect us to the past, prepare us for the future, and enable us to develop our talents in the present.

There are many different societies to which we belong. Think of yourself at the heart of a series of concentric circles, each one representing a particular association to which you belong. First and most basic is your family, both immediate and extended. Then you belong to a neighborhood, go to a particular school, and perhaps play on a team or belong to several clubs. You belong to a parish community, live in a certain city, reside in a given state. You are the citizen of a nation. The world is your home, too. You belong to the society of the world's citizens. Everyone is your neighbor. Everyone shares with you space on this planet. Think of all the other groups or associations to which you belong. You might be surprised at how long the list is.

Each society is different according to its purpose of existence. Each has its own set of rules. But the one thing all societies have in common is the human person. Individual persons are "the foundation, cause, and end of all social institutions" (*On Christianity and Social Progress*, §219). What follows from this is that "the social order and its development must invariably work to the benefit of the human person" (*The Church in the Modern World*, §26). This means that society is made for the benefit of people and not the other way around. Jesus said the same thing when he warned that the Sabbath was made for people, not that people were made for the Sabbath. The rules, laws, and procedures of society must serve people and not vice versa.

This principle is very clear when we think about our participation in both the family and the community, both of which correspond most directly to our nature. We cannot survive infancy and childhood without our families; we cannot survive living together as a collection of people without the governmental authority of the state. Yet, both of these essential societies exist to promote the individual, to help the individual develop his or her talents.

Beyond the family and the state, we need to participate in a variety of associations in all areas of life—economic, political, professional, social, religious, cultural, and the like. Organizations like sports teams, political parties, religious groups, neighborhood associations, and so many others, help us achieve goals that we could never do alone.

PRINCIPLE OF SUBSIDIARITY
(CCC, 1897-1904)

The Church is wise in encouraging us to join in a variety of associations so that everyone has "the ability to participate actively in the economic, political, and cultural life of society" (*Economic Justice for All, §78*). However, the Church warns about the tendency of the state to usurp authority to control persons, thereby destroying individual liberty and initiative. Therefore, the Church promotes the principle of subsidiarity, which teaches that justice and human welfare are best achieved at the most immediate level. Pope Pius XI defined this principle:

Just as it is gravely wrong to take from individuals what they can accomplish by their own initiative and industry and give it to the community, so also it is an injustice and at the same time a grave evil and disturbance of right order to assign to a greater and higher association what lesser and subordinate associations can do. For every social activity ought of its very nature to furnish help to the members of the body social, and never destroy and absorb them.

The supreme authority of the State ought, therefore, to let subordinate groups handle matters and concerns of lesser importance, which would otherwise dissipate its efforts greatly. Thereby the State will more freely, powerfully, and effectively do all those things that belong to it alone because it alone can do them: directing, watching, urging, restraining as occasion requires and necessity demands

(On Reconstructing the Social Order, *§79-80*).

Under the principle of subsidiarity, people should take responsibility to provide for their own welfare, given the situation they are dealing with. It is wrong for the government to take over what families or voluntary organizations can do for themselves. For example, it is wise for the local community to elect a dog catcher to handle strays in the neighborhood, not the federal government. The government should only get involved when the needs of people cannot be met in smaller groupings.

The principle of subsidiarity discourages attempts to maximize or centralize the power of the state at the expense of local institutions. The principle of subsidiarity wisely supports the sharing of power and authority on the grassroots level. It prefers local control over central decision-making. The sign of a just government is one that frees people to exercise their own responsibility. A just government is one that is small enough not to intrude unnecessarily into people's lives, yet is large enough

subsidiarity—The principle of Catholic social teaching that holds that a higher unit of society should not do what a lower unit can do as well (or better).

Share an example of a decision that should be made by a family, a local community agency, a state government, and the federal government.

to promote the common good and guarantee basic human rights.

The principle of subsidiarity implies the existence of a variety of associations and institutions below the level of the central government. Examples include neighborhood associations, school boards, zoning commissions, city councils, and political action committees. Some of these associations or institutions are responsible for making decisions that

affect individual citizens. For example, the city council may pass a curfew law after consulting citizen groups. This ordinance is designed to protect minors from criminal elements that roam the streets at night. It affects individuals. Other associations have the purpose of influencing how decisions are made at higher levels of government. For example, the National Right to Life Association lobbies legislators to pass a pro-life amendment. Or, labor unions lend financial support to legislators who support raising the minimum wage.

The principle of subsidiarity is not meant to maintain a status quo that denies individuals their rights. It can never be an excuse for selfishness, ignoring the common good or human solidarity. It should not be used as an excuse to support governmental policies that work against the poorest in our midst. It cannot be used to silence those whose voices have difficulty getting heard.

Consider how it is sometimes impossible for people to obtain justice on the local level because of ingrained prejudice or local customs and laws. A good historical example took place in states that set up "separate but equal" schools for African Americans. Unfortunately, the schools were not equal. So ingrained was discrimination against African Americans that the national government had to get involved to ensure the basic human rights of citizens of all states. Civil rights laws on the national level were (and are) necessary to guarantee that basic human rights are respected in all states of the union. In this example, and others like it, the proper application of the principle of subsidiarity allows the larger governmental unit to step in and take action when necessary. The federal government is often the only agency that can effectively achieve a desired goal. Sometimes only at this level can the common good of all citizens be guaranteed.

Political Advocacy Associations, including faith-based organizations, try to influence decisions on higher levels of government. Check the website of these two advocacy groups. Read about their purpose or mission. Then briefly summarize the most recent press release from one of them.
• Bread for the World: www.bread.org
• Network: www.networklobby.org

SUBSIDIARITY: VIOLATION OR NOT?

Decide whether the principle of subsidiarity is being violated in the following scenarios:
- the federal government legislates the speed limit for interstate highways;
- the state government passes a law dictating which books must be read in senior high school English classes for each school district;
- your school administration passes a rule that student athletes must have a 2.0 grade point average to participate in sports; the state standard is 1.5 on a 4.0 scale;
- the Congress of the United States passes an environmental law that limits the amount of emissions which Midwest factories may spew from their smokestacks.

PRINCIPLE OF THE COMMON GOOD
(CCC, 1905–1912; 1924–1927)

A just society must promote the **common good**. But what is meant by the common good? The Second Vatican Council document *Pastoral Constitution on the The Church in the Modern World* defines the common good as "the sum of those conditions of social life which allow social groups and their individual members relatively thorough and ready access to their own fulfillment" (§26).

The common good concerns our life together, protecting the welfare of each individual who must in turn be concerned with the welfare of each other person. Human dignity requires that we work for the common good, that we create and support institutions that improve our human life, individually and collectively.

The *Catechism of the Catholic Church* teaches that the common good entails three essential elements. Each of us, and especially our governmental officials, must take all these into account in any moral or social decisions we make. They are:

1. *Respect for the person.* Public authorities must respect the fundamental and inalienable rights of each human being. Society must allow each individual to fulfill his or her vocation, respecting individual conscience, privacy, and freedom of religion.
2. *Social well-being and development.* Public authorities must enable various groups to develop—socially, economically, politically, culturally, spiritually. Moreover, social policy should see to it that every person has what is necessary to live a full human life: food, clothing, health, education, work, and the like.
3. *Peace.* Without peace and stability, secured by legitimate and moral personal and collective defense, it would be impossible to establish a just society.

A nation's government has the important responsibility of promoting the common good of the various associations and groups, as well as the individuals, within the society. Their efforts, and those of individual citizens, must be based on truth, justice, and love. These three virtues remind us that the common good applies to future generations as well. Therefore, individuals and societies must not engage in practices that waste our material or social resources

common good—The sum of the spiritual, material, and social conditions needed for a person to achieve full human dignity.

and thereby deprive future generations of their ability to prosper.

Furthermore, in today's world, we must also recognize that we are one human family. There is a universal common good that applies to everyone in every place. To promote human rights throughout the world requires international cooperation, for example, by seeing that all people have access to the basic necessities of life like food and clothing. International cooperation is an exercise of the virtue of solidarity.

RESPECT AND THE COMMON GOOD

The common good cannot be promoted without respecting individuals and groups of people. Justice is impossible to attain without simple, down-to-earth, common respect. What is *respect*? *The American Heritage Dictionary* tells us that when we respect others we "feel or show esteem for" or "honor" them. It also defines respect as "to show consideration for; avoid violation of; treat with deference."

FROM THE DOCUMENTS

Everyone must consider his every neighbor without exception as another self, taking into account first of all his life and the means necessary to living it with dignity, so as not to imitate the rich man who had no concern for the poor man Lazarus.

In our times a special obligation binds us to make ourselves the neighbor of every person without exception, and of actively helping him when he comes across our path, whether he be an old person abandoned by all, a foreign laborer unjustly looked down upon, a refugee, a child born of an unlawful union and wrongly suffering for a sin he did not commit, or a hungry person who disturbs our conscience by recalling the voice of the Lord, "As long as you did it for one of these the least of my brethren, you did it for me" (Mt 25:40).

—*The Church in the Modern World*, §27

The Church favors governments that foster the common good by respecting human rights and promoting freedom and participation. The best governments have just systems that neither oppress nor enslave people.

However, the Church is realistic. It knows all too well the reality of sin and human selfishness. It knows that the best governmental and institutional structures can quickly turn callous "if the inhuman inclinations of the human heart are not made wholesome, if those who live in these structures or who rule them do not undergo a conversion of heart and of outlook" (*Evangelization in the Modern World*, §36).

Political, economic, and social structures depend on human hearts that have turned from selfishness, pride, and greed. They require conversion, a need to see and treat other people not as objects but as brothers and sisters of a common, loving Father. Two virtues that will help in this conversion are **solidarity** and a **preferential option for the poor**. More information on each follows.

Solidarity (CCC, 1939–1942; 1948) Solidarity is the Christian virtue of social charity. This virtue helps us see that we are all members of one human family, sharing equal human dignity. Solidarity realizes

solidarity—The virtue of social charity, friendship, and responsible sharing whereby we recognize our interdependence on others and that we are all brothers and sisters of one family under a loving Father.

preferential option for the poor—A preferential love for the poor that allows one to see things from the perspective of the poor and powerless and to assess lifestyle, policies, and social institutions in terms of their impact on the poor. This choice for the poor follows the example of Jesus who sided with those most in need.

that we share certain values, goals, standards, and interests. We are all responsible for each other. As individuals, groups, societies, and nations we depend on each other. We can make claims on each other. This is true not only within the smaller structure of the family but also for the larger structures in the human community. We are all interdependent. Therefore, we should all commit ourselves to work for the common good of all, locally, nationally, and internationally. Solidarity is exemplified when we share both spiritual and material goods with others, especially the poorest in our midst. Pope John Paul II wrote:

The fact that men and women in various parts of the world feel personally affected by the injustices and violations of human rights committed in distant countries, countries which perhaps they will never visit, is a further sign of a reality transformed into awareness, thus acquiring a moral connotation.

It is above all a question of interdependence, sensed as a system determining relationships in the contemporary world, in its economic, cultural, political and religious elements, and accepted as a moral category. When interdependence becomes recognized in this way, the correlative response as a moral and social attitude, as a "virtue," is solidarity. This then is not a feeling of vague compassion or shallow distress at the misfortunes of so many people, both near and far. On the contrary, it is a firm and persevering determination to commit oneself to the common good; that is to say to the good of all and of each individual, because

we are all really responsible for all (*On Social Concern, §38, emphasis added*).

In the practical order, how can an individual make any kind of difference for our distant brothers and sisters?

Minimally, we can pray for them. We can support international relief agencies like the Catholic Relief Services or the International Red Cross to help relieve the suffering of disaster victims or come to the aid of refugees. We can cultivate a lively interest in world news. We can support political candidates who have a global vision that reaches out to other nations to help them develop. Some people do choose the more personal, hands-on effort of traveling to faraway lands and serving the people there as teachers, doctors, scientists, missionaries, and in a host of other jobs.

What we may never do is be so self-absorbed or self-concerned that "looking out for number one" becomes our only concern. Such an attitude demands a conversion of heart, repentance so we can look on others as our brothers and sisters.

How can you make a difference for your faraway neighbors? List a specific response.

Make a list of all those you consider to be your neighbors. How might recognizing these people as neighbors make a difference in your treatment of people? Explain.

CATHOLIC RELIEF SERVICES

Research Catholic Relief Services and read about the work of CRS and ways you and your school can get involved.

Pay special attention to the CRS Fair Trade Program. In contrast to the usual trading system, which looks to the bottom line and often exploits low-income workers in other nations, Fair Trade puts into practice the virtue of solidarity by respecting human dignity and promoting global economic justice. The goal of Fair Trade is to connect us to the persons in other nations who actually make products we use. It gives us opportunities to positively impact their lives by the conscientious decisions we make when we buy products. Here are some things you can do:

- Find out where the persons responsible for buying coffee for your school or parish currently purchase it. Tell them about Fair Trade coffee and request that they give serious consideration to buying coffee from a Fair Trader. (CRS lists many of them on their website.)
- Examine the SERVV International Catalog for Fair Trade Handcrafts. This catalog can be found on the CRS website. Consider buying Christmas and birthday presents from this nonprofit organization that helps promote the social and economic progress of developing regions of the world.

Option for the poor (CCC, 2443–2447) Christians have a special concern for the poor. Through the ages, the Church has always ministered to the poor, whether through medical care, education, almsgiving, or caring for orphans and widows.

In the past few decades, the popes and bishops have recalled time and again our responsibility to do justice by looking out for the poor, that is, those who lack the necessities for a decent human life and cannot do anything about it. The American bishops termed the responsibility and tasks as the "preferential option for the poor":

Jesus takes the side of those most in need, physically and spiritually. The example of Jesus poses a number of challenges to the contemporary Church. It imposes a prophetic mandate to speak for those who have no one to speak for them, to be a defender of the defenseless, who in biblical terms are the poor. It also demands a compassionate vision that enables the Church to see things from the side of the poor and powerless, and to assess lifestyle, policies, and social institutions in terms of their impact on

the poor. It summons the Church also to be an instrument of assisting people to experience the liberating power of God in their own lives, so that they may respond to the Gospel in freedom and in dignity. Finally, and most radically, it calls for an emptying of self, both individually and corporately, that allows the Church to experience the power of God in the midst of poverty and powerlessness (Economic Justice for All, §52).

The purpose of this special consideration of the poor is so the poor can grow to take an active role in society and share in and contribute to the common good. This option (choice) for the poor is a practical application of the virtue of solidarity. It puts into practice the works of mercy. It requires involvement in changing political and economic policies that create structures that hurt the poor. It means living more simply as we share more of our own wealth with those who lack the basics.

All of this, of course, demands a conversion of heart from selfishness. Justice can sometimes require the giving up of some of one's own privileges and goods so others can have at least the chance to live and to participate in the system. This can be tough to do in a consumer society that tells us to buy more and measures us on what we have, not who we are.

Before God we are all poor. God is the source of our goodness. When we include the poor in our outlook, we get a very realistic view of who we really are. Without God and God's goodness, we are nothing, and we have nothing of real worth. Opting for the poor makes us true followers of Jesus Christ and living symbols of justice.

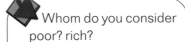

Whom do you consider poor? rich?

How can you "see things from the side of the poor"?

Discuss tax or health reform as an example of how this might be done.

What can the poor offer you? What can you offer the poor?

15 THINGS YOU CAN DO FOR THE POOR

1. Conduct a school or parish clothing or food drive. Distribute your collection to some needy families.
2. Clean up the yard of an elderly couple.
3. Call shut-ins to chat. Offer to run errands.
4. Tutor at an elementary school in a poor neighborhood.
5. Volunteer at a food bank or a clothing bank.
6. Raise funds to take poor children to the movies or an amusement park.
7. Visit a nursing home, especially one that serves the more neglected in our society. Try to befriend an elderly person there.
8. Attend services at a church that is poorer than yours.
9. Write a letter to a policy-maker to encourage him or her to keep the needs of the poor in mind.
10. Volunteer at a literacy organization to help teach English to immigrants.
11. Volunteer at a hotline for the troubled.
12. Baby-sit for a mother who needs to get out to do some shopping.
13. At school or in the parish, collect essentials for good grooming for poor families: soap, toothpaste, toiletries, detergents, etc.
14. Make greeting cards for kids who are in the hospital for lengthy stays.
15. Collect recent issues of magazines for distribution to hospitals.

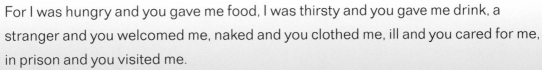

For I was hungry and you gave me food, I was thirsty and you gave me drink, a stranger and you welcomed me, naked and you clothed me, ill and you cared for me, in prison and you visited me.

—Matthew 25:35-36

■ *SCRIPTURE LINK*

Read the following passages. Answer the questions that follow.

Read Leviticus 19:9–18: Love of neighbor
1. List three practices that demonstrate love of neighbor.

Read Deuteronomy 15:1–15: Just practices
2. How often should debts be cancelled?
3. What is the purpose of this practice? (See v. 11)

Read Matthew 25:31–46: Those we should love
4. Whom does Jesus identify as our neighbor?

Read Romans 12:3–21: Instructions for living
5. According to Saint Paul, why should we love each other?

6. List three instructions for living as discussed by Paul.

Read 1 John 4:7–21: Love
7. Why should we love one another?

Proverbs: Write out the following verses from Proverbs in your journal.
  Proverbs 19:17:
  Proverbs 21:13:
  Proverbs 31:8-9:

THE HUMAN FAMILY AND NATURAL LAW
(CCC, 1954-1960; 1978-1979)

God's revelation to us, especially the teaching and life of Jesus Christ, is the primary source of the Church's social teaching. The **natural law** is another key source of Catholic social teaching.

The natural law is an expression of the moral law. Because the natural law is written on the human heart (see Rm 2:14–15) and can be discovered through human reason, every thinking person can discover it. Therefore, even people without faith can use the natural law as a source of moral guidance. People of good will, believers or not, can draw on the natural law to discover how God intends for us to live in society. Much of Catholic social teaching draws on this natural law. This is why much of the Church's teaching makes good sense to many people not of our faith.

Quoting Saint Thomas Aquinas in his encyclical *The Splendor of Truth* (§12), Pope John Paul II defined the natural law as "the light of understanding infused in us by God, whereby we understand what must be done and what must be avoided. God gave this light and this law to man at creation." The natural law is the imprint of divine light in our hearts so that every human being can discover what is true and how we should act in relationship to God and others. The natural law is human reason commanding us to do good and counseling us to avoid evil. It is God's law written on our hearts.

Natural law and divine revelation are closely related. The Ten Commandments, which God revealed to Moses, were already present in the hearts and minds of the Chosen People in the form of the natural law (e.g., the fifth commandment—"Thou shalt not kill"—is written on the human heart). All societies have discovered that if you allow indiscriminate killing (or adultery or dishonesty

NATURAL LAW—God's plan written into the way He made things. The light of understanding infused in us by God, whereby we understand what must be done and what must be avoided.

or theft, etc.), then people cannot live together in harmony. The natural law can be found in the moral teachings of all the world's great religions.

The precepts of the natural law are *universal*, and apply to each person and every society for all time. The natural law discovers and expresses human dignity, which is the basis for all rights and responsibilities. Although societies may apply the natural law in different ways throughout the ages, the natural law itself is *unchangeable* and *permanent*. For example, the killing of innocent human beings was, is, and will always be wrong and a great offense against human dignity. In protecting human life, though, one society might have cars drive only on the right side of the street, while another society will permit driving on the left side alone. The natural law of protecting human life by not killing is the same; its application differs according to law and custom.

Because of our sinful nature, figuring out the exact precepts of the natural law is not always easy. This is where God's grace and divine revelation help us learn what is morally right. For example, the natural law reveals that human life has dignity and should be protected. But divine revelation adds to this and tells us to take special care for those who are weak, defenseless, poor, or otherwise unable to secure their rights ("preferential option for the poor" and "solidarity").

Natural law not only governs individual conduct; it is the foundation for the civil law. A civil law that is good will always be in harmony with the natural law. If it is not in harmony, it is not a binding law. For example, consider the horrific anti-Semitic laws of Nazi Germany. These were evil to the core, contrary to God's law written on the human heart. Laws like these must not only

be disobeyed; they should be resisted. Pope John Paul II wrote:

> *I repeat once more that a law which violates an innocent person's natural right to life is unjust and, as such, is not valid as law. For this reason I urgently appeal once more to all political leaders not to pass laws which, by disregarding the dignity of the person, undermine the very fabric of society* (The Gospel of Life, §90).

Auschwitz

RESPONSIBILITIES OF INDIVIDUALS AND SOCIETY
(CCC, 1913-1923; 2235-2246; 2255-2256)

Because we have a social nature, we have responsibilities toward the communities in which we live. Similarly, because societies exist primarily to promote the welfare of individuals, they and those who hold positions of authority in them have obligations toward individual persons. The following chart emphasizes some key responsibilities of both.

What are other historical examples of unjust laws that have undermined human dignity?

NATURAL LAW VIOLATIONS
Explain exactly how each of the following would violate the natural law.
- using Weapons of Mass Destruction (WMD)
- slavery
- the sexual abuse of children
- drinking to get intoxicated

OBLIGATIONS OF INDIVIDUALS	SOCIETAL OBLIGATIONS
1. Help shape a just, loving society so it promotes love of God and neighbor. A key way to do this is to live a life of inner conversion so that the individual is a just, loving, moral person. Minimally, be on the alert to root out any laws or practices that cause sin or undermine human dignity.	1. Guarantee the conditions that allow associations and individuals to obtain their due, according to their vocation and nature.
2. Take special vigilance to see that God's little ones are cared for in society. Support those causes, laws, and institutions that guarantee the rights of the poor in our midst.	2. Root out any form of social, religious, cultural, racial, economic, ethnic, or sexual discrimination that denies people their fundamental human rights.
3. Treat each person as another self. Exercise the virtue of solidarity by viewing others as members of one family under a loving God.	3. Guarantee the most basic right of all, the right to life. Outlaw unspeakable crimes like abortion, murder, euthanasia, assisted suicide, fetal experimentation.
4. Exercise one's right to participate in society. Everyone has a duty to engage in voluntary and generous social interchange according to one's position, role, talents, and interests. Minimally, one must meet family and work obligations, contribute to the Church community, and be involved in public affairs.	4. Create a climate where people can participate and contribute to the common good. See to honest, just, and open communication based on truth, freedom, justice, and solidarity.
5. Respect those who have legitimate positions of authority and obey established laws. As good citizens, pay taxes, exercise the right to vote, and defend one's country. Welcome immigrants. Protest, even through civil disobedience, unjust laws that undermine human dignity.	5. Those who hold public authority must always promote the common good, recognize the sovereignty of the law, promote the principle of subsidiarity and the practice of limited government. Besides certain duties listed above: * support and defend the family, * look out for the needs of the poor and defenseless through distributive justice, * guarantee the right of religious freedom, * promote peace within and outside the country, * see that all have access to the economic and political spheres, * ensure a morally fit environment where virtue can thrive, for example, by outlawing pornography.

This chart is not an exhaustive list of duties of individuals toward society or of government toward its citizens. However, it does highlight many key duties that both individuals and societies have that flow from our social nature.

CENTRALITY OF THE FAMILY

(CCC, 2201–2213; 2234–2246)

The foundation of all society is the family. It is the "original cell of social life" (CCC, 2207) and introduces us to the life of society. If the rights of families are not protected, we simply cannot have a just society. A society is only as strong as its individual families.

The Church has been a staunch defender of the family. Its many social teachings are strongly pro-family. Consider the following statement:

The first and fundamental structure for "human ecology" is the family, in which man receives his first formative ideas about truth and goodness, and learns what it means to love and to be loved, and thus what it actually means to be a person. Here we mean the family founded on marriage. . . .

It is necessary to go back to seeing the family as the sanctuary of life. The family is indeed sacred: it is the place in which life—the gift of God—can be properly welcomed and protected against the many attacks to which it is exposed, and can develop in accordance with what constitutes authentic human growth. In the face of the so-called culture of death, the family is the heart of the culture of life (On the Hundredth Anniversary of "Rerum Novarum," §39).

Society and government have a duty to honor and assist the family and to guarantee basic rights. *The Charter of the Rights of the Family*, presented by Pope John Paul II at the request of the Synod of Bishops, spelled out some of these rights:

1. All persons have the right to the free choice of their state of life and thus to marry and establish a family or to remain single.

2. Marriage cannot be contracted except by free and full consent duly expressed by the spouses.

3. The spouses have the inalienable right to found a family.

4. Human life must be respected and protected absolutely from the moment of conception.

Analyze a "smaller" society to which you belong, for example, a club or sports team.
- List some duties you have because you belong to this group.
- List some responsibilities this group has to you.

CIVIC INVOLVEMENT

Here are some things you can do to be an informed and involved citizen.
- Read your daily newspaper.
- Watch the local and national news on television, if only for fifteen minutes each day.
- Listen to a political talk-radio station.
- In your reading, watching, and listening, be sure to check sources that promote views contrary to your own.
- Discuss current news events with your family at the dinner table.
- Find out when you are eligible to vote. Register. Then vote in the next election.

Find a copy of the *Charter of the Rights of the Family* online. (Type the title in quotes in a search engine and you will locate it at the Vatican's website, www.vatican.va, or at the website of the United States Conference of Catholic Bishops, www.nccbuscc.org. After reading the entire Charter, list in your journal five other rights that you find critical to family life that are listed as subsets under the main articles.

* Name one or more rights for the family you would add to these articles.

* List any violations of these rights that you are aware of by employers, local governments, or the federal government.

5. Since they have conferred life on their children, parents have the original, primary, and inalienable right to educate them; hence they must be acknowledged as the first and foremost educators of their children.

6. The family has the right to exist and to progress as a family.

7. Every family has the right to live freely its own domestic religious life under the guidance of the parents, as well as the right to profess publicly and to propagate the faith, to take part in public worship and in freely chosen programs of religious instruction, without suffering discrimination.

8. The family has the right to exercise its social and political function in the construction of society.

9. Families have the right to be able to rely on an adequate family policy on the part of public

authorities in the juridical, economic, social and fiscal domains, without any discrimination whatsoever.

10. Families have a right to a social and economic order in which the organization of work permits the members to live together, and does not hinder the unity, well-being, health, and the stability of the family, while offering also the possibility of wholesome recreation.

11. The family has the right to decent housing, fitting for family life and commensurate to the number of the members, in a physical environment that provides the basic services for the life of the family and the community.

12. The families of migrants have the right to the same protection as that accorded other families.

---

case study ▶ SHOULD THE STATE GIVE VOUCHER CREDITS FOR PAROCHIAL AND PRIVATE SCHOOLS?

Background:

Some states and local governments, including Florida and the city of Milwaukee, support legislation giving parents tax credit that can be applied to private and parochial schools.

Con:

Read an article that argues that school vouchers will either destroy the separation of church and state or will undermine the public school system. (Do a web search under the title "school vouchers." You might also wish to check out www.schoolchoices.org for links to several articles.)

Pro:

Read an article supporting the premise that voucher tax credits will strengthen both parochial and public school systems.

Discuss and Debate:

Share the information you found. Take a stand on the issue. Explain why you believe as you do.

SAINT THÉRÈSE OF LISIEUX (1873–1897) THE LITTLE WAY OF HOLINESS

Without love, deeds, even the most brilliant, count as nothing.
— *Saint Thérèse of Lisieux*

It is surprising that the Church should name a cloistered nun, Saint Thérèse of Lisieux, a patron saint of the missions. After all, she died of tuberculosis at the young age of twenty-four in a Carmelite convent in France having never put a foot on mission soil. But her love for the missions, her remarkable prayers and support for them, and her "little way" to holiness have taught Christians around the world how to do God's work in a hidden yet powerful way. Her example and her teachings, especially in her autobiography, *The Story of a Soul*, are so powerful a path to holiness that the Church named her a Doctor of the Church in 1997 on the centennial of her death. ("Doctor of the Church" is a designation bestowed on outstanding leaders, writers, teachers, and theologians.)

Thérèse grew up in a Christian family surrounded by love. Her father, Louis Martin (1823–1894), was a watchmaker who wanted to be a monk but could not master the Latin required for entrance into the community. Her mother, Zelie Guerin (1831–1877), after unsuccessfully trying to enter religious life, mastered lace-making. Zelie's talent, brains, and hard work enabled her to run a successful business enterprise. When she and Louis met, they married but vowed to live a celibate life as a way to show their love for God. When their priest said this is not how married people should show their love, Louis and Zelie made an about-face and became the very loving parents of nine children!

However, tragedy pursued the Martins. Within a three-year period, they lost two baby boys, an infant daughter, and a five-year-old girl. Many couples would have despaired at this, but they trusted God and relied on him to get them through their tough times.

Their last child was Thérèse, born on January 2, 1873. Thérèse began life weak and frail; the family thought they would lose her. But she survived, becoming the favorite of her parents and her four sisters: Marie, Pauline, Leonine, and Celine.

A loving and adorable little girl, Thérèse possessed a fierce temper which she spent a lifetime mastering. A major setback in her life took place when she was four. Her beloved mother died of breast cancer after fighting it heroically and without complaint for twelve years. Her sisters, especially Pauline, helped raise Thérèse. When Pauline left for the Carmelite convent, Thérèse said she lost her second mother, but was determined to join her there one day.

Eventually Marie entered the Carmelite convent, and Leonine joined the Visitation Convent. Louis Martin was very close to Thérèse but did not hesitate to help her when she announced at the age of fourteen that she wanted to follow in Pauline's footsteps. The local bishop was astounded that Louis would be willing to sacrifice yet another daughter to convent life. Louis's response was, "A father is as eager to give his child to God as this child was eager to offer herself to him."

In due course, the authorities permitted the young Thérèse to enter the convent. She lived a hidden life for nine years before her painful death by tuberculosis. But in her nine years she drew on the solid Christian foundation she learned from her loving family and continued to master the spiritual life. In brief, she learned how a small, insignificant, unnoticed "flower" like her could do great things for God.

Through her prayer, spiritual reading, and lived experience, Thérèse learned a "little way" to God. It consisted in simply accepting his love for us—after all, God's great love for us in Christ Jesus is pure gift, something we cannot earn. She also pointed out that we should seek the Lord's help in all that we do. Next, we should keep trying to do good and never ever get discouraged by any setbacks. Finally, we should welcome God's forgiveness.

For her part, Thérèse grew in holiness by fighting her own impatience and by controlling her temper. She always tried to anticipate the needs of others. She smiled at someone when she did not necessarily feel

Obtain a copy of Saint Thérèse's *Story of a Soul: The Autobiography of Saint Thérèse of Lisieux* and use it for spiritual reading in the coming weeks.

Read more about Saint Thérèse at The Society of the Little Flower's website: www.littleflower.org

like it. She went out of her way to help an old crotchety nun who never tired of belittling Thérèse. She tried to take an interest in boring people. She resisted the urge to scream when a nun drove her crazy in Church by making an annoying, clacking sound. She silently endured the misunderstanding of others. She prayed for priests who worked in the missions. She prayed for the conversion of sinners.

Nothing "great" here. But the give-and-take of daily loving and living is a sure path to heaven. And these little battles of love gave her the strength to endure an excruciatingly painful illness. She died as we would all hope to die with these words on her lips, "Oh! I love Him! My God, I love you!"

Thérèse's "little way" can teach us how to fight the fight. We do not necessarily have to perform notorious acts of bravery to be God's instruments of justice. But we can accept his love and then spread it around by treating everyone with respect and kindness, even if they annoy us to no end. We can seek out both the physically and spiritually hungry and thirsty in our midst and do some kind deed for them. We can find a stranger in our midst—even among our own classmates—and extend a friendly smile. We can look out for the needs of others in our neighborhood and do a "random act of kindness."

Doing justice by giving others what is their due is a great opportunity to grow in holiness. Just deeds, tempered with love, count for a lot in God's eyes.

- All of Louis and Zelie's five daughters became nuns, "brides of Christ." This heroic generosity in service of Christ and his Church is extremely rare today. Why do think this is so?
- What do you consider to be qualities of a good Christian family today?
- What qualities would you look for in a potential marriage partner? in the father or mother of *your* children? in a person who will share your faith life "until death do you part"?
- Choose a religious community of men or women. Write to or interview in person a member of the community to find out how he or she and the community are engaged in promoting justice in the world.

CHAPTER SUMMARY

- God made us social beings—with and for other persons. We belong to many different societies, groups bound by a principle of unity that goes beyond the individual. Every society has its own reason for being and its own set of rules. However, individuals must always be the foundation, cause, and end of all social institutions. Societies must exist for the benefit of the human person.
- The Church promotes individual freedom and initiative. Therefore, it subscribes to the principle of subsidiarity. This principle holds that larger social organizations, like the federal government, should not take over what individuals or lower associations can accomplish on their own.
- Just societies always promote the common good, the sum of those social conditions which allow individuals to achieve fulfillment as human beings. Societies that promote the common good respect persons, encourage development and social well-being, and foster peace.
- Christians committed to justice practice the virtue of solidarity, or social charity, which views others as brothers and sisters with whom we must share. This is true not only with groups we are closest to, like our families, but also with people on the other side of the globe. As God's children, we are interdependent and responsible for one another.

- Christians, in imitation of Jesus, will also have a preferential love for the poor. The poor are often powerless and unable to secure their own rights. Therefore, they need our help so they can take an active role in society and share in and contribute to the common good.
- Besides divine revelation, the Church draws on natural law as a key source in its social teaching. All people can discover the natural law by using their intellects. The natural law is the light of understanding which God implants in our hearts so we can discover good and evil.
- Because we are social beings, we have responsibilities to the larger society. We must help shape a just and loving society and contribute to the common good. We must participate in social interchange according to our position, role, talents, and interests. We must especially look out for the interests of the poor and view and act toward each person as another self. We must be good citizens by voting, paying taxes, and so forth.
- In turn, society has obligations toward individuals. It must see that everyone has access to the political, economic, social, and cultural arenas. It must outlaw any form of discrimination. It must create a wholesome climate that does not undermine virtuous living. Government must always protect innocent human life, support the family, guarantee that distributive justice is meeting the needs of the poor and defenseless, promote peace, and the like.
- The family is the foundation of society. All families have fundamental rights. For example, spouses have the right to found a family. Each human life deserves respect from the first moment of conception. Every family has the right to pursue a religious life according to its conscience. Parents have the right to educate their children according to their conscience and so forth.
- An example of a Christian saint who grew out of a loving family environment was Saint Thérèse of Lisieux. She exemplifies a "little way" of justice and love, that is, by living each day simply and doing the ordinary things in an extraordinary way. She teaches us to see others as another self, as a hidden Jesus.

REVIEW QUESTIONS

1. Explain how human life is like a spider web.
2. Why do we have a social nature?
3. Define society. What should all societies have in common?
4. Define the principle of subsidiarity. Give an example of the principle being correctly applied. Give an example of the principle being violated.
5. Define the common good. What are its three essential elements?
6. What is the virtue of solidarity? Give an example of this virtue in action.
7. What is meant by "the preferential option for the poor"?
8. List five ways you can exercise an option for the poor.
9. What is meant by the "natural law"?
10. What do we mean when we say the natural law is universal, permanent, and unchangeable?
11. List and discuss three duties individuals have toward society.
12. List and discuss three duties society has toward its individual members.
13. Why is the family the central social unit? List three basic family rights.
14. Briefly explain Saint Thérèse's "little way" to holiness. Give an example of how you might put it into practice in your daily life.

MAKING A DIFFERENCE

Do your little bit of good where you are; it's those little bits of good put together that overwhelm the world.

—*Archbishop Desmond Tutu*[2]

Respect, solidarity, caring for the poor, and harmonious family life all thrive when kindness is present. Synonyms for the word *kindness* include: good will, tenderness, compassion, humanity, gentleness, goodness, generosity, and favor.

- Devise a plan of action for "random acts of kindness." Your active goodness for others will help build up the virtue of solidarity. Check the website of The Random Acts of Kindness Foundation for some ideas: www.actsofkindness.org
- Saint Thérèse of Lisieux taught us the power of one life, simply lived for others. The Creed of the Christopher Organization—"It is better to light one candle than to curse the darkness"—shares her philosophy. The name *Christopher* means "Christ bearer." You can be a Christ-bearer simply by making a difference in someone's life, by getting involved in your community, by looking out in a special way for the least among us. Visit the Christophers' website at www.christophers.org. Next, do at least one of the following:
  - Read about their variety of works.
  - Sign up to receive the free News Notes.
  - Consider entering their art contest for high-school students.
  - Watch one of their *Closeup* video clips.

RESEARCHING ON THE INTERNET

The ultimate injustice is for a person or group to be treated actively or abandoned passively as if they were nonmembers of the human race. To treat people this way is effectively to say that they simply do not count as human beings.

— *U.S. Bishops,* Economic Justice for All, *§77*

1. Visit the United States Conference of Catholic Bishops website—www.nccbuscc.org. Under their departments page, locate the Social Development and World Peace Office. Read and report on one of the bishops' recent statements in the news.
2. *The Common Good and the Catholic Church's Social Teaching* is an important social teaching document written by the bishops of England and Wales. Report on all or part of §24–53 of this pastoral letter. Search for this document on the Internet.

PRAYER REFLECTION

Pope Pius XII lived during the trying times of World War II. Pray his heartfelt words in his "Prayer for Justice and Peace."[3]

> *Almighty and eternal God,*
> *may your grace enkindle in all of us*
> *a love for the many unfortunate people*
> > *whom poverty and misery reduce to a*
> > *condition of life*
> > *unworthy of human beings.*
> *Arouse in the hearts of those who call you Father*
> *a hunger and thirst for justice and peace,*
> > *and for fraternal charity in deeds and in truth.*
> *Grant, O Lord, peace in our days,*
> *peace to souls, peace to families, peace to*
> > *our country,*
> *and peace among nations.*
> *Amen.*

NOTES

1. These facts are reported by Brian Cavanaugh, T.O.R., in his *Fresh Packet of Sower's Seeds: Third Planting* (New York: Paulist Press, 1994), pp. 52–54.
2. Found at The Random Acts of Kindness Foundation, "Inspirational Quotes" <http://www.acts ofkindness.org/inspiration/quotes.asp>.
3. Reproduced in *Day by Day: The Notre Dame Prayerbook for Students* (Notre Dame, IN: Ave Maria Press, 1975), p. 28.

CHAPTER OVERVIEW

Assaults Against Life
The most basic right of life has been assaulted in several ways.

Abortion
Abortion is a grave act of injustice against the child, the mother, and the whole human family.

Stem Cell Research
There is a moral difference between research with adult stem cells and embryonic stem cells.

Euthanasia
Euthanasia, or "mercy killing," is a crucial issue for today. The Church reminds us that we do not have the "right" to die. Our life and death is in God's hands.

Capital Punishment
This section presents both traditional and contemporary Church teachings on capital punishment.

Saint Gianna Beretta Molla
This recently canonized saint gave up her life to save the life of her newborn child.

The Seamless Garment
Catholic social teaching promotes a "consistent ethic of life" from conception to natural death.

Respect, protect, love and serve life, every human life!
Only in this direction will you find justice, development, true freedom,
peace and happiness!

— **Pope John Paul II,** *The Gospel of Life,* **§5**

4
JUSTICE AND
THE RIGHT TO LIFE

ASSAULTS AGAINST LIFE

This chapter focuses on the fundamental principle of social justice: the right to life for all human beings from conception to natural death. Unfortunately, this most basic of all rights has been assaulted at all stages and in many horrific

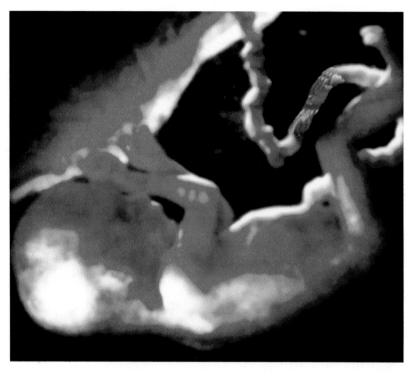

ways in recent years. As a preview to this chapter, consider these facts that describe some assaults against life:

- In 96 percent of the states where there have been reviews of race and the death penalty, there was a pattern of either race-of-victim or race-of-defendant discrimination, or both.
- Capital punishment does not deter crime: states that have the death penalty have higher murder rates than those that do not.[1]
- The system of capital punishment is flawed: On the federal level, 3.5 percent of persons whom the Attorney General has attempted to execute have been innocent. In one example of state-level problems, Illinois (prior to the governor's blanket commutation) had an error rate of at least 4.5 percent.[2]
- Suction aspiration is the abortion technique used in most first trimester abortions. This technique inserts into the mother's womb a powerful suction tube with a sharp cutting edge. This device dismembers the body of the baby and tears the placenta from the uterine wall, sucking blood, amniotic fluid, placental tissue, and fetal parts into a collection bottle.
- Salt poisoning (saline amniocentesis) is often used to abort babies after sixteen weeks of pregnancy. A needle is inserted through the mother's abdomen to withdraw amniotic fluid and replace it with a solution of concentrated salt. The baby breathes in and swallows the salt and dies, usually within an hour. The saline solution also causes painful burning and deterioration of the baby's skin. The mother goes into labor about 33–35 hours after instillation of the salt and delivers a dead, burned, shriveled baby.[3]
- A National Cancer Institute study of over 1,800 women in Washington state found a 50 percent increased risk among women who had abortions. The risk was more than double for women whose first abortion took place before age eighteen or over age thirty.[4]
- In a rare 9–0 vote, the United States Supreme Court in a 1997 decision found that the average American does not have a constitutional right to physician-assisted suicide. However, the court implied that individual states could pass laws to permit doctors to help people commit suicide in the future.
- Requests for voluntary **euthanasia** are rarely free and voluntary. Patients with terminal illnesses are vulnerable and anxious about their medical treatment and the effect of their illness on loved ones. Patients cannot be entirely objective. They are often suffering depression, are confused, and are suffering from troublesome dementia often caused by inappropriate treatment. After their symptoms have been given proper treatment, many patients are glad that their request "to just let me die" was not honored.[5]
- Besides considering in more depth the scope of some of these assaults against life, this chapter will present several ways Christians promote life and will look at the Church's outline of a consistent ethic of life.

WHAT DO YOU THINK?

Test your knowledge on the following questions related to the Church's teaching on life. Check either the true or false column as appropriate.

The Questions	T	F
1. Papal encyclicals on social justice treat the topic of abortion more frequently than the theme of poverty.		
2. The Church teaches that you do not have to use "extraordinary" measures to maintain life.		
3. In rare cases, like to extract secrets from captured spies in wartime, government officials can torture their prisoners.		
4. To treat a worker as a tool for profit is an infamy (a wicked, depraved act).		
5. Killing in self-defense violates the divine law.		
6. The Church forbids the death penalty under all circumstances.		
7. Artificial reproduction—like test-tube babies—is morally acceptable.		
8. Not to help alleviate the misery of starving people makes society guilty of murder.		
9. Rape is an allowable exception for abortion.		
10. Organ donation is permitted if done morally.		

In your opinion, which is the greatest life issue facing our country today? Explain.

EUTHANASIA—"AN ACT OR OMISSION WHICH of itself and by INTENTION CAUSES DEATH, with the purpose of eliminating all suffering" (*The Gospel of Life*, §65). EUTHANASIA is a violation of the fifth commandment which forbids killing; it CAN NEVER BE justified.

ABORTION

(CCC, 2258; 2270-2275; 2318-2320; 2322-2323; 2331-2350; 2393-2395)

Perhaps the most compelling justice issue of our day is abortion, the unjustified killing of unborn human beings. What makes abortion wrong is that human life is a gift from God which everyone must protect, nurture, and sustain from *the first moment of conception*. The right to life is the foundation on which rests all other inalienable rights and from which they develop.

If the most fundamental right—the right to life—is not protected, then every other human right is under threat. Laws must guarantee this most basic human right or society is under threat of collapse. The common good can only be served when the right to life is acknowledged and defended.

Abortion assaults human dignity and one's worth as a unique child of God redeemed by Christ Jesus. It is a grave act of injustice against the child. It also violates the mother and the whole human family. When society tolerates abortion, or even encourages it as a way to deal with unwanted pregnancies, all human life—womb to tomb—is threatened. The old, the handicapped, and anyone else termed "undesirable" are soon considered bothersome. Before long, voices in what Pope John Paul II called a "culture of death" will find "rational" arguments to kill them, too. As the Second Vatican Council warned:

ABORTION—THE deliberate killing of unborn human life by means of medical or surgical procedures. DIRECT ABORTION is seriously wrong because it is an unjustified attack on innocent human life.

I SWORE NEVER TO BE SILENT WHENEVER AND WHEREVER HUMAN BEINGS ENDURE SUFFERING AND MUTILATION. WE MUST ALWAYS TAKE SIDES. NEUTRALITY HELPS THE OPPRESSOR, NEVER THE VICTIM. SILENCE ENCOURAGES THE TORMENTOR, NEVER THE TORMENTED.

—ELIE WEISEL,
HOLOCAUST SURVIVOR

THE ONLY LEGITIMATE OBJECT OF GOOD GOVERNMENT IS THE CARE AND PROTECTION OF ITS PEOPLE, NOT THEIR DESTRUCTION.

—THOMAS JEFFERSON

Whatever is opposed to life itself, such as any type of murder, genocide, abortion, euthanasia or willful self-destruction . . . all these things and others of their like are infamies indeed. They poison human society, but they do more harm to those who practice them than those who suffer from the injury. Moreover, they are a supreme dishonor to the Creator (The Church in the Modern World, §27).

WHY LEGALIZED ABORTION?

In 1973 in the United States of America, the Supreme Court in its *Roe v. Wade* decision held that a woman's right to privacy includes her decision to have an abortion. This famous case declared abortion a constitutional right in the United States, a country that once prided itself on defending the weak. (It is interesting to note that the original litigant in this famous case, Jane Roe—whose real name is Norma McCorvey—converted to Catholicism. She is now dedicating her life to reversing the infamous case that legalized abortion in the United States.)[6]

NORMA McCORVEY

YOU DO SOLEMNLY SWEAR . . . THAT YOU WILL EXERCISE YOUR ART SOLELY FOR THE CURE OF YOUR PATIENTS, AND WILL GIVE NO DRUG, PERFORM NO OPERATION, FOR A CRIMINAL PURPOSE, EVEN IF SOLICITED, FAR LESS SUGGEST IT.

— HIPPOCRATIC OATH

Today, its abortion policies are among the most permissive of any industrialized nation of the West. The statistics are both shameful and staggering:

- though the rate of abortions has decreased in recent years, most estimates say there are still around 1.3 million abortions performed each year in the United States;
- over 3,700 abortions are performed per day, 155 per hour, 1 every 24 seconds;
- 48 percent of the pregnancies among American woman are unintended; half of these are terminated by abortion;
- for every 1,000 live births there are 314 abortions;
- an estimated 46 million abortions occur worldwide each year.[7]

How did legalized abortion in the United States come about? Years ago, the vast majority of people viewed abortion as an unspeakable crime, an act of desperation, the killing of one's own child. Today, our society has adopted an abortion mentality that has blinded even people of good will from seeing that unborn, innocent humans have a God-given right to life, acceptance, respect, help, and love. This mentality is a cancer that has eaten into our society, leading to more and more people supporting euthanasia, assisted suicide, organ harvesting, and similar assaults on the dignity of humans.

The mindset and language of abortion are part of a "culture of death," that does not guarantee life to those who most depend on us to protect them. We find this mindset and language in the media—in the news, on television, in the movies and contemporary music. The mentality that sees little or nothing wrong with abortion praises unlimited freedom of choice, an unbridled individualism that sees no responsibility to others, and an absolute right to privacy.

The pope and the American bishops,[8] among other Church leaders, trace the roots of today's disrespect for the sanctity of life to two major factors:

1. **Breakdown of the family.** In the words of Pope John Paul II in *The Gospel of Life* (§11), the family is the "sanctuary of life." The family teaches fidelity, loyalty, and devotion

to those who are young and old, disabled or sick, that is, to those who depend on others for their very existence. Yet, contemporary society has undermined the family, changing traditional views on marriage and divorce. Today, marriage is often seen as optional for couples who live together, even for those who want to be parents. The legal system has also largely allowed people to divorce for virtually any reason, expanding the grounds for divorce far beyond the serious offenses of adultery and desertion. Commitment and responsibility are not valued as they once were. As a result, family life erodes, and the innocents who need the protection of families suffer the most.

2. *Freedom is the absolute value.* Many in the fields of education, the various media, and politics preach the pursuit of individual happiness as the supreme value. The values of fidelity to duty and service to others often meet ridicule. The Church respects the exercise of freedom, especially in religious and moral matters, but teaches that the "exercise of freedom does not entail the putative right to say or do anything" (CCC, 1747).

Unchecked personal freedom leads to an excessive individualism that ignores other people, and especially those too weak or dependent to defend their own rights. Within the past generation a "me-first" culture has led to the idea that an unplanned baby somehow destroys individual freedom. Therefore, the undesirable, unborn child can be dispensed with before seeing the light of day. This "me-first" attitude has also given birth to the idea that a spouse or parent who is too old or sick or "unproductive" can have his or her life ended as an act of mercy.

OPPOSITE OF ABORTION: PRO LIFE

From its beginning, the Church has strongly opposed abortion. For example, the first-century catechetical document known as the *Didache* reflects the teaching of the apostles: "You shall not kill by abortion the fruit of the womb and you shall not murder the infant already born" (§6). Through the centuries, the Church always considered abortion a mortal sin.

Today, the Church teaches that our opposition to abortion is consistent with a profound respect for life, a seamless garment of respect from womb to tomb.

Christians who stand for life must be educated so we can respond to those in our pluralistic society who would permit abortion. As people who are pro-life, we must always proclaim:

God conveys the gift of life, not the state. The state sometimes has immoral laws on its books. Recall how the laws of America once permitted slavery, treating human beings as objects to buy and sell and not as persons to love and to cherish. Bad laws must be changed, even disobeyed. The right to life is so basic that society must make it a crime to take an innocent human life. Abortion is the moral equivalent of murder.

Human life begins at conception. Human life begins from the time the ovum is fertilized. Genetics has shown that a new human being—genetically distinct from both mother and father—has begun the process of his or her growth at the moment of conception. As the Vatican's *Declaration on Procured Abortion* emphatically states, "Any discrimination based on the various stages of life is no more justified than any other discrimination" (§12).

A child's right to life outweighs a mother's freedom of choice or her right to privacy. No doubt abortion involves privacy and choice issues.

However, the most fundamental right—the right to life—outweighs either a woman's right to privacy or her right to choose an abortion. We must always choose the greater good and side with life. In the case of abortion, this means siding with the unborn child. As our laws against suicide exemplify, no one has an absolute right over his or her own body. As social beings, we belong to each other. This is most dramatically true of a mother who carries an unborn child who is totally dependent on her.

Abortion should be made illegal. In a pluralistic society, we may often hear the argument that making abortion illegal forces one's own personal beliefs on others. However, abortion deals with an assault on the most basic right of all—the right to life. The role of government is to protect human rights, especially the fundamental right to life. As citizens in a democracy, we have the right and duty to make laws that protect human beings. The life of a defenseless child is more valuable than the opinion that human life is dispensable as an exercise of one's freedom.

Making abortion illegal through a constitutional amendment, backing efforts to restrict access to abortions by eliminating government support of abortions, and voting for laws that provide morally acceptable alternatives to abortion will not prevent all abortions. However, these efforts would greatly cut down the number being performed today. In any case, Catholics are not bound to obey any permissive abortion law. Pope John Paul II wrote:

> *Abortion and euthanasia are thus crimes which no human law can claim to legitimize. There is no obligation in conscience to obey such laws; instead there is a grave and clear obligation to oppose them by conscientious objection (The Gospel of Life, §73).*

Concerning an unjust law, we may never take part in a propaganda campaign in favor of such a law or vote for it.

We should cultivate a correct view of the sacredness of sex. Many unplanned pregnancies occur because people behave immorally concerning sex. Many people want sex for pleasure alone, without responsibility and commitment. This view comes from a sex-saturated and hedonistic society. Various media sell a message to teens that says that it is impossible for them to control their sexual urges; therefore, they should indulge in "safe" sex.

This view of sex demeans humans. We are free and, with God's grace, are capable of controlling our sexual appetite. We need a proper education on the beauty and holiness of human sexuality. Sexual sharing is God's gift to a committed married couple to express love and to share life. When sex and committed, monogamous married love are separated, people get hurt. They often use each other and cause unplanned pregnancies. If more people would learn and then pay attention to God's plan for sexual sharing, there would be far fewer unwanted pregnancies.

There are always alternatives to abortion. Unfortunately, unborn children are at the mercy of those who contemplate abortion as their only alternative. Sadly, some women consider abortion because they conceived children as a result of the tragic crimes of rape or incest. However, the unborn child conceived in these circumstances did not commit these infamies. The innocent child has a right to life, regardless of how he or she was conceived. Two wrongs do not right the situation in which the violated woman finds herself. Adoption is always a viable alternative to abortion. Life is always a greater good than death.

All too often young teenage girls find themselves pregnant after an affair with a boyfriend. He may push for abortion because he does not want to accept responsibility. To complicate matters, the girl's family may also pressure her to have an abortion. Despite these pressures and her feeling of being trapped, the young mother always has alternatives. For example, she can turn to an organization like Birthright where she can go for material, psychological, spiritual, and medical help.

With loving and caring Christians and others committed to life reaching out to those who find themselves with an unwanted pregnancy, abortion is never the only option.

One final word: We know that many times women and girls abort their children because of grave psychological strain. Although they have committed an objectively serious evil by killing innocent human life, their diminished freedom may well lessen their moral blameworthiness for the act. While condemning the serious sin of abortion, as Christ's followers, we must never judge a person's condition before God, either the person who aborted, or the person who encouraged or cooperated in an abortion. Jesus told us to preach God's forgiveness and compassion for everyone, including sinners. Those who have aborted out of fear and psychological pressure need our help and support, not our condemnation.

We live in a violent society; abortion is an obvious quick-fix, but a violent solution to a complex social problem. Any society that kills its

QUESTIONS FOR CATHOLIC VOTERS

We urge those Catholic officials who choose to depart from Church teaching on the inviolability of human life in their public life to consider the consequences for their own spiritual well being, as well as the scandal they risk by leading others into serious sin. We call on them to reflect on the grave contradiction of assuming public roles and presenting themselves as credible Catholics when their actions on fundamental issues of human life are not in agreement with Church teaching. No public official, especially one claiming to be a faithful and serious Catholic, can responsibly advocate for or actively support direct attacks on innocent human life. [N]o appeal to policy, procedure, majority will or pluralism ever excuses a public official from defending life to the greatest extent possible. As is true of leaders in all walks of life, no political leader can evade accountability for his or her exercise of power (Evangelium Vitae, 73–4). *Those who justify their inaction on the grounds that abortion is the law of the land need to recognize that there is a higher law, the law of God. No human law can validly contradict the Commandment: "Thou shalt not kill."*
—Living the Gospel of Life: A Challenge to American Catholics *(1998), §32*

Recent elections have raised the important issue of whether Catholics may vote for political candidates who endorse pro-abortion views. The issue is especially controversial when the candidate who is running for office identifies himself or herself as a Catholic.

Debate this issue. The following two documents can help you formulate your arguments. You might also want to consult what the bishop of your diocese has said about this topic:
- United States Conference of Catholic Bishops, *Catholics in Political Life*: www.usccb.org/bishops/catholicsinpoliticallife.shtml
- Congregation for the Doctrine of the Faith, *On Some Questions Regarding the Participation of Catholics in Political Life*: www.vatican.va/roman_curia/congregations/cfaith/documents/rc_con_cfaith_doc_20021124_politica_en.html

children and its old and sick, while neglecting the needy, is a failed society. Violent acts like bombing abortion clinics only help to create a more violent society. Some of these acts have led to death. They are unacceptable and un-Christian. They violate the principle that a good end or reason for doing something does not justify an evil means to attain it.

Fighting abortion must fit into a larger picture of promoting life. What can we do? First, we can pray for a change in hearts, so people may see the most vulnerable in our midst as brothers and sisters, and not as objects for disposal. As Christians, we can also speak of Christ's loving forgiveness and compassion for repentant sinners, especially women who have had an abortion. Pope John Paul II addressed these words to women who have had an abortion:

The Church is aware of the many factors which may have influenced your decision, and she does not doubt that in many cases it was a painful and even shattering decision. The wound in your heart may not yet have healed. Certainly what happened was and remains terribly wrong. But do not give in to discouragement and do not lose hope. Try rather to understand what happened and face it honestly. If you have not already done so, give yourselves over with humility and trust to repentance. The Father of mercies is ready to give you his forgiveness and his peace in the Sacrament of Reconciliation. You will come to understand that nothing is definitively lost and you will also be able to ask forgiveness from your child, who is now living in the Lord. With the friendly and expert help and advice of other people, and as a result of your own painful experience, you can be among the most eloquent defenders of everyone's right to life. Through your commitment to life, whether by accepting the birth of other children or by welcoming and caring for those most in need of someone to be close to them, you will become promoters of a new way of looking at human life (The Gospel of Life, §99).

In addition, the American bishops urge Catholics to get involved in pastoral care programs for pregnant women, especially those who would be most vulnerable to abortion and find it difficult to get quality medical care. Compassionate pastoral care programs would include:

- factual and educational information on alternatives to abortion;
- nutritional, prenatal, childbirth, and postnatal care for the mother, including information about the latest developments in prenatal and neonatal medicine;
- nutritional and pediatric care for the child;
- agency-sponsored adoption and foster care services to all who want them, as well as an educational effort presenting adoption in a positive light;
- counseling and spiritual assistance that supports those facing difficulties related to pregnancy and parenting, including engaged or married couples who may have concerns about the health of their future offspring;
- opportunities for teen and college-age parents to continue their education during pregnancy and after childbirth, including school policies that encourage and enable them to complete their high school education, and counseling and assistance encouraging continued undergraduate or graduate studies;
- compassionate understanding, encouragement, and support for victims of rape and other forms of abuse and violence;
- education in the virtue of chastity, as well as education in fertility awareness for young men and women, enabling them to take responsibility for their power to generate life;
- expansion of natural family planning programs and education in their mission as responsible parents for married and engaged couples.[9]

CASE STUDY: PREGNANT TEENAGER

Background:

Tammy is fifteen. She lives with her single mother and two younger siblings. Tammy has told her boyfriend, Ted, seventeen, that she is pregnant. He is "freaked out" and unwilling to take responsibility. Tammy is distraught. If she chooses to have her baby, she knows she'll have to leave school to support the child. At this point, to her abortion looks like the only alternative.

What Would You Do?

- Tammy confides in you as her best friend. What would you advise?
- Imagine you are Tammy's mother and that Tammy told you of her crisis. What would you tell her? What should you tell her?
- Ted confides in you as his best friend. What would you tell him? What should you tell him?

SCRIPTURE LINK

The Bible is pro-life. Six Scripture themes convincingly prove this statement:

1. *God outlaws the killing of innocent people.*
2. *God loves everyone, including unborn babies.*
3. *God alone is in control of human life.* We are creatures whose lives are not absolutely our own.
4. *Christ Jesus is Lord and Life.* In Jesus, sin and death are conquered.
5. *We must love.* Made in God's image and likeness and redeemed by Christ, we must love others as ourselves. We must have preferential love for the weak and defenseless.
6. *God is a just God.* He intervenes for the helpless. So must we if we want to be called God's people.

Read and summarize the following Scripture passages. Point out which themes above are represented in each passage.

1 John 3:11–23	Psalm 139
Genesis 4:1–15	Proverbs 24:8–12
Psalm 72	John 1:1–5

STEM CELL RESEARCH

In recent decades, medical science has been moving at a lightning pace. One area that has taken on special urgency in the public arena is stem-cell research, both for its potential benefits to medical science and its moral and ethical side effects due to the use of living human embryos to harvest stem cells.

Just what is a stem cell? In brief, stem cells are a vital way for the body's cells to be replenished. A stem cell is an unspecialized cell that has the potential to become one of many specific types of cells—a cell like itself or a more specialized cell, for example, a cell that can produce new white blood cells. *Embryonic stem cells* have the potential to become *any* kind of body cell. *Adult stem cells* have the potency to

PROMOTING LIFE

Promote life by doing one of the following in the coming weeks:

- Pray daily for an end to abortion, for women tempted to have abortions, for doctors and nurses, for legislators, for clergy, for those who work in the pro-life movement, and for those who do not realize how wrong abortion is.

- Read. Be more informed about abortion from such books as *Abortion: Questions and Answers*, by Dr. and Mrs. J.C. Willke (available from Hayes Publishing, (513)681-7559).

- Wear the "Precious Feet" pin which shows the baby's feet at 10 weeks after conception (available from Heritage House, 1-800-858-3040). You can also wear the pro-life red rose (available from NRLC Rose Account, 51 Candice Circle, Springfield, MA 01107).

- Find out who the local abortionists are. Some of them do it "on the side." Let them know your opposition to abortion. Pray for them by name.

- Conduct fund raising efforts for pro-life groups: car washes, bake sales, raffles, dinners, penny drives, etc.

These and many other ideas can be found on the Priests for Life website. Please check this website frequently for many great helps to promote life: www.priestsforlife.org/brochures/youcan.html

become *many* different cells, *but not all*. The goal of some scientists is to work on lines of embryonic stem cells to develop them into becoming specific kinds of cells, thus hoping to cure diseases like diabetes and Alzheimer's disease.

The Church supports most stem cell research which typically obtains cells from adult tissue, umbilical cord blood, and other sources. This type of research poses no moral problem. On the other hand, the ethical issue involved in *embryonic* stem cell research is that researchers must harvest stem cells from living human embryos, thus destroying them. Scientists do this by collecting or harvesting stem cells from the very early stages of a fertilized egg, called a *blastocyst*.

Even though the purpose of this type of research might produce a good result, it does not justify the evil means of the destruction of innocent human life. It is a clear principle of Catholic morality that we may not use a good end or purpose for doing an act to justify an evil means. And it is evil to treat human life as disposable commodities, as beings created in order to kill them for their cells. The Church's consistent teaching opposes the direct destruction of

human life from these earliest stages. For example, the Congregation for the Doctrine of the Faith's document, *The Gift of Life (Donum Vitae)*, teaches that

from the first moment of its existence, that is to say from the moment the zygote has formed, demands the unconditional respect that is morally due to the human being in his bodily and spiritual totality. The human being is to be respected and treated as a person from the moment of conception; and therefore from that same moment his rights as a person must be recognized, among which in the first place is the inviolable right of every innocent human being to life (§I, Q1).

An argument used by those promoting embryonic stem-cell research is that stem cells from adults are difficult to obtain. Adult stem cells are collected from a limited number of types in the body. Typically these are bone marrow from the very early stages of development. Current research has had some success in isolating and developing adult stem cells. If this trend continues, there will be no reason to employ embryonic stem cells, which requires the destruction of embryos.

The fact is that adult stem cell research has saved thousands of lives to date. In contrast, embryonic stem cell research has promised much more than it has delivered. The American bishops have called attention to contrasting outcomes between adult stem cells and embryonic stem cells. Their "Reality

Check" contrasts the relative merits of adult and embryonic stem cell research related to several medical problems.[10] Consider the following:

JUVENILE DIABETES	*Adult Pancreatic Islet Cells* Fifteen people with serious Type I (juvenile) diabetes became "insulin free" after adult pancreatic islet cell transplants; nine still need no insulin injections. —AMERICAN DIABETES ASSOCIATION REPORT, JUNE 24, 2001	*Embryonic Stem Cells* No person has benefited.
SPINAL CORD INJURY	*Adult Immune-System Cells* A young woman rendered paraplegic by a car accident can move her toes and legs after injection of her own immune-system cells into her severed spinal cord. —TORONTO GLOBE AND MAIL, JUNE 15, 2001	*Embryonic Stem Cells* No person has benefited.
IMMUNE DEFICIENCY	*Adult Bone Marrow Stem Cells* Two children born without immune systems ("bubble boy" syndrome) have left their sterile environment and lead normal lives after bone marrow stem cell treatment. —"SCIENCE," THE WASHINGTON POST, APRIL 28, 2000	*Embryonic Stem Cells* No person has benefited.
CORNEAL REPAIR	*Adult Corneal Stem Cells* Several legally blind people can now see more clearly after their corneas were reconstructed with corneal stem cells. —NEW ENGLAND JOURNAL OF MEDICINE, JULY 13, 2000	*Embryonic Stem Cells* No person has benefited.

Do one or more of the following:

1. Answer the following questions and debate your responses with classmates: Do you believe the government should promote research into high-tech and expensive therapies that may not be available to the millions of citizens who don't have access to them because of lack of insurance? Why? Or should the government devote the majority of its resources to preventing disease? Explain.

2. Locate *The Gift of Life* on the U.S. Bishops' or Vatican's website. Do one of the following:

Write a brief report on questions 2, 3, 4, 5, or 6 in part 1.

Read the introductory section of part 2 and the response to question 1.

Then report on the answer given in question 2, 3, 4, 5, or 6 in part 2.

3. Research and report on some other aspect of the moral issues involved in embryonic stem-cell research or the cloning of humans.

EUTHANASIA
(CCC, 2276–2283; 2324–2325)

The popular definition of *euthanasia* is "mercy killing." *The Gospel of Life* defines euthanasia as "an act or omission which of itself and by intention causes death, with the purpose of eliminating all suffering" (§65).

There is a growing move to legalize euthanasia in the United States and other Western nations. Three reasons for this mindset are:

1. A cultural climate that sees no value in suffering, in fact, views it as the worst of all evils. When people abandon God, they often see life as simply the pursuit of pleasure. If pain enters the picture, and death looms

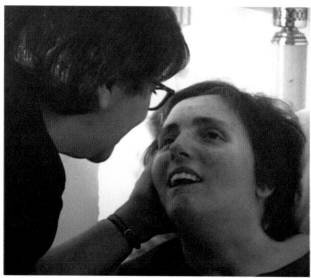

Terri Schiavo

Besides those at right, what are some other pitfalls of legal, voluntary euthanasia?

on the horizon, then hastening death seems like the best choice to be free from suffering.

In contrast, Christians have a God-inspired view of suffering. Not all suffering is meaningless. In fact, if we unite suffering to the Lord, especially in the last moments of life, we can share in Christ's passion. We can join his sacrifice offered to the Father for the sake of our sins. We should view impending death as a chance to say goodbye to our loved ones and to prepare to meet the Lord Jesus.

Offering our suffering to the Lord is heroic. However, the Church recognizes that we are not required to do so. Nor does God desire us to suffer needlessly. Therefore, Christian teaching authorizes the use of painkilling drugs as long as the intent is not to hasten death or cause unconsciousness.

2. People who neglect God often think they have sole control over life and death. Excessive individualism and the belief in an absolute right to freedom can influence godless people to believe they are the masters of death. Advances in medical science can contribute to "playing god" in life-and-death situations. Also, contemporary culture has a preoccupation with efficiency and judges the old and infirmed as unproductive and therefore dispensable.

3. An aging population puts pressure on a costly healthcare system. Some see euthanasia and assisted suicide as "cost effective." Sad to say, there are those who promote a "right to die" mentality, not because they are compassionate, but because keeping old people alive is expensive. Some people support abortion simply because babies cost money. Others foster assisted suicide and euthanasia because caring for the elderly or those with mental or physical disabilities costs money. A mentality exists that those who are a burden threaten the lifestyles of those who are better off. The solution: disposal, elimination. This mindset is a key ingredient in a society that has adopted a culture of death.

WHY LEGAL, VOLUNTARY EUTHANASIA IS WRONG

- It would deny patients the final stage of growth and, for example, the chance to mend broken relationships.
- It would become more widely accepted just like abortion has. The public conscience would become numb against this assault on human life, just as has happened with abortion.
- It violates the Hippocratic Oath, the ancient medical oath which physicians have traditionally taken. A doctor's duty is to preserve life, not end it.
- It would give too much power to doctors.
- Voluntary euthanasia would inevitably lead to involuntary euthanasia. This is precisely what has happened in Holland, which has legalized euthanasia.

ANOTHER OPTION: COMPASSION FOR THE DYING

Some believe that those with a terminal illness have only two options: unrelieved suffering or euthanasia. However, a third option of creative and compassionate care is also available. This option involves administering palliative medicine that can relieve or greatly reduce the pain associated with terminal illness. This third option is compatible with Church teaching. It recognizes that we promote life when we *compassionately* care for the sick and dying:

Those whose lives are diminished or weakened deserve special respect. Sick or handicapped persons should be helped to lead lives as normal as possible (CCC, 2276).

In caring for the sick, we must always use ordinary and morally acceptable means to preserve life, even of those who face death. However, the Church distinguishes between ordinary care and the decision not to employ "aggressive medical treatment," traditionally known as "extraordinary means." Church teaching holds that the decision to forego using extraordinary or disproportionate means to sustain life is morally acceptable and in no way equated with euthanasia or suicide. Rather, such a decision often signals a willingness to accept God's will in the face of death.

Quoting the Vatican's *Declaration on Euthanasia* (§IV), *The Gospel of Life* tells us that "aggressive medical treatment" refers to:

medical procedures which no longer correspond to the real situation of the patient, either because they are by now disproportionate to any expected results or because they impose an excessive burden on the patient and his family. In such situations, when death is clearly imminent and inevitable, one can in conscience "refuse forms of treatment that would only secure a precarious and burdensome prolongation of life, so long as the normal care due to the sick person in similar cases is not interrupted" (§65).

The *Declaration on Euthanasia* says we can judge whether the means are ordinary or extraordinary by analyzing:

• the kind of treatment to be used;

• its complexity and risk; and

• its costs and possibilities of using it.

Then, we must study these elements with the expected result, looking at the sick person's physical and psychological resources. For example, most reasonable people would agree that a heart transplant operation for a ninety-year-old would qualify as an aggressive medical procedure. One would not be obligated to undergo or to provide such an operation to prolong life.

CHURCH TEACHING ON EUTHANASIA, SUICIDE, AND ASSISTED SUICIDE

The Church strongly condemns euthanasia, suicide, and assisted suicide despite how or why they are done. Life is sacred, a gift from God. Euthanasia gravely violates God's law which forbids "the deliberate and morally unacceptable killing" of a human person. Similarly, suicide is always the moral equivalent of murder, a gravely evil act forbidden by the fifth commandment. It rejects God's absolute sovereignty over life and death.

Assisted suicide is also gravely wrong. By definition, "assisted suicide" is concurring with the intention of another person to commit suicide. It is helping someone to take his or her life. To do so is to cooperate in a grave injustice. Saint Augustine wrote that it is never moral to kill another person "even if he should wish it, indeed request it" (quoted in *The Gospel of Life*, §66).

Euthanasia and assisted suicide might appear compassionate. But they involve a false mercy. As Pope John Paul II explained:

Even when not motivated by a selfish refusal to be burdened with the life of someone who is suffering, euthanasia must be called a false mercy, and indeed a disturbing "perversion" of mercy. True "compassion" leads to sharing another's pain; it does not kill the person whose suffering we cannot bear. Moreover, the act of euthanasia appears all the more perverse if it is carried out by those, like relatives, who are supposed to treat a family member with patience and love, or by those, such as doctors, who by virtue of their specific profession are supposed to care for the sick person even in the most painful terminal stages.

What government policies would you recommend to support life at both its beginning and its end?

How do you answer someone who claims that life is valuable only when it is healthy?

The choice of euthanasia becomes more serious when it takes the form of a murder committed by others on a person who has in no way requested it and who has never consented to it. The height of arbitrariness and injustice is reached when certain people, such as physicians or legislators, arrogate to themselves the power to decide who ought to live and who ought to die (The Gospel of Life, §66).

Euthanasia and assisted suicide are part of today's "conspiracy against life." To combat this grave problem, we must give each human being the respect due him or her as God's unique child with profound dignity. Society must guarantee the right of each person to be born as well as to die a natural death. Again, if society fails to protect a person's right to life when he or she is most vulnerable and helpless, then all human rights are gravely threatened.

WHAT IS THE "RIGHT TO DIE"?

We do not have a right to die. A right is a moral claim. Death claims us; we do not claim death. No one is in total control of his or her own life—when it begins or when it ends. Only God has absolute control. As God's child, however, we do have a right to proper care when we are sick or dying. And proper care does not include killing (euthanasia) or suicide (assisted or not).

case study ▶ ### BETTER TO LIVE OR DIE?

Background:

Joseph is a severely brain-damaged forty-seven-year-old man. Though he has control of his muscular functions, mentally he is around the age of three. Many years of special education have taught Joseph how to do simple tasks like dress himself, but he has never been capable of holding down any kind of job. Care-taking has exhausted his family's financial resources. Joseph's parents are now in their seventies, and in need of care themselves. Joseph's dad suffers from Alzheimer's. Nevertheless Joseph's family has always resisted putting Joseph in a state institution, preferring instead to share care among family members, but mostly his parents.

Physically, Joseph is sometimes prone to serious, life-threatening infections that he gets over with ample doses of powerful antibiotics. Now, at this stage of all their lives, Joseph's parents are seriously considering not administering drugs the next time Joseph gets one of these periodic infections. They think it would be much better for everyone involved—Joseph, the family, and the taxpaying community—if he would just die.

Debate:

- What would you advise Joseph's parents?
- What, if anything, would Joseph's parents be guilty of if they "forgot" to give Joseph his antibiotics the next time he suffered an infection? Explain.
- What limits, if any, should a community put on the resources it commits to caring for people like Joseph?

CAPITAL PUNISHMENT
(CCC, 2263-2267; 2321)

Consider the following criminals:
- a serial killer of small children,
- a terrorist who bombs a building containing hundreds of innocent people,
- a thoroughly perverted leader who orders millions of his fellow citizens to the gas chamber, and
- a rapist who tortures his victims.

Certainly, people like these deserve justice. Many people—including many Catholics—believe that the only just punishment for criminals like these is the death penalty, that is, capital punishment. The question considered in this section is whether state-sanctioned killing can be understood as just punishment by Christians. Today, the bishops of the United States and Pope John Paul II ask us to question seriously the appropriateness of capital punishment in our day and age. They ask us to reflect on the truth that "not even a murderer loses his personal dignity" (*The Gospel of Life*, §9). They challenge Catholics, Christians, and all people of good will to look for ways to punish and rehabilitate criminals, while protecting society, and yet not inflict the death penalty.

TRADITIONAL CHURCH TEACHING ON CAPITAL PUNISHMENT

Christians who struggle with the morality of the death penalty must first begin with Jesus. His teachings are a major challenge to anyone who would justify the violence of death as a solution to social problems. For example, he taught the new law of non-retaliation in the Sermon on the Mount:

You have heard that it was said, "An eye for an eye and a tooth for a tooth." But I say to you, offer no resistance to one who is evil. When someone strikes you on (your) right cheek, turn the other one to him as well" (Mt 5:38–39).

Minimally, this stark teaching seems to rule out revenge as a motive for punishing evildoers.

Jesus also taught nonviolence in the Garden of Gethsemane when he told his followers to sheathe their swords, observing that violence only leads to violence (Mt 26:52). Jesus taught the way of forgiveness to his followers, instructing them to forgive their enemies not just seven times, but seventy-seven times (that is, an infinite number of times; see Mt 18:21–22). His own example teaches a powerful lesson of how to give forgiveness. Though innocent, Jesus was condemned to death as a common criminal. As he

hung on the cross, he prayed, "Father, forgive them, they know not what they do" (Lk 23:34). Christians can never ignore the teaching and example of Jesus.

In trying to formulate a realistic approach to dealing with serious crime, the Church has recognized the right of both individuals and the state to self-defense, using the minimum force necessary to stop unjust aggressors. For the sake of the common good, according to Saint Thomas

Aquinas, criminals who are destructive of the community may even be put to death. The *Catechism of the Catholic Church* has confirmed this teaching:

> The traditional teaching of the Church does not exclude recourse to the death penalty, if this is the only possible way of effectively defending human lives against the unjust aggressor (2267).

CONTEMPORARY CHURCH TEACHING ON CAPITAL PUNISHMENT

The question today, however, is whether contemporary conditions warrant recourse to the death penalty. Church teaching holds that if "bloodless means are sufficient to defend against the aggressor and to protect the safety of persons" the states should limit themselves to these means. Non-lethal means "better correspond to the concrete conditions of the common good and are more in conformity to the dignity of the human person" (CCC, 2267). The *Catechism* adds:

> Today, in fact, given the means at the State's disposal to effectively repress crime by rendering inoffensive the one who has committed it, without depriving him definitively of the possibility of redeeming himself, cases of absolute necessity for suppression of the offender "today . . . are very rare, if not practically non-existent" (2267 quoting The Gospel of Life, §56).

In the *Statement on Capital Punishment* (1980), the American bishops agree that modern governments have many ways to repress crime so as to make the need for capital punishment unnecessary. They strongly urge Catholics and American citizens to work to abolish the death penalty.

In urging abolition of the death penalty, the bishops are not ignorant of the rising problem of crime. They are very aware of the need to preserve order in society and to work for justice through law. They are also extremely sensitive to both the victims of crime and law enforcement officers who risk their lives defending us. And the bishops are realistic enough to recognize that crime is part of the great mystery of evil and the abuse of human freedom. They know that crime is a very complex reality with no easy answers. Criminals deserve punishment. However, the bishops note that punishment needs justification. The bishops simply do not believe that killing another person is justifiable punishment.

Rather, the American bishops remind us that *retribution*, *deterrence*, and *reform* are the three traditional reasons for punishing someone. However, in the case of capital punishment, the reform of the criminal is impossible as a dead criminal cannot be reformed.

Second, there is little evidence to prove that the death penalty deters crime. For example, the National Coalition to End the Death Penalty reports on a *New York Times* survey that showed that the homicide rate in states with capital punishment have been 48 percent to 101 percent higher than those without the death penalty.[11] Most violent criminals act irrationally. The remote threat of death does not usually enter their minds.

Third, retribution refers to the restoration of the order of justice violated by the criminal acts. But taking the life of a criminal is not necessary to restore the order of justice. For example, consider how barbaric it would be to mutilate a criminal who maimed his victim. By the same token, why do we not consider it inhumane to kill a criminal? Truth be told, revenge often lurks under the surface of why many citizens want to inflict the death penalty. Recall, however, that revenge can never be a just motive for Christians.

BREAKING THE CYCLE OF VIOLENCE

Those who argue for keeping the death penalty must especially take note of some disturbing realities and problems. Among those noted by the bishops are these:

- A dead criminal cannot be reformed; nor is he or she able to make any effort to compensate for the crime committed.
- Mistakes are and have been made in administering capital punishment. We can never correct the mistake of killing an innocent person.
- Since 1973 at least one hundred people were exonerated and released from death row in the United States. Reacting to the reporting of these statistics, Cardinal Theodore McCarrick, the Archbishop of Washington, eloquently wrote:

The report that at least 100 people have now been found to be innocent of the crimes that put them on death row are 100 reasons to turn away from capital punishment. The 101st reason is not what was done to them, but what is being done to the rest of us. The increasing reliance on the death penalty diminishes all of us, increases disrespect for human life, and offers the tragic illusion that we can teach that killing is wrong by killing. It's time to "Choose life, then, that you and your descendants may live" (Dt 30:19).[12]

- Executions attract enormous, unhealthy publicity. The media circus accompanying them negatively inflames people's emotions.

- A growing body of evidence shows that the death penalty is disproportionally administered to poor persons and members of minority groups, especially black males. (Those who have money also commit violent crimes, but their resources allow them to work the system to their advantage and typically avoid the death penalty.)

To combat these injustices, the American bishops see four benefits to abolishing the death penalty:

- It would tell society that we can break the cycle of violence, that there are more humane and effective ways to deal with violent crimes.

- It would manifest "our belief in the unique worth and dignity of each person from the moment of conception, a creature made in the image and likeness of God" (*Statement on Capital Punishment*, §11).

- It would testify to our belief that God is the Lord of life and emphasize our belief that life is sacred in all its stages. The bishops write:

We do not wish to equate the situation of criminals convicted of capital offenses with the condition of the innocent unborn or of the defenseless aged or infirm, but we do believe that the defense of life is strengthened by eliminating exercise of a judicial authorization to take human life (Statement on Capital Punishment, §12).

- Outlawing capital punishment is more in line with Jesus who taught and embodied forgiveness.

Crime is part of the great mystery of evil. Violent criminals are a threat to society. Ending the death penalty will not solve either of these problems.

The Church calls on lawmakers to make changes in the criminal justice system so that it can reform criminals more effectively. Moreover, Church leaders call on citizens to deal with issues of poverty and injustice that create environments where hopelessness leads to crime. The Church also supports gun control and opposes media presentations that glamorize violence, especially to the young and vulnerable.

- Survey several adults as to their opinions on the death penalty. Share with them some key points of Church teaching as presented above. Report on their reactions.
- Locate either the U.S. Bishops' 1980 *Statement on Capital Punishment* or their 2005 statement entitled *A Culture of Life and the Penalty of Death*. You can find both online in the Social Justice issues section of the United States Conference of Catholic Bishops' website: www.usccb.org. Prepare a report on the bishops' teaching concerning the death penalty.
- Locate a copy of the Pontifical Council for Justice and Peace's *Compendium of the Social Doctrine of the Church* (Washington, D.C.: United States Conference of Catholic Bishops, 2005). Read and report on the section that discusses the political community's right to inflict punishment, #402-405. Refer to the *Compendium* for other research projects during your course of study on Catholic Social Justice.
- For more information on the death penalty, visit and report on the Death Penalty Information website: www.deathpenaltyinfo.org
- Also, visit the website of Catholics Against Capital Punishment for some more useful information on the subject: www.cacp.org/pages/585134/index.htm
- Helen Prejean, CSJ, a member of the Sisters of St. Joseph of Medaille, burst into the limelight when her book, *Dead Man Walking*, was turned into an award-winning film of the same name. Because of the notoriety of her book and the film, Sister Helen has become one of America's most eloquent spokespersons against the death penalty. Read about Sister Helen and her work at her website: www.prejean.org. Write a report on what you find out.

How can the Church, society, and individuals offer their love and support to victims of crime?

What is your opinion on the death penalty?

"States can adequately defend themselves without exercising the death penalty." Discuss the truth of this statement.

SAINT GIANNA BERETTA MOLLA (1922–1962)
ALWAYS CHOOSING LIFE

Gianna was born to Maria and Albert Beretta in Magenta (near Milan), Italy, on October 4, 1922. She was the tenth of thirteen children. As a child she was raised in a loving home by parents who educated her in the Catholic faith. They implanted in her a strong faith in God's watchful providence and taught her the need for and effectiveness of daily prayer.

As a teen and young adult, Gianna was a diligent student. During these years she got involved in Catholic Action and joined the Saint Vincent de Paul Society. As a member of these charitable organizations, she devoted many hours of generous service caring for the needs of others.

Gianna graduated from the University of Pavia in 1949 with a degree in medicine and surgery and opened a clinic in Mesero, Italy, in 1950. With further medical studies at the University of Milan, Gianna specialized in pediatrics and thereafter her medical practice gave special attention to babies, mothers, the elderly, and poor people.

Blessed with a great love for life and physical activity, Gianna took up skiing and moutaineering in these years. She continued to serve in Catholic Action and considered for a time whether she had a vocation to the religious life. After much prayer and reflection, she decided that God was calling her to Christian family life. So in September of 1955, she married Pietro Molla, and in the following years became the devoted mother of three. She was a loving and dedicated wife and mother who continued to serve as a doctor, especially to the poor of her town. She saw her life as a mission from God to help others. Gianna wrote down four goals every doctor should have:

- To do his or her part well by studying science diligently and not seeking after money.
- To be honest and a doctor of faith.
- To show loving care, thinking of the sick person as a brother or sister.
- To always remember the patient's soul by striving to always do good for the patient.

Gianna's true Christian character shone forth when she was diagnosed with a large ovarian cancerous tumor during her pregnancy with her fourth child. She was confronted with three choices. The first was recommended by her doctor: Kill the growing baby in her womb by removing both the tumor and the uterus. The second option was to remove the tumor and perform a therapeutic abortion, thus resulting in the death of the baby. The third choice was to have the tumor removed and not touch the baby. This choice would save the baby's life but perhaps threaten Gianna's own over time.

Gianna chose the third way. She ordered her doctor to save her baby and told her husband: "If you must decide between me and the child, do not hesitate: choose the child—I insist on it."

On April 21, 1962, a beautiful baby girl named Gianna Emanuela was born. Despite the best efforts of her doctor, a week later, Gianna died after suffering unspeakable pain. The thirty-nine-year-old mother of four went to eternal life after saying over and over again, "Jesus, I love you. Jesus, I love you."

In the gospel, Jesus told us that no one can show greater love than to lay down one's life for another. This is exactly what Gianna Beretta did when she sacrificed her life for the sake of her child. That child, named after her mother, is today also a physician and active in the pro-life movement.

Gianna was canonized in May of 2004. She is the patron saint of physicians and mothers of families. She left us with some powerful words for living:

> The secret of happiness is to live moment by moment and to thank God for all that He, in His goodness, sends to us day after day.
>
> God's providence is in all things, it's always present.
>
> One cannot love without suffering or suffer without loving.[13]

PRAYER OF SAINT GIANNA

O Jesus, I promise You to submit myself to all that You permit to befall me, make me only know Your Will. My most sweet Jesus, infinitely merciful God, most tender Father of souls, and in a particular way of the most weak, most miserable, most infirm which You carry with special tenderness between Your divine arms, I come to You to ask You, through the love and merits of Your Sacred Heart, the grace to comprehend and to do always Your holy Will, the grace to confide in You, the grace to rest securely through time and eternity in Your loving divine arms.[14]

- Pray these words of Saint Gianna. In your journal, write your own prayer for life.
- Further Reading: To learn more about Saint Gianna, check the Catholic Forum's website and the links that are listed there: www.catholic-forum.com/saints/saintgaq.htm

THE SEAMLESS GARMENT

Catholic social justice teaching promotes a "**consistent ethic of life.**" The late Cardinal Joseph Bernardin of Chicago termed the Catholic position a "seamless garment," referring to the tunic Jesus wore at the crucifixion (cf. Jn 19:23). In brief, this viewpoint holds that we must respect life from the moment of conception until natural death, from womb to tomb. We must not only guarantee a child the right to life, but as a society we must support the quality of life of the weak and powerless in our midst: old and young, the homeless and the hungry, undocumented immigrants and those unemployed. The government must guarantee the right to life. But it must also create the economic, social, and political conditions that enable those born to have a decent life of dignity.

This is why the Church has taught about almost every topic related to human dignity under the social-justice umbrella. Abortion and euthanasia are not the *only* issues the Church has written about. However, note the wise words of the American bishops:

To focus on the evil of deliberate killing in abortion and euthanasia is not to ignore the many other urgent conditions that demean human dignity and threaten human rights. Opposing abortion and euthanasia "does not excuse indifference to those who suffer from poverty, violence and injustice. Any politics of human life must work to resist the violence of war and the scandal of capital punishment. Any politics of human dignity must seriously address issues of racism, poverty, hunger, employment, education, housing and health care" (Living the Gospel of Life, no. 23). We pray that Catholics will be advocates for the weak and the marginalized in all these areas. "But being 'right' in such matters can never excuse a wrong choice regarding direct attacks on innocent human life.

CONSISTENT ETHIC OF LIFE—The viewpoint of Catholic social teaching that calls for the respect of all human life, especially the most defenseless in our midst, a "SEAMLESS GARMENT" of protection, womb to tomb.

Indeed, the failure to protect and defend life in its most vulnerable stages renders suspect any claims to the 'rightness' of positions in other matters affecting the poorest and least powerful of the human community" (Living the Gospel of Life, no. 23).[15]

Since 1975, the American bishops have issued several statements on the common good and the need for citizens to participate responsibly in the electoral process. These statements appear about a year before the national election for president. A good example of such a document is *Faithful Citizenship: A Catholic Call to Political Responsibility* issued for the 2004 election cycle.[16] This document summarizes Catholic teaching on the public life and on certain important moral issues. Its reflections and teachings on many diverse issues are organized around the general themes of respecting human life, promoting family life, pursuing social justice, and practicing global solidarity.

Drawing on papal teaching, their own past political responsibility statements, a statement from the Congregation for the Doctrine of the Faith on Catholics in public life, and important themes from bishops' statements like *Living the Gospel of Life* and *A Place at the Table*, the bishops exemplify the seamless garment, manifesting a consistent ethic of life. Listed below are only a few of the issues (besides those discussed in this chapter) that reveal the Church's commitment to life.

PROTECTING HUMAN LIFE

- The bishops support aid to those who are sick and dying by encouraging health care coverage for all as well as effective palliative care.
- The bishops encourage national leaders "to strengthen barriers against the use of nuclear weapons, to expand controls over existing nuclear materials and other weapons of mass destruction, and to ratify the Comprehensive Test Ban Treaty."

PROMOTING FAMILY LIFE

- Laws should support marriage as a lifelong commitment between a man and a woman. "Policies related to the definition of marriage, taxes, the workplace, divorce, and welfare must be designed to help families stay together and to reward responsibility and sacrifice for children."
- The bishops support their commitment to protect children in all settings and at all times, and to safeguard their well-being. For example, they support a TV-rating system and technological advancements that will help parents supervise what their children view. They also believe the Internet should be available to all students regardless of income. However, because the Internet can give easy access to pornography and violent material, they support laws and efforts to block out unwanted material.

PURSUING SOCIAL JUSTICE

- The bishops support policies that create jobs for everyone who can work, decent working conditions, a living wage, and equitable pay for women. Small family farmers also deserve a decent return for their labor. In a special way, society should look out for farm workers so that they have adequate pay and decent housing and health care.
- The goal of welfare reform should not be simply to cut money and programs, but to reduce poverty and dependency. Tax credits for children should be increased.
- In reforming Social Security, a decent and reliable income should be guaranteed for the neediest of workers and their families.
- Affordable and accessible health care is a fundamental human right; it should be a top national priority.
- The bishops support wise affirmative action programs as one way to overcome discrimination and its continuing effects.
- They also support energy conservation and the development of alternative, renewable, and clean-energy resources.

PRACTICING GLOBAL SOLIDARITY

- The nation must not define national security primarily in military terms. With other nations, it must assess those situations that are breeding grounds for terrorism.
- The United States should lead in the fight against global poverty by increasing development aid for the poorest countries, by practicing more equitable trade policies, and by working to eradicate the crushing burdens of debt and disease.
- The United States must do all in its power "to reverse the spread of nuclear, chemical, and biological weapons, and to reduce its own reliance on weapons of mass destruction by pursuing progressive nuclear disarmament. It also should reduce its own predominant role in the conventional arms trade."
- We should also adopt a more generous immigration and refugee policy.

ANALYZING CANDIDATES ON MORAL ISSUES

In *Faithful Citizenship*, the bishops raise a series of questions to help us to discover which candidates and policies best serve the moral and human choices facing voters. Several of the questions are listed here. Use them to do the following:

- Personally interview and report on the views of a politician (local, state, or national) on these various issues.
- Research the platforms of several political parties and their approaches to these questions. Create a chart using a grid to compare and contrast their views.
- Write a letter to a political figure. Identify who you are as a student committed to social justice. Share with the person several of the important themes of Catholic social teaching (discussed in Chapter 1 of this text). Then ask the person for his or her views on several of these questions:
  - How will the weakest in our midst—innocent unborn children—be protected? How will the nation resist what Pope John Paul II termed a "culture of death"? How can we keep from turning to violence to solve some of the most difficult problems—abortion to deal with difficult pregnancies; the death penalty to combat crime; euthanasia and assisted suicide to deal with the burdens of age, illness, and disability; and war to address international disputes?
  - How will the tragic fact that more than 30,000 children die every day as a result of hunger, international debt, and lack of development around the world be solved?
  - How can society defend the central institution of marriage and better support families in their moral roles and responsibilities, offering them real choices and financial resources to obtain quality education and decent housing?
  - How will the situation of the growing number of families and individuals without affordable and accessible health care be addressed? How can health care better protect human life and respect human dignity?

Read all the bishops' questions in *Faithful Citizenship: A Catholic Call to Political Responsibility*. View the website of the American bishops: www.usccb.org.

CHAPTER SUMMARY

- Abortion, the unjustified killing of innocent unborn humans, is the compelling social justice issue of our day. If we do not respect the fundamental right to life, God's great gift to us, then all human lives and rights are threatened. Abortion assaults human dignity and a person's worth as God's unique child, redeemed by Christ Jesus. Regardless of the motive, abortion is always seriously wrong.

- The breakdown of the family and the cult of the individual in his or her quest for absolute freedom have helped to create a "culture of death" that permits abortion, euthanasia, and other crimes against human dignity.
- A child's right to life outweighs a mother's right to choose. Human life must be protected from the first moment of conception. The legal system should guarantee the right to life by banning abortion, acknowledging that God—not the state—conveys life. A proper view of the sacredness of human sexuality would help combat the permissiveness that often leads to unplanned pregnancies. But if an unwanted child should be conceived, adoption is always an alternative to abortion.
- The Church supports adult stem cell research. However, embryonic stem cell research is immoral because in order to obtain the cells, researchers must harvest stem cells from living human embryos, thus destroying innocent human life, a grave assault on human dignity.
- Popularly, euthanasia is called mercy killing. But euthanasia is a perverted mercy. True compassion leads to sharing another's pain. For Christians, suffering can be redemptive, a sharing in Christ's own passion and death for the sake of sin. An alternative and acceptable way between unrelieved suffering and euthanasia is palliative care that medically reduces the pain of terminal illness. Though we must always use ordinary care to preserve our lives, we are not required to use "extraordinary means," that is, aggressive medical procedures that no longer correspond to the real situation of the patient.
- The Church condemns euthanasia, suicide, and assisted suicide as a violation of God's fifth commandment not to kill. These acts can never be justified.
- The Church has traditionally permitted the death penalty as a last resort for a society to defend itself against violent criminals. Today, however, Church leaders teach that states have enough means to repress crime and control violent criminals without inflicting the death penalty.
- Abolishing capital punishment would break the cycle of violence, manifest our belief in the unique dignity of each person, and testify to our belief that God is the Lord of life. Moreover, it would be most consistent with Jesus' teaching about forgiving the enemy.
- Church leaders call on a reform of the criminal-justice system to better rehabilitate criminals. Furthermore, we should all deal forthrightly with issues of poverty and injustice that create environments that lead to violence. Such efforts would manifest a "consistent ethic of life," the showing of concern that we should be pro-life from womb to tomb.
- Being pro-life means fighting abortion and euthanasia. It means finding alternatives to the death penalty. And it means so many other things as well: fighting poverty, prejudice, gross economic inequalities. It requires being pro-family, advocating rights of workers, cutting back on arms trade. It means seeing that everyone has access to a decent education, food, shelter, and clothing. In short, a pro-life social justice outlook must be like a "seamless garment," a defense of the rights of everyone, but especially the weakest in our midst, at every stage of their life's journey.

REVIEW QUESTIONS

1. Why is abortion the most compelling justice issue of our day?
2. List some effects of the *Roe v. Wade* decision in the United States.
3. Discuss two reasons why there is disrespect for unborn human life today.
4. Respond to the argument that by making abortion illegal you are denying a woman her right to choose.
5. Respond to the argument that you are forcing your morality on others by working to make abortion illegal.
6. Discuss the connection between abortion and an incorrect view of human sexuality.
7. What might you say to a young girl contemplating an abortion? What could you do for her?

8. Discuss a pro-life activity that can help combat abortion.
9. What is euthanasia? Discuss two reasons why people promote it.
10. List three pitfalls of legalizing euthanasia.
11. What is Church teaching concerning the use of "extraordinary means," or aggressive medical treatment, in sustaining life?
12. What is assisted suicide? Why is it wrong?
13. According to Church teaching, under what circumstances is capital punishment justifiable?
14. What can Jesus' words and actions teach us about the viability of the death penalty?
15. What are the three purposes of punishment?
16. List and discuss four benefits to abolishing the death penalty.
17. Discuss some problems with supporting the death penalty.
18. Identify Saint Gianna Beretta Molla.
19. What is meant by the terms "seamless garment" or "consistent ethic of life" as applied to Catholic social teaching?
20. List five issues besides fighting abortion, euthanasia, and capital punishment that would reflect a consistent ethic of life.

RESEARCHING ON THE INTERNET

There are six things the LORD hates,
*   yes, seven are an abomination to him;*
Haughty eyes, a lying tongue,
*   and hands that shed innocent blood;*
A heart that plots wicked schemes,
*   feet that run swiftly to evil,*
The false witness who utters lies,
*   and he who sows discord among brothers.*
*   —Proverbs 6:16–19*

1. Check out the National Right to Life web page at: www.nrlc.org. Report on one of the techniques of abortion or on a recent news alert posted on the website.
2. Check out and report on something you discovered at the excellent Priests for Life website: www.priestforlife.org
3. Report on some aspect of the aftermath of abortion and Project Rachel at: www.hopeafterabortion.org
4. Research some basic facts about abortion at Second Look Project: www.secondlookproject.org
5. Report on some aspect of the ethics surrounding the stem cell research debate at the site of Do No Harm: The Coalition for Americans for Research Ethics: www.stemcellresearch.org
6. Report on something you found on this website: International Task Force on Euthanasia and Assisted Suicide: www.internationaltaskforce.org
7. Research what the Vatican and the American bishops have to say about cloning.

PRAYER REFLECTION

Lord and giver of all life,
help us to value each person, created in love by you.
In your mercy, guide and assist our efforts
to promote the dignity and value
of all human life, born and unborn.
We ask this through Christ our Lord. Amen.[17]

NOTES

1. Death Penalty Information Center, "Facts about the Death Penalty."
2. National Coalition to Abolish the Death Penalty, "Fact Sheet: Innocence."
3. You can read about these two methods and many other methods online from the excellent book *Abortion: Questions and Answers* by Dr. and Mrs. J.C. Willkie at: www.ohiolife.org/qa/qatoc.asp.
4. Abortion *facts*.com, "Abortion Information You Can Use: Studies."
5. The source of this information is the British Christian Medical Fellowship. Among the goals of this organization is to unite Christian doctors in their pursuit of the highest standards in Christian and professional life. Research their articles on euthanasia and abortion, parts 1 and 2, under the Ethics section of their website: www.cmf.org.uk.
6. You can read about Norma's story at her website: www.roenomore.org/crossing_over/welcome.html
7. Christian Life Resources, "General Abortion Stats."
8. See, for example, Pope John Paul II's *The Gospel to Life* (1995) and various statements of the American Bishops: www.usccb.org/prolife/tdocs/index.htm.
9. Excerpted from *Pastoral Plan for Pro-Life Activities: A Campaign in Support of Life*. Copyright © 2001, United States Conference of Catholic Bishops, Inc., Washington, D.C. All rights reserved.
10. Secretariat for Pro-Life Activities, U.S. Conference of Catholic Bishops, "Stem Cell Reality Check #1" <http://www.usccb.org/prolife/issues/bioethic/stemfax1.htm> (18 February 2005).
11. National Coalition to End the Death Penalty, "Fact Sheets" cites the original study conducted by Raymond Bonner and Ford Fessenden, "Absence of Executions," *New York Times*, September 22, 2000.
12. United States Conference of Catholic Bishops, Office of Communications, "Cardinal Cites '101 Reasons to Abandon the Death Penalty'" <http://www.usccb.org/comm/archives/2002/02-062.htm>.
13. Found at the website of The Society of Blessed Gianna Beretta Molla <http://www.gianna.org/>.
14. Gianna Beretta Molla <http://www.catholic-forum.com/saints/saintgaq.htm>.
15. United States Conference of Catholic Bishops, *Pastoral Plan for Pro-Life Activities: A Campaign in Support of Life*, 2001 <http://www.usccb.org/prolife/pastoralplan.htm#implementing>.
16. United States Conference of Catholic Bishops, *Faithful Citizenship: A Catholic Call to Political Responsibility*, 2003.
17. You can find this and many other prayers on the Internet. This one originally came from www.web desk. com/catholic/prayers/forthedignityofhumanlife.html.

CHAPTER OVERVIEW

Go and Worship with Your "Own" People
Jesus preached love for all people without discrimination.

Real-Life Prejudice
Several contemporary examples of prejudice are cited based on its definition as a "prejudgment based on insufficient data."

Stages of Prejudice
Prejudice proceeds in degrees of seriousness from antilocution to avoidance to discrimination to physical attack to extermination.

Attempting to Explain Prejudice
This section offers several reasons for why people may be prejudiced and how people typically become prejudiced.

Jean Vanier
Jean Vanier organized a community to serve people with mental handicaps.

Do to others whatever you would have them do to you.

—Matthew 7:12

There is neither Jew nor Greek, there is neither slave nor free person, there is not male and female; for you are all one in Christ Jesus.

—Galatians 3:28

JUSTICE AND PREJUDICE

5

GO AND WORSHIP WITH YOUR "OWN" PEOPLE

As a young man, Mohandas Gandhi, a Hindu, seriously considered converting to Christianity after reading about Jesus in the gospels. He saw the Christian message of God's unconditional love for everyone as a possible solution to the Indian caste system, a great source of division in his country.

In his autobiography, Gandhi relates how he attended Sunday services at a Christian church, fully intending to seek further instructions from the minister afterwards. However, when he went into the church's sanctuary, the ushers rudely refused to seat the dark-skinned Gandhi. They told him that he should go worship with his "own" people. Without making a fuss, Gandhi left. He never returned. He decided if Christians also have a caste system, he might as well remain a Hindu.

Gandhi

Jesus preached God's love for everyone. He told us we are all children of his loving Father. He gave us the Holy Spirit to form us into a community of love. This Spirit of love bestows on us the power to look into the eyes of another human being and see—not differences of skin color, age, sex, religion, national origin, physical and mental attributes, or whatever—but a sister or a brother.

Unfortunately, sin has infected the human condition. We do not always treat others as God's special creations, beings of incomparable worth, redeemed by Jesus Christ and destined for eternal life.

This chapter will focus on the sin of *prejudice* and, conversely, on the ways we are called to treat *all* people with respect.

WHAT DO YOU THINK?

How good are you at recognizing prejudicial statements? A working definition of *prejudice* is "a prejudgment based on insufficient data." If you think a statement is prejudicial, mark **P**; if you do not think it is prejudicial, mark **N**; if you are not sure, mark **?**.

	N	P	?
1. Minorities flagrantly violate the welfare system.			
2. People are poor because they refuse to take advantage of our "free" public school system.			
3. Most gay people do not choose their sexual orientation.			
4. Immigrants come to America to seek greater religious, economic, or political freedom.			
5. In point of fact, not everyone is created equal.			
6. Today's teens are carefree, with little that is serious on their minds.			
7. Catholics rarely think for themselves since they are so used to taking marching orders from the pope.			
8. America's crisis isn't with terrorists; the problem is with Islam and those who practice it.			

- Could you "prove" that one or more of these statements is based on fact? is a prejudicial opinion?
- How do you define equality as stated in number 5?
- In your opinion, which people are the greatest victims of prejudice today? Why do you think this is so?

REAL-LIFE PREJUDICE

According to Tolerance.org, in the United States:

- every hour someone commits a hate crime;
- every day at least eight blacks, three whites, three gays, three Jews, and one Latino become hate crime victims; and
- every week a cross is burned.[1]

Consider, too, how prejudice is involved in the following situations:

- Joan interviewed for a computer data entry job. Her skills are superior. But her potential employer did not hire her. She is fifty pounds overweight and forty years old. She suspects, but cannot prove, that her age and physical condition kept her from getting a job.
- Bob has graduated at the top of his class from a highly regarded law school. Unfortunately, he is having a hard time finding a position even though many of his classmates whose class rank is lower than his have been hired by good firms. Bob is legally blind.
- Tom and Bill, both age sixteen, enter a computer store to purchase a new printer. The sales clerks ignore them and focus their attention instead on the middle-aged man in a business suit who comes in behind them.
- In the Bronx, New York, four young white males attacked a fourteen-year-old African American brother and sister while they were walking home from school. The bullies took $3 from the girl and cut her hair. They also sprayed the brother and sister with white paint and taunted them.
- Alfredo and Rita, professionals of Puerto Rican descent, moved into an upscale neighborhood with their two young children. The week after they settled in they found a sign on their front lawn that read: "You people don't belong here. Go back to Puerto Rico!"
- In Germany, some teens are playing computer games which have Jewish inmates of Nazi death camps being sent to the gas chamber. Historians fear that people have either forgotten the Holocaust or are denying its horrific reality.

- After teaching for four years in a Catholic school, a young female teacher is hired by a public school district. At the same time, the district issues a contract to a male teacher with identical qualifications. However, his salary is $5,000 more than his female counterpart. The district's reasoning for the discrepancy is that the male teacher is also going to coach. However, the male teacher will receive a supplementary contract for this additional responsibility.
- A social studies teacher at a New York high school said to a Muslim girl returning from an illness that he was "pleased to see that she did not become a suicide bomber."

prejudice—An unsubstantiated or preformed judgment about an individual or group.

Prejudice

The word **prejudice** comes from the Latin *praejudicium*, a word that we translate as *prejudge*. Prejudice, then, is a prejudgment based on insufficient data. One dictionary definition holds that prejudice is a favorable or unfavorable feeling toward a person or thing, prior to, or not based on, actual fact. In one form or another, prejudice is present in each of the scenarios above.

This definition is interesting because it points out that prejudice involves feelings. Also, it challenges the usual notion people have of prejudice as always a negative, sinful reality. Interestingly, the definition itself can connote a positive or even neutral reality, in addition to the negative image of prejudice we commonly understand. Examples of positive and neutral prejudice follow.

Prejudice can be positive. For example, let's say a teacher judges that you are going to be a great student because she taught your brother. He was a sterling scholar,

and the teacher thinks you will be too. She has a positive prejudice toward you. She is predisposed to give you the benefit of the doubt because of your sibling. Her initial positive impression of you certainly will not hurt you; in fact, it might even bolster your confidence and help you perform well in her class.

But the teacher has to be careful that she forms an accurate image of you as she gets to know you. You are not your brother. You are a unique person. The teacher must guard against favoring you to the detriment of her other students. What appears to be a positive prejudgment about you can become a negative prejudice towards others if the teacher refuses to have an open mind or if she is an unfair teacher, favoring you over her other students.

Prejudice can also be neutral. For example, making a prejudgment about some*thing*. Suppose a friend tells you he hates raw oysters. You may ask, "Have you ever eaten raw oysters?" His response: "To be honest, no, I haven't." Is your friend prejudiced against oysters? It appears that he is because he has judged them negatively without ever tasting them.

Your friend's prejudgment against raw oysters seems neither good nor bad. His prejudice has not really harmed anyone or anything. One warning, though: even a simple neutral prejudice like this one can have some negative aspects. For example, it can reveal a closed-mindedness on your friend's part. Also, being rigid in one's opinions and beliefs about *things* one has not experienced can easily transfer to being inflexible and negatively judgmental about *people*.

NEGATIVE PREJUDICE

Our concern in this chapter is with *negative prejudice*, the kind we typically mean in the expression "racial prejudice." (From now on, when we speak of prejudice we will be talking about the negative variety.) This type of prejudice infects humanity like a virus. Negative prejudice finds its roots in original sin.

Negative prejudice is, of itself, sinful. It violates the virtue of justice which calls on us to respect the dignity of others. Three conditions make prejudice wrong.

First, prejudice is wrong when it threatens the rights of people, that is, when it denies people their just due.

Second, prejudice is wrong when it is illogical or when it exhibits stereotypical thinking.

Stereotypes are oversimplified generalizations about some aspect of reality. They result from over-categorization, of prejudging a whole group based on one or two faulty assumptions. (Examples: "All blond-haired girls are air-heads." "All jocks are dumb.")

Third, prejudice is a fault when it resists new information, when one is unwilling (or even unable) to change his or her mind when confronted with the truth. This last trait especially is what makes someone with a negative prejudice a "prejudiced person," that is, someone who is unwilling to change.

EXAMPLE OF NEGATIVE PREJUDICE

An example of negative and sinful prejudice is that against persons with a homosexual orientation (CCC, 2357–2359). Many homosexual persons are stereotyped in a degrading way and are often the object of scorn, hatred, and discrimination. There are

STEREOTYPE—AN OVERSIMPLIFIED GENERALIZATION.

many different reasons for this, of course; however, ignorance is perhaps the most prominent factor in this kind of prejudice. At the root of this prejudice might be ignorance, for example, the conviction that homosexual people choose their sexual orientation.

As far as science can determine, no one chooses to have a homosexual orientation. In their pastoral letter, *Always Our Children*, the American bishops wrote:

There seems to be no single cause of a homosexual orientation. A common opinion of experts is that there are multiple factors—genetic, hormonal, psychological—that may give rise to it. Generally, homosexual orientation is experienced as a given, not as something freely chosen. By itself, therefore, a homosexual orientation cannot be considered sinful, for morality presumes the freedom to choose.[2]

The *Catechism of the Catholic Church* goes on to say that "This inclination, which is objectively disordered, constitutes for most

105

[persons with the homosexual inclination] a trial" (2358). Although the orientation is not sinful, just like being right-handed or having brown eyes is beyond a person's control, what is wrong is homosexual activity because it is contrary to God's intention for male-female bonding. The *Always Our Children* pastoral adds:

First, it is God's plan that sexual intercourse occur only within marriage between a man and a woman. Second, every act of intercourse must be open to the possible creation of new human life. Homosexual intercourse cannot fulfill these two conditions. Therefore, the Church teaches that homogenital behavior is objectively immoral, while making the important distinction between this behavior and a homosexual orientation, which is not immoral in itself. It is also important to recognize that neither a homosexual orientation, nor a heterosexual one, leads inevitably to sexual activity. One's total personhood is not reducible to sexual orientation or behavior.[3]

The Church teaches that every human being deserves respect. This includes persons of both heterosexual and homosexual orientation. Every person is a child of God, our sister or brother. To call people derogatory names, to tell vicious jokes, to engage in prejudicial behavior including violence—all these acts are condemnable and unworthy of Christians. "The fundamental human rights of homosexual persons must be defended and . . . all of us must strive to eliminate any form of injustice, oppression or violence against them."[4]

Let's say that a person who has been prejudiced against homosexuals admits that his or her former views were wrong. This admission reveals an open-mindedness and a willingness to accept homosexual persons as brothers and sisters in Christ. This willingness to drop ignorant stereotypes is a good sign that he or she is not a bigoted person. Bigots are truly "prejudiced persons," that is, those who out of pride and stubbornness hold on to their beliefs and erroneous opinions contrary to the evidence. Bigots, in short, are infected with a massive dose of negative prejudice. They neither listen to nor consider the views of others. They have closed minds and act out of sinfulness.

CHECKING FOR STEREOTYPES IN THE MEDIA (CCC, 2493FF)

The media influence society in many direct and indirect ways. Four principles about media are commonly recognized.[5]

1. **The media construct reality.** Television, movies, pop music, and the like create in their studios the effects we see and hear. The media are our modern storytellers.
2. **The media use identifiable techniques.** For example, television shows use various camera angles, musical underscores, and lighting to affect our moods, attitudes, and thoughts.
3. **Media are businesses with commercial interests.** They are in the business of making money and selling products. For example, news shows have sponsors who are selling products. Nothing the media promotes is really "free." They want us to consume.
4. **The media present ideologies and value-messages.** Media producers operate on a philosophy and a set of values.

With these principles of media literacy in mind, check to see if you can discover any stereotypes portrayed in a current television program. Watch the program carefully to see how it portrays people. Here are some questions to help you look out for prejudicial messages.

- What type of work is represented and how was it stereotyped? For example, were athletes pictured as intellectually challenged? Were teachers portrayed as absent-minded? Scientists as eccentric? Blue-collar workers as unpolished?
- How were men and women portrayed? What qualities are depicted in each? Are they stereotyped? Are women seen as sex objects? Men as sexual predators?
- How are teens portrayed? older people? For example, are the elderly depicted as weak, old-fashioned? Are teens seen as irresponsible or pleasure-seekers?
- What roles do people of color and various ethnic groups have? Are people with accents poked fun at?

Checking Out Stereotypes

Literally, *stereotype* means "set image." The word derives from the fabrication of metal plates for printing. Stereotyping of people refers to having a fixed picture of a group of people, usually based on incomplete or false information. Stereotypes result from faulty over-generalizations or over-categorization. Many stereotypes are negative.

Below is a list of various groups of people with some common stereotypes attached to them. Check off those statements which you have actually heard someone say about a person in that group or that you yourself once believed based on your first impressions.

TEENS are:	PHYSICALLY DISABLED PEOPLE are:	OLD PEOPLE are:
❑ rude	❑ below average in IQ	❑ senile
❑ poorly dressed	❑ fearful	❑ moody
❑ promiscuous	❑ unskilled	❑ unhappy
❑ lazy	❑ overly sensitive	❑ fearful
❑ untrustworthy	❑ overly dependent	❑ set in their ways
Add another: _____	Add another: _____	Add another: _____

- Why do people hold these particular stereotypes about each of the groups above?
- Give specific examples of people you know who totally disprove each of the stereotypes listed above.
- Develop a list of at least five stereotypes for each of the following groups of people. Discuss the probable origin of each stereotype. Note any that are "positive" stereotypes.

Men	Women	Catholics
African Americans	Hispanic/ Latin Americans	Native Americans
Asian Americans	Jews	Professional athletes
Whites		

In our post-9/11 world, Arab and Muslim Americans are on the receiving end of a number of negative stereotypes. What are some stereotypes of Muslims that you are aware of?

"Muslim," "Arab," and "Islam" are not interchangeable terms. Islam refers to the religion itself. Muslims are the followers of Islam. Arabs are a linguistic and cultural community with a common history. Most but not all Arabs are Muslims. Most Muslims are not Arabs. About 85 percent of the world's Muslims are not Arabs. Indonesia has the largest Muslim population in the world. About 12 million Arabs are Christian and thousands are Jewish.

Source: American-Arab Anti-Discrimination Committee, www.adc.org

STAGES OF PREJUDICE

Prejudice prejudges and harbors negative attitudes. Judgments and attitudes are primarily internal, though our tendency is to translate them into action. Very few people keep their negative prejudices to themselves. Eventually, strong negative feelings will find expression.

The noted psychologist Gordon Allport, in his classic *The Nature of Prejudice* (Perseus, 1988), distinguishes certain degrees of negative action that prejudice takes. The degrees discussed below proceed from the least to the most energetic forms of prejudice.

ANTILOCUTION

The name for this stage, "antilocution," means "speaking against." Eventually, most people will express their negative feelings for others by talking against them. Sometimes the negative speech emerges almost unconsciously, for example, in the cliché expressions we hear daily. Some examples include: "He Jew'd me down." "Why you being so white?" "She's an Indian-giver." Imbedded in these apparently innocent, everyday expressions are stereotypes about Jews, Caucasians, and Native Americans. Not challenging expressions like these only reinforces stereotypes.

Ethnic jokes are often considered a mild form of antilocution. "Have you heard the one about . . . ?" (fill in the group). Though innocent-sounding enough, some of these jokes can be vicious, cruel, and degrading to the humanity of the "out" group. (The groups you belong to and associate with are your "in" groups. Everyone else is a member of an "out" group. We tend to be wary of and prone to be prejudiced toward "out" group members.)

We have all heard the expression, "Sticks and stones may break my bones but words will never hurt me." Not true. Think of how angry and hurt you would be if someone who disliked you called you a "fag" or a "dyke." These derogatory epithets not only insult persons with a homosexual orientation, but they demean the victims of the nasty comment, often making them the objects of cruel derision.

It is true that antilocution can be mild. But it is always demeaning and un-Christian. We ought to root this kind of language out of our own vocabulary and gently challenge any friends who use it.

AVOIDANCE

A more progressive way of expressing bias or prejudice is avoidance of members of the disliked group. Sometimes prejudiced persons will go to great extremes to avoid people they dislike. Not sitting on a city bus next to an old person, crossing the street to avoid walking by a black couple, going out of one's way not to associate with people in an "out group" in the school cafeteria—all of these exemplify *avoidance*.

Avoidance behavior does not directly inflict harm on members of the "out" group; the one most often inconvenienced is the prejudiced person. However, those who are avoided do feel hurt and dehumanized. Reflect on how you personally feel when someone ignores you. It is dehumanizing and un-Christian to treat others as though they do not exist. Another problem with this kind of behavior is that it often leads to worse manifestations of overt prejudice.

What are some common, everyday expressions that have imbedded in them subtle prejudice based on stereotypes?

What are the names of various groups, organizations, and clubs that make up your "in" groups?

DISCRIMINATION

Discrimination involves harmful actions against disliked persons. Discrimination denies people their fundamental human rights, not treating them as equals.

Examples of discrimination in our society abound, including:

- denying people jobs simply because of race, ethnicity, sex, religion, age, etc.;
- excluding people from certain neighborhoods;
- restricting people's educational or recreational opportunities;
- excluding people from joining churches or other social groups;
- segregating people in neighborhoods, schools, hotels, trains and buses, etc.

An enduring example of discrimination is **sexism**, that is, the misguided belief that one sex is superior to the other by the very nature of things. Historically, in almost every society, men were considered superior to women. In fact, only in recent years has *feminism* (the belief that sexes are equal and should be treated equally) been able to challenge *patriarchy*, the institutionalized belief that men should dominate women whom they consider inferior to them. Examples of the evils which sexism has brought about include:

- In no country in today's world are women treated as well as men.
- There is a much higher incidence of poverty among households headed by women. This goes by the name "feminization of poverty" and is true in both developing and industrial societies (see chapter 7 for more information on this topic).

- Women suffer from the "glass ceiling" effect, that is, being able to advance only so far and not being able to advance higher. This discrimination shows itself in employment, wages, and promotion. For example, in the United States, women receive about 75 percent of the wages that men receive for doing comparable work.
- Countries like Iran, South Korea, and Nigeria, among many others, restrict the political participation of women.

- In many countries worldwide, the lot of women in the home is that of condemnation to unending menial labor.
- The most serious problem confronting women is how men victimize them with violence through assaults, beatings, and rape.

> What kind of avoidance behavior have you witnessed at your school? What can be done to overcome it?
>
> What cliques are prominent at your school? How do they engage in avoidance behavior?

SEXISM—THE WRONG OPINION THAT ONE SEX IS SUPERIOR TO THE OTHER BY THE VERY NATURE OF THINGS, LEADING TYPICALLY TO PREJUDICE AGAINST WOMEN.

AGEISM—Prejudice exhibited against the elderly because of their age.

Another example of discrimination is **ageism**, prejudice manifested against old people. For example, discrimination against the elderly

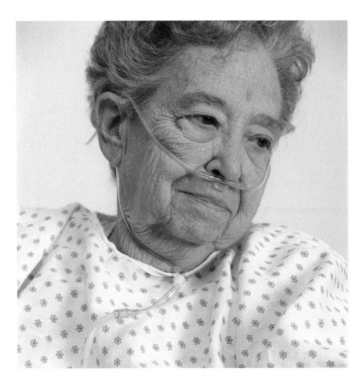

includes forced or early retirement as companies "downsize" to enhance the profit line.

Our society is "graying," and as it does there is an ever-increasing danger that more and more elderly people will be living in poverty. Current statistics reveal that the poverty rate among the elderly tops ten and a half percent, with elderly women having a significantly higher poverty rate than elderly men and with a disproportionate number of the elderly poor being members of minorities. The stability of Social Security and Medicare are of great concern as more people retire and a reduced work force is expected to help support the system. The move to legalize euthanasia is an attempt by some elements in society to remove sick elderly persons because they are "unproductive" and "burdensome."

In their statement entitled *Society and the Aged: Toward Reconciliation* (1976), the American bishops remind us that each person has dignity as a child of God, and has something to offer our society. For example, the wisdom and experience of many older people can be a real treasure for society. They are entitled to the basic rights: to life, to a decent home, to a job if they want one, to health care, to food, to a decent income, and to equal treatment. Pope John Paul II wrote of our obligations to the elderly and to the contributions they can make:

Neglect of the elderly or their outright rejection are intolerable. Their presence in the family . . . is of fundamental importance in creating a climate of mutual interaction and enriching communication between the different age groups. It is therefore important to preserve, or to reestablish where it has been lost, a sort of "covenant" between generations. . . . The elderly are not only to be considered the object of our concern, closeness and service. They themselves have a valuable contribution to make to the Gospel of life. Thanks to the rich treasury of experiences they have acquired through the years, the elderly can and must be sources of wisdom and witnesses of hope and love (The Gospel of Life, 94).

CHURCH TEACHING ON PREJUDICE AND DISCRIMINATION (CCC, 1934–1948)

Based on the teaching of Jesus, the Church vigorously condemns all forms of prejudice, including discrimination. The Second Vatican Council's *The Church in the Modern World* firmly states:

With respect to the fundamental rights of the person, every type of discrimination, whether social or cultural, whether based on sex, race, color, social condition, language or religion, is to be overcome and eradicated as contrary to God's intent (§29).

Discrimination is evil because it denies the equality of people, based simply on personal qualities like color, sex, race, religion, or the like. Although people differ according to physical attributes, moral aptitudes, intellectual gifts, and benefits derived from social commerce and the distribution of wealth, everyone has equal dignity (cf. CCC 1936).

God has blessed us with different gifts and talents. These talents have not been distributed equally. This is part of God's plan for each of us to receive what we need from others. However, the Lord also requires those who have been endowed with particular talents to develop them and then generously and charitably share them with others. Having or not having these gifts does not make us either superior or inferior to others. We are equal in our humanity as creatures of a loving God who endows us with dignity. The *Catechism of the Catholic Church* states it this way:

Created in the image of the one God and equally endowed with rational souls, all men have the same nature and the same origin. Redeemed by the sacrifice of Christ, all are called to participate in the same divine beatitude; all therefore enjoy an equal dignity (1934).

Because we are all children of God, we are essentially brothers and sisters. We share and deserve equal rights before God and each other. Discrimination dishonors a loving Father and the human family. According to the Vatican II documents:

We cannot truly call on God, the Father of all, if we refuse to treat in a brotherly way any man, created as he is in the image of God. Man's relation to God the Father and his relation to men his brothers are so linked together that Scripture says: "He who does not love does not know God" (1 John 4:8).

No foundation therefore remains for any theory or practice that leads to discrimination between man and man or people and people, so far as their human dignity and the rights flowing from it are concerned.

The Church reproves, as foreign to the mind of Christ, any discrimination against men or harassment of them because of their race, color, condition of life, or religion (Declaration on the Relation of the Church to Non-Christian Religions, §5).

Read:

List examples of how discrimination violates each of the following elements mentioned in the passage from the *Catechism of the Catholic Church* (1934).

- We are all created in God's image.
- We all have a rational soul with the same nature.
- We all have the same origin.
- Christ redeemed everyone.
- God calls everyone to share in the divine beatitude (the happiness of heaven).

Research:

Find examples in the newspapers and weekly news magazines of discrimination in today's world.

THE RIGHTS OF WOMEN (CCC, 369–373)

Pope John Paul II's *Letter to Women* highlighted the following:

Transcending the established norms of his own culture, Jesus treated women with openness, respect, acceptance and tenderness. In this way, He honored the dignity which women have always possessed according to God's plan and in His love (§3).

As far as women's rights are concerned, there is an urgent need to achieve real equality in every area: equal pay for equal work, protection for working mothers, fairness in career advancements, equality of spouses with regard to family rights . . . and to rights and duties of citizens in a democratic state. This is a matter of justice but also of necessity (§4).

Read the following passages from Luke's gospel and write answers to the questions that follow.

- **Luke 7:36–50**
  The woman who was a sinner
- **Luke 8:40–48**
  The woman with the hemorrhage
- **Luke 10:38–42**
  Mary and Martha
- **Luke 21:1–4**
  The widow's mite
- **Luke 24:1–11**
  The women at the tomb
- How did Jesus defend women when they were attacked?
- How did he encourage women? Warn women? Comfort women?
- What is an issue of women's rights today about which you are most concerned? Explain.

CHURCH TEACHING ON PREJUDICE AND DISCRIMINATION *continued*

Report:

Write a report on one of the following topics:
- Financial challenges for the elderly today (interview your grandparents or great-grandparents on this one)
- Health care for the elderly
- Nursing home issues
- Caring for elderly parents
- Elder abuse
- The aged and loneliness
- Scam artists and the elderly

Share:

Tell of a time when you were the victim of discrimination because of your age, sex, national origin, religion, socio-economic background, or some other personal quality. Report on how you felt at the time the discrimination took place.

PHYSICAL ATTACK

Heightened emotions associated with prejudice often lead to violence and to the commission of hate crimes. The daily newspapers report acts like desecrating graveyards or painting swastikas on synagogues. Spitting on people and throwing stones at cars or houses are also examples of physical attack. More serious examples include forcible ejection from neighborhoods and gang violence. Other violent and loathsome incidents include "gay-bashing," a favorite sport of insecure and immature males, and the terrible crimes of rape and sexual assault committed against women.

Everyone has the right to be free from these kinds of violence. Society has a duty to prevent and punish such behaviors. Some suggest that the potential victims of such violence should voluntarily restrict their own movements. But these proposals smack of discrimination. They are really saying that some classes of people should forgo their basic human rights.

Of course, potential victims of prejudice must use ordinary prudence to prevent becoming targets of violent crimes. However, to accept that some people must not live in nor visit certain neighborhoods, for example, is to promote prejudice and discrimination. To tolerate prejudice against some classes of people, or to conclude that some victims are acceptable or must forgo their basic human rights, is to take the path that leads to the destruction of everyone's rights.

EXTERMINATION

The ultimate form of prejudice is killing the "undesirable," eliminating either the individual or the whole group to which he or she belongs. Assassinations, lynchings, massacres, terrorist bombings, and "ethnic cleansings" are all horrific examples of prejudice gone mad.

Historians rightly term the twentieth century the most violent in human history. A fitting symbol for this violence was Adolf Hitler and his immoral collaborators attempting to inflict genocide on the Jewish people. This gross barbarity resulted from **anti-Semitism**, prejudice against the Jewish people exhibited down through the ages and even in our own time. The Holocaust (referred to as *Shoah* by the Jewish people) was a vivid enfleshment of the evil of prejudice. Pastor Martin Niemoeller, a victim of Nazism, wrote these chilling words:

*First they came for the Jews
and I did not speak out—
because I was not a Jew.
Then they came for the Communists
and I did not speak out—
because I was not a Communist.
Then they came for the trade unionists
and I did not speak out—
because I was not a trade unionist.
Then they came for me—
and there was no one left
to speak out for me.*[6]

ANTI-SEMITISM—Prejudice manifested in word or deed against people of Jewish origin.

WHAT TO DO?

Imagine that your school recently enrolled some Arab students who feel uncomfortable because both teachers and fellow students do not know much about Arab customs and traditions.

In addition, a small, obnoxious group of fellow students have decided to make life miserable for the new students. They joke about Arabs, linking them to terrorists. An Arab boy was verbally attacked with comments like, "Terrorist! Go back to your country before we kill you and your family off!" One Muslim girl, who was allowed to wear the *hijab*, was physically harassed when other students tore it off her head. Lately, the harassment has escalated to shoving matches and knocking food trays out of the hands of the Arab students at lunch.

- Write your opinion on what should be done to resolve this situation.

Also read:
- For more information on how to foster better relationships with Arab Americans, check out the American-Arab Anti-Discrimination Committee at www.adc.org. The case above is a modification of one on this website.
- Search the internet for this article originally published in the *Detroit Free Press*: "100 Questions and Answers about Arab Americans."

Interview a non-Catholic. Discover and then report on five beliefs you hold in common with this person of another faith.

Check an encyclopedia article on a non-Christian religion. Report on some feature of this religious tradition that you find interesting or attractive.

Report on examples of anti-Catholicism in American history.

Report on a specific example of anti-Semitism that occurred in history.

Scapegoating—Blaming an individual or group for something that the individual or group is not responsible for. Blaming another person or group for societal problems because of that person's group identity.

THE CHURCH AND THE JEWS (CCC, 595–598)

Bigotry against the Jewish people has been a sad chapter throughout history. In the Middle Ages, hatred of Jews led to the destruction of synagogues, the burning of books, and the periodic expelling of Jews from their native lands. In times of economic hardship, Jews have often been scapegoats for people's frustrations. For example, Nazi hatred of European Jews began with attacks on their economic livelihood, blaming them for the hard times people were having. It soon escalated into violence directed against Jewish homes, synagogues, and work places. Next came the isolation of the Jewish people into ghettos, culminating in the systematic attempt to exterminate every last Jew in death camps like Treblinka and Auschwitz.

Anti-Semitism and discrimination against any people because of their religious faith contradict Jesus' teaching. Jesus' own example was one of acceptance and love of people of other faiths, for example, he made the hated Samaritan into the hero of a parable.

The Church firmly teaches love of people of all faiths. It rejects anti-Semitism. The Second Vatican Council taught:

True, the Jewish authorities and those who followed their lead pressed for the death of Christ; still, what happened in His passion cannot be charged against all the Jews, without distinction, then alive, nor against the Jews of today. Although the Church is the new people of God, the Jews should not be presented as rejected or accursed by God, as if this followed from the Holy Scriptures. All should see to it, then, that in catechetical work or in the preaching of the word of God they do not teach anything that does not conform to the truth of the Gospel and the spirit of Christ.

Furthermore, in her rejection of every persecution against any man, the Church, mindful of the patrimony she shares with the Jews and moved not by political reasons but by the Gospel's spiritual love, decries hatred, persecutions, displays of anti-Semitism, directed against Jews at any time and by anyone. (Declaration on the Relationship of the Church to Non-Christian Religions, §4).]

WHY PREJUDICE IS WRONG: A BIBLICAL VIEW

If we believe in God's word, we must uproot prejudice from our own lives and fight it wherever we find it. Here is a brief list of Scripture-based statements that reveal the necessity to love and accept everyone. Our love should be inclusive, not exclusive.

1. God makes each person in his image and likeness. We possess a human soul with the ability to think and the ability to love. Therefore, every human being has basic dignity and deserves respect.
   Genesis 1:26–27

2. We are creatures of God. We all have the same origin, belonging to the same race, the human race. We are all equal in our creaturehood. No one is superior to anyone else. No one is inferior to anyone else.
   Acts 17:26–29

3. God loves everyone unconditionally, saint and sinner alike. We should love everyone, too, especially those whom society deems losers. We should love even our enemies.
   Luke 6:27, 15:1–2; Matthew 5:43–48

4. Jesus died for every human being. He loves everyone. He wants us to imitate his love.
   John 15:9–13

5. God calls everyone from the first moment of his or her conception to eternal life with the Blessed Trinity. We should help each other on our journey to our loving God and not neglect anyone, especially those who need us.
   Matthew 25:31–40

6. God is Abba, Father, papa. This makes us God's children. We are fundamentally brothers and sisters. We must treat each other not as strangers but as brothers and sisters.
   Matthew 6:7–15

7. We simply must love everyone if we want to be called disciples of Christ. We must treat others the way we want to be treated. Prejudice is unloving.
   Matthew 7:12

8. We simply must love everyone if we want Jesus to be our friend. He commands us, his friends, to love.
   John 15:14–17

9. We must eradicate negative thoughts and feelings about others from our minds and hearts because they lead to violent behavior.
   Mark 7:21–23; Matthew 5:21–26

> Transcribe into your journal three favorite Scripture quotes from those given here. Write a paragraph explaining how you can put one of them into action.

Research the pamphlet "101 Ways to Combat Prejudice" on the Anti-Defamation League's website: www.adl.org

• Write five ways you can personally root out prejudice in your own life.

Read Leviticus 16:8–22 to learn of the derivation of scapegoating. It tells how, on the eve of the Day of Atonement, the high priest puts his hands on a goat's head and confesses Israel's sins. The guilt of the people is transferred to the goat who is then driven into the desert bearing the sins of the people.

NINE WAYS YOU CAN FIGHT PREJUDICE

1. *Pray for your own conversion.* All of us have some prejudice in our hearts, recognized or not. Ask God to help you identify and root out any unfounded opinions you might have that keep you from looking on others as equals before God.

2. *Learn to celebrate cultural differences.* People are sometimes xenophobic, that is, they hate or fear strangers, foreigners, people from other ethnic groups. Learn something about an ethnic group that is different from yours. Listen to its music. Read about its traditions. Visit its churches. Enjoy its foods. You might like what you discover.

3. *Look for inequalities in your school, work place, and parish.* Note how minorities are represented. Encourage those in leadership positions to allow greater representation of those who are different.

4. *Avoid racial stereotypes, jokes, slurs.* Refuse to laugh. Don't repeat. Don't become part of a willing audience that encourages these things.

5. *Refuse to participate in any verbal attacks on homosexual persons.* Avoid stereotypes, jokes, and slurs. Gently challenge those who insist on attacking others in this vicious way.

6. *Treat those with disabilities as unique individuals.* Speak directly to them. Use common sense. Ask to help if assistance seems necessary. Establish contact, for example, by calling a blind person by name or by touching her arm. Never mock someone who is mentally slow or physically disabled.

7. *Visit a nursing home with some friends.* Take along some magazines for the residents. Talk with some of the lonely people there.

8. *Avoid sexist comments.* Treat girls and women with respect and dignity. Recognize and praise their gifts.

9. *Include rather than exclude.* Be the first to welcome a new classmate, club member, co-worker, or neighbor. Ask a lonely classmate to sit with your group at lunch. Help create an atmosphere where prejudging people because they are different simply won't be tolerated.

ATTEMPTING TO EXPLAIN PREJUDICE

Prejudice is a serious effect of original sin. It comes from human fallen nature that Jesus Christ has redeemed. Sociologists and psychologists point to some of the following factors to help explain why people hold on to their prejudices.[7]

People are too lazy to think. Prejudice is oversimplification. For example, it is easier to say "Poor people are shiftless" than to search out all the causes of poverty.

Scapegoats are an easy way to deal with negative emotions. Prejudice helps people deal with the frustrations in life instead of dealing with the real source of problems.

Prejudice makes people feel superior. Prejudiced people divide the world into simple categories of good and bad, right and wrong. Their "in" groups are always good and right. The "out" groups are always bad and wrong.

Prejudice thrives because it pays—both psychologically and financially. Psychologically, it makes people feel "better" than others. Financially, prejudice keeps "in" group members in power.

HOW DO PEOPLE BECOME PREJUDICED?

Psychological studies reveal that no one is born prejudiced. Prejudice is something we learn. And it is a complex process. Here are two important factors in the formation of prejudice in people.

1. *The home is the central school for learning prejudice.* Parents pass on their own biases to their children. Furthermore, if they raise their children in a fearful, threatening atmosphere, then children grow suspicious of others. Children in this type of home situation also view relationships in terms of power rather than sharing and give-and-take. These attitudes contribute to forming prejudiced personalities. Schools, neighborhoods, and church groups often reinforce the prejudices. For example, sometimes people feel superior to others when churches preach "We are saved, and nonbelievers are not."

2. *Sexism is key in forming early prejudices.* If boys and girls are taught that society values maleness more than femaleness, that males should have more power than females, then it follows that feelings of superiority might easily emerge among the boys, while the girls might struggle with a sense of inferiority. It is easy to transfer this hierarchical way of relating between the sexes to other relationships. For girls, the temptation is to identify some group they can feel superior to, while for boys, the tendency is simply to identify anyone who is different— by sex or race or religion, etc.—as inferior.

WHO ARE THE PREJUDICED?

Psychological studies agree to the following characteristics of people who are prejudiced:

Prejudiced people have difficulty dealing with ambiguity. Simple "either-or" explanations are what they want. They cannot deal with fuzziness, with shades of gray. Their thinking is rigid.

Prejudiced people have low self-esteem. They lack self-esteem and self-appreciation. They desperately want to feel good about themselves.

Unfortunately, the way many prejudiced people get a sense of self-worth is to tear others down.

Prejudiced people are authority-oriented. They do not like change or unstable institutions. They want well-defined chains of command.

OVERCOMING PREJUDICE

Psychological studies have discovered that the following practices can help people overcome prejudice[8]:

- Working with a different group at a task in a cooperative and interdependent manner in pursuing common goals. Doing so helps all to discover that it is no longer just "us and them" but "we."

- Participating in programs where we put ourselves in the shoes of another.

- Becoming aware of how inconsistent prejudice is with one's values, attitudes, and behaviors.

- Establishing laws, regulations, and social norms that require the fair treatment of others.

Compose ten rules or policies that you think parents should follow to raise children who accept others as equals and persons worthy of respect.

HIRING

Background:

This case involves you and your classmates. You were elected to represent them to serve on a committee to select a teacher for a new program in Fine Arts to start in the fall term. Two highly qualified individuals applied for the job. One is a Catholic; the other, an evangelical Christian.

What Would You Do?

- Who would you recommend for the job?
- Would it make any difference if one candidate were a woman and the other a man?
- Both applicants are women, but one is young and attractive, graduated from college three years ago. The other is matronly. She has experience in the public schools.
- What if the evangelical Christian is black? (Your school has only one other black teacher on staff.)
- Both applicants are men. One is slightly effeminate. Would this make any difference?

After discussing these situations with your classmates, determine if any of the comments shared demonstrated prejudice.

JEAN VANIER (1928–)
A CHAMPION FOR PERSONS WITH DEVELOPMENTAL DISABILITIES

In 1964, after a successful stint as a naval officer, Jean Vanier gave up a promising career as a college professor of philosophy. He met a Dominican priest who introduced him to a world of persons with developmental disabilities.

Jean began to visit psychiatric hospitals, institutions, and asylums. He gradually discovered the despair of those suffering mental disabilities and learned of the enormity of the problem. In an asylum near Paris, he met two men with mental disabilities: Rafael, who had meningitis when he was young, and Philippe, who suffered from the effects of encephalitis. Both orphaned in childhood, they had been placed in an asylum and remained there until Jean met them.

In 1964 Jean Vanier bought a small, dilapidated house in a small village not too far from Paris. He called the house l'Arche after Noah's ark, a symbol of God's covenant with humanity and a symbol of hope and of life. Jean invited Rafael and Philippe to live with him. They accepted. What began was a small community of hope and of life. Two men were treated with the respect humans deserve, living in an ordinary family-type atmosphere.

There was so much good about Jean's approach to serving and living with his friends, that his original *l'Arche* community has grown to more than 400 people: 200 with disabilities and 200 assistants living in about twenty houses spread across five villages. Worldwide, more than 120 other *l'Arche* communities exist in thirty countries. All these communities are committed to a new type of family where the strong help the weak, and the weak help the strong.

Jean's openness to people who are different has led to a great outpouring of love that has created houses and communities for those society has so often and easily spurned. These special people have given as much as they have received.

In their thirst and their gift for friendship and communion the weaker people in society can touch and transform the strong, if the strong are only prepared to listen to them.[9]

—*Jean Vanier*

CHAPTER SUMMARY

- Prejudice, a prejudgment based on insufficient information, is a source of many injustices. Negative prejudice is sinful because it threatens the rights of people, boxes people into categories, and often resists truth. Many prejudices are rooted in stereotypes, oversimplified generalizations that pigeonhole a whole group based on faulty assumptions.

- Examples of prejudice that plague our contemporary society include hatred of persons with a homosexual orientation, sexism, ageism, and anti-Semitism. The five stages of prejudice are: antilocution—speaking against a person; avoidance; discrimination—denying a person his or her rights; physical attack; and extermination. Genocide, the killing of an entire people, is the worst form of prejudice.

- Prejudice persists because people are often too lazy to think. It also helps them deal with their negative emotions and gives them feelings of superiority over others. There are both psychological and financial payoffs to being prejudiced.

- People basically learn prejudice in the home. Early doses of sexism can teach boys especially that males are superior to females and leave girls vulnerable to feelings of inferiority for which they may compensate by holding onto prejudicial opinions of others. Many prejudiced people lack self-esteem, have difficulty dealing with ambiguity, and are authority-oriented.

- Prejudice can be lessened when groups work cooperatively together and engage in empathy training. Reflecting on how prejudice conflicts with one's core values and passing laws that require fair treatment of others also help individuals and groups to overcome prejudice.

- The Church's bottom line teaching is that prejudice is a serious evil because it refuses to treat each person as a child of God, a person of incomparable dignity whom Christ redeemed and destined for eternal happiness. Christians especially know that if we want to accept the friendship of Jesus, then we must love everyone without distinction.

> It is easy to judge others, but so difficult to look critically at ourselves and the groups to which we belong. The person who is different, the stranger, makes us feel uneasy. . . . We find it difficult to listen to them, to respect them and above all to integrate them into our own convictions and way of looking at life.
>
> —Jean Vanier[10]

List some examples to illustrate Jean Vanier's quote about the weak helping the strong.

Do you know, either as a friend or relation, a person with a mental disability? If so, describe your relationship with this person.

Visit the official international website of L'Arche: www.larche.org.

Report on some core beliefs of this remarkable organization.

REVIEW QUESTIONS

1. Define the term *prejudice*.
2. Give an example of a "positive" prejudice and a "neutral" prejudice. How might these turn into a "negative" prejudice?
3. What is the ultimate source of prejudice?
4. When is prejudice sinful and wrong?
5. Define the term *stereotype*. Give some examples of stereotypes related to your own ethnic background or religion.
6. Why do people exhibit prejudice toward persons with a homosexual orientation? Why is this wrong?
7. List the five stages of prejudice. Give an example of each.
8. What is sexism? Why is it wrong? How does it encourage other prejudices in boys? girls?
9. Discuss the meaning of these terms: feminism, patriarchy, glass ceiling.

10. What is ageism? Give an example.
11. Discuss two specific Church teachings that tell us that prejudice and discrimination are wrong.
12. What is anti-Semitism?
13. Discuss five specific biblical teachings that show the immorality of prejudice.
14. Discuss three specific things you can do to combat prejudice.
15. Describe the prejudiced personality.
16. Identify Jean Vanier. How does he embody Christian love?

 RESEARCHING ON THE INTERNET

The first principle, which is one that must be stated clearly and firmly, is that the disabled person (whether the disability be the result of a congenital handicap, chronic illness or accident, or from mental or physical deficiency, and whatever the severity of the disability) is a fully human subject, with the corresponding innate, sacred and inviolable rights.
—from "Basic Principles", §I, of the Document of the Holy See for the International Year of Disabled Persons, To All Who Work for the Disabled, *1981.*

1. Look up this excellent bibliography on race, ethnicity, and multiculturalism. Locate a recommended site, read an article, and report to class on your findings: http://ethics.acusd.edu/Applied/race/
2. Visit the Anti-Defamation League website: www.adl.org/adl.asp. Do one of the following:
   • Report on examples of anti-Semitism in the United States
   • Report on how denial of the Holocaust is an example of anti-Semitism.
3. Visit the National Council of La Raza website, which is dedicated to making a difference for Hispanic Americans: www.nclr.org. Read and report on a recent news item.

PRAYER REFLECTION

Dear Heavenly Father—
You have made each of us
male and female,
black and red and brown and white and yellow,
tall and short, old and young.
We speak a symphony of tongues.
We come from all around this beautiful globe you put us on.
Please send us your Holy Spirit to teach us
to see everyone as a brother or sister,
to respect and not to criticize,
to understand rather than to revile.
May the Spirit give us the courage
to love rather than hate,
to include rather than exclude,
to welcome rather than turn away.
Father, we ask this in the name of your Son, Jesus Christ,
who came to give us, one and all, salvation and
eternal joy with you forever. Amen.

NOTES

1. "10 Ways to Fight Hate" from Tolerance.org.
2. Secretariat for Family, Laity, Women & Youth, United States Conference of Catholic Bishops, *Always Our Children: A Pastoral Message to Parents of Homosexual Children and Suggestions for Pastoral Ministers: A Statement of the Bishops' Committee on Marriage and Family*.
3. Ibid.
4. Ibid., citing *The Pastoral Care of Homosexual Persons*, 1986, no. 10.
5. The four principles were taken from a special issue of *Media & Values*, No. 57, Winter, 1992, pp. 21–22. This issue is copyrighted by the Center for Media and Values and was co-sponsored by the Catholic Communication Campaign.
6. Quoted in Tony Castle, *Quotations for All Occasions* (London: Marshall Pickering, 1989), p. 264.
7. Drawing on the work of Gordon Allport and others, David L. Shields reports on these findings in "The Psychology of Prejudice," *PACE 16*, pp. 135–139.
8. The summary of this research can be found at Scott Plous, "The Psychology of Prejudice, Stereotyping, and Discrimination: An Overview," pp. 3–48, in Scott Plous, ed., *Understanding Prejudice and Discrimination* (New York: McGraw Hill, 2002), pp. 23–24.
9. Jean Vanier, *Our Journey Home* (Maryknoll, NY: Orbis Books, 1997), p. xi.
10. Ibid., pp. 25–26.

CHAPTER OVERVIEW

When Night Ends
This section introduces racism, one of the ugliest forms of prejudice.

Institutional Racism
Institutional racism refers to occasions when racism infects every aspect of society.

Racism Against Certain Groups
This section focuses on specific examples of racism against people of African, Hispanic, and Native American origin.

Being Inclusive
Christians must work to avoid exclusion that results from prejudice, stereotyping others, and discrimination and create inclusive communities instead.

Saint Katherine Drexel
Katherine Drexel used her inheritance to build missions and schools to benefit many minority children.

Racism is an evil which endures in our society and in our Church. Despite apparent advances and even significant changes . . . the reality of racism remains. In large part it is only the external appearances that have changed.

—American Bishops, Brothers and Sisters to Us, §1

6

JUSTICE AND RACISM

WHEN NIGHT ENDS

An old Jewish tale reveals how God intends for us to love everyone.

An old Rabbi once asked his pupils how they could tell when the night had ended and the day begun.

"Could it be," asked one of the students, "when you can see an animal in the distance and tell whether it's a sheep or dog?"

"No," answered the Rabbi.

Another asked, "Is it when you can look at a tree in the distance and tell whether it's a fig tree or a peach tree?"

"No," answered the Rabbi.

"Then, when is it?" the pupils demanded.

"It is when you can look on the face of any man or woman and see that it is your sister or brother. Because if you cannot see this, it is still night."[1]

Racism is one of the ugliest forms of prejudice. The Vatican document, *The Church and Racism*, defines racial prejudice as:

> *Awareness of the biologically determined superiority of one's own race or ethnic group with respect to others (§2).*

Racism leads to the mistreatment of people based on their race, color, national origin, religion, place of origin, or ancestry. This mistreatment can take place on a person-to-person basis. Racism can also be institutional, that is, legalized or tolerated in the very structures of society, favoring the majority and hindering the success of the minority.

No one is immune from racism. Even Christian churches, including the Catholic Church, have been racist. Further,

> *Racism is a sin: a sin that divides the human family, blots out the image of God among specific members of that family, and violates the fundamental human dignity of those called to be children of the same Father. Racism is the sin that says that some human beings are inherently superior and others essentially inferior because of race. It is the sin that makes racial characteristics the determining factor for the exercise of human rights. It mocks the words of Jesus: "Treat others the way you would have them treat you." Indeed, racism is more than a disregard for the words of Jesus; it is a denial of the truth of the dignity of each human being revealed by the mystery of the Incarnation* (Brothers and Sisters to Us, §9).

In this chapter, we will examine in more detail three manifestations of racial prejudice that continue to haunt contemporary society.

WHAT DO YOU THINK?

Chapter 5 pointed out that prejudice often results from stereotyping, that is, making oversimplified generalizations. Stereotypes also result from exaggerating some quality or trait exhibited by individuals or groups. Although some stereotypes can be favorable, most are harmful and even degrading.

Below is a list of seven statements. See if you can recognize which are racial stereotypes. Mark according to this scale: **1—clearly a stereotype; 2—a provable statement; 3—I'm not sure.**

	1	2	3
1. Blacks are athletically superior to whites.			
2. Mexican Americans have large families.			
3. Societal institutions need to celebrate racial and ethnic diversity more to tap into all the gifts with which God has blessed all his people.			
4. No wonder blacks and Hispanics are poor; there is something in their culture that discourages the work ethic.			
5. If the dominant white culture were not reluctant to share its wealth or power, people of color would undoubtedly assume greater leadership roles in the institutions of society.			
6. If Native Americans were not so super sensitive about their identity, they would not be fighting to change the names and mascots of collegiate and professional sports' teams.			
7. Progress has been made in racial justice in the United States; however, we have a way to go for the principle of equality to become a reality for all Americans.			

- How would you go about proving or disproving any of the statements above?
- List some positive stereotypes about African Americans, Hispanic Americans, Native Americans, and Asian Americans.

INSTITUTIONAL RACISM

When racism infects every aspect of society it is known as *institutional racism*. A modern historical example was apartheid in South Africa, a form that the Vatican has termed racism's worst modern-day example. South African blacks could not vote, were not allowed to travel freely, and had to live in certain restricted areas. In effect, they were prisoners in their own country.

In the United States, slavery of African Americans was the most notorious example of institutional racism. Since then, America has fought a Civil War, passed an amendment that guarantees the basic human rights of all people regardless of race, handed down Supreme Court decisions banning segregated schools and approving some forms of **affirmative action**, passed Civil Rights legislation, and the like. Though the United States has gone a long way to eradicate the evil effects of racism, its institutions are still not entirely free of its insidious effects.

Take one example: education. Many of the economic disadvantages for minorities stem from a lack of good schools and educational opportunity. Note how poverty and inferior school systems perpetuate themselves. In most states, the schools are funded by local property taxes. If you live in a poor area, there

RACISM—"Awareness of the biologically determined superiority of one's own race or ethnic group with respect to others" (The Church and Racism, §2).

AFFIRMATIVE ACTION—The policy and programs established to correct past discrimination in educational and employment opportunities directed against women, blacks, and members of other minorities.

125

will not be enough of a tax base to fund superior schools. The lack of money results in schools that simply cannot compete with either private schools or those in the wealthy suburbs.

If you are from an African- or Hispanic-American family with no option but to go to an inferior, perhaps even unsafe school, you have two strikes against you from the outset. A poor school leads to a poor education which leads to an inferior, low-paying job that keeps you poor and disadvantaged. This is an example of institutional racism, how the system perpetuates the disadvantages the victims of racism have suffered for decades.

CASE STUDY: LOW COST HOUSING

Background:

The county government has approved funds to erect a low-income housing development near your neighborhood. Many in your neighborhood are dead-set against this idea and are circulating a petition to stop progress on the proposal. Their main worry is that such a development will negatively affect the value of the homes in your neighborhood. In addition, some are worried about the safety of the neighborhood once low-income people move in.

The opponents of the housing development claim that their only concerns are economics and safety, even though they admit that many of the likely future residents will be people of color. They insist that race is not an issue.

Discuss and Debate:

- Is this an example of institutional racism? Explain.
- Would your parents sign the petition? Would you? Would you be racist if you did? Explain.
- How is justice served or not served in a situation like this? (For example, what about the children of the potential residents who might now be denied a good education from schools in your area?)

A WIDENING WEALTH GAP

Fact 1: Black and Hispanic household incomes are two-thirds that of white households.

Fact 2: The median net worth of a white family is ten times that of black and Hispanic families.

Contributing Factor: A major reason for the wealth gap is that minorities have historically been forced to buy homes in less-desirable neighborhoods and to finance the homes at higher interest rates that led to early foreclosures.[2]

RACISM AGAINST CERTAIN GROUPS

Below you will find a brief discussion of three examples of racism that have victimized our brothers and sisters of African, Hispanic, and Native American origin. As you read about the discrimination committed against their ethnic group, see if you can discover examples of how societal institutions contribute to putting these groups at a disadvantage.

AFRICAN AMERICANS

A newspaper report recounts that two off-duty police officers drew a gun on a man. The potential suspect had left his truck to approach a teller at a bank drive-through to cash a check. The man's truck would not fit under the overhang. The officers thought the man was going to rob the teller. Their evidence that the man's action was threatening: the man was black.[3]

This sad story reveals that racial prejudice is alive and well in the United States. The horrible effects of slavery are with us yet, both in prejudiced individuals and in societal structures that help to promote acceptance of a status quo that favors whites over blacks.

As the American bishops' pastoral letter *Brothers and Sisters to*

Us puts it, "Racism has been part of the social fabric of America since its European colonization" (§20). This is especially true for the history of African Americans who were first brought to this country as slaves in 1607. To support an economic system built on slavery, slave-owners and others justified slavery by treating blacks as property and claiming they were not fully human. As such, they could not vote, were denied the right to an education, had no choice in where to live, and suffered many other injustices contrary to human dignity.

1887 NEBRASKA HOMESTEADERS

Slavery continued in the United States until the Emancipation Proclamation of 1863. At the end of the Civil War, the Thirteenth Amendment to the Constitution outlawed slavery. The period of history that followed—Reconstruction—did result in a more humane existence for former slaves. However, when the troops were withdrawn, "Jim Crow" laws came into being and African Americans were again treated as second-class citizens.

Segregation was enforced in the South, resulting in a mentality that blacks were inferior to whites. African Americans were not allowed to compete on an equal basis economically. This resulted in widespread poverty, health problems, lack of a decent and competitive education, and a host of other social injustices. Lurking in the background were groups like the Ku Klux Klan which resorted to intimidation, violence, terrorism, and deplorable crimes like lynchings. Nor was the situation rosy for blacks once they began to move to the North in the twentieth century. Settling largely in industrial cities, African Americans were victimized by widespread and pervasive discrimination in employment and education and de facto segregation in housing and schools.

The civil rights movement of the 1950s and 1960s began to bring relief. The famous 1954 *Brown v. Board of Education of Topeka* Supreme Court decision desegregated public elementary and secondary schools. Nonviolent acts by silent heroines like Rosa Parks, who refused to give up her bus seat to a white person in Montgomery, Alabama, in December of 1955, mobilized the black community. Demonstrations led by civil rights heroes like Dr. Martin Luther King, Jr., helped to raise public consciousness concerning the inequalities suffered by blacks. Nonviolent marches, sit-ins, and boycotts led to voter registration drives and programs to combat poverty. Eventually, Congress passed into law the Civil Rights Act of 1964. Since then, major strides have been made to combat the injustices of the past. For example, affirmative action programs have helped blacks and other minorities gain a more equitable footing in employment and housing and have helped right some excesses of past discrimination.

However, we still live in an unequal society. There exists a large income and employment gap between African Americans and whites. Blacks suffer much more from the effects of a violent society, are incarcerated disproportionally according to their numbers, and have shorter life spans. The following facts support these statements:

- In a recent year, the U.S. Census reported that the poverty rate for non-Hispanic whites was 8.2 percent; for blacks it was almost three times as high at 24.4 percent. This translates

Rosa Parks

to the fact that nearly one in four blacks lives below the poverty line.[4]

- The death rate for African American women during childbirth is 3.5 times higher than it is for white women.[5]
- Life expectancy for black newborns is five years less than white newborns.[6]
- The 2000 census found that 91.8 percent of white students graduated from high school, compared with 83.7 percent of black students.
- On average, blacks are twice as likely to die from disease, accident, and homicide as whites.
- The average prison sentence for a black person is six months longer than that for whites.[7]

The list goes on. Past racial hatred against African Americans has helped to create a black underclass. For various complex reasons, this underclass is victimized by a vicious cycle of poverty and violence.

apartheid—The long-term policy in South Africa of strict racial segregation and economic and political discrimination against nonwhites.

Differences in education can partly explain the income gap between black and white Americans, but many of these differences are also the result of prejudice and discrimination. Part of this gap can also be explained by the large number of black families headed by single women. But again, this condition also partly results from prejudice that makes it extremely difficult for black men to find work. This in turn has put many young black men at risk for many crimes including violence leading all the way to death.

The Catholic Church strongly condemns racism against all minorities. It has singled out the **apartheid** ("separate development") policy in South Africa from 1948–1991 as the most extreme and condemnable form of segregation, prejudice, and racial inequality against blacks (*The Church and Racism*, §9). The Church points to the Bible and God's gracious liberation of the Israelites from slavery and proclaims that God frees everyone from slavery and calls each of us to be responsible for each other.

The Church has also admitted that Christian nations have been guilty of supporting slavery and that Christian churches have been prejudiced against blacks.

All too often the Church in our country has been for many a "white Church," a racist institution. . . . Each of us as Catholics must acknowledge a share in the mistakes and sins of the past. Many of us have been prisoners of fear and prejudice. We have preached the Gospel while closing our eyes to the racism it condemns. We have allowed conformity to social pressures to replace compliance with social justice (Brothers and Sisters to Us, §31–32).

Simply put, Church teaching tells us to fight racism. For example, the victims of racism, wherever they may be, must be defended. Acts of discrimination among persons and peoples for racist or other reasons *—religious or ideological—and which lead to contempt and . . . exclusion, must be denounced and brought to light . . . and strongly rejected in order to promote equitable behavior, legislative dispositions, and social structures* (The Church and Racism, §26).

In addition, various Church documents, especially *Brothers and Sisters to Us*, outline steps the Church itself can take to combat racism. For example:

- Catholic institutions should check their own policies to see if they treat minorities justly.
- The Church should continue to run and even expand Catholic schools in inner city neighborhoods.
- The Church should be a model equal opportunity employer.
- Catholics should become more aware of the history and culture of black Catholics.

LIVES OF GREAT AFRICAN SAINTS

Write a report on the life of one of the following African saints:
- Saint Augustine of Hippo
- Saint Benedict the Moor
- Saints Felicitas and Perpetua
- Saint Josephine Bakhita
- Saint Martin de Porres, patron saint of interracial justice and harmony
- Saint Moses the Black

Use one of the following websites to help in your research:
- www.catholic_forum.com/ saints/indexsnt.htm
- Catholic Online: www.catholic.org
- American Catholic.org: www.americancatholic.org

Extra Credit: Visit the website of the National Black Catholic Congress. Read and report on an article from *The Black Catholic Monthly* at www.nbccongress.org.

AFFIRMATIVE ACTION

Affirmative action programs seek to correct past discrimination against minorities and women by increasing recruitment, promotions, retention, and on-the-job training and by removing barriers to admission to educational institutions. Laws have created some affirmative action programs. Some employers have voluntarily initiated others. The American bishops have supported the idea of affirmative action:

Where the effects of past discrimination persist, society has the obligation to take positive steps to overcome the legacy of injustice. Judiciously administered affirmative action programs in education and employment can be important expressions of the drive for solidarity and participation that is at the heart of true justice. Social harm calls for social relief (Economic Justice for All, §73).

A study on the effectiveness of affirmative action, completed in 1998 by Harvard sociologist Barbara Reskin, concluded that affirmative action programs have been "moderately successful." She holds that it would be a costly and dangerous experiment to roll these programs back. The study claimed that racial discrimination in employment is still widespread, that affirmative action programs have lessened racial bias in the workplace, and that the dominant racial group is not suffering to any significant degree because of affirmative action, despite popular perceptions.[8]

Concerning opposition to affirmative action programs, the American bishops warned:

Racism is sometimes apparent in the growing sentiment that too much is being given to racial minorities by way of affirmative action programs or allocations to redress long-standing imbalances in minority representation and government-funded programs for the disadvantaged. At times, protestations claiming that all persons should be treated equally reflect the desire to maintain a status quo that favors one race and social group at the expense of the poor and nonwhite (Brothers and Sisters to Us, §18).

129

Do you think affirmative action and welfare programs have gone too far to help racial minorities? Explain.

Other than affirmative action, what should our country do to help correct the injustices committed in the past against minorities?

Research the pros and cons of affirmative action. Write a summary of your findings.

Locate and read the following articles on affirmative action:
- Scott Plous, "Ten Myths about Affirmative Action," in Scott Plous (ed.), *Understanding Prejudice and Discrimination* (New York: McGraw Hill, 2003), pp. 206–212. Find this article online at: www. understandingprejudice. org/readroom/articles/ affirm.htm.
- Father Bryan Massengale, "Catholics Should Stand Firm on Affirmative Action," *Salt of the Earth Magazine:* http://salt.claretianpubs. org/issues/racism/affirm. html.

Chicano—A person of Mexican American heritage.

HISPANIC AMERICANS

Hispanic Americans are descended from Spanish-speaking peoples. They represent a mix of cultures, national groups, and races (*mestizos*—people of mixed European and Native American ancestry; *mulattos*—people of mixed African and European ancestry). The Hispanic presence in America is the result of a rich and varied history and a culture connected to the far-flung Spanish Empire of old.

Hispanic Americans predate English-speaking colonists in America. For example, in the 1500s, Spanish explorers helped to discover the Americas. St. Augustine, Florida, was the first European settlement in North America, founded in 1565. Spanish explorers were also active in the West and Southwest in the 1500s, later settling in states like California, New Mexico, Texas, and Arizona. Spanish presence is strongly felt in these states today, for example, in Santa Fe, the beautiful capital of New Mexico.

In 2003, the Census Bureau designated Hispanics as the largest minority group in the United States several years before they had been forecast to reach that size. What is remarkable about this designation is that in 1980 the Latino population was barely more than 50 percent of the African American population.

"While today one of every eight residents of the United States is Latino, it is projected that Latinos could account for one of every five residents by 2035, one of every four by 2055, and one of every three by 2100."[9]

Most Hispanics come from Mexico, Central and South America, Puerto Rico, and Cuba. Information about prejudice against people from each of these regions is highlighted in the rest of this section.[10]

Around two out of three Hispanics come from Mexico, thus comprising the largest subgroup of Latinos in the United States. After the Mexican War, the Treaty of Guadalupe Hidalgo (1848) forced Mexico to cede Texas to the United States. America also took control of a vast territory encompassing lands in California, Nevada, Utah, Arizona, New Mexico, and parts of Colorado and Wyoming. Citizenship was given to Spanish-speaking people living in these territories. These were the first **Chicanos**, that is, Hispanic Americans of Mexican ancestry.

Many Mexicans also came to America after the Mexican Revolution in 1910; almost 700,000 immigrated between 1910 and 1930. They took low-paying jobs on ranches and farms, in the mines, and on the railroad. Local inhabitants resented their presence. An immigration law of 1917 required adult immigrants to read and write one language; another in 1924 established a border patrol. Both laws discouraged Mexican immigration to America. During the Depression, when jobs were tight, many Mexicans living in the United States were forced to go back to Mexico.

Also, Chicanos were not allowed in public swimming pools or theaters. They could not speak Spanish in the public schools. After World War II, the government allowed thousands of Mexicans into the country to work as cheap labor, most notably in California and Texas. Five million immigrants entered the United States as *braceros* (manual laborers). Many were uneducated and had to live in substandard housing, for example, in *barrios* (neighborhoods) in the poorest section of towns. Some Mexican Americans lost their jobs because of the cheap labor of the *braceros*. Unfortunately, their unemployment helped contribute to the stereotyping of all Chicanos as lazy.

It was especially tough for the children of migrant workers to get a decent education because their parents had to move from place to place.

In the 1950s the United States government made a special push to rid the country of undocumented Mexicans who entered the country illegally. The Immigration and Naturalization Service would periodically arrest and detain Hispanic-looking persons to send them back to Mexico. Even in our day, abuses are reported in handling the cases of the thousands of Mexicans who cross the border for economic opportunity. Lacking citizenship, they are often detained without any regard for due process of law.

Many Hispanic Americans toil as migrant farm workers because of their inability to speak English and their lack of job skills and education. They have been ripe for exploitation by the owners of large farms. Chicanos suffer the abuses of low wages, the lack of health care and decent education, unsafe and congested housing, and spotty enforcement of child labor laws.

About 15 percent of the Hispanic people in America today come from Central American countries like Nicaragua, El Salvador, Guatemala, and the Caribbean nation, the Dominican Republic. Political oppression in their homelands forced many to seek refuge in the United States, the "nation of immigrants." Economic opportunity is also a motivation for immigration, as it has been since America's earliest days.

Hispanics from Central America have mostly settled in New York and California. Unfortunately, many of them are *undocumented* immigrants, that is, lacking the papers ensuring their legal entrance into this country.

Largely, Hispanics from South America have not immigrated to America to escape poverty. Many are middle-class with above-average education and good technical skills. They have been able to contribute to life in the United States in their chosen fields, including the sciences, medicine, the arts, and business.

Puerto Rico, an island one thousand miles southeast of Florida, became a protectorate of the United States after the Spanish-American War in 1898. The Jones Act of 1917 gave Puerto Ricans U. S. citizenship. Thousands of Puerto Ricans immigrated to large Eastern cities, especially New York City, to help escape the poverty of their homeland. They found work in factories, hospitals, laundries, and in the garment industry. Puerto Ricans make up close to nine percent of the Latino population in the United States.

Their language and color have targeted them for prejudice. Unskilled and low-paying jobs have resulted in poor housing conditions. Humiliation in schools contributed to a high drop-out rate. Tragically,

FOUR WAYS TO FIGHT RACISM

1. *Understand.* It is outright wrong to believe that one race or ethnic or religious group is inherently superior to another. Evaluate how you speak with and act toward others who come from different backgrounds. Resolve to change.

2. *Watch your tongue.* Analyze the need to mention someone's race or ethnicity when talking about them. If it is not relevant, then don't. Learn how people like to be described: for example, some like Black, others African Americans; some prefer Hispanic, others Latino/a. If in doubt, ask. Avoid racial epithets at all costs.

3. *Avoid stereotypes.* Learn more about the culture and customs of a group unfamiliar to you. To expand your horizons, talk to classmates who come from different backgrounds, read books, or visit websites.

4. *Speak out.* Interrupt racial jokes or smears. Simply say something like this, "I don't like hearing jokes like that." Remember this axiom: "If I omit, I permit." By not challenging bigots, you are giving them permission to continue their slurs.

Brainstorm other practical ways you can fight racism at your school.

ENCYCLICAL—A PASTORAL PAPAL LETTER SENT TO THE WHOLE CHURCH, AND SOMETIMES TO ALL PEOPLE, ON SOME IMPORTANT ASPECT OF CHURCH TEACHING.

The Church acknowledges the right of governments to limit the number of refugees and immigrants entering a country, "taking into consideration its possibilities for employment and its perspectives for development but also the urgency of the need of the other people" (*The Church and Racism*, §29). Discuss what your class believes would be a just immigration policy, especially for Hispanics who wish to enter the United States.

Report on Our Lady of Guadalupe, a popular devotion Mexican Americans have toward our Blessed Mother.

more than 50 percent of Puerto Rican American children live in poverty.

The third largest Hispanic group in America comes from Cuba. Cuban Americans have the highest median income of any Hispanic group in the United States.

After Fidel Castro's revolution in Cuba in 1959, many middle- and upper-middle-income Cubans left their island homeland and settled in Miami, Florida, which today is a bilingual city. More than 155,000 Cubans immigrated between 1959 and 1962. The American government welcomed them as refugees. Another group of less privileged Cubans immigrated in 1980 when Castro relaxed his emigration policy due to a bad economy. Included in this group were drug addicts, people with mental disorders, prisoners, and sick people.

Many Cuban exiles remain tight-knit, intellectually sophisticated, and committed to return to Cuba one day.

The American bishops have reminded us that American Catholics should especially hate racial prejudice:

The members of every racial and ethnic group are beings of incomparable worth, yet racial antagonism and discrimination are among the most persistent and destructive evils in our nation. Those victims of discrimination of whom we are most conscious are Hispanic Americans, black Americans, and native Americans. The Catholic community should be particularly sensitive to this form of prejudice because it, too, has experienced prejudice and discrimination in America based on national origin and religion (To Live in Christ Jesus, §70).

According to a recent study, nearly 73 percent of Hispanics residing in the United States are

Catholic. Sixty-four percent go to church on a regular basis.[11] Yet, because the Church in the United States has lacked a Spanish-speaking clergy, they have often been treated as second-class citizens in the Church. The American bishops want to change this: "All of us in the Church should broaden the embrace with which we greet our Hispanic brothers and sisters and deepen our commitment to them" (*The Hispanic Presence: Challenge and Commitment*, §5).

In various Church documents, the American bishops denounce prejudice against Hispanics, for example, in parishes that segregate Anglo and Hispanic events. Parishes must find ways to embrace Hispanic Catholics, for example, by celebrating Spanish and bilingual worship services; by promoting evangelization efforts that celebrate Hispanic devotions and prayer forms; and by holding religious education and Bible study programs in Spanish.

In a recent document entitled *Encuentro and Mission: A Renewed Pastoral Framework for Hispanic Ministry* (2002), the bishops also enthusiastically support the creation of small faith communities within a parish under the direction of pastors because they promote experiences of faith and conversion. "They are a prophetic challenge for the renewal of our Church and the humanization of our society and can serve to stem the loss of Hispanic Catholics to other faith traditions."[12]

In this same document, the bishops also urge pastoral leaders:

- to plan with the people, and not simply for them;
- to promote and support more vigorously vocations to the priesthood, diaconate, and consecrated life;

- to support efforts at forming lay leaders to serve as bridge-builders for today's culturally diverse Church; and
- to promote intercultural dialogue and collaboration.

Given the fact that the Hispanic population in the United States is now the fifth largest in the world—after Mexico, Spain, Argentina, and Colombia—the bishops also urge Church leaders to send pastoral letters, statements, and other Church documents and resources to parishes in Spanish as well.

SCRIPTURE LINK

Read the following passages. Answer the questions that follow.

Read Psalm 103: A loving God
1. Why should we love God?

Read Matthew 5:46–47: Love
2. What is the meaning of this passage?
3. How could the application of this passage reduce racial tensions?

Read Luke 14:7–14: Humility
4. What will happen to those who think they are better than others?

Read Luke 15:1–3: Jesus' associates
5. Why does Jesus get in trouble with the Pharisees and others?
6. What does this passage reveal about Jesus' true character?

Read Acts 10:34–35: Learning from God
7. What lesson can we learn from God?

Read 1 John 2:9–11: Light
8. What keeps us in the dark?

Report on the Cursillo Movement, a Church renewal program important to many Catholics of Hispanic origin.

Attend a Mass celebrated in Spanish. Report on your reactions to this celebration of the liturgy.

Visit one of these websites devoted to Hispanic issues. Read and report on an article from one of the websites you visited.
Pew Hispanic Center: www.pewhispanic.org/index.jsp?page=index
National Council of La Raza: www.nclr.org
Hispanic Online: www.hispaniconline.com

DEBATE THESE ISSUES:

1. Should undocumented immigrants be allowed to obtain a driver's license in a state where they are living and working, for example, as part of a construction crew?
2. Should a person be allowed to vote in an election if he or she is not able to speak English?
3. Should a community extend health-care treatment to the children of non-legal immigrants?

NATIVE AMERICANS

Native Americans (those indigenous to the Americas, also called Indians) have suffered greatly from the effects of racism. The hundreds of Native American nations may have numbered from 4.5 million to 10 million people north of Mexico at the time of Columbus' "discovery" of America. By the end of the nineteenth century, their population had decreased to an estimated quarter million people.

Many factors brought about the decline in the Native American population and culture:

- Diseases like smallpox, measles, and tuberculosis—against which Native Americans had no immunities—resulted in the decimation of whole populations. Sometimes Native Americans were purposely infected with these diseases.

- Loss of cultural identity as missionaries and government agencies worked to stamp out Native American religion and customs. (Some viewed Native Americans as "savages" who needed to be converted to an ideal yeoman farmer. Others, like those on the frontier, thought Native Americans should be exterminated.)

- Vicious wars waged by the English in the seventeenth and eighteenth centuries devastated various tribes in the East. Later wars with Native Americans led to policies like the Indian Removal Act of 1830. Mandatory forced marches, many of them in the dead of winter, killed countless Native Americans as they were moved West to make room for white settlers.

- The willful destruction of buffalo on which nations like the Lakota (Sioux) depended for life.

- Expansion of the railroads which deprived the Native Americans of valuable range lands they needed to sustain their people.

- The gobbling of lands by Anglos in the move to expand West. All too often these lands were taken after treaties were broken. For example, whites broke a treaty with the Lakota so they could extract gold in the Black Hills of the Dakotas, a land sacred to the people.

In 1870, the Reservation system was introduced. It forced whole nations to live on barren land that no one else wanted.

This system confined the people so they could not support themselves in their accustomed way. It has led to the institutional racism Native Americans experience to this day.

Some negative effects of this enforced segregation include:

- Housing Needs: An estimated 200,000 housing units are needed immediately in reservations.

- Homelessness: Approximately 90,000 Native American families are homeless or under-housed.

- Poverty Rate: The poverty rate for Native Americans is approximately 26 percent—2.6 times higher than that for whites and more than twice the average for all Americans, at approximately 12 percent.

- Unemployment Rate: Compared to 5.8 percent of the general U.S. population, 13.6 percent of the workforce on reservation areas is unemployed.[13] However, there are pockets on certain reservations where unemployment is as high as 75 percent.[14]

- Death Rates Among Youth: Alcohol-related deaths among Native Americans ages fifteen to twenty-four are seventeen times higher than the national averages. The suicide rate for Native American youth is three times the national average.[15]

- Education: The public high school graduation rate for Native American youth in 2000 was 57 percent; for whites, it was 76 percent.[16]

In addition, Western Native Americans have experienced chronic exposure to low doses of radiation for over forty years. This was due to uranium mining and nuclear testing programs that took place on or near reservation lands. Many Indians worked for the government and large energy consortiums for substandard wages and working conditions and are today experiencing the effects of radiation poisoning.[17]

Many Spanish and Portuguese colonizers treated Native Americans as inferiors, often enslaving them and trying to destroy their "savage" cultures. However, some Catholic leaders stood up for the rights of indigenous peoples. For example, the one-time soldier turned Dominican priest, and later bishop, Bartolome de Las Casas (1474–1566) defended Native American rights. Popes also intervened. In 1537, Pope Paul III denounced in a papal bull those who claimed "the inhabitants of the West Indies and the southern continents . . . should be treated like irrational animals and used for our profit and service. . . . The . . . Indians . . . must be left to enjoy their freedoms and possessions."[18] A later pope—Urban VIII (1623–1644)—even excommunicated anyone who kept Indians as slaves.

Looking back, we can admit honestly that some Church practices to Christianize Native Americans were prejudicial, for example, treating indigenous peoples as children, destroying cultural artifacts, and creating boarding schools which unintentionally undermined Native American family life. The Church has confessed that, although motivated by the good intention of bringing people to Christ, it did not always best serve the Native Americans.

As a Church, we often have been unconscious and insensitive to the mistreatment of our Native American brothers and sisters and have at times reflected the racism of the dominant culture of which we have been a part. . . . We

extend our apology to the native peoples and pledge ourselves to work with them to ensure their rights, their religious freedom and the preservation of their cultural heritage (Heritage and Hope, *p. 2*).

However, many missionaries were sensitive to Native Americans. For example, they would learn their language and help them form a written language by creating grammars, dictionaries, and catechisms. An outstanding example of this identification and respect for a Native American culture was the Franciscan Berard Haile who toiled for many years among the Navajo nation. Haile assembled a grammar and transcribed Navajo religious myths to help preserve their culture.[19]

Today, the Church is very sensitive to defending Native American rights.

Christian teaching [on racism] . . . can be summarized in three key words: respect for differences, fraternity, and solidarity. . . . No human group . . . can boast of having a natural superiority over others, or of exercising any discrimination that affects the basic rights of the person (The Church and Racism, *§23*).

The right of the first occupants to land, and a social and political organization which would allow them to preserve their cultural identity while remaining open to others, must be guaranteed. With regard to indigenous peoples, often numerically small, justice demands that two opposing risks be avoided: on the one hand, that they be relegated to reservations as if they were to live there forever, trapped in their past; on the other hand, that they be forced to assimilate without any concern for their right to maintain their own identity (The Church and Racism, *§7*).

The American bishops have also called for self-examination. They challenge Catholics to look at their own perceptions of Native Americans and to examine how they are shaped by stereotypes and distorted by ignorance or media portrayals. In addition,

We must first of all increase our understanding of the present needs, aspirations, and values of

the American Indian peoples. This responsibility can only be carried out effectively in dialogue with American Indians (Statement of U.S. Catholic Bishops on American Indians, §20).

The bishops also call for an examination of government policy and legislation, including:
- "the speedy and equitable resolution of treaty and statute questions;
- protection of Indian land and resource rights;

- more adequate housing and delivery of social, education and health care services; and
- increased levels of funding and technical assistance necessary to aid American Indians in achieving political and economic self-determination and full employment" (*Statement of U.S. Catholic Bishops on American Indians,* §25).

RESEARCH PROJECTS

Many Native Americans want sports teams that have names like Indians or Braves to change them to less offensive names. Research various sports teams' names on both the professional and college levels that bear Native American names. Find out specific reasons some Native Americans want these names changed. Research colleges that have already changed the names of their teams (e.g., Stanford, St. John's). Explain the decision-making process that took place in these cases.

Read a general article on Native Americans. Then choose a particular nation, read another article on it, and report on some of that nation's history and favorite customs.
To help your research, check out these excellent links:
- Native American Resources: www.cowboy.net/native/index.html
- Index of Native American Resources on the Internet: www.hanksville.org/NAresources
- American Indian Cultural Resource Center: www.bluecloud.org/dakota.html
- Lakota Dakota Information Home Page: http://puffin.creighton.edu/lakota/index.html

Report on the life of a Catholic missionary who worked among Native Americans. Some possibilities:
- Father Eusebio Francisco Kino
- Blessed Junipero Serra
- Blessed Marie of the Incarnation (Ursuline)
- Saint Isaac Jogues
- Father Pierre DeSmet
- Saint Phillippine Rose Duchesne

Another group that racism has victimized in the United States are people from Asia: Chinese, Filipinos, Japanese, Indochinese (Cambodians, Laotians, Vietnamese), Koreans, Indian Americans, and others. Do one of the following:
1. Research an Asian American group and report on examples of prejudice it has suffered in the United States.
2. Learn about the family customs and holiday celebrations of an Asian American subgroup.

BEING INCLUSIVE (*CCC, 2196; 2822*)

The Christian message contradicts the practice of exclusion. Jesus includes; he does not exclude. For example, Jesus associated with outcasts like lepers, with "respectable" people like the Pharisees, with women who were considered inferior to men, with children who had no social status at all, with the hated Samaritans, and with public sinners. Jesus' love excluded no one. The apostle to the Gentiles, Saint Paul, taught that external differences among people are nothing compared to oneness in Christ Jesus. Paul wrote to his converts, instructing them to see through the external differences that separate us. He told them to look into the hearts of people who are different and see neighbors, not strangers. We follow Paul's advice when we embrace and celebrate diversity, when we accept other people as brothers and sisters in Christ. Why? Paul writes:

There is neither Jew nor Greek, there is neither slave nor free person, there is not male and female; for you are all one in Christ Jesus (Gal 3:28).

Furthermore, Jesus founded a community of disciples, that community which today we recognize as the Catholic Church. Note the name catholic, a term that means "universal." The Lord commissioned this community to preach the good news of God's love to everyone, to spread the truth of salvation in his name to all people, to announce and live the sisterhood and brotherhood of each human who is a child of an incredibly generous Abba.

Exclusion results from prejudice, stereotyping others, and active discriminatory practices. When people are excluded, their right to participate in community life is affected negatively. Rights are denied. People suffer.

Christians are obligated to fight the exclusion of anyone based on race, sex, religion, ethnic background, national origin, or any other arbitrary designation. Christians must be in the vanguard in creating inclusive communities. Christians must call both individuals and societies to racial justice. Minimally, this means:

1. We must root prejudice out of our own lives. We need to allow God's love to touch us at the core of our beings to reassure us that we too are lovable. So much prejudice results from an inferiority complex, of not feeling worthy of love. This is why so many people display prejudice by attacking others, by tearing others down to build themselves up.

2. We must appreciate our common humanity. We need to realize that we have more in common with people of various races and cultures and nationalities and religions than we have differences. All of us need love and understanding. All of us cherish our families, love our children, and value our education. If we scratch beneath the surface, we recognize our common dependency on God, our craving for unity with others, our mortality. It is very short-sighted and

narrow not to recognize our relationship to each precious human being whom our loving God created in his divine image and likeness.

3. We must celebrate diversity. How boring a colorless world would be. How dull music would sound on a one-note scale. How impoverished would be the human race if we were all clones who looked alike, talked alike, thought alike. Part of God's plan is to endow his children with a variety of gifts, just as in a family each member has unique talents. As our world grows in interdependence, it becomes ever more important to celebrate the differences among the people whom Abba created.

4. We must learn from others. One way to celebrate differences is to learn from others. A great way to do that is to befriend someone from a different racial group. We have a wonderful opportunity to develop an interracial friendship with a classmate, a teammate, a co-worker, a neighbor.

We can appreciate other racial and ethnic groups by learning about their culture: holidays, foods, music, clothing, family customs, religious services, and so forth. Learning about a particular group's contributions to our country is also an excellent way to appreciate others. Committing ourselves to grow in knowledge about other groups helps dispel ignorance, a major source of ongoing prejudice.

5. We must empathize with others. Though not overtly prejudiced toward others, many people are oblivious to the plight of the victims of racial discrimination and other forms of prejudice. In contrast to this approach, we must display empathy, being always attentive to those whom society ignores.

6. We must support societal efforts to eradicate racial and other discrimination. The American bishops have outlined what society as a whole should do to help attain the dual goals of racial and economic justice. As citizens, we should vigorously support the following general guidelines:

[Within our own nation,] justice demands that we strive for authentic full employment, recognizing the special need for employment of those who, whether men or women, carry the principal responsibility for the support of a family. Justice also demands that we strive for decent working conditions, adequate income, housing, education, and health care for all. Government at the national and local levels must be held accountable by all citizens for the essential services which all are entitled to receive. The private sector should work with various racial communities to insure that they receive a just share of the profits they have helped to create (Brothers and Sisters to Us, §56).

Concerning our relationship to other nations, our Christian faith suggests several principles.

First, racial differences should not interfere with our dealing justly and peacefully with all other nations. Secondly, those nations which possess more of the world's riches must, in justice, share with those who are in serious need. Finally, the private sector should be aware of its responsibility to promote racial justice, not subordination or exploitation, to promote genuine development in poor societies, not mere consumerism and materialism (Brothers and Sisters to Us, §58).

SAINT KATHARINE DREXEL (1858–1955)
WORKING FOR RACIAL JUSTICE

Katharine Mary Drexel was born November 26, 1858. Four weeks later, her mother died. Katharine's father, Francis A. Drexel, was a rich international banker who amassed a great fortune. Two years later, he married Emma Bouvier Drexel, a devoted Catholic from a prominent Philadelphia family. Unfortunately, in 1879, Emma contracted cancer and suffered intensely for three years. During this period, Katharine lovingly nursed her stepmother and began to think of a life of service in religious life.

The death of Katharine's stepmother in 1883, and her father's sudden death two years later, imprinted on Katharine a deep realization of the transitory nature of life. Her father left her and her two sisters a vast fortune which Katharine immediately began to use for charitable works, especially for missionaries who were laboring among Native Americans. She gave money to support Catholic missions and build schools, and even made trips out West to see that her money was being used wisely.

Katharine's spiritual advisor was Bishop O'Connor. He counseled Katharine not to join a religious community because of the great good she was doing for the Native Americans. She was not happy with this advice because she ardently longed for the contemplative life, permitting others to distribute her money, while she did penance and received the Eucharist daily.

On a trip to Rome in 1887, Katharine had an audience with the pope. She asked the Holy Father to send an order of priests to the Indian missions. Pope Leo XIII replied, "Why not, my child, yourself become a missionary?" By the next year, she could hold back no longer and decided, with the blessing of her once reluctant spiritual director, to establish a new religious order for "the Indian and Colored People." After a period of formation, she professed her vows as the first member of the Sisters of the Blessed Sacrament, with the Motherhouse located nineteen miles outside of Philadelphia. By 1894, nine members of her community, formed in a spirit of prayer, humility, and service, went to staff a school in Santa Fe, New Mexico. Thus began the work of Mother Katharine and her remarkable order.

For the next forty years, Mother Katharine crisscrossed the country, at times at great personal sacrifice, to oversee the building of missions and schools. She believed Catholic education greatly benefited children from minorities by drawing them closer to the Lord and equipping them with the basic skills necessary to escape poverty.

She extended her works of love into the South by building schools to educate black children who were not allowed to attend the more prosperous schools of white children. Eventually, her congregation set up schools in the ghettos of cities like New York and Chicago. Mother Katharine kept up a tremendous pace of work, drawing inner strength from the Eucharist and hours spent in quiet, devotional prayer in front of the Blessed Sacrament.

At the age of seventy-seven, Mother Katharine suffered a massive heart attack. Amazingly, she lived another twenty years in contemplative prayer, sacrificing for others. She died in 1955. Though financially a millionaire, Mother Katharine Drexel lived a life of poverty, even drinking day-old coffee to save money. She spent her life and fortune establishing 145 Catholic missions, twelve schools for Native Americans, and fifty schools for African American children, most of them staffed by her congregation of the Blessed Sacrament. She became a canonized saint in 2000.

One of Mother Katharine's last meditations reveals the source of her strength in working for those neglected ones in society. Her words deserve our attention:

> Love! Love! Let us give ourselves to real pure love. Devotion to the Sacred Heart is a devotion which alone can banish the coldness of our time. The renewal which I seek and which we all seek is a work of love and can be accomplished by love alone.[20]

DO SOMETHING TO COMBAT RACISM

- As a class, sponsor an activity to commemorate Martin Luther King, Jr., Day at your school. For example, perhaps you could join a March for Justice or sponsor a day of community service in a poorer neighborhood to honor the slain civil rights hero.
- Brainstorm ways minorities in your school might be made to feel inferior. Devise strategies to combat current attitudes and practices.
- Write articles for the school newspaper that celebrate the racial and cultural diversity of your school or local community.
- Invite a speaker to address your class on a topic about racism and human rights.
- Organize a cultural-sharing music festival at your school.
- Organize a school-wide poster contest on the theme of inclusion. Raise funds for a prize for the award-winning production.
- Organize a lunch-time film festival. Show and discuss films that depict prejudice and discrimination.

CHAPTER SUMMARY

- Racism is the belief that one's own race is biologically superior to other racial or ethnic groups. Racism leads to the mistreatment of people based on their skin color, race, national origin, and the like. This mistreatment can be on an individual basis or can manifest itself institutionally whereby societal organizations, laws, customs, and so forth, work to keep minorities in an inferior and disadvantaged position. A notorious example of institutional racism was the apartheid policy practiced against nonwhites in South Africa.

- Racism is a sin that blots out the image of God among those who are its victims. It violates the essential dignity that every person possesses as God's unique child. It mocks Jesus' command to treat others as we would want to be treated. Racism must be fought and its victims actively defended. As individuals, we must root prejudice and racism out of our hearts, work for conversion, and right past wrongs. We must include groups that are different from us, not exclude them. We do this by celebrating differences, affirming our common humanity, and learning from and empathizing with others in imitation of Jesus whose love embraces all people.

- As societies, we must eradicate racial and other discrimination by supporting full employment at home. We must also support family life and back a living wage and decent housing, education, and health care for all. At times, this may mean supporting affirmative action programs designed to right past injustices. Abroad, we should deal justly with nations regardless of racial differences, share economic resources, and encourage the private sector to promote genuine development and not mere materialism and consumerism.

- Major victims of racial discrimination in the United States include African Americans, Hispanic Americans, and Native Americans. African Americans suffered greatly and still suffer from the legacy of slavery. Hispanic Americans were often exploited as cheap labor in the farm fields. Native Americans were decimated by horrific practices; they suffer greatly from the negative effects of the Reservation System. Also, Asian Americans are the victims of racism.

- As a product of its time and culture, the Church has also historically been guilty of racial prejudice. However, specific Church leaders condemned racial injustice and countless missionaries demonstrated compassionate and enlightened views and practices. Today, the Church repents of past racial injustices. It calls on all Catholics to imitate Jesus by responding in love and justice to the needs of the most powerless in our midst.

REVIEW QUESTIONS

1. What is racism? Why is it a sin?
2. What is "institutional" racism?
3. Give examples to support the thesis that institutional racism exists today.
4. Discuss three points in the history of racism directed against African Americans in the United States.
5. List three facts that support the theory that blacks and whites live in an unequal society.

6. How can the Church fight racism within the Church itself?
7. Identify *Brothers and Sisters to Us*.
8. What does affirmative action attempt to do? Is the Church generally for or against it? Explain.
9. What are the four major Hispanic American groups in the United States of America today?
10. How have Chicanos suffered discrimination?
11. Discuss three things the Church can do to combat prejudice against Hispanic American Catholics.
12. Discuss three factors that decimated the Native American population.
13. Give some evidence that shows that Native Americans suffer from institutional prejudice.
14. How did the Church historically both help and hurt Native Americans?
15. What policies do the American bishops support to help Native Americans?
16. Why is exclusion anti-Christian?
17. Discuss several practices that can help us be inclusive of others.
18. Identify Saint Katharine Drexel. How did she promote racial justice?

RESEARCHING ON THE INTERNET

Faith in the one God, Creator and Redeemer of all humankind made in his image and likeness, constitutes the absolute and inescapable negation of any racist ideologies.
—The Church and Racism, §19

1. Visit this Canadian website—Say No to Racism: www.gnb.ca/hrc_cdp/e/sayno.htm. Read and report on some ideas on how you can stop racism.
2. Research and report on an article from this excellent website, Ethics Updates at the University of San Diego: Literature on Race, Ethnicity and Multiculturalism: http://ethics.acusd.edu/Applied/race/index.asp.
3. Visit the Salt of the Earth website and report on an article on racism printed in the Archive section: http://salt.claretianpubs.org.

PRAYER REFLECTION

Wake me up Lord, so that the evil of racism
*   finds no home within me.*
Keep watch over my heart Lord,
*   and remove from me any barriers to your grace*
*   that may oppress and offend my brothers and sisters.*
Fill my voice Lord, with the strength to cry freedom.
Free my spirit Lord, so that I may give services
*   of justice and peace.*
Clear my mind Lord, and use it for your glory.
And finally, remind us Lord that you said,
*   "Blessed are the peacemakers,*
*   for they shall be called children of God."*
*   Amen.[21]*

NOTES

1. From *Tales of the Hasidim*, cited in Robert J. Wicks, *Touching the Holy* (Notre Dame, IN: Ave Maria Press, 1992), pp. 124–125.

2. Griff Witte and Nell Henderson, "Wealth Gap Widens for Blacks, Hispanics: Significant Ground Lost After Recession," *Washington Post*, October 18, 2004, A-11.

3. Joe Dirck, "Plea for Witnesses of Bank Altercation," *Cleveland Plain Dealer*, September 12, 1998, p. B-1.

4. U.S. Department of Commerce, U.S. Census Bureau, "Income Stable, Poverty Up, Numbers of Americans With and Without Health Insurance Rise, Census Bureau Reports."

5. A Harvard study reported by For Faith and Family Issues, "Racial Reconciliation Fact Sheet___2004."

6. Child Trends Data Bank, "Life Expectancy" <http://www.childtrendsdatabank.org/pdf/78_PDF.pdf>(21 February 2005).

7. These last three facts come from a study by the National Urban League as reported at REDNOVA NEWS, "Report: Black, White Disparities Abound," March 23, 2003.

8. Reported in *The Christian Science Monitor*, August 24, 1998.

9. Rogelio Saenz, "Latinos and the Changing Face of America," Population Reference Bureau, August 2004 .

10. Recent statistics reveal that two-thirds (66.9 percent) of the Hispanic population were of Mexican origin, 14.3 percent were Central and South American, 8.6 percent were Puerto Rican, 3.7 percent were Cuban, and the remaining 6.5 percent were of other Hispanic origins. Roberto R. Ramirez and G. Patricia de la Cruz, *The Hispanic Population in the United States: March 2002*, Current Population Reports, P20-545 (Washington, D.C.: Census Bureau, 2002), p. 2.

11. Survey commissioned by The Latino Coalition and conducted by McLaughlin & Associates' Opiniones Latinas, August 2002. Reported by the United States Conference of Catholic Bishops, Hispanic Affairs.

12. United States Conference of Catholic Bishops, *Encuentro and Mission: A Renewed Pastoral Framework for Hispanic Ministry*, §41 (Washington, D.C.: USCCB, 2002).

13. National American Indian Housing Council, "FactSheet: Native Americans and Housing."

14. National Center for Family Literacy, Momentum, "American Indian Facts," August 1999.

15. Building Blocks for Youth, "Native American Youth: Fact Sheet" <http://www.buildingblocksforyouth.org/issues/nativeyouth/facts.html>.

16. Jay P. Greene, Ph.D. and Marcus A. Winters, "Public School Graduation Rates in the United States," Center for Civic Innovation at the Manhattan Institute, No. 31, November 2002.

17. Andreas Knudsen, "Native Americans Bear the Nuclear Burden." Reprinted at Native Americans and the Environment from *Indigenous Affairs*, January/February/March 1996.

18. *Sublimis Deus* of Pope Paul III quoted in the Pontifical Commission on Justice and Peace, *The Church and Racism*, §3.

19. For a fascinating look at Father Berard's story, see Fr. Murray Bodo, O.F.M., *Tales of an Endishodi: Fr. Berard Haile and the Navajos, 1900-1961* (Albuquerque: University of New Mexico Press, 1998).

20. The source of this information was originally found at www.wau.org/current/drexel.html. Two current and good sources of information on St. Katharine can be found at the official website of the Sisters of the Blessed Sacrament and Catholic Forum's feature on the saints.

21. National Conference of Catholic Bishops' Committee on Black Catholics quoted in the Bilingual Edition of *Brothers and Sisters to Us* (Washington, D.C.: United States Catholic Conference, 1979), revised to include *For the Love of One Another*, p. 43.

CHAPTER OVERVIEW

The Scourge of Poverty
The gap between rich and poor persists in our nation and throughout the world.

Definitions of Poverty
While poverty is most often associated with a lack of means for material needs, it can also include poverty of the soul and poverty of the spirit.

The Bible and Poverty
Examples from the Old Testament and New Testament reveal God's deep concern for the poor.

The Scandal of Hunger
This section examines the causes of world hunger and a Christian's expected responses.

A Christian Response to Poverty: Preferential Option for the Poor
A preferential option for the poor means that we cannot love immoderately or use our wealth selfishly. It means we must practice the spiritual and corporal works of mercy.

Eliminating Poverty
The United States Catholic Bishops offer several suggestions for living a just economic life and working toward an elimination of poverty. There are several Catholic agencies that serve the poor.

Dorothy Day
Dorothy Day helped found the Catholic Worker movement that worked to transform society in peaceful ways.

If a brother or sister has nothing to wear and has no food for the day, and one of you says to them, "Go in peace, keep warm, and eat well," but you do not give them the necessities of the body, what good is it? So also faith of itself, if it does not have works, is dead.

—James 2:15–7

7

JUSTICE AND POVERTY

THE SCOURGE OF POVERTY

Is it tough for you to imagine how rich you are compared to more than a billion of the world's people who face the all too real struggles of daily **poverty**? The famous economist Robert Heilbroner provides a mental exercise in which those who are rich can imagine how poor people live in contrast. Do the imagination exercise yourself:

POVERTY–From a Latin word *paupertas*, it literally translates as *pauper*, or poor.

- Remove all the furniture in your home except for one table and a couple of chairs. Use a blanket and the chair pads for beds.
- Throw away all your clothes except for your oldest dress, pants, and shirt or blouse. Keep only one pair of shoes.
- Empty the pantry and the refrigerator except for a small bag of flour, some sugar and salt, a few potatoes, some onions, and a dish of dried beans.
- Dismantle the bathroom, shut off the running water, and remove all the electrical wiring in your house.
- Take away the house itself and move your family into the toolshed. This "house" should be placed in a shantytown.
- Cancel all subscriptions to newspapers, magazines, and book clubs. No one can read anyhow. Leave only one radio for the whole shantytown.
- Move the nearest hospital or clinic ten miles away. A midwife, not a doctor, is in charge.
- Throw away all monetary assets of any kind. The family has a total savings of ten dollars.
- Permit the head of the family a few acres to farm a few hundred dollars of cash crops. A third of the proceeds will go to the landlord and one tenth to the money lenders.
- Shorten everyone's life by twenty-five years.[1]

Americans are very rich indeed in comparison to so many of God's children. Being blessed with so much wealth imposes a tremendous duty on us to use our wealth wisely, to avoid waste at all costs, to share our abundance with others, and to reform all political, economic, and social structures that keep desperately poor people in this unacceptable state of existence.

It is a sad fact that humanity has not escaped the noose of poverty. Even in America, the infant mortality rate in some inner-city neighborhoods ranks with the poorest countries worldwide. Statistics reveal that the gap between the rich and the poor widens domestically as well as between the developed, industrialized nations and the poor, developing nations. This situation is deplorable and sinful because our God of abundance has blessed the earth with enough wealth and material goods to take care of the needs of each of his precious children.

In this chapter, we will look at various types of poverty and the causes of material poverty and ways to begin to solve some of the problems that it creates.

WHAT DO YOU THINK?

Here are some statements on poverty and hunger. Check the statement that best reflects your own personal view: **SA=strongly agree; A=agree; DK=I don't know what to think; D=disagree; SD=strongly disagree.**

Some Statements to Think About	SA	A	DK	D	SD
1. Christ said the poor we will always have with us (Mt 26:11); therefore, we should not make that big a deal out of poverty.					
2. In our country especially, if some people go hungry, it is their own fault.					
3. The cause of hunger and poverty is simple: human greed and selfishness.					
4. It is a sin to overeat and to buy nonessential luxuries as long as we have poor in our midst.					
5. We cannot call ourselves Christians if we fail to help those less fortunate than ourselves.					

- Share your responses to the various items. Explain your choices. Do you have any Biblical support for your views?
- How does the following quote apply to the way the poor are treated in our society?
  Give a man a fish and he'll eat for a day
  But teach a man to fish and he'll eat for a lifetime . . .
  is the greatest half-truth ever spoken, for . . .
  If the man has no tools to fish with nor a place to fish,
  All the knowledge in the world will not produce the next day's catch.

DEFINITIONS OF POVERTY

The word poverty, from a Latin word *paupentas*, literally translates as pauper, or poor. Poverty is most commonly associated with the lack of means to provide for material needs or comforts. But poverty can also refer to different realities, too. Listed below are three:

Poverty of the soul. This type of poverty is often present in people with a lack of purpose in life, a sense of hopelessness about any lasting meaning. Sadly, the psychological and spiritual suffering brought on by this poverty of the soul typically involves people who are materially well off but who look for meaning in the acquisition of more things. Instead of searching for love, forgiveness, and redemption in an all-holy God, they make gods out of created goods like possessions, power, prestige, physical beauty, and sex. Only the Lord can quench their hunger and thirst for meaning and purpose in life. As Jesus said:

It is written: "One does not live by bread alone, but by every word that comes forth from the mouth of God" (Mt 4:4).

Poverty of the spirit. In contrast to the kind of poverty that ignores God, Christian tradition recognizes a genuine "poverty of the spirit." This is a positive type of poverty, the kind Jesus praised in the first Beatitude when he said,

Blessed are the poor in spirit,

for theirs is the kingdom of heaven (Mt 5:3).

Poverty of the spirit recognizes that we totally depend on God. It affirms that God alone is our Savior, the sole source of all good gifts. This positive sense of spiritual poverty is the source of true humility. The virtue of humility prompts us to express our gratitude to God by sharing our personal gifts, talents, and wealth with others, but especially with our most needy neighbors. It helps us see these very neighbors as our brothers and sisters, other Christs whom we are privileged to serve.

Out of love, this poverty of spirit moves us to share our blessings with the truly poor. It compels us to fight for justice so that the most defenseless, powerless, and impoverished may obtain what they truly need to live in dignity as human beings, children of a loving Father.

Material poverty. In its prime sense, poverty means "the lack of sufficient material means to meet basic human needs." This type of poverty is scandalous. It manifests itself in the lack of the necessary means of survival like nutritious food and safe drinking water and basic health care such as immunizations against preventable diseases. It includes the lack of a home or woefully inadequate, unsafe, unhealthy, crowded living conditions. Poverty of this type involves not having adequate clothing and shoes to ward off the ill effects of the weather.

Material poverty takes the form of chronic unemployment or jobs that do not earn enough money to take care of one's own needs or those of one's family. Material poverty means being lonely and having no one to count on for help. It means being voiceless and powerless in the political and economic sectors where decisions are made that keep people poor. It means accepting the terrible consequences that accompany poverty, including broken homes, drug addiction, unplanned pregnancies. Material poverty involves living in crime-infested neighborhoods, being looked down on, living with chronic fear.

EVIDENCE OF MATERIAL POVERTY

There is ample evidence of the presence of material poverty both on the world scene and in the United States.

On the world scene:

* Twenty percent of the population in the developed nations consume 86 percent of the world's goods.
* Nearly 1.3 billion people live on less than one dollar a day; 3 billion live on under two dollars a day.
* Nearly 1.3 billion people have no access to clean water; 3 billion have no access to sanitation; 2 billion have no access to electricity.
* The richest 50 million people in Europe and North America have the same income as 2.7 billion poor people. The size of the world's goods consumed by 1 percent of the population is the same as that handed to the poorest 57 percent.

- A mere 12 percent of the world's population uses 85 percent of its water, and these 12 percent do not live in the Third World.[2]
- In developing countries, 91 children out of 1,000 die before their fifth birthday. By comparison, in the United States eight children in 1,000 will die before turning five years old.
- Each day in the developing world, more than 30,000 children die from mostly preventable and treatable causes such as diarrhea, acute respiratory infections, measles, or malaria. These diseases are far more deadly to children who are stunted or underweight.
- Nearly 12 million people die each year from lack of water, including 3 million children from waterborne disease.[3]
- Every year, more than 500,000 women die from complications of pregnancy and childbirth; 99 percent of such deaths occur in the developing world.
- Almost 4 million babies die annually in the developing world during their first week of life. These deaths are often the result of limited prenatal health care and births spaced closely together.
- Malaria threatens the lives of more than 2.2 billion people in over 100 countries, about 40 percent of the world's population. Each year, an estimated 300 million to 500 million clinical cases of malaria are recorded.[4]
- On average, 840 million people go hungry everyday.
- Approximately 31 percent of the world's urban population lives in slums.[5]

In the United States:
- The United States Census Bureau reported that the official poverty rate for a recent year was 12.7 percent, numbering almost 37 million Americans.
- Nearly 16 percent of the population did not have health insurance.
- African Americans had the lowest median income.[6]

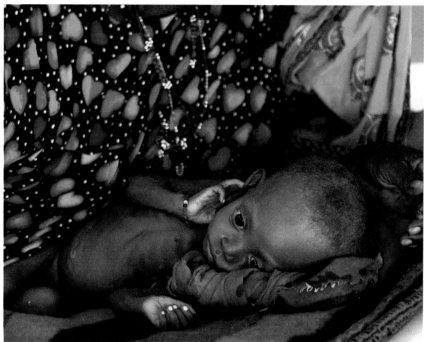

- In 2005, the U.S. Census Bureau defined a family of four as poor if they earned less than $20,144 per year. But the Economic Policy Institute claims that a more realistic threshold for a family of four should be $30,000 per year, making the poverty rate in America around 30 percent.[7]
- There are 3.5 million homeless people in the United States; the average age of a homeless person is nine years old. The majority of homeless adults work.
- 18,000 people die in the United States each year because they lack medical care.[8]
- The rate of poverty among children was 16.7 percent, significantly higher than the poverty rate for the population as a whole. Child poverty in the United States is much higher—often two-to-three times higher—than that of most other major Western industrialized countries.
- Nearly 40 percent of America's poor over the age of sixteen worked either part-time or full-time in 2001, yet could not earn enough to secure even the basic necessities of life.[9]
- Bill Gates alone has as much wealth as the bottom 40 percent of U.S. households combined.[10]

FIGHTING POVERTY WITH SIMPLICITY

Greed is one of the causes of poverty. Some people go after material possessions with a vengeance. Along the way, they ignore poor people. Consumerism—the practice of "buy, buy, buy"—is a trap that blinds us to other people by turning material possessions into gods. The following quotation from Pope John Paul II offers an understanding of the dangers of consumerism:

. . . [A]N EXCESSIVE AVAILABILITY OF EVERY KIND OF MATERIAL GOODS FOR THE BENEFIT OF CERTAIN SOCIAL GROUPS, EASILY MAKES PEOPLE SLAVES OF "POSSESSION" AND OF IMMEDIATE GRATIFICATION, WITH NO OTHER HORIZON THAN THE MULTIPLICATION OR CONTINUAL REPLACEMENT OF THE THINGS ALREADY OWNED WITH OTHERS STILL BETTER. THIS IS THE SO-CALLED CIVILIZATION OF "CONSUMPTION" OR "CONSUMERISM," WHICH INVOLVES SO MUCH "THROWING-AWAY" AND "WASTE." AN OBJECT ALREADY OWNED BUT NOW SUPERSEDED BY SOMETHING BETTER IS DISCARDED, WITH NO THOUGHT OF ITS POSSIBLE LASTING VALUE IN ITSELF, NOR OF SOME OTHER HUMAN BEING WHO IS POORER.

ALL OF US EXPERIENCE FIRSTHAND THE SAD EFFECTS OF THIS BLIND SUBMISSION TO PURE CONSUMERISM: IN THE FIRST PLACE A CRASS MATERIALISM, AND AT THE SAME TIME A RADICAL DISSATISFACTION, BECAUSE ONE QUICKLY LEARNS—UNLESS ONE IS SHIELDED FROM THE FLOOD OF PUBLICITY AND THE CEASELESS AND TEMPTING OFFERS OF PRODUCTS—THAT THE MORE ONE POSSESSES THE MORE ONE WANTS, WHILE DEEPER ASPIRATIONS REMAIN UNSAT-ISFIED AND PERHAPS EVEN STIFLED.

— ON SOCIAL CONCERN, §28.

WAYS TO FIGHT CONSUMERISM

An important way to fight back against consumerism is to live more simply. A life of simplicity can free us from unnecessary possessions so they do not own or enslave us. Simplicity is not poverty. Material poverty disfigures the person and wears down the human spirit. Simple living is letting go of excessive and non-essential posses-sions. It frees us from being tied down so we can help others, espe-cially the needy.

Simplicity begins with the simple truth of gratitude. Pray this daily prayer:

THANKS, LORD, FOR A NEW DAY. FOR THE GIFT OF LIFE. FOR MY HEALTH. FOR MY FRIENDS. FOR ALL MY GIFTS. FOR EVERYTHING. HELP ME USE MY TIME AND MY POSSESSIONS WISELY, LORD, NOT TO INFLATE MY OWN EGO, BUT TO HELP ALL THE WONDERFUL PERSONS YOU WILL SEND TO ME TODAY. THANKS, LORD. AMEN.

Richard Foster, author of *Celebration of Discipline*, lists ways to live more simply.[11] Here are some:
1. Develop a habit of giving things away.
2. Enjoy things without owning them.
3. Buy items for their usefulness rather than their status.
4. Enjoy all the beauty in God's creation.
5. Give up anything you find addictive.
6. Sparingly use credit cards. Reject any "by now, pay later" schemes.
7. Reject anything that oppresses others.
8. Ignore propaganda from sellers of useless products that you don't really need.
9. Seek God's kingdom first and foremost.

THE BIBLE AND POVERTY

Sacred Scripture reveals that God is compassionately concerned for the welfare of the poor. In the boldest language possible, the scriptures proclaim that God has a preferential option for the poor. In the words of the American bishops in their brief pastoral message prefacing *Economic Justice for All*, we must also choose for the poor and respond to their needs:

From the Scriptures and Church teaching, we learn that the justice of a society is tested by the treatment of the poor (§16).

The Bible also names those who are poor. They include:

- the materially impoverished, members of the lower class whom the powerful exploited;
- the afflicted and powerless;
- the hungry, the unclothed, the homeless, prisoners;
- orphans who have no parental love to support them;
- lepers whom society feared and isolated, forbidding them to have normal contact with people;
- sinners like the women caught in adultery whom society was going to destroy because the law was broken;
- strangers and outsiders;
- widows who had no social status, who could not inherit from their husbands, who were totally dependent on the whims of judges; and
- outcast tax collectors, some of whom were even wealthy (for example, Zaccheus), but no longer accepted as true sons of Abraham.

Like a true Israelite, Jesus came to embrace the poor. His first public speech announced that as God's agent he came to reach out to the most needy:

The Spirit of the Lord is upon me,
because he has anointed me to bring glad tidings to the poor.
He has sent me to proclaim liberty to captives and recovery of sight to the blind, to let the oppressed go free,
and to proclaim a year acceptable to the Lord (Lk 4:18–19).

Jesus' was a prophetic voice repeating God's love for the poor and God's command for the well-off to respond to the needy—a message announced time and again in the Old Testament.

TREATMENT OF THE POOR IN THE OLD TESTAMENT

The Israelites of the Old Testament were chosen by God to be a just community, a beacon among the nations, which would draw others to the just God who created and sustained them. The Israelites showed their love for God by their love for neighbor—especially the most afflicted members of their community. Part of their commitment to caring for the impoverished were two important practices: the Sabbatical Year (the seventh year) and the Jubilee Year (every fifty years, the Grand Sabbatical). During the Sabbatical Year, land was not to be farmed, debts were to be forgiven, and slaves were to be let go. During the Jubilee Year, people were supposed to return to their proper place in the community and original owners were to lay legal claim to their property. The idea behind this practice was to try to keep the various tribes of Israel in some kind of equal balance so some would not get excessively wealthy nor others inordinately impoverished.

Observing these years was a reminder to the Jewish people that they were former slaves whom a just and loving God rescued. In return, they had a duty to care preferentially for the oppressed and the poor in their midst.

Ideally, the Sabbatical and Jubilee years were to be a great help to reduce poverty and to help the poor assume a respectable position in society. But because the Israelites, like all people, were sinners, all too often the needs of the poor were ignored. Because of this Yahweh sent prophets to warn the Israelites about their wickedness, to call people back to justice.

The prophet Zechariah taught the Israelites how to be just:

Render true judgment, and show kindness and compassion toward each other. Do not oppress the widow or the orphan, the alien or the poor; do not plot evil against one another in your hearts (Zec 7:9–10),

The prophet Amos taught that injustice will be punished:

Hear this, you who trample upon the needy and destroy the poor of the land! . . .
I will turn your feasts into mourning and all your songs into lamentations. I will cover the loins of all with sackcloth and make every head

bald. *I will make them mourn as for an only son, and bring their day to a bitter end (Am 8:4, 10).*

Time and again, the Old Testament teaches about injustice and reassures the poor that God indeed hears their cries:

Injure not the poor because they are poor, nor crush the needy at the gate;
For the Lord will defend their cause, and will plunder the lives of those who plunder them (Prv 22:22–23).

SCRIPTURE LINK

Read these passages from the Old Testament. They reveal God's relationship with the poor and what he expects of the rich. Answer the questions that follow.

Read Psalm 34:1–11: The unfortunate
1. What will the Lord do for the unfortunate who call out for his help?

Read Exodus 3:4–10: Injustice
2. To what injustice is God responding?

Read Leviticus 25:8–17: Jubilee Year
3. What is the purpose of the Jubilee Year?

Read Deuteronomy 26:12–13: Tithing
4. To whom should the tithe be given?
5. What is its purpose?

TREATMENT OF THE POOR IN THE NEW TESTAMENT

The Incarnation is the great proof of God's love for humanity and his great love and compassion for the poor. The letter to the Philippians reminds us of this teaching:

Jesus Christ, being in the form of God, did not count equality with God something to ge grasped. But he emptied himself, taking the form of a slave, becoming as human beings are; and being in every way like a human being, he was humble yet, even to accepting death, death on a cross (Phil 2:6–8).

The Son of God became lowly and lived a life of poverty. He called no place home (Mt 8:20). He relied on the generosity of others for support (Lk 8:3). He died with no possessions (Jn 19:23–24). Jesus chose this lifestyle of openness and dependence on the Father to teach us about Truth, to show us what it means to love, and to sacrifice his life to gain eternal life for all humanity.

Throughout his earthly ministry, Jesus associated with the poor and the outcast: lepers, despised women, children, tax collectors, common folk, and so on. He responded to their needs, for example, by feeding them loaves and fishes when they came to hear his life-giving words (see Mk 6:30–44 and Jn 6:1–13). He healed those who were ill: the blind, the lame, the deaf and mute, even lepers. He took pity on a widow by bringing her son back to life (see Lk 7:11–17).

Jesus' parables reveal his attitude toward the poor and lowly. For example, when asked who is our neighbor, he told the parable of the Good

Samaritan (Lk 10:30–37). The hero of this parable—a hated Samaritan—went out of his way to minister to the wounds of a beaten traveler. He even spent his own money to help him recover his health. Among the lessons this famous parable teaches is that we must go out of our way to help those in need. This love of neighbor is mandatory. And note another important truth: our neighbor is everyone, especially the person in need, *even our enemies.*

Another parable—Lazarus and the Rich Man (Lk 16:19–31)—teaches that we must first notice and then respond to the needs of the poor in our midst. We cannot ignore them. To do so risks eternal separation from God. It is the Lord himself who will separate the sheep from the goats on judgment day. The goats are those who refuse to respond to the needy. In Jesus' words:

Then he [the king] will say to those on his left, "Depart from me, you accursed, into the eternal fire prepared for the devil and his angels. For I was hungry and you gave me no food, I was thirsty and you gave me no drink, a stranger and you gave me no welcome, naked and you gave me no clothing, ill and in prison, and you did not care for me. . . . [W]hat you did not do for one of these least ones, you did not do for me." And these will go off to eternal punishment, but the righteous to eternal life (Mt 25:41–43; 45–46).

Another parable, that of the wealthy farmer (Lk 12:16–21), warned how riches can make us arrogant and neglectful of others' needs. We must have our priorities straight. Jesus teaches:

Sell your belongings and give alms. Provide money bags for yourselves that do not wear out, an inexhaustible treasure in heaven that no thief can reach nor moth destroy. For where your treasure is, there also will your heart be (Lk 12:33–34).

Jesus does not condemn wealth or rich people. He does, however, warn us:

No one can serve two masters. He will either hate one and love the other, or be devoted to one and despise the other. You cannot serve God and mammon (Mt 6:24).

The danger with money is that it can control us when we should be controlling it:

Take care to guard against all greed, for though one may be rich, one's life does not consist of possessions (Lk 12:15).

Jesus' standard for how we should treat poor people is simple, straightforward, compelling, and can be summarized as follows:

Do to others whatever you would have them do to you (Mt 7:12).

As the facts cited above attest, poverty results in great anguish. However, the severest human tragedy of all is that poverty leads to hunger and, ultimately, death. The link between poverty and hunger is ironclad. We will examine this link in the next section of the chapter.

▶ SCRIPTURE LINK

Read the following passages. Answer the questions that follow.

Read Mark 10:17–31: Rich young man
1. Why was it difficult for the rich young man to give up his possessions?
2. How can a rich person get to heaven? Explain.

Read Luke 16:19–31: Lazarus and the rich man
3. Retell this parable in your own words.
4. What is the moral of the story?

Read Luke 12:13–21: Greed
5. What is the meaning of this parable?
6. Rewrite this parable in a modern context.

Read Acts 2:44–47; 4:32–35: Way to live
7. How did the early Christians deal with poverty?

Read Mark 12:38–44: What it means to give
8. What message might this have for individuals? for governments?

Read James 2:1–13: How to treat others
9. What does James say about class distinctions?

THE SCANDAL OF HUNGER

The most basic right of each human being is the right to life. To live, we need food. Denying people the right to food is a fundamental injustice of the highest order. For Christians, feeding the hungry is one of the corporal works of mercy. So basic is the injunction of feeding the hungry that the Second Vatican Council called our attention to the saying of the Church Fathers, "Feed the man dying of hunger, because if you have not fed him, you have killed him" (*The Church in the Modern World*, §69).

Worldwide, millions are hungry and malnourished. Chronic hunger includes both starvation and malnourishment. The body starves when it does not take in enough calories to sustain itself. The body turns in on itself and consumes muscle, fat, and tissue for food. It quickly deteriorates as its immune system fails and opens itself to diseases. Brain function slows. When the starving person loses approximately 40 percent of his or her body weight, death is inevitable.

Malnourishment is the silent killer that may not be immediately obvious. The body gets enough calories to sustain life, but the subsistence level of food intake does not provide the proper amount of vitamins and minerals for a healthy life. Strength is weakened and the malnourished person is subject to infection and disease.

The chief victims of hunger and malnutrition are poor people: children, pregnant women, nursing mothers, the sick, the elderly, refugees, and the victims of political turmoil. This link between poverty and hunger is dramatically highlighted by the Bread for the World Institute which reports the following facts:

- Approximately 5 billion people live in the developing world. This world is made up of about 125 low and middle-income countries in which people generally have a lower standard of living with access to fewer goods and services (such as soup kitchens, food stamps, and job training programs) than people in high-income countries.

- In this developing world, more than 1.2 billion people currently live below the international poverty line, earning less than $1 dollar per day.

- Among this group of poor people, many have problems obtaining adequate, nutritious food for themselves and their families. As a result, 815 million people in the developing world are undernourished. They consume less than the minimum amount of calories essential for sound health and growth.[12]

The injustice of hunger is that the world is not lacking in any way in food resources. Citing the *Food and Agriculture Organization of the United Nations' Final Report of the International Conference on Nutrition*, the important Vatican document, *World Hunger—A Challenge for All: Development in Solidarity* (1996), concludes:

In the world as a whole, an average of about 2,700 calories of food is available per person per day, enough to meet everyone's energy requirements. But food is neither produced nor distributed equally. Some countries produce more food than others, while distribution systems and family incomes determine access to food (§1).

CAUSES OF HUNGER

World Hunger—A Challenge for All: Development in Solidarity addresses the cause of hunger in considerable detail. The primary cause of hunger is poverty. Related to poverty are the following issues.

- Various forms of corruption contribute to poverty. Greedy officials engage in policies and practices that undermine the authentic development that poor nations need to escape poverty and hunger. For example, poor nations may export certain crops like sugar or coffee to boost their economies. However, government officials neglect developing a sound economy that rewards the growing of diverse foodstuffs that could feed the entire population, and especially the poor.

- Unfair and high interest on foreign loans is another contributing factor. Often poor nations have to go into extreme debt to foreign investors. The interest on these foreign loans is usually unreasonably high. This takes resources away from vital programs that could help poor nations combat poverty and work for development. In desperate times, when money is tight or inflation is out of control, creditors might impose severe borrowing restrictions on the debtor nations, further plunging them into poverty and despair.

- Demography shows that as a nation becomes richer, higher birth and death rates are reversed. However, as this process is taking place, technology must keep up with population growth so farmlands are not depleted. Developing countries must take great care not to exploit limited resources. When lands are raped and deforestation happens uncontrollably, the environment can be affected so negatively that famine-inducing droughts take place. It takes many years for damaged land to be made fertile again. (Incidentally, contrary to a popular myth, except in extreme cases, population density does not account for hunger.)

- Politics is another factor as food is often used as a political or military pawn. A recent historical example was Bosnia where humanitarian aid was held hostage for political purposes. In the meantime, thousands of innocent people starved. A related problem in the political sphere is "strings-attached" foreign aid.

These various causes of hunger do not, however, argue that the world is unable to feed itself. On the contrary, the solid research of many organizations, including the United Nations, shows that the world produces enough food to feed every human being. *World Hunger—A Challenge for All* concludes:

The fact that people continue to starve . . . shows that the problem is structural, and that "inequitable access is the main problem." Hunger is not a problem of availability, but of meeting demand. It is an issue of poverty (§19).

RESPONSE TO WORLD HUNGER

A moral response to the hunger problem involves the following:

We must manage earthly goods more efficiently. This management means that people cannot worship the false gods of money, power, and reputation.

For up-to-date statistics on world hunger, check one of these websites. Report on two new facts that you discovered. Bread for the World Institute: www.bread.org United Nations World Food Programme: www.wfp.org World Hunger Education Service: www.worldhunger.org

Everyone must respect the social teaching of the "universal and common destination" of the goods of the earth. Consider the words of Pope John Paul II:

> *God gave the earth to the whole human race for the sustenance of all its members, without excluding or favoring anyone. This is the foundation of the universal destination of the earth's goods* (On the Hundredth Anniversary of "Rerum Novarum," §31).

Everyone has a right to food. If people are not getting the food necessary to live, injustice is taking place.

We must apply the principle of subsidiarity so power is not taken from those who rightly possess it. This requires the participation of poor people in decisions that affect them.

We must practice the principle of solidarity. We are indeed our brothers' and sisters' keepers. The principles of subsidiarity and solidarity require that we be careful to guarantee that rich people do not exclude poor people from social and economic life. Governments should financially support international organizations that are working to solve the hunger problem. They should establish fair trade relations with poorer nations so they have a chance at development. They should see that poor people have access to credit so they can become a more vital part of society.

Solidarity with the poor means that governments and individuals must also back emergency food aid during times of famine and other crises. We must carefully heed the words of Pope John Paul II:

> *Love for others, and in the first place love for the poor, in whom the Church sees Christ himself, is made concrete in the promotion of justice. Justice will never be fully attained unless people see in the poor person, who is asking for help in order to survive, not an annoyance or a burden, but an opportunity for showing kindness and a chance for greater enrichment. Only such an awareness can give the courage needed to face the risk and the change involved in every authentic attempt to come to the aid of another. It is not merely a matter of "giving from one's surplus," but of helping entire peoples which are presently excluded or marginalized to enter into the sphere of economic and human development. For this to happen, it is not enough to draw on the surplus goods which in fact our world abundantly produces; it requires above all a change of lifestyles, of models of production and consumption, and of the established structures of power which today govern societies* (On the Hundredth Anniversary of "Rerum Novarum," §58).

WHAT CAN YOU DO?
A CALL TO SELF-EXAMINATION

World Hunger—A Challenge for All: Development in Solidarity challenges each of us to listen to the poor in our midst:

> *Wherever in the world God has placed them, Christians must respond to the call of those who are hungry by personally questioning their own lives. The call of the hungry urges one to question the meaning and the value of daily actions. . . . One must gauge the magnitude . . . of the consequences of all one does, even the most ordinary things, and hence appraise real responsibility. . . . [Christians must] discreetly and humbly . . . listen to and serve anyone in need (§66).*

You can help hungry people by doing one or more of the following:

- Collect food for a local hunger center. Do so at a non-traditional time, remembering that people are hungry year round, not just at Thanksgiving and Christmas.
- Volunteer your time at a local soup kitchen.
- Sponsor a food waste awareness campaign at your school.
- Assist at a local Meals-on-Wheels program.
- Write a letter to your congressional representative encouraging him or her:

  - to support long-term solutions to the hunger problem abroad;
  - to sponsor foreign-aid bills that support land reform and literacy programs; or
  - to inquire about our arms trading policy to poor countries so that tax dollars go for food and not guns.

- Join a hunger-action group like Bread for the World.
- Fast from a favorite food item for a month. Donate the money you save on this item to a hunger-fighting program.
- Examine your own eating habits. This will help you become more aware of food waste and good nutrition. It will also help you become more sensitive to hungry people in other parts of the world. Consider your health by:
  - Eating less meat, white bread, foods with refined sugars, foods with saturated fats, and highly processed foods.
  - Consuming more legumes (beans and nuts), fresh fruits and vegetables, and whole grains.

PROJECT

PART 1: RESEARCH

1. Work with a partner for this project.

2. Select one or two countries to research and report on. Do not choose a country chosen by another pair of students. Here are your choices:

Afghanistan	France	Norway
Argentina	Germany	Pakistan
Australia	Ghana	Philippines
Bangladesh	Guinea	Russian Federation
Bhutan	India	Saudi Arabia
Brazil	Iraq	Sri Lanka
Cambodia	Kenya	Turkey
Canada	Mexico	Uganda
Chad	Netherlands	United States
El Salvador	North Korea	Zaire

3. Discover the following facts about your country:
   a. What is the country's population?
   b. What is the country's population density?
   c. What percent of the population is hungry?
   d. What is the fertility rate?
   e. What is the infant mortality rate?
   f.   What is the life expectancy at birth?
   g. What is the GNP (Gross National Product) per capita?
   h. Find three other interesting facts about your country or countries.

PART 2: REPORT

Report your findings to the class. Record information from the reports of other students. Then answer these questions.

1. What are the three countries with the highest percentage of hunger?

2. What are the three richest countries?

3. Which country has the fastest rate of population growth?

4. What two countries can most afford to share their resources with the poorer countries?

PART 3: RESULTS

Participate in class discussion.

1. Brainstorm five ideas of how the rich nations can help the poor nations with their hunger problem.

2. Brainstorm five things you as individuals can do to help solve worldwide or local hunger problems.

THE EUCHARIST AND THE HUNGRY

Another way Catholics respond to the problem of world hunger is through participation in the Eucharist. As the U.S. Catholic Bishops state:

The most important setting for the Church's social teaching is not in a food pantry or in a legislative committee room, but in prayer and worship, especially gathered around the Eucharist.[13]

In the Eucharist, the Catholic community gathers around the altar to receive the Lord himself in the form of bread and wine. Jesus is the "bread of life," the Father's gift to us and the gift we offer to the Father on our behalf. Jesus is our Savior, the perfect "person for others" who poured out his life so we might have eternal life. When we receive him into our hearts in holy communion, we ask him, by power of the Holy Spirit, to make us like him—to be other Christs. The Eucharistic meal forms us into God's family, the Body of Christ. It nourishes us with the life of Christ. It empowers us to live in solidarity with one another for one another.

In his earthly ministry Jesus responded to the basic needs of people, often within the context of food. For example, he performed his first miracle at a wedding feast. He fed the hungry crowds when he multiplied the loaves of bread and fishes. He shared a last supper with his apostles before his great sacrifice. Moreover, he taught that he is the cure for all of our hungers:

I am the bread of life;
whoever comes to me will never hunger,
and whoever believes in me will never thirst (Jn 6:35).

We come to the Eucharist to receive the bread of life. However, our Eucharist is empty if we do not become the bread of life for others. Jesus tells us to come and receive him so that we may go and serve the Lord and each other. The Eucharist is not meant to be an isolated affair among Christians who simply enjoy each other's and the Lord's company. Rather, the Eucharist is meant to help us become Christ's body so we may continue his work of feeding people, not just their spiritual hungers, but also their physical hungers. We pray for all of God's children at the Eucharist. But when we are dismissed from the Eucharist, we must become the "persons for others" that our Master calls us to be. We must be people who serve the needy in our midst and around the world. Minimally, this means we must respond to our brothers and sisters who are crying out for food. We must become Christ's hands and his feet to feed the hungry, to clothe the naked, to give drink to the thirsty, and so forth. Not to do so is to receive the Eucharist unworthily.

> Read 1 Corinthians 11:17–34.
>
> 1. Why did Saint Paul have to correct the Corinthian community when it celebrated the Eucharist?
> 2. In what ways do we make a mockery of the Eucharist if we do not respond to Christ in others?

A CHRISTIAN RESPONSE TO POVERTY: PREFERENTIAL OPTION FOR THE POOR (CCC, 2402-2406; 2443-2448; 2450-2454; 2462-2464)

As Christians, a great measure of our response to Jesus, indeed a test of our love for him, is what we do for the poor. The Church must display *a preferential option or love for the poor*. What does it mean to have special love for the poor?

First, and most basic, it means we cannot love immoderately, or selfishly use, riches and wealth. Saint John Chrysostom warns us: "Not to enable the poor to share in our goods is to steal from them and deprive them of life. The goods we possess are not ours, but theirs" (quoted in CCC, 2446).

Second, we must put into practice the spiritual and corporal works of mercy "by which we come to the aid of our neighbor in his spiritual and bodily necessities" (CCC, 2447). Despite the sins and shortcomings of Christians through the ages, the Church has always responded to the whole person—physically, socially, psychologically, and spiritually. It has, through the centuries, responded by instructing, advising, consoling, comforting, forgiving, and enduring wrongs patiently (the spiritual works of mercy). Further, Christians have fed the hungry, sheltered the homeless, clothed the naked, visited the sick and imprisoned, and buried the dead (the corporal works of mercy). "Among all these, giving alms to the poor is one of the chief witnesses to fraternal charity: it is also a work of justice pleasing to God" (CCC, 2447).

In their pastoral letter, *Economic Justice for All* (§52), the American bishops spell out the challenges which the "preferential love for the poor" requires for today's Church:

1. We must speak for those who have no one to speak for them. We must defend the defenseless, those whom the Bible calls "the poor."
2. We must look at things from the side of the poor and powerless.
3. We must evaluate lifestyle, policies, and social institutions in terms of how they affect the poor.
4. We must help people experience God's saving love and liberating power so they may respond to the gospel in freedom and dignity.
5. As individual Christians and a Church community, we must empty ourselves so God's power can touch us in the midst of poverty and powerlessness.

The core of the fundamental option or preferential love for the poor is evaluating social and economic activity from the viewpoint of the poor and the powerless. This vantage point will help us understand better the problems of poverty and work more intelligently towards their solutions. The purpose of a special commitment and love for the poor is not to pit various economic groups against each other. Its main purpose is to help poor people to become active participants in society.

CATHOLIC FRAMEWORK FOR ECONOMIC LIFE

In an appendix to their pastoral reflection on poverty entitled *A Place at the Table: A Catholic Recommitment to Overcome Poverty and to Respect the Dignity of All God's Children*, the American bishops outline ten important themes that represent a "Catholic Framework for Economic Life."[14] They give direction to reflecting on, making judgments about, and then putting into action economic reforms and policies. These slightly reworded principles come from the American bishops' pastoral letter *Economic Justice for All* and other pastoral letters, the *Catechism of the Catholic Church* (2458–2462), and recent papal encyclicals:

1. The economy exists for the person, not the person for the economy.
2. Moral principles should shape economic life. Choices and institutions should be judged by how they protect or undermine human life, the dignity of the human person, and whether they serve the family and the common good.
3. A basic way of measuring the morality of any economy is how the poor and vulnerable are faring.

4. Each person has a right to life and the basic necessities of life (e.g., food, shelter, education, health care, safe environment, economic security).

5. All people have the right to economic initiative, to productive work, to just wages and benefits, to decent working conditions. They also have the right to join unions or other associations.

6. To the extent that they can, all people have a corresponding duty to work, a responsibility to provide for their families' needs, and the obligation to contribute to the broader society.

7. In economic life, free markets have both clear advantages and limits and governments have essential responsibilities and limits. Voluntary groups have irreplaceable roles, but they cannot substitute for the proper working of the market and the just policies of the state.

8. Society has a moral obligation, including government actions when necessary, to assure opportunity, meet basic human needs, and pursue justice in economic life.

9. Workers, owners, managers, stockholders, and consumers are moral agents in economic life. By our choices, initiative, creativity, and investment, we enhance or diminish economic opportunity, community life, and social justice.

10. The global economy has moral dimensions and human consequences. Decisions on investment, trade, aid, and development should protect human life and promote human rights, especially for those most in need wherever they might live on this globe.

A PLACE AT THE TABLE

In *A Place at the Table,* the United States Catholic Bishops invite us to envision a table where everyone is able to gather to eat, to make decisions, and to worship. Unfortunately, poverty keeps some from having enough to eat or even to own a table. Many are also excluded from sitting at the table because they are powerless and their voices are not heard.

We gather at the table of the Lord to worship. And it is the Eucharist that challenges us to be the Christ for others that we have received. As the *Catechism of the Catholic Church* puts it: *"The*

Eucharist commits us to the poor. To receive in truth the Body and Blood of Christ given up for us, we must recognize Christ in the poorest" (CCC, 1397).

The bishops recognize that there are four institutions that can help us as individuals and as a society to stand with the poor. Continuing the analogy of the table as having four legs, they explain how these four institutions support the table around which *all* are invited to dine and participate in mutual decisions that affect all. The first leg is what *families and individuals* must do. For example, each person must respect the dignity of others and see that their rights are secured. Support for marriage and family life must take center stage in the campaign to restore dignity and overcome poverty for children.

The second leg of the table is the role and responsibility of *community organizations and faith-based institutions*. These groups can be advocates for families and confront unjust structures that keep people poor. They can demand accountability from public officials. They can continue to be beacons of hope for poor families. Good examples of these kinds of faith-based organizations are Catholic schools that provide quality education to inner city youth, health care institutions, and the many works of Catholic Charities.

For each of the following situations, list the three most important principles, criteria, and/or directions from the ten listed in this section that you feel must absolutely be considered. Be prepared to give reasons for your choices.

- Congress is proposing an income tax cut.

- An auto company is proposing to move its factory to Mexico.

- A soft-drink company is considering a vigorous ad campaign in an under-developed country.

- You are considering investing a $500 gift from your grandparents in a drug company

- To ensure the viability of the Social Security System for future generations, political leaders are considering cutting benefits by 20 percent to current recipients.

The third leg of the table is *the marketplace and institutions of business, commerce, and labor.* The private sector must not only provide economic growth, but must also contribute to the common good by avoiding greed and by helping the poorest workers secure decent wages and working conditions; health care; vacation time and medical leave; an opportunity to participate in the workplace; and the hope for a decent retirement.

Finally, the *government* has the vital role of helping to accomplish what all the above groups cannot accomplish on their own. Its role is to serve the common good, provide a safety net for those who are vulnerable, pass laws to overcome discrimination, guarantee equal opportunity for all, and overcome structures of injustice and misuse of power that contribute to poverty and assaults on human dignity.

The bishops remind us that all four of these legs are essential and complementary to overcome poverty.[15]

ELIMINATING POVERTY (CCC, 2426–2430)

The American bishops' letter, *Economic Justice for All,* offers many down-to-earth ideas for eliminating poverty in the United States. The bishops reject the idea that poverty is an impossible problem to address. People have created the economy; they can change it. In its analysis of economic policies, the Church is not bound by any political, economic, or social system. It asks a simple question: "Does it support or threaten human dignity?" (§130). A high social priority must be

increasing active participation in economic life by those who are presently excluded or vulnerable.... The human dignity of all is realized when people gain the power to work together to improve their lives, strengthen their families, and contribute to society (§91).

Some specific directives to help fight poverty, enhance human dignity, and increase participation in economic life by our most vulnerable brothers and sisters are:

1. *Those who are well off must change their attitudes toward the poor.* We must be careful not to let greed and consumerism blind us to the poverty in our midst. We must examine how we talk about poor people. For example, we should refrain from actions, words, and attitudes that stigmatize the poor. Nor should we exaggerate the welfare benefits they receive or distort the abuses of the welfare system. The bishops challenge the persistent belief that poor people are poor out of laziness or by choice, that poor people could escape poverty if they only worked harder, or that welfare programs are an excuse not to work. These attitudes punish the poor. They also conveniently ignore the many social and generous subsidies that corporations and individuals receive. Note how these are termed "entitlements" rather than "benefits" (§194).

A Christ-like attitude toward the poor recognizes that we must absolutely make the fulfillment of their basic human needs our highest priority.

Basic justice also calls for the establishment of a floor of material well-being on which all can stand. This is a duty of the whole of society and it creates particular obligations for those with greater resources (§74).

Meeting the fundamental human needs of the poor must precede our desire for luxury consumer goods, profits that do not serve the common good, or for unnecessary military hardware (§90).

The bishops put it well in *A Place at the Table: Those who have more can make choices to use less, to share more, and to advocate for greater justice so that all people have the resources to provide for themselves and their families. For all to have a place at the table, some of us may have to take a smaller place at the table.*[16]

2. *We must support full and equal employment as well as a just wage.* Employment is the first line of defense against poverty. Therefore, society must work for a healthy economy that will provide full employment with just wages to all adults who want a job and are able to work. Since jobs are a way out of poverty, society should also see that women and minorities have free access to work.

Concerted efforts must be made through job training, affirmative action, and other means to assist those now prevented from obtaining more lucrative jobs (§199).

3. *Society must empower the poor to help themselves.* Private charity and voluntary action are certainly necessary to help the poor, but they are not enough. We must also work through the government to set up just and effective public policies. However, paternalistic programs that "do too much for and too little with the poor" (§188) are wrong-headed. One effective technique to combat poverty is through small-scale, locally based programs that empower the poor to

become self-sufficient. Examples of such self-help programs include worker cooperatives, credit unions, legal assistance, and various community organizations. The Church sponsors a self-help program called the Catholic Campaign for Human Development.

4. *We must make education of the poor our top priority.* There are many inequities in our school system, both public and private. Without an adequate education suitable for our information age, poor people will have a difficult time being adequately prepared to participate competitively in economic life.

5. *The tax system must be continually evaluated based on how it affects the poor.* First, there should be enough taxes to pay for the public needs of society, especially of the poor. Second, the principle of progressivity should come into play so that those with more wealth pay a higher rate of taxes. Third, families below the poverty line should not pay taxes.

6. *Reforms in the nation's welfare programs must help recipients, when possible, to become self-sufficient through gainful employment. They must enhance their lives and protect their dignity.* Welfare programs must provide a safety net of support to cover basic human needs. In the words of *Faithful Citizenship*, "The measure of welfare reform should be reducing poverty and dependency, not cutting resources and programs."[17] Besides job creation, meaningful welfare reform should include child tax credits; health care; child care; and safe, affordable housing.

FAIR HOUSING

Everyone has the God-given right to decent housing. The American bishops hold that America's housing goals should include:

- Policies that help to preserve, maintain, and improve the existing low-cost, decent housing.
- Creative, cost-effective programs to increase the supply of quality housing for poor families as well as the elderly and other vulnerable people.
- The active involvement of the homeless and others to accomplish the national tradition of homeownership, self-help, and neighborhood participation.
- Support for effective partnerships among various community groups, churches, the private sector, banks, governmental agencies, and the like to build and preserve affordable housing.
- Helping families afford decent housing in a way that their other basic necessities are not neglected.
- Ongoing efforts to fight any form of housing discrimination based on race, ethnic or national origin, sex, and so forth.[18]

7. *The bishops support governmental efforts to preserve and protect family-operated, moderate-sized farms.* Loss of farms, the concentration of agriculture in the hands of large conglomerates, and the exodus of farmers from the land have led to the loss of a valued way of life. The government should sponsor measures to support family farms, reassess benefits and tax policies that go disproportionately to large farms, encourage conservation efforts by all farmers, and support research efforts to help land productivity of smaller farms. Furthermore, the government should see that hired farm workers and migrant workers are protected by minimum wage and basic benefits laws (*Economic Justice for All*, §241–247).

CATHOLIC ORGANIZATIONS HELPING THE POOR

The Catholic Campaign for Human Development is one Church-sponsored organization that serves the poor. Read about that and other Catholic social ministry organizations here. Check these websites and report on a current project of one of these organizations.

Catholic Campaign for Human Development

Begun in 1969 with the philosophy of "a hand up, not a handout," the Catholic Campaign for Human Development (CCHD) is the domestic anti-poverty, social justice program of the United States Catholic bishops. It tries to address the root causes of poverty in America by promoting and supporting community-controlled, self-help organizations and by advancing education. Its mission is empowerment and participation for the poor. By aiding poor people to participate in decisions and actions that affect their lives, CCHD helps them move beyond poverty. It has funded more than 4,000 self-help projects developed by grassroots groups of poor persons. It receives its support through private donations, owing its success to Catholic parishioners who contribute through an annual parish appeal. The CCHD web site is: www.usccb.org/cchd. (Be sure to check the link to PovertyUSA for some interactive and multimedia presentations on poverty.)

Catholic Relief Services

Founded by the American bishops in 1943 to help the disadvantaged outside the country, Catholic Relief Services (CRS) serves millions of poor people around the world. CRS provides disaster relief (for example, for the victims of the historic tsunami of December 2004 in countries like Indonesia and Sri Lanka), supports community self-help projects, and contributes in many other ways to building just societies. Its motivating force is the gospel as it pertains to relieving human suffering, developing people, and fostering justice and charity. CRS also educates United States citizens on their moral duty to help practice the virtue of solidarity toward our impoverished brothers and sisters around the world and to help remove the causes of poverty and to promote social justice. By engaging in Christ's work, CRS empowers those who lack a political voice, have little economic power, and have no social status. By supporting CRS, we put into action Christ's mandate to serve the poor. We also express our solidarity with Christ's little ones in over ninety countries worldwide. Read about the work of CRS by contacting its website: www.crs.org.

Catholic Charities USA

Founded in 1910, Catholic Charities USA is one of the largest non-profit social services network in the United States. One of its founding principles was to become an "attorney for the poor," that is, an advocate for America's most vulnerable people and communities. The mission of Catholic Charities is threefold: to provide service for needy people; to promote justice in social structures; to challenge the entire Church and other people of good will to join in these same efforts. Local Catholic Charities' staff members and volunteers help people become self sufficient. They engage in many services including adoption, child care, disaster relief, elderly services, family support, housing assistance, parenting education, pregnancy counseling, prison ministry, refugee and immigration assistance, soup kitchens, treatment for alcohol and drug abuse, and many others. The Catholic Charities USA website is: www.catholiccharitiesusa.org.

WELFARE REFORM

In 1996 the United States Congress passed, and the president signed, the Personal Responsibility and Work Opportunity Reconciliation Act. This historic welfare-reform bill shifted funding and control of assistance for needy people back to the states via block grants. It also placed a five-year limit on a person's eligibility to receive public assistance, increased work requirements for welfare recipients, and ended most federal benefits for noncitizens.

Assess the impact of this bill on the poor. Has it provided the needed flexibility for community-based programs to fight poverty as promised? Or has it simply been a scheme for the rich and middle class to save money ($55 billion over five years)?

- Have changes in the food-stamp program left more or less people hungry? Have churches and other hunger-fighting agencies been able to take up the slack?
- Do the new jobs that have been created to hire the poor pay a decent and just living wage? Who can live on a minimum-wage job?
- Are the states addressing the problem of the lack of low-cost housing?
- Do cities support a public transportation system that allows the urban poor to get to and from jobs? for all shifts?
- What is the state of child-care choices for welfare recipients or those with low-paying jobs?
- How have legal immigrants fared under this welfare-reform bill?

Do an Internet search under the topic "welfare reform" to find current articles that will help you answer some of these questions. For more in-depth research, pick up the widely praised *American Dream* by Jason Deparle chronicling three women's experience of welfare reform in Milwaukee and also examining the greater impact of welfare reform.

TEN WAYS YOU CAN HELP THE HOMELESS

The following are some suggestions on what you can do to help the homeless in your area:

1. Contact Catholic Charities and learn about who the homeless are in your area.
2. Have a fund-raising drive at your school to purchase some fast-food certificates. Donate these to a halfway house for the homeless.
3. Compile a list of homeless shelters in your county.
4. Collect food, money, toys to donate to the homeless.
5. Volunteer at a soup kitchen.
6. Tutor homeless children.
7. Collect and clean recyclables and donate them to a thrift shop.
8. Play with children in a shelter.
9. Join Habitat for Humanity. Volunteer your services.
10. Write to your local government representatives and inquire what they are doing for the homeless.

Learn more about the homeless from the National Coalition for the Homeless at: www.nationalhomeless.org.

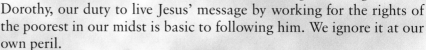
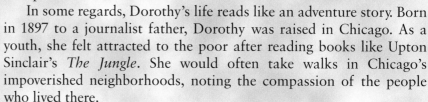

DOROTHY DAY (1897–1980)
A CATHOLIC WORKER FOR THE POOR

After her many years of unflagging devotion to her beloved poor, many people spoke of Dorothy Day as a saint. Her attitude to this assessment? "Don't call me a saint. I don't want to be dismissed so easily."

This abrupt response seems strange to many of us because we would take it to be a high compliment to be known as saints in our own lifetimes. But Dorothy felt that we put many saints on pedestals and see them as plaster-perfect people not relevant to everyday life. Dorothy did not want her message of the need to be just to God's poor to be perceived as old-fashioned, out-of-date, and something we can ignore. For

Dorothy, our duty to live Jesus' message by working for the rights of the poorest in our midst is basic to following him. We ignore it at our own peril.

In some regards, Dorothy's life reads like an adventure story. Born in 1897 to a journalist father, Dorothy was raised in Chicago. As a youth, she felt attracted to the poor after reading books like Upton Sinclair's *The Jungle*. She would often take walks in Chicago's impoverished neighborhoods, noting the compassion of the people who lived there.

A bright young woman, she won a scholarship to college but dropped out after two years of reading radical literature. Dorothy moved to New York to write for a socialist newspaper and got involved in socialist causes. She was convinced that injustice infected the social order of the day. She had several job changes that took her to various cities, but she ended back in New York where she had a common-law marriage for four years to an atheist anarchist. Though not a Catholic at the time, Dorothy slowly began to be attracted to the Catholic Church, and after the birth of a daughter, she broke off her relationship with her common-law husband and converted to Catholicism.

When writing for the Catholic magazine *Commonweal*, Dorothy met a remarkable man, Peter Maurin. Peter was a former Christian Brother who embraced celibacy and voluntary poverty to identify with poor people and to be free to serve them. With his encouragement, she began a newspaper—*The Catholic Worker*—to make public the social teaching of the Church and to suggest ways to transform society in peaceful, just ways. She charged 1¢ a copy so anyone could buy the paper. To this day, *The Catholic Worker* costs one penny.

Started during the Great Depression, the message of *The Catholic Worker* met great success. It sided with labor unions and challenged the social order. Peter Maurin's essays encouraged Christian hospitality. Before long, homeless people started to knock on Dorothy's door. Volunteers came to join Peter and Dorothy as they began an apartment of hospitality, first for women and then for men. By 1936, there was a growing Catholic Worker movement with thirty-three houses across the country. These centers of charity took not only the "deserving poor" down on their luck, but also the "good-for-nothings," drunks, and the lazy poor. In Dorothy's eyes these were all her brothers and sisters in Christ. They all deserved companionship, food, a place to live, and even a decent burial. To aid in these goals, Catholic Workers also experimented with farming communes, some more successful than others. What always worked, though, was Christian hospitality extended to the poor.

The Catholic Worker movement was radical, teaching social change and preaching nonviolence. Dorothy thought a nonviolent life of serving others was the heart of Jesus' gospel. She could not tolerate war and, in her columns, railed against Catholic participation in the Spanish Civil War and World War II.

She preached that the works of mercy rather than the works of war win over and change hearts.

These views were not popular with many Catholics and others in the country. The newspaper lost readers; some hospitality houses closed because not all the volunteers agreed with Dorothy.

During the Cold War, Dorothy witnessed for world peace and justice for the poor. Through sit-ins, public demonstrations, stays in prison, and various fasts she preached that the arms race was a devious and destructive lie that most hurt the poor. She preached that no nuclear war was winnable and that the billions of dollars spent on the weapons of death assaulted the poor who go hungry. During the Vietnam War, many involved with the Catholic Worker movement, and many young men who thought Dorothy's reading of the gospel was correct, refused conscription. Some went to prison, while others performed alternative service.

Under Dorothy's leadership, *The Catholic Worker* also worked tirelessly for civil rights for blacks, justice for farm workers, and the like.

Toward the end of her life, many Catholic organizations recognized Dorothy's witness to peace, work for the poor, and being a voice of conscience that called Catholics to works of justice, for "comforting the afflicted and afflicting the comfortable." Dorothy died in 1980 with love for the poor in her heart. In 2000, the Vatican approved the late Cardinal John O'Connor's request to consider Dorothy Day's "cause," the first step on the road to official canonization.

At the conclusion of his masterful biography of Dorothy Day, Jim Forest tells us that Dorothy Day helped bring a reformation,

> . . . one rooted in the sacredness of life, the truth that we are each made in the image and likeness of God, and the real presence of Christ in the poor. She gave an example of hospitality and mercy as a way of life. "We are here to celebrate Him," she declared, "through works of mercy."
>
> To put it as simply as possible, she gave an example of active love. "Love is the measure," she so often said, "by which we will be judged."[20]

LEARNING MORE ABOUT THE CATHOLIC WORKER

Visit the Catholic Worker website: www.catholicworker.org. Do each of the following:

- Learn how to obtain a copy of *The Catholic Worker*. Report on an article from a recent issue.
- Read more about the mission of the Catholic Worker movement, Dorothy Day, and Peter Maurin.
- Read some of the writings of Dorothy Day and Peter Maurin. Choose something of interest to you and report on it.

The Catholic Worker—The newspaper and movement founded by Dorothy Day and Peter Maurin to make public the social teaching of the Church.

IMITATING DOROTHY DAY

THE MYSTERY OF THE POOR IS THIS: THAT THEY ARE JESUS, AND WHAT YOU DO FOR THEM YOU DO FOR HIM. IT IS THE ONLY WAY WE HAVE OF KNOWING AND BELIEVING IN OUR LOVE. THE MYSTERY OF POVERTY IS THAT BY SHARING IN IT, MAKING OURSELVES POOR IN GIVING TO OTHERS, WE INCREASE OUR KNOWLEDGE OF AND BELIEF IN LOVE.[21]

— *Dorothy Day*

EXERCISES

WAYS TO HELP THE POOR

To respond to the poor takes a spirit of generosity, a recognition that other people, especially the weakest in our midst, are Christ in disguise.

Justice educator Jack Jezreel offers six concrete ways to help the poor.[22] He reminds us that there are two classes of people in the world: the rich and the poor. The rich know what they are going to eat tomorrow. The poor do not know. Here's how you can help the poor:

1. Be directly connected to the poor. Volunteer at a shelter for the homeless or working once a week in a soup kitchen.
2. Ask questions and search for answers. For example, "Who are the homeless? What keeps them that way? What is my city doing about it?" Your search for answers may move you to start reading some social justice magazines.
3. Start to advocate. For example, write a letter on behalf of anti-hunger legislation. Bread for the World, a Christian lobby on hunger and poverty issues, claims that one letter written saves one human life.
4. Work with the poor as they help themselves. This is an exercise in the virtue of solidarity and combines the first three points above. An example might be to volunteer to help at a soup kitchen.
5. Watch your money. For example, who made the item you are planning to buy? Was it made by child labor in a foreign country? Were the makers of the product exploited? If so, don't buy the product. Your purchasing habits do have an effect.
6. Give some of your money to the poor—both in your local community and worldwide. For example, donate to a local crisis center that serves the poor or raise funds for the Catholic Relief Services.

GROUP RESEARCH PROJECT: WHERE DOES MY MONEY GO?

Christians committed to doing justice have an obligation to know the consequences of their buying decisions. Research the following:

Think about a brand name athletic shoe (or clothing item) that you wear.

Answer these questions:

1. Who made the item?
2. What materials were used? Are any of these materials in scarce supply?
3. Did the processing of the materials or the manufacturing of the item cause any harmful byproducts?
4. Describe the working conditions of the place of manufacture.
5. What wages were paid to the workers? Were they given any benefits? Can a person live on these wages?
6. Describe some of the ads the seller of the item uses to advertise it. (For example, do they appeal to feelings of inadequacy if you do not buy it? Do they use big-name people to endorse it?)
7. How is the item displayed in the store?
8. What is the markup on the product? What percentage of the selling price do the workers who made it receive?
9. Why did *you* buy the product? After researching this topic, will you be likely to buy it again? Why or why not?
10. How did you learn about the product?

CHAPTER SUMMARY

- Poverty can refer to "poverty of the soul," a spiritual emptiness sometimes caused by a love of material goods; "poverty of the spirit" which recognizes our total dependence on a good and generous God; and "material poverty," defined as the lack of material means to meet basic human needs. Material poverty in a world of plenty is a scandal that contradicts God's plan for his children.

- Greed is a major cause of poverty; simplicity of lifestyle is a good antidote to greed.

- Both the Old and New Testaments reveal God's compassionate concern for the poor, a preferential option for their welfare. The Israelites strove to dedicate themselves wholeheartedly to the cause of justice, especially in defense of the poor. Jesus' example of a life of voluntary poverty, his ministry to God's forgotten ones, and his teaching that we must respond to the least in our midst if we want to be called his disciples—all these show his compassionate commitment to the poor.

- Hunger and malnutrition are two of the worst effects of poverty. This is tragic because everyone has the God-given right to life and the food necessary to live it. Further, it is an outrage that 40,000 children die each day of starvation or diseases associated with malnutrition. And this in a world that produces enough food to feed every human being an adequate diet.

- Many other social and cultural factors contribute to hunger. To combat these vices we must manage earthly goods more wisely and practice the principles of subsidiarity and solidarity. Furthermore, individuals, corporations, and nations must respect the universal and common destination of the earth's goods.

- Catholics must see the connection between the Eucharist and hungers of the world. Our celebration of the Eucharist is empty unless we become the bread of life for others.

- The Church must display a preferential option for the poor. We do this by putting into action the spiritual and corporal works of mercy and by speaking for those who have no one to speak for them. We must look at everything from the side of the poor and powerless. We must evaluate lifestyle, policies, and social institutions on how they affect the poor. We must help people experience God's saving love and power. We must empty ourselves so God's power can touch us, too. At heart, though, we must evaluate social and economic activity from the viewpoint of the poor and powerless.

- In combating poverty, the well-off must change their attitudes toward the poor, never allowing greed or consumerism to blind us to the poverty in our midst. We must also examine how we talk about the poor. Other ways to side with the poor include supporting full and equal employment and just wages, reforming the tax and welfare systems to better help the poor, and making the education of the poor our top priority. A key point is that society must empower the poor to help themselves, guarding against paternalistic programs that do too much for and too little with the poor. The bishops also support governmental efforts that preserve and protect family-operated, moderate-sized farms.

- Dorothy Day, a founder of *The Catholic Worker*, is an inspiring example of a Christian who saw Jesus Christ in the face of the poor person.

REVIEW QUESTIONS

1. What is the difference between "poverty of the soul" and "poverty of the spirit"?
2. Define material poverty.
3. Cite three facts about poverty that alarm you.
4. List three practices you can engage in to simplify your own life.
5. According to the Bible, who are the poor?
6. Write out two specific Old Testament passages that show that God is on the side of the poor.
7. Write three words or actions of Jesus that reveal how he thinks Christians should treat the poor.
8. "People do not have to be hungry." Why is this statement true?
9. List five causes of hunger.
10. Discuss three moral responses to the hunger problem.
11. How does the Eucharist teach us to care for the world's poor?
12. What is "the preferential option for the poor"?
13. List the spiritual and corporal works of mercy.
14. What does the preferential option for the poor require of today's Church?
15. List five principles that form a Catholic framework for economic life.
16. Identify: *Economic Justice for All; No Place at the Table.*
17. Discuss three concrete strategies that the American bishops support to combat poverty in the United States of America.
18. List three Catholic agencies that serve the poor.
19. How did Dorothy Day respond to the needs of the poor?
20. Discuss three practical things you can do to help the poor.

RESEARCHING ON THE INTERNET

There is sufficiency in the world for man's needs but not for man's greed.
—*Mohandas Gandhi*

1. Read and report on one of the Center for Concern's focus areas: www.coc.org.
2. Report on some interesting topic you read about at Food First: www.foodfirst.org.
3. Read and report on a feature from Second Harvest: www.secondharvest.org.
4. Read and report on a recent press release from the United Nations: Food and Agricultural Organization: www.fao.org.
5. Check out one of the links from WHY (World Hunger Year): www.worldhungeryear.org.
6. Report on the work of Covenant House: www.covenanthouse.org.
7. Report on the work of Habitat for Humanity: www.habitat.org.

PRAYER REFLECTION

PRAYER FOR BREAD AND JUSTICE

O God.
To those who have hunger
give bread;
And to those who have bread
give the hunger for justice.[23]

NOTES

1. Steve Williams reported this exercise in a short piece entitled "Material Poverty," Bible.org.
2. The first five facts and their original sources are reported by Anup Shah, "Causes of Poverty: Poverty Facts and Stats."
3. The three previous stats were reported by Hearts & Minds[SM], "Facts on World Hunger and Poverty" <http://www.heartsandminds.org/poverty/hungerfacts.htm>.
4. The previous three facts were reported by Care, "Facts about Health and Poverty" <http://www.careusa.org/features/rhealth/facts.asp?source=ghp>.
5. These two stats were found at "Hunger and Poverty Quick Facts" <http://borgenproject.org/Hunger.html>.
6. These three facts are reported in U.S. Census Bureau, *Income, Poverty and Health Insurance Coverage in the United States: 2004*, Current Population Reports, August 2005.
7. See the U.S. Census Bureau's website on poverty and the Catholic Campaign for Human Development, "Poverty USA: The State of Poverty in America" at www.nccbuscc.org/cchd/poverty usa/povfacts.htm.
8. "Poverty Facts" <http://www.geoclan.com/politics/articles/04/oct/PovertyFacts.htm>.
9. The previous two facts were reported by the Office for Social Justice of the Diocese of St. Paul and Minneapolis, "Facts About Poverty That Every American Should Know."
10. Office for Social Justice of the Diocese of St. Paul and Minneapolis, "Facts About Wealth That Every American Should Know."
11. With some modification cited from *Christopher News Notes*, "The Simple Life," No. 381, January 1996.
12. Bread for the World Institute, "Hunger Basics: World Hunger and Poverty: How They Fit Together."
13. United States Conference of Catholic Bishops, *Communities of Salt and Light: Reflections on the Social Mission of the Parish*, the Appendix in *Communities of Salt and Light: Parish Resource Manual* (Washington, D.C.: United States Catholic Conference, 1994), p. 5.
14. United States Conference of Catholic Bishops, *A Place at the Table: A Catholic Recommitment to Overcome Poverty and to Respect the Dignity of All God's Children* (Washington, D.C.: United States Conference of Catholic Bishops, Inc., 2002), pp. 25–26.
15. Ibid., pp. 15–18.
16. Ibid., p. 19.
17. *Faithful Citizenship: A Catholic Call to Political Responsibility* (Washington, D.C.: United States Conference of Catholic Bishops, 2003).
18. United States Conference of Catholic Bishops, Office of Social Development & World Peace, "Housing and Community Development," February 2002.
19. Adapted from Rabbi Charles A. Kroloff, *54 Ways You Can Help the Homeless*.
20. Jim Forest, *Love Is the Measure: A Biography of Dorothy Day* (Maryknoll, NY: Orbis Books, 1994), p.156.
21. Dorothy Day, "The Mystery of the Poor," *The Catholic Worker*, April 1964, p. 2.
22. Jack Jezreel, "Why the Preferential Option for the Poor Is Not Optional," *U.S. Catholic*, Vol. 62, No. 11, November 1997, pp. 30–35.
23. Quoted in *A Justice Prayer Book* (Washington, D.C.: United States Catholic Conference, 1998), p. 13. Original source acknowledged as *The Gift of Prayer: A Treasury of Personal Prayer from the World's Spiritual Traditions*, copyright 1995 by The Fellowship in Prayer and used by permission of The Continuum Publishing Group. All rights reserved.

CHAPTER OVERVIEW

Moving Forward, Making Peace
Among Abraham Lincoln's qualities was the ability to make peace with his enemies and move forward from there.

Christians and Peace
Christians must be peacemakers. To engage in the work of peace means we must work for justice.

The Meaning of Peace in the Bible
Peace is a central theme in Scripture, but also embraces a variety of meanings in both the Old Testament and New Testament.

Nonviolence
The option of strict nonviolence combats injustice with peaceful means like dialogue, negotiations, protests, boycotts, civil disobedience, strikes, citizen resistance, and the like.

The Just-War Tradition
The just-war tradition provides ethical guidelines for using military force.

Peacemaking Strategies
Working for peace involves working for a global option for the poor and global solidarity.

Franz Jägerstätter
Franz Jägerstätter died resisting induction into the Nazi army during World War II.

Blessed are the peacemakers,
for they will be called children of God.
—Matthew 5:9

JUSTICE AND PEACE

8

ABRAHAM LINCOLN

MOVING FORWARD, MAKING PEACE

Abraham Lincoln's virtues were many, not the least of which was his ability to love his enemies. When Lincoln was running for president, one of his greatest opponents was Edwin McMasters Stanton, a man who hated Lincoln with every fiber of his being. Stanton berated Lincoln for his physical appearance (calling him the "original gorilla") and castigated everything Lincoln did and said. His attacks were cruel and unrelenting.

Despite Stanton's efforts, Lincoln was elected sixteenth president of the United States. When he was considering a replacement for an inefficient Secretary of War, Lincoln named Stanton to that post. His closest advisors were dumbfounded. "Aren't you mistaken, Mr. President? Don't you remember the vicious attacks Stanton made about you? He will work to undercut your agenda. Have you really considered this decision?"

Lincoln assured his friends that he was well aware of Stanton's hateful opinions of him. "But after looking over the nation, I find he is the best man for the job." Thus Stanton became Lincoln's Secretary of War and served with honor during the Civil War.

After Lincoln was assassinated, Stanton proclaimed quite correctly, "He now belongs to the ages." Not the least of Lincoln's many qualities was his ability to make peace with his enemies and move forward from there.

This chapter will look at a major fruit of doing justice—peace. All Christians are called to imitate Jesus and to work wholeheartedly for peace. It is our vocation. Working for peace marks us as brothers and sisters living in the one family of God.

It is hard to be a world peacemaker if we don't learn the skills of conflict resolution in our personal relationships. Examine your own interactions with others. How do you fare? Answer the following.

During the past two weeks, did you:	Yes	No
1. Badmouth someone to his or her face?		
2. Refuse to talk to someone out of anger?		
3. Honestly and calmly tell someone how bad you felt when you were treated shabbily?		
4. Lose your temper because you were very upset at what the person said or did?		
5. Seek different ways to solve a problem you were having with someone?		
6. Ask for a friend or adult to run interference for you in a bad relationship with another person?		
7. Try to see another person's point of view when you disagreed about something?		
8. Do or say nothing when someone hurt you, allowing your feelings to simmer below the surface?		
9. Compromise with a friend or family member in a situation where you both wanted to do two different things?		
10. Cave in and not assert yourself when you were afraid someone might disagree with or think poorly of you because of your independent thinking?		

- Which of the questions above might reveal that a person is prone to violence and needs help with conflict resolution?
- Which questions reveal that a person handles conflict well?
- Which questions indicate a person's unwillingness to deal with conflict?
- What are three common conflicts you experience in your daily life? What are some possible ways you can resolve these conflicts?

CHRISTIANS AND PEACE

Saint James wrote: "The peace sown by peacemakers brings a harvest of justice" (Js 3:18, NJB).

In the Beatitudes, Jesus teaches, "Blessed are the peacemakers, for they will be called children of God" (Mt 5:9).

Pope Paul VI observed, "If you want peace, work for justice." And Pope John Paul II, in his World Day of Peace message following the terrorist attacks of September 11, 2001, added to this, "No peace without justice; no justice without forgiveness."

These statements reveal two profound truths: *Christians must be peacemakers.* To be a follower of Jesus is to have the vocation of peacemaking. To work for peace is an essential task for disciples of Jesus.

To engage in the work of peace means we must work for justice, and justice requires forgiveness. True peace is the fruit of justice which is completed by "forgiveness which heals and rebuilds troubled human relations from their foundations."[1]

DEFINITION OF PEACE

Peace is, ultimately, a blessing of Jesus Christ. It is "the tranquillity of order" (CCC, 2304). Both Jesus and the Church teach that peace results from both justice *and* love. Peace exists when people are treated with dignity, are allowed to communicate freely, and relate to each other lovingly as brothers and sisters.

Peace for the earth images the peace that Christ won for us when he sacrificed his life on the cross. The gift of his life, death, and resurrection reconciled us to God and each other. The fruit of reconciliation is the peace of Christ (CCC, 2305).

An important teaching on peace comes from the Vatican II document *The Church in the Modern World*. It delves further into a definition of peace:

Peace is not merely the absence of war; nor can it be reduced solely to the maintenance of a balance of power between enemies; nor is it brought about by dictatorship. Instead, it is rightly and appropriately called an enterprise of justice. Peace results from that order structured into human society by its divine Founder, and actualized by men as they thirst after ever greater justice. The common good of humanity finds its ultimate meaning in the eternal law. But since the concrete demands of this common good are constantly changing as time goes on, peace is never attained once and for all, but must be built up ceaselessly. Moreover, since the human will is unsteady and wounded by sin, the achievement of peace requires a constant mastering of passions and the vigilance of lawful authority.

But this is not enough. This peace on earth cannot be obtained unless personal well-being is safeguarded and men freely and trustingly share with one another the riches of their inner spirits and their talents. A firm determination to respect other men and peoples and their dignity, as well as the studied practice of brotherhood are absolutely necessary for the establishment of peace. Hence peace is likewise the fruit of love, which goes beyond what justice can provide.

> What does it mean to say that peace results from justice and love?
>
> What does it mean to say that peace is also the "fruit of love"?

That earthly peace which arises from love of neighbor symbolizes and results from the peace of Christ which radiates from God the Father. For by the cross the incarnate Son, the prince of peace, reconciled all men with God. By thus restoring all men to the unity of one people and one body, He slew hatred in His own flesh; and, after being lifted high by His resurrection, He poured forth the spirit of love into the hearts of men (The Church in the Modern World, §78).

SPIRITUALITY OF PEACEMAKING

In their pastoral letter on peace, *The Challenge of Peace* (1983), the American bishops discussed a spirituality of peacemaking. In this document, the bishops told us that peacemaking begins in a person's heart. However, because we are prone to sin, peace is a difficult task. We need conversion of mind and heart so we can be open to God's healing grace working within us. Saint Paul writes:

Do not conform yourselves to this age but be transformed by the renewal of your mind, that you may discern what is the will of God, what is good and pleasing and perfect (Rm 12:2).

In *The Harvest of Justice Is Sown in Peace*, a letter commemorating the tenth anniversary of the publication of *The Challenge of Peace*, the American bishops note two sets of virtues we need to be more peaceful. On the one hand, we must—like our Savior—be humble, gentle, and patient with people. On the other hand, we must be strong, active, and bold to spread the gospel of peace. The gospel of peace is best exemplified when we forgive and love our enemies and, in a spirit of generosity, perform good deeds for them. Jesus commands, "Love your enemies and do good to them. . . . Be compassionate, just as your Father is compassionate" (Lk 6:35–36).

Peacemaking is enhanced by our practice of the virtues, habits that empower us to be good. For example, *faith* and *hope* enable us to put our trust in God, not ourselves. *Courage* and *compassion* move us to action. *Humility* and *kindness* empower us to put others' needs first. *Patience* and *perseverance* help us stay the course as we fight for justice. *Civility* and *charity* enable us to treat others with respect and love.

Finally, prayer is essential for developing a spirituality of peacemaking. In prayer, God can calm our anxieties, challenge us to greater compassion and love for others, and energize us to keep working for peace despite frustration, setbacks, and defeats. Prayer teaches us many important lessons:

Prayer for peace is not an afterthought to the work of peace. It is of the very essence of building the peace of order, justice, and freedom. To pray for peace is to open the human heart to the inroads of God's power to renew all things. With the life-giving force of his grace, God can create openings for peace where only obstacles and closures are apparent; he can strengthen and enlarge the solidarity of the human family in spite of our endless history of division and conflict. To pray for peace is to pray for justice, for a right-ordering of relations within and among nations and peoples. It is to pray for freedom, especially for the religious freedom that is a basic human and civil right of every individual. To pray for peace is to seek God's forgiveness, and to implore the courage to forgive those who have trespassed against us (Pope John Paul II, Message of the World Day of Peace, 1 January 2002, §14).

THE CHURCH'S VISION OF PEACEMAKING

The Church's vision of peacemaking consists of three major elements:

1. *The Universal Common Good.* A peaceful society can only be built when people's rights are honored and respected. Governments, endowed with political authority, must promote the common good, especially by defending human rights. However,

When a government clearly fails in this task or itself becomes a central impediment to the realization of those rights, the world community has a right and duty to act where the lives and the fundamental rights of large numbers of people are at serious risk (The Harvest of Justice, p. 3).

2. *The Responsibility for the Development of Peace.* Peace is more than the absence of war. Achieving peace means alleviating the injustices individuals and society suffer by promoting their individual and collective development. Pope John Paul II wrote:

Another name for peace is development. Just as there is a collective responsibility for avoiding war, so too there is a collective responsibility for promoting development. Just as within individual societies it is possible and right to organize a solid economy which will direct the functioning of the market to the common good, so too there is a similar need for adequate interventions on the international level. For this to happen, a great effort must be made to enhance mutual understanding and knowledge, and to increase the sensitivity of consciences (On the Hundredth Anniversary of "Rerum Novarum," §52).

Development contributes to a peaceful world because underlying most wars are serious grievances like the denial of human rights, frustrated

one human family and that we are required to respond to others' needs, not only in our own country, but around the world, despite any differences of race, religion, or nationality. Human solidarity recognizes that people have a common destiny—that being our brothers' and sisters' keepers means we must reach out globally in an interdependent world.

The American bishops write:

We are responsible for actively promoting the dignity of the world's poor through global economic reform, development assistance and institutions designed to meet the needs of the hungry, refugees and the victims of war (The Harvest of Justice, p. 4).

Human solidarity put-into-practice is a rock-solid building block for permanent peace.

The section on Peacemaking Strategies (pages 190–196) lists some concrete strategies for implementing this vision of peace.

aspirations, exploitation of desperate people, and extreme poverty. On the one hand, development promotes justice; on the other, it provides the foundation for a peaceful world.

3. *Human solidarity*. The virtue of solidarity is a "firm and persevering determination" to seek the good of all. It recognizes that we belong to

WAR

How do you feel about the following statements? Do you agree, or are you unsure?

1. All war is evil. You can never justify war.

2. "The best offense is a good defense." To prevent war and deter potential enemies, our country should increase its defense budget.

3. I would serve in a war if drafted because serving in the military is honorable.

4. I could never fight in a war. "Thou shalt not kill" means exactly that.

5. "What's sauce for the goose is sauce for the gander." If men have to be drafted, so should women.

6. If our country could end a war on foreign territory through the use of limited nuclear weapons, then it should do so.

7. "All's fair in love and war."

8. Large amounts of money spent on the military establishment is a gross injustice to the poor.

Experts generally acknowledge three major causes of war:

1. *Political*. A properly constituted government is obliged to protect its citizenry and defend human rights. But some political leaders cave in to power and greed and begin wars by overrunning their neighbors. Case in point: the Persian-Gulf War (1991) was a response to Iraq's unwarranted invasion of Kuwait. It was also, at least in part, an attempt to ensure that Iraq was unable to withhold oil from the West, thus raising oil prices dramatically and threatening the economies of the United States and other western nations.

Some revolutions and civil wars result from political tyranny within a particular country. Guerilla warfare is waged against the general population to gain political advantage for a rebel group.

2. *Economic.* People go to war when their means of livelihood are attacked. Abject poverty, hunger, colonialism that exploits a less developed nation's vital natural resources, frustrated dreams of a better life—all these and similar situations have led to wars between nations and to conflict among various classes within nations.

3. *Cultural/religious.* Ethnic conflict between and within nations and religious wars fought to force one's beliefs on other peoples are often the source of many wars. A good example of this type of conflict is the decades-long civil war in Sudan where the Christian minority was oppressed and massacred by the Muslim majority. Other factors in the longest civil war in history involved racial and regional differences (Arab northerners versus African southerners) as well as economic factors involving access to oil and the waters of the Nile River.

THE MEANING OF PEACE IN THE BIBLE

A brief survey of the Scriptures reveals that peace is a central theme. However, note that in Scripture, the term peace embraces a variety of meanings. For example, peace can refer to an individual's sense of security. It can also mean the cessation of armed hostility among nations. In addition peace refers to a right relationship with God. This relationship includes the ideas of union, forgiveness, and reconciliation. Finally, the Bible talks about a peace to come at the end of time when God's salvation will transform all of creation and make it whole.

PEACE IN THE OLD TESTAMENT

In the early part of Jewish history, violence and war played a key role as God led the people to freedom and helped them create a monarchy. Thus, a *warrior God* who rescues and protects his people—and who requires obedience—is a prominent image in biblical books like Joshua and Judges. However, over time, and especially after the Exile, the image of a warrior God is transformed. God is no longer identified with military victory and might.

Peace develops as a rich image in the Old Testament. Peace is understood in light of Israel's relationship to God; it is a gift from God and a fruit of God's saving activity. The individual's personal peace is not greatly stressed; rather the unity and harmony of the whole community with other peoples and with creation itself have primary focus.

Peace is also an element of the covenant with God. When Israel is obedient to God's commands, God dwells among the people. The Lord says,

I will set my Dwelling among you, and will not disdain you. Ever present in your midst, I will be your God, and you will be my people (Lv 26:11–12).

Peace, therefore, is one fruit of keeping the covenant. But recall that fidelity to the covenant is related to integrity and justice. Unless true justice takes place—like care of the poor—then prophets like Isaiah and Jeremiah warn that there is no true peace.

The Israelites looked forward to a Messianic age when God's righteousness would come among the people. At this time, the Spirit would be poured down from on high, creation would be made whole, and justice would take root everywhere. A lasting

From a current weekly news magazine, discover and report on the causes of an ongoing war in the world.

peace would take hold. In the words of the prophet Isaiah:

In days to come . . .

They shall beat their swords into plowshares
and their spears into pruning hooks;
One nation shall not raise the sword against
another,
nor shall they train for war again (Is 2:2, 4).

PEACE IN THE NEW TESTAMENT

Jesus preached the coming of the reign of God, a new reality. He proclaimed this reign in his words and made it present in his actions. The poor will inherit the kingdom, mourners will be comforted, the meek will inherit the earth, and peacemakers are to be called God's children (Mt 5:3–10).

Christ's proclamation of God's reign calls us to conversion. We must now embrace a new way of life that both fulfills and goes beyond the law. This love requires us to put into action an active, life-giving, and inclusive love. This love must go beyond family and friends. It must reach out even to our enemies. This love must always reject revenge and violence and embrace forgiveness. "Put your sword back into its sheath, for all who take the sword will perish by the sword" (Mt 26:52). This Christian love is merciful even in the face of threat or opposition. Jesus' command to forgive and to love undercuts the revenge and hate that cause conflict.

Jesus left the Church both the gift of his peace and the gift of the Holy Spirit. These gifts go hand-in-hand. The Spirit enables us to recognize God's goodness to us in and through Jesus. The Spirit empowers us to preach Jesus to a world that is still struggling with violence, hatred, and war. And the Lord's gift of peace gives us a foretaste of what is in store for all humanity which will one day accept him as the Prince of Peace.

The gifts of the Lord's peace and the Holy Spirit help Jesus' disciples to be missionaries of peace, people who reveal the reign of God by being agents of reconciliation, forgiveness, mercy, justice, and love. Being a disciple of Jesus Christ means being an ambassador of reconciliation among all people so God's plan "to unite all things" in Christ can be accomplished.

SCRIPTURE LINK

Read the following passages. Answer the questions that follow.

Read Isaiah 11:6–9: The peaceful kingdom
1. What are three qualities of the just?

Read Isaiah 32:16–20: Fruit of justice
2. What is the result of doing justice?

Read Micah 4:1–4: God's reign
3. What will happen when God establishes his reign of peace?

Read James 4:1–3: The root of the problem
4. What is the source of conflict?

Read 1 Corinthians 13:1–13: Love
5. What are qualities of love that can help one in the work of peace?

Read Matthew 5:44–45: Jesus' command
6. What reward is given to those who love their enemies?

NONVIOLENCE (CCC, 2302-2317; 2327-2330)

Christians live in a sinful world that is, at times, a violent world. Violence involves conflict; its antidote is peace. Jesus commands us to be peacemakers. We have "no choice but to defend peace. . . . This is an inalienable obligation. It is the how of defending the peace which offers moral options" (*The Challenge of Peace*, §73).

Through the centuries, the Church has given witness to two ways of responding to armed conflict: nonviolence and the just war. Both traditions call us to pray for peace and to devote all our efforts to avoid war.

Church teaching always begins with a presumption against war, advocating instead the peaceful settlement of disputes. As far as possible, conflict situations should be resolved justly through nonviolent means. Having said that, the Church also recognizes the right and duty of legitimate political authorities to employ limited force to save innocent people and to establish justice. But this can only be a last resort when sustained nonviolent action has failed to protect the innocent from fundamental injustice.

Within the Catholic community there is a diversity of opinion over the morality of armed conflict. Many Catholics support the traditional "just-war theory" as a necessary response to evil, all the while acknowledging that armed force must be strictly limited by specific ethical considerations.

Other Catholics argue that a total commitment to nonviolence better conforms to the gospel witness to peace. This opinion further holds that just-war thinking is extremely difficult to apply under the conditions of modern warfare or in an age of independent terrorist organizations that are not affiliated with a particular state.

Those who disagree with the position of strict nonviolence argue that this approach closes its eyes to grave evil in the world and flees from our responsibility to resist evil.

The Church teaches that both traditions hold moral insight; either position could be argued by sincere Christians of good conscience.

LEVELS OF VIOLENCE

Violence, the use of some form of physical force to injure, damage, or destroy other people or their property, is with us today. Since the original sin, violence has always been a part of humanity. For example, today violence is often hidden in our homes: some parents beat their children, some husbands abuse their wives. Other forms of violence are reported daily by the media: rape, armed burglary, terrorism, and war. All too often violence results in death.

Since Cain laid hands on Abel, human history has been engaged in a struggle between peace and violence, rich and poor, black and white, workers and employers, nation and nation. One analysis of this constant struggle images a spiral of violence with three levels:

- *The first level of violence* ("institutional violence") denies basic human rights. The denial of rights results in unemployment, poverty, hunger, loss of participation, and early death. This leads to . . .
- *The second level of violence* ("counter-violence") is where the oppressed group tries to correct the wrong through violence. The oppressed may resort to individual acts of force, or armed resistance to fight the denial of human rights. This leads to . . .
- *The third level of violence* ("repressive violence") is where those in power repeat the cycle of violence. To solidify their power over others, those in power (like governmental authorities or military regimes) further solidify the injustices committed against people. And the whole cycle starts over again.

Examples of each level of violence in family, school, and society follow.

Levels	Family	School	Society
LEVEL 1: INSTITUTIONAL VIOLENCE	Parents set unreasonable rules for a teen.	A teacher is notorious for grading unfairly.	A minority suffers discrimination in housing, education, and employment.
LEVEL 2: COUNTER-VIOLENCE	The teen rebels, deliberately breaking one or more of the parents' rules.	Students are disruptive and disrespectful.	The minority rebels through civil disobedience. This leads to riots and looting.
LEVEL 3: REPRESSIVE VIOLENCE	Parents ground the teen and become more unreasonable in their demands.	The teacher becomes even more demanding and unfair.	The government cracks down. For example, it issues an order to "shoot to kill" looters.

The Church teaches that violence must always be the last possible resort to solve conflict. Peaceful communication through dialogue, exchange, compromise, negotiation, and arbitration should be tried over and over again to try to secure rights and resolve conflicts. This is the Christian way. Why? Because violence escalates. Violence almost always leads to more violence and is rarely the foundation for lasting peace and harmony.

What are two other examples in each of the levels of violence?

What is needed to break the cycle of violence in each of the examples given?

THE OPTION OF NONVIOLENCE

Nonviolence is an option for dealing with violence. We should not confuse nonviolence, however, with passivity, with a "sit-back-and-do-nothing approach" to confronting evil. Nonviolence requires courage, patience, action, creativity, and a passionate commitment to seek justice and truth no matter what the price. Nonviolence combats injustice and resists evil by using peaceful means like dialogue, negotiations, protests, boycotts, civil disobedience, strikes, citizen resistance, and the like.

> The ultimate weakness of violence is that it is a descending spiral, begetting the very thing it seeks to destroy. . . . Returning violence for violence multiplies violence, adding deeper darkness to a night already devoid of stars. Darkness cannot drive out darkness; only light can do that. Hate cannot drive out hate; only love can do that.
>
> MARTIN LUTHER KING, JR.

In the past, nonviolence was often seen as simply an individual option to resist war and other violent actions. For example, **conscientious objectors** (COs) are people who refuse to engage in armed conflict. Historically, one type of CO opposes all war on principle. A second type refuses to participate in wars considered to be unjust. Members of the Society of Friends (Quakers) and the Mennonite religion usually are COs of the first type. Many American young men who protested the Vietnam War in the 1960s and 1970s were COs of the second type because of their belief in the injustice of that particular war.

Some COs are **pacifists** who not only object to and refuse to participate in wars, but they also reject any recourse to violence regardless of the circumstances. The Catholic tradition supports both a pacifist response and conscientious objection to unjust wars. In fact, Christians must object to unjust wars.

Today, nations are beginning to realize that nonviolent actions have the power to bring about change, even under repressive dictatorial regimes. Successful examples of nonviolent action in the latter half of the twentieth century included:

- Mohandas Gandhi's (1869–1948) nonviolent protests (what he termed "truth and firmness") that helped lead to India's gaining independence from British colonial rule in 1947.
- The Solidarity Movement in Poland in the 1980s, mobilized by Lech Walesa, used strikes, labor meltdowns, prison hunger strikes, boycotts, marches, and the power of an underground press to topple a communist regime.
- The Filipino people, armed with rosary beads in their hands, knelt in front of armored tanks sent to intimidate them. This was part of a 1986 People Power Movement that resulted in a four-day nonviolent protest that brought down the Marcos dictatorship in the Philippines.
- Massive nonviolent resistance to a coup attempt against Mikhail Gorbachev and other nonviolent actions helped bring freedom to states forced by communist regimes to be part of the former Soviet Union.

These nonviolent revolutions prove the power of systematic, organized, nonviolent activity. The American bishops support the belief in solving problems and conflicts with nonviolent means. They also call for the promotion of education, research, and training in nonviolent ways to combat evil (*The Harvest of Justice*, p. 5).

CONSCIENTIOUS OBJECTOR—A PERSON WHO REFUSES TO PARTICIPATE IN A WAR OUT OF REASONS OF CONSCIENCE EITHER BECAUSE A GIVEN WAR IS UNJUST OR BECAUSE OF RELIGIOUS CONVICTIONS AGAINST ALL WAR.

PACIFIST—SOMEONE WHO OPPOSES ALL WAR AS A MEANS OF SETTLING DISPUTES.

NON-VIOLENCE IN ACTION

Here are some suggestions for promoting peace through nonviolent actions:

1. Pray for peace daily. Use the Prayer for Peace of Saint Francis of Assisi.

    Lord, make me an instrument of your peace.
    Where there is hatred, let me sow love;
    > where there is injury, pardon;
    > where there is doubt, faith;
    > where there is despair, hope;
    > where there is darkness, light;
    > where there is sadness, joy.

    O Divine Master, grant that I may not seek
    > so much to be consoled as to console;
    > to be understood, as to understand,
    > to be loved, as to love.

    For it is in giving that we receive,
    > it is in pardoning that we are pardoned,
    > and it is in dying that we are born to eternal life.

2. Become an "instrument of peace" by learning about the causes of conflict, war, and the like. Amass some facts and figures about the economic and political factors that cause nations to fight. Keep informed about some of the hot spots of conflict in the world by reading the daily newspaper.

3. Learn the position of your representatives in Congress and the Senate on weapons' spending versus foreign aid for development. Write letters to encourage them to work against the arms race and other policies that cause international conflict. Be an instrument of peace by writing to the newspaper to express your opinion.

4. "Sow love" by being gentle in how you treat others: your family members, fellow classmates, students from other schools, your coworkers, others you meet each day. Take the Pledge Against Violence, which can be found on the Institute for Peace and Justice website: www.ipj_ppj.org.

5. Where there is personal injury to you, learn to pardon the offender. Celebrate the sacrament of reconciliation regularly.

6. Engage in the works of mercy: feed the hungry, give drink to the thirsty, clothe the naked. For example, support an organization like Catholic Relief Services which works to alleviate some of the misery of people abroad.

7. Shed light by dispelling ignorance. Learn about people who are different from you. For example, read a publication from another country. Correspond with a student in another part of the world. Attend an ethnic festival in your area to learn about the customs of a nationality with which you are unfamiliar.

8. Console and understand others when conflict arises by trying to resolve the tension nonviolently. Don't use inflammatory words or gestures. If you meet originally with little success, ask for someone to act as a mediator.

9. Love by befriending a lonely person at school, by verbally defending a member of a minority who is being badmouthed, by volunteering at a hunger center, by joining a branch of Amnesty International at your school, by organizing a fund-raising project for a peace-and-justice group, etc.

THE JUST-WAR TRADITION

The Church's **just-war tradition** tries to provide guidelines for three things:

1. the conditions under which armed force might be used in a conflict;
2. the limits that should constrain resort to force; and
3. ethical norms on restraining damage caused by military forces in a war.

As is true of all Church efforts at peacemaking, just-war teaching always begins with a strong presumption against the use of force. However, it sets out those conditions that enable properly constituted governments to use force when the common good demands it to protect human dignity and human rights.

We live in a sinful world. Unfortunately, peaceful, nonviolent resolution to conflicts does not always work. The just-war tradition makes a major contribution to the ethical climate. It helps to restrain and to regulate the force governments and international organizations like the United Nations can use to right serious injustices as a last resort.

Church teaching on the just-war tradition is summarized in the *Catechism of the Catholic Church* (2307–2309; 2312–2314; 2327–2328; 2330). The Church holds that all the following criteria must be present before a government can declare war and subsequently use lethal force:

Just cause. There must be a real, lasting, grave, and certain damage inflicted by an aggressor on a nation or a community of nations. If a situation threatens the lives of innocent people, if basic human rights are violated, or if there is an imminent need

for self-defense, then there would be just cause.

Legitimate authority. The right to declare a war of defense belongs to those who have the legitimate responsibility to represent the people and are entrusted with the common good.

Comparative justice. The rights and values in the conflict must be so important that they justify killing.

While there may be rights and wrongs on all sides of a conflict, to override the presumption against the use of force the injustice suffered by one party must significantly outweigh that suffered by another (The Harvest of Justice, *p. 5*).

Right intention. To be just, a war must be waged for the best of reasons and with a commitment to postwar reconciliation with the enemy. Needless destruction, cruelty to prisoners, and other harsh measures cannot be tolerated.

Probability of success. The odds of success should be weighed against the human cost of the war. The purpose of this criterion is to prevent irrational use of force or hopeless resistance when either will prove futile.

JUST-WAR TRADITION—A set of principles developed through the centuries by the Church that clearly outlines when a nation may ethically participate in a war. It also sets clear limits on armed force once a war is engaged.

Proportionality. The damage to be inflicted and the costs incurred by the war must be proportionate to the good expected. Armed conflict must not produce evils and disorders graver than the evil to be eliminated. For example, if a large number of people would be destroyed over a dispute that only slightly affects the two countries, the decision to go to war would violate proportionality.

Last resort. War must be a last resort, justifiable only if all peaceful efforts have been tried and exhausted and there are no alternatives.

To override the strong presumption against the use of force, all the above criteria must be satisfied.

The Church's just-war tradition also imposes a moral standard of restraint once there is armed conflict. This standard includes:

Immunity of noncombatants. Civilians may not be the object of direct attack. Military strategies must avoid and minimize any indirect harm inflicted on noncombatants.

Proportionality. Minimum force necessary to obtain military objectives should be carefully adhered to so undue collateral damage to civilians and property may be avoided.

Right intention. Political and military leaders must always see that peace with justice is the only reason for the use of arms. Vengeful acts and indiscriminate killing—committed by individuals, military forces, or governments—are forbidden and immoral. Therefore, mass extermination of a people, nation, or ethnic minority is morally reprehensible and gravely sinful. Furthermore, blind obedience to unjust orders, for example, participation in genocide, cannot excuse one's responsibility for participating in such a heinous crime.

Applying these principles requires the virtue of prudence. It also requires resisting the various political forces that can affect the accuracy of the information which is needed to make a decision about the morality of a particular war.

The American bishops caution that military strategies that involve air strikes that target civilian infrastructures or the use of overwhelming force usually contradict the **principle of proportionality** and the necessity of sparing noncombatants from violence.

Finally, the bishops hold that in a violent society that fosters a culture of death, it may be more difficult in the future to apply these principles in an honest and a restrained way. Nevertheless, the *Catechism of the Catholic Church* and *The Challenge of Peace* clearly outline what may never be permitted in a war:

pRiNciple of pRopoRTioNaliTy—The rule that requires the damage inflicted and the costs incurred in a war (or a particular action in a war) to be commensurate with the good expected.

- Any act of war aimed indiscriminately at entire cities or extensive areas and their populations is a crime against God and humanity. Both actions merit total condemnation.

- Any act, including nuclear attack, that has great potential for widespread and indiscriminate destruction. *The Challenge of Peace* condemns nuclear war. There are major problems in trying to apply the just-war criteria to any kind of nuclear war. The bishops do not perceive any situation in which the first use of nuclear weapons could be justified. And they question whether there can be such a thing as a limited nuclear war. They argue that one of the criteria of the just-war teaching is that there must be reasonable hope of success in bringing about peace and justice. They question whether there can be this reasonable hope once nuclear weapons have been used. The American bishops also argue that good ends (defending one's country, protecting freedom) cannot justify immoral means (the use of weapons which kill indiscriminately and threaten whole societies).

- Further, the *Catechism of the Catholic Church* (2314–2317) warns that the arms race does not insure peace. Rather, it aggravates the causes of war; namely, it contributes to injustice, excessive economic and social inequalities, envy, distrust, and pride. The accumulation, production, and sale of arms are dangerous to international order and a grave injustice to the poor and needy. Over-armament intensifies the threat of conflict and squanders money that should be spent on the starving in our midst.

PERSONAL CONSCIENCE

The decision to fight in a just war, or to be a nonviolent witness to peace as a conscientious objector or a pacifist is a difficult one. To form one's conscience on this issue requires that a person regularly reflect on God's word in the scriptures, live the Christian virtues, cultivate an active prayer life, and study and apply the Church's teachings on peace and justice.

The Church respects the personal conscience of those who enter military service out of loyalty to their country and views them as the custodians of the security and freedom of the nation. When they carry out their duties properly, "they are contributing to the maintenance of peace" (*The Church in the Modern World*,

THE WAR IN IRAQ

The Vatican and the American bishops spoke out against the war on terrorism in Iraq declared by the United States in 2003 according to the criteria of the just-war doctrine. Most of the Church's questions concerned the criteria of last resort and proportionality. The Church also warned that

- a significant increase in terrorist activity was likely to happen;
- the war might escalate into a "clash of civilizations" between Islam and Christianity;
- revengeful acts against the small Christian communities in the Middle East might result;
- the Israeli-Palestinian "peace process," especially as it concerns the protection of the Holy Land, would suffer;
- a so-called "pre-emptive," preventive war waged by a country like America (and her allies), acting unilaterally without the support of United Nations, would be a dangerous precedent against the rule of international law.

ANALYSIS

- Were Church authorities correct in their pre-war assessment? Find facts to back up your conclusion.
- Read and report on some of the statements of the bishops and the Vatican leading up to the war:

www.usccb.org/sdwp/peace/churchleaders.htm

www.osjspm.org/iraq.pdf

www.vatican.va/holy_father/special_features/peace/prayer_peace_index.html

EXTRA CREDIT

Research and debate whether or not another recent war (e.g., Vietnam, Persian Gulf, Kosovo, Afghanistan) could be justified using traditional just-war teaching.

§79). Noting that no government can demand blind obedience from its citizens, the American bishops go on to teach that

A citizen may not casually disregard his country's conscientious decision to call its citizens to acts of "legitimate defense." Moreover, the role of Christian citizens in the armed forces is a service to the common good and an exercise of the virtue of patriotism, so long as they fulfill this role within defined moral norms (The Challenge of Peace, §232).

On the one hand, the Church values conscientious military service in defense of the common good. On the other, the Church also respects those

who forego the use of violence to vindicate their rights and resort to other means of defense which are available to weaker parties, provided it can be done without harm to the rights and duties of others and of the community (The Church in the Modern World, §78).

Furthermore, the Church supports laws which would make humane provision for conscientious objectors who refuse to bear arms, "provided they accept some other form of community service" (*The Church in the Modern World*, §79).

Note the duty here to serve one's fellow citizens—whether in the military to fight injustice or as a conscientious noncombatant who serves the cause of peace in some nonviolent way.

THE JUST-WAR TRADITION AND THE WAR ON TERRORISM

America and all the world changed on September 11, 2001, when fanatical extremists hijacked jets and used them as weapons of destruction in New York City and Arlington, Virginia. On that day, Americans came face to face with a new kind of threat that international law has had difficulty dealing with, namely, terrorist organizations that are not themselves part of an organized state. The international legal

What type of war would you conscientiously object to?

What are some ethical ways a person could protest an unjust war?

The American bishops call for the progressive disarmament of both nuclear and conventional weapons.

How might this be done effectively worldwide to insure the safety of all nations?

What is the current defense budget of the United States? Compare this amount to the budget allotted for poverty programs.

system that developed through the centuries has established norms to discipline sovereign states that assault human rights. But how should civilized countries respond to terrorist organizations and atrocities like those committed on 9/11?

Pope John Paul II defined "terrorism" as "the intention to kill people and destroy property indiscriminately, and to create a climate of terror and insecurity, often including the taking of hostages" (*Solicitudo Rei Socialis*, §24). Terrorist actions or threats to commit violence against innocent people are used to sow fear or seek revenge for the ideological purposes of the terrorist groups. "*Terrorism is built on contempt for human life. For this reason, not only does it commit intolerable crimes, but because it resorts to terror as a political and military means it is itself a true crime against humanity.*"[2]

Terrorist actions are objectively a grave evil that can *never* be justified. The *Catechism of the Catholic Church* clearly teaches:

Kidnapping and hostage taking bring on a reign of terror; by means of threats they subject their victims to intolerable pressures. They are morally wrong. Terrorism threatens, wounds, and kills indiscriminately; it is gravely against justice and charity (CCC, 2297).

Governments and citizens, of course, have the right of self-defense against terrorists and their heinous actions. But Pope John Paul II taught that to win the fight against terrorism, repressive and punitive operations are not the final solution. He wrote,

It is essential that the use of force, even when necessary, be accompanied by a courageous and lucid analysis of the reasons behind terrorist attacks. The fight against terrorism must be conducted also on the political and educational levels: on the one hand, by eliminating the underlying causes of situations of injustice which frequently drive people to more desperate and violent acts; and on the other hand, by insisting on an education inspired by respect for human life in every situation: the unity of the human race is a more powerful reality than any contingent divisions separating individuals and people.[3]

Pope John Paul II acknowledged that the fight against terrorism is necessary, but that international law must find ways to prevent, monitor, and suppress crime. Furthermore, democratic governments must never renounce the rule of law and use methods that undermine basic human rights. A good end or purpose for doing something can never justify evil means to attain it. This is why, for example, the torture of suspected terrorists can never be permitted:

Torture which uses physical or moral violence to extract confessions, punish the guilty, frighten opponents, or satisfy hatred is contrary to respect for the person and for human dignity (CCC, 2297).

The most effective remedy for the scourge of terrorism is to remove its causes, including poverty and the powerlessness felt by so many people around the world because of oppression and the lack of respect for their basic human rights. These situations are the breeding ground for terrorists. Limiting a response to terrorism to revengeful acts will only breed more hatred and violence and will not get at the root of the problem. Nations must band together to help struggling nations to develop. They must respect international law, and cooperate with organizations like the United Nations, because they are the foundation for peace among nations.

Pope John Paul II "often reminded Christians and all persons of good will that forgiveness is needed for solving the problems of individuals and peoples. There is no peace without forgiveness!"[4]

PROFILE OF A PROMINENT PEACEMAKER: THOMAS MERTON (1915–1968)

Thomas Merton was one of the most famous American Catholics of the twentieth century. A prolific writer who has over sixty books in print in English today, his works are widely read around the world decades after his untimely death.

Born in France of artist parents, Merton studied for a brief time at Cambridge University in England before obtaining his master's degree at Columbia University in 1939. While there, young Thomas began his conversion to Catholicism, a conversion that moved him eventually to join the Trappist order of monks, noted for their strict discipline of silence and solitude. In 1948, he published his best-selling autobiography titled *Seven Storey Mountain*, one of the most influential works authored by a twentieth-century Catholic.

While at the Abbey of Gethsemani in Kentucky, Merton served as novice master for a number of years and began a writing career that included a vast array of works on prayer and meditation, historical and biographical works on his religious order, poetry, and a voluminous correspondence with leading thinkers of his time. Merton also wrote many essays commenting on the society of his day. Some of his key interests were racism, economic injustice, and war and peace. He was a leading Catholic voice in his criticism of the Vietnam War.

Merton died in 1968 when an electric fan accidentally electrocuted him while he was attending a religious conference of Buddhist and Christian monks held in Bangkok, Thailand.

MERTON QUOTES

Peace demands the most heroic labor and the most difficult sacrifice. It demands greater heroism than war. It demands greater fidelity to the truth and a much more perfect purity of conscience.[5]

So instead of loving what you think is peace, love other [people] and love God above all. And instead of hating the people you think are warmakers, hate the appetites and the disorder in your own soul, which are the causes of war. If you love peace, then hate injustice, hate tyranny, hate greed—but hate these things in yourself, not in another.[6]

- Read more about the Trappist life at Gethsemani at: www.monks.org/monasticlife.html
- Read more about Thomas Merton at The Thomas Merton Center and International Thomas Merton Society: www.merton.org.

Research and report on the pacifist positions of religious groups like the Amish, Mennonites, or Quakers (Society of Friends).

PEACEMAKING STRATEGIES (CCC, 2437–2442)

Peacemaking is a task for both individuals and societies. As individuals, we must be Christlike, living loving and just lives. We must be truthful, exercise our freedom responsibly, and respect and defend the rights of others, especially the weak in our midst. In *The Challenge of Peace*, the American bishops encourage everyone who wants to end war to begin by defending the lives of the unborn. In the words of Pope Paul VI, "If you wish peace, defend life" (quoted in *The Challenge of Peace*, §289). Furthermore, the bishops urge us to perform the traditional acts of holiness that Jesus teaches in the Sermon on the Mount (Mt 6:1–18): to pray, to perform acts of penance, and to give alms to the poor. All of these should be done with the goal of converting our hearts and minds to become peacemakers. Concerning the evil of the nuclear arms race, the bishops wrote:

We are called to turn back from this evil of total destruction and turn instead in prayer and penance toward God, toward our neighbor, and toward the building of a peaceful world (§300).

Nations must also commit themselves to build a just and peaceful world. This commitment takes political will. It requires steady work and the implementation of policies to build structures of peace. It demands building and supporting an international order that protects human rights and ensures peace among nations.

Catholic teaching on social justice especially calls us to implement the key principles of a global option for the poor and global solidarity in our peacemaking efforts. Information on these principles and an agenda for peace follows.

GLOBAL OPTION FOR THE POOR

Catholic social teaching sees a definite link between poverty and war and reiterates society's strong option for the poor. Nations promote peace when they work for the common good of all people. They promote peace when they work to solve economic and social inequalities through distributive justice. In the words of the *Catechism of the Catholic Church*:

Injustice, excessive economic or social inequalities, envy, distrust, and pride raging among men and nations constantly threaten peace and cause wars. Everything done to overcome these disorders contributes to building up peace and avoiding war (CCC, 2317).

Recall that each human posesses dignity and deserves the right to life and all that is necessary to sustain life. Recall also the universal destination of human goods, that is, that God made creation for the benefit of everyone and not just a select few.

God gave the earth to the whole human race for the sustenance of all its members, without excluding or favoring anyone (On the Hundredth Anniversary of "Rerum Novarum," §31).

Yet, we live in a world where there is a shocking inequality between the rich and the poor. One of the eight goals of the United Nations for the millennium is to halve the world's poverty by the year 2015. Yet, little progress is being made on the hunger front. The World Health Organization reports that hunger and malnutrition claim 10 million lives every year, 25,000 lives *every day*, one life every five seconds.[7] This is simply wrong and, sadly, the situation worsens.

Peace and justice are linked. But providing a global option for the poor requires conversion. Pope John Paul II challenges:

Love for others, and in the first place love for the poor, in whom the Church sees Christ himself, is made concrete in the promotion of justice. Justice will never be fully attained unless people see in the poor person, who is asking for help in order to survive, not an annoyance or a burden, but an opportunity for showing kindness and a chance for greater enrichment. Only such an awareness can give the courage needed to face the risk and the change involved in every authentic attempt to come to the aid of another.

It is not merely a matter of "giving from one's surplus," but of helping entire peoples which are presently excluded or marginalized to enter into the sphere of economic and human development. For this to happen, it is not enough to draw on the surplus goods which in fact our world abundantly produces; it requires above all a change of lifestyles, of models of production and consumption, and of the established structures of power which today govern societies (On the Hundredth Anniversary of "Rerum Novarum," §58).

GLOBAL SOLIDARITY

International solidarity is a requirement of the moral order; world peace depends in part upon this (CCC, 1941).

Christian teaching has always recognized what the world is now discovering for itself due to things like the globalization of economic markets and the explosion in communication networks: we are members of one human family who depend on each other. Catholics must increasingly be aware that their name refers to their universality. Our love must embrace everyone.

Today, to take care of our brothers and sisters requires a global outlook. Pope John Paul II wrote:

Sacred Scripture continually speaks to us of an active commitment to our neighbor and demands of us a shared responsibility for all of humanity. This duty is not limited to one's own family, nation, or state, but extends progressively to all . . . so no one can consider himself extraneous or indifferent to the lot of another member of the human family (On the Hundredth Anniversary of "Rerum Novarum," §51).

The virtue of solidarity requires us to commit ourselves to the common good of all people. This means that the world's rich nations especially will make a conscientious effort to promote development of the poorer nations. This effort "involves sacrificing the positions of income and of power enjoyed by the more developed economies" so there will be "an overall human enrichment to the family of nations" (*On the Hundredth Anniversary of "Rerum Novarum,"* §52).

The American bishops described the requirements of solidarity:

Solidarity is action on behalf of one human family; calling us to help overcome the divisions in our world. Solidarity binds the rich to the poor. It makes the free zealous for the cause of the oppressed. It drives the comfortable and secure to take risks for the victims of tyranny and war. It calls those who are strong to care for those who are weak and vulnerable across the spectrum of human life. It opens homes and hearts to those in flight from terror and to migrants whose daily toil supports affluent lifestyles. Peacemaking, as Pope John Paul II has told us, is the work of solidarity.[8]

AGENDA FOR PEACE

The Harvest of Justice Is Sown in Peace, Economic Justice for All, The Challenge of Peace, various papal social-justice encyclicals, and messages for the celebration of the world day of peace indicate the following steps that individual nations can take to help build a more peaceful international community:

1. Strengthen international institutions. The way to a peaceful world is to exercise the option for the poor and to promote the global common good. This requires an international system that will ensure human rights, work for peace within and among nations, and help develop political and economic interdependence that works for the common good. In today's world this means that citizens and nations should support the efforts of the United Nations—not to replace the sovereignty of individual nations, but to address problems that no individual nation can face alone.

Since the fall of the Soviet Union, it is even more necessary for the United States and other countries to strengthen the United Nations and other international institutions so they might be more "effective, responsible, and responsive. . . . Effective multilateral institutions can relieve the United States of the burden, or the temptation, of becoming of itself the world's peace force" (*The Harvest of Justice*, p. 8). Minimally, this requires that the United States pay its United Nation's assessments and accept the authority of the United Nations in international disputes, including submitting to the compulsory jurisdiction of the International Court of Justice.

For its part, the United Nations must reform its sometimes unwieldy bureaucracy to better build up peace and serve the common good.

In addition, a healthy international order requires strong non-governmental groups like human rights organizations, humanitarian aid organizations, businesses and labor groups, media, churches, and the like to promote international understanding, cultural exchanges, mutual understanding, and so forth—all of which help the cause of peace.

2. Work to secure human rights. There can never be a just and peaceful world without the promotion and defense of human rights both within and among nations. These rights include religious, civil, political, social, cultural, and economic rights.

As reported, respect for human rights must begin with the defense of life. Other rights that need special protection and promotion are those of families, women, children, workers, and those who are most vulnerable, especially the poor. This will require a foreign policy that makes human rights a top priority and the support of

international organizations that challenge the violation of human rights around the world. Examples of such violations that affect many countries throughout the world include religious intolerance and persecution; the undermining of human rights in the so-called "war on terror"; the ill-treatment and torture of prisoners of war and political dissidents; violence committed against women and children; social exclusion based on race, sex, or class; and the marginalization and denial of justice to native peoples on every continent in the world.

Of special concern today is terrorism committed in the name of religion. Pope John Paul II firmly stated:

Terrorism is often the outcome of that fanatic fundamentalism *which springs from the conviction that one's own vision of the truth must be forced upon everyone else. Instead, even when the truth has been reached—and this can happen only in a limited and imperfect way—it can never be imposed. Respect for a person's conscience, where the image of God himself is reflected (cf. Gn 1:26–27), means that we can only propose the truth to others, who are then responsible for accepting it. To try to impose on others by violent means what we consider to be the truth is an offence against human dignity, and ultimately an offence against God whose image that person bears. For this reason, what is usually referred to as fundamentalism is an attitude radically opposed to belief in God.* Terrorism exploits not just people, it exploits God: *it ends by making him an idol to be used for one's own purposes.*
Consequently, no religious leader can condone terrorism, and much less preach it. *It is a profanation of religion to declare oneself a terrorist in the name of God, to do violence to others in his name. Terrorist violence is a contradiction of faith in God, the Creator of man, who cares for man and loves him. It is altogether contrary to faith in Christ the Lord, who taught his disciples to pray: "Forgive us our debts, as we also have forgiven our debtors"* (Mt 6:12).[9]

Catholic teaching holds that, at times, forceful humanitarian intervention into the internal affairs of other nations is required where the survival of populations or entire ethnic groups are under fatal assault. Though non-military forms of intervention (like economic sanctions or humanitarian relief efforts for starving civilian populations) should take precedence over force, military intervention may sometimes be justified, for example, in the case of genocide. However, these interventions should be restrained by the principles of a just war and,

Multilateral interventions, under the auspices of the United Nations, are preferable because they enhance the legitimacy of these actions and can protect against abuse (The Harvest of Justice, p. 16).

3. *Promote true development for the poorer nations.* In his Message for the Celebration of the World Day of Peace for 2005 just weeks before he died, Pope John Paul II said, "Since the good of peace is closely linked to the development of all peoples, the *ethical requirements for the use of the earth's goods* must always be taken into account."[10] This means that as citizens of the world, we must always remember that God intended the earth and all it contains for the use of everyone in each generation. Therefore, both justice and charity require that the goods of creation should be available to all. Yet, consider the following two glaring facts about the disparity of wealth in today's world:

- Globally, 20 percent of the world's richest people account for 86 percent of total private consumption expenditures, while the poorest 20 percent account for a mere 1.3 percent.
- The U.S. population, 4.55 percent of the world population, consumes 25 percent of the world's energy resources.

Steps need to be taken to right these inequities. They include the following:

Improving Foreign Aid The United States used to be the pioneer in foreign aid. Today, it lags far behind most industrialized countries in percentage of its gross national product devoted to foreign aid. The amount of aid given must be increased and it must be given with no conditions attached. The American bishops

call for a U.S. international economic policy designed to empower people everywhere and enable them to continue to develop a sense of their own worth, improve the quality of their lives, and ensure that the benefits of economic growth are shared equitably (Economic Justice for All, §292).

Less foreign aid should be earmarked for military and security purposes; more should be targeted primarily for the elimination of poverty:

It is a fundamental obligation of solidarity on the part of those who enjoy a plentiful share of earth's riches to promote the rightful development of those who have barely enough to survive (The Harvest of Justice, p. 11).

For their part, developing countries have the right to direct their own social and economic development, cooperating on an equal footing with other nations in working for the common good. In the words of Pope John Paul II:

Development demands above all a spirit of initiative on the part of the countries which need it. Each of them must act in accordance with its own responsibilities, not expecting everything from the more favored countries, and acting in collaboration with others in the same situation. Each must discover and use to the best advantage its own area of freedom. . . . The development of peoples begins and is most appropriately accomplished in the dedication of each people to its own development, in collaboration with others (On Social Concern, §44).

Rectifying Trade Relationships A key drawback to authentic development for poor nations is fair access to international markets. The principle of the preferential option for the poor will see that poor countries receive fair prices for their products and that they have access to the markets in the wealthier countries.

Foreign aid should focus more on empowering the poor to improve the quality of their lives than in shoring up the international economic system or pursuing national interest or competitive advantage (The Harvest of Justice, *p. 10).*

Rich nations should be encouraged to share their technological resources with the developing nations; the poorer nations should in turn learn how to use them properly.

On Social Concern (§45) encourages the formation of new regional organizations among developing nations based on equality and freedom so the poorer nations can participate more fully in the international community.

Relieving International Debt In *On Social Concern* (§43), Pope John Paul II calls for reforming the world monetary and financial system because it is marked by excessive fluctuation in exchange and interest rates to the detriment of poorer nations. Without a doubt, there must be ways found to reduce the crushing international debt of the poorer nations. Consider the following:

Dozens of countries, large and small, have foreign debts so large that their interest payments on the debt are a crushing burden. The Republic of the Congo, for example, has annual debt service payments equal to 50 percent of its export earnings; Uganda's debt service equals 44 percent of its exports. Not surprisingly many countries cannot keep up with their interest payments, let alone ever hope of paying off the principal.[11]

Renegotiated, longer repayment periods, lower interest rates, and debt forgiveness are some of the suggestions the American bishops called for in *Economic Justice for All* (§271–277) to alleviate the major debt problem. This problem especially affects the poor because when debtor nations tighten their economic belts, austerity measures like lower wages and a reduction in basic services most affect them. Pope John Paul II wrote of the basic morality involved in this issue:

The principle that debts must be paid is certainly just. However, it is not right to demand or expect payment when the effect would be the imposition of political choices leading to hunger and despair for entire peoples. It cannot be expected that the debts which have been contracted should be paid at the price of unbearable sacrifices. In such cases it is necessary to find—as in fact is partly happening—ways to lighten, defer or even cancel the debt, compatible with the fundamental right of peoples to subsistence and progress (On the Hundredth Anniversary of "Rerum Novarum," *§35).*

In recent years, some wealthier nations have cancelled some debt of impoverished nations. Pope John Paul II observed:

Recent moves in favor of debt reduction, centered mainly on the needs of the poor, have certainly improved the quality of economic growth. Yet, because of a number of factors, this growth is still quantitatively insufficient, especially in relation to the millennium goals. Poor countries remain trapped in a vicious circle: low income and weak growth limit savings and, in turn, weak investments and an inefficient use of savings do not favor growth.[12]

Ending the Arms Race, Halting Arms Trade, and Banning Landmines Pope John XXIII was ahead of his time when he wrote:

Justice, then, right reason and consideration for human dignity and life urgently demand that the arms race should cease; that the stockpiles which exist in various countries should be reduced equally and simultaneously by the parties concerned; that nuclear weapons should be banned; and finally that all come to an agreement on a fitting program of disarmament, employing mutual and effective controls. (Peace on Earth, *§112).*

Although the American bishops judge that our country may possess nuclear weapons to deter others from using them, they abhor any use of these weapons and call for progressive disarmament. They call for the elimination of all nuclear weapons as a policy goal and support a halt to all nuclear testing.

In the words of the fathers at the Second Vatican Council, "The arms race is an utterly treacherous trap for humanity, and one which ensnares the poor to an intolerable degree" (*The Church in the Modern World*, §81). Pope John Paul II called excessive levels of spending on arms a "serious disorder" and the moral judgment about the arms trade "is even more severe" (*On Social Concern*, §24).

In addition, arms trading fuels dozens of regional conflicts around the world. The American bishops wrote:

As the world's largest supplier of weapons, the United States bears great responsibility for curbing the arms trade by taking concrete actions to reduce its own predominant role in this trade. . . . Neither jobs nor profits justify military spending beyond the minimum necessary for legitimate national security and international peacekeeping obligations. (The Harvest of Justice, *p. 14*).

CASE STUDY: VIOLENCE OR NONVIOLENCE?

Background:

You are working the closing shift at a fast food retail store. Just minutes from closing a man approaches, pulls a gun, and demands the money from the cash register. After you give him the money he lays down his gun on the counter and begins to stuff the money in his coat pocket. You grab the gun and point it at the man.

What Do You Do?

- Do you point the gun at the man and demand that he leave the store?
- Do you point the gun at the man and tell him to return the money?
- Do you point the gun at the man as you back away from him?
- Do you shoot the man point blank?
- Do you shoot the man as he walks away?

Debate:

- Explain your action.
- Are any of the actions listed above morally wrong?

FRANZ JÄGERSTÄTTER(1907–1943): ICON OF CONSCIENCE

"Actions speak louder than words." An enduring example of this time-tested principle was an Austrian farmer, Franz Jägerstätter, who at the age of thirty-seven was executed for refusing to enter Hitler's army. By refusing to cave into peer pressure, Franz did what he thought was right in the face of evil. He followed his conscience, saying he would rather die following the Lord's teaching than live and betray what he knew was the right thing to do.

Franz was born out of wedlock on May 20, 1907, to a man killed in World War I. His birthplace was a small Catholic village of St. Radegund on the border of Austria and Germany. He took the Jägerstätter name from a farmer who eventually married his mother and adopted him. Franz grew up on a farm, and like most of his peers, left school at the age of fourteen.

As a young man, Franz had a wild side. According to his biographer, the American Catholic pacifist Gordon Zahn, Franz enjoyed fighting, bowling, card-playing, dancing, and women.[13] At the age of twenty-seven, he fathered a child out of wedlock, as had his own father. The birth of this child, however, converted Franz from his wild ways and set him on a spiritual journey that transformed him into a new person.

Franz made a pilgrimage to a local shrine and even considered entering a religious order. However, he returned to the farm and married a loving wife with a similar religious outlook on life. Franz became active in his local church as a sexton and would often be heard singing religious songs or reciting the rosary as he worked in the fields or walked to the church. He went to daily Mass and often fasted until noon out of deep respect for the Blessed Sacrament. At sacrifice to his own family, he shared food with the poor living in his area.

When Hitler marched into Austria, Franz Jägerstätter was the only one in his community who voted against *Anschluss* (the annexation of Austria by Germany in March of 1938). He saw Hitler as an evil man who wanted allegiance to him to replace one's allegiance to Christ Jesus. When his contemporaries, even leading Churchmen, would salute "Heil Hitler!" rather than "Jesus is Lord!" Jägerstätter would often reply "Gross Gott!" which means "God's greetings!"

In February 1943 Franz received a draft notice. By then he had three young daughters, the oldest of whom was only six. Franz refused to serve in the army of the Third Reich. His neighbors thought him a fanatic. Even his pastor, a good priest who also opposed Nazism, urged him to serve for the sake of his family. The local bishop joined in, arguing that Franz was not knowledgeable enough to oppose the government's position. Franz continually refused to submit himself to what he considered an evil regime. He was eventually imprisoned for his convictions.

In prison his wife was allowed to visit him. She tried to get him to change his mind. So did the prison chaplain who insisted that Franz was an extremist for refusing to join the army. After six months of refusal to relent, Franz Jägerstätter underwent a military trial in Berlin. He was sentenced to death by decapitation on August 9, 1943.

Franz left behind only thirty-three pages of collected writings. In one letter he composed from prison, he wrote:

Today one can hear it said repeatedly that there is nothing any more an individual can do. If someone were to speak out, it would only mean imprisonment and death. True, there is not much that can be done anymore to influence the whole course of world events. . . . But as long as we live in this world, I believe it is never too late to save ourselves and perhaps some other soul for Christ. . . . Do we no longer want to see Christians who are able to take a stand in the darkness around us in deliberate clarity, calmness, and confidence—who, in the midst of tension, gloom, selfishness, and hate, stand fast in perfect peace and cheerfulness—who are not like the floating reed which is driven here and there by every breeze—who do not merely watch to see what their friends will do but, instead, ask themselves, "What does our faith teach us about all this," or "Can my conscience bear this so easily that I will never have to repent?"[14]

Franz Jägerstätter died resisting induction into Hitler's army.

- Do you believe Franz was foolish to die for his beliefs? Why or why not?
- Name a cause you would be willing to die for. Explain.
- Read a short biography of Franz Jägerstätter at: http://justus.anglican.org/resources/bio/224.html or www. c3.hu/~bocs/jager_a.htm

BECOME A PEACEMAKER

Here are some positive actions you can take to grow in an awareness of global solidarity. Choose one to do as an individual or with several classmates.

- Read and report on a news profile that details the major beliefs of Islam.
- Partake in a learning simulation that will help you understand more about poverty, one of the scourges that leads to conflict: Hungry Decisions: www.churchworldservice.org/ decisions/index.htm.
- Sponsor a needy child. The National Council of Catholic Women and Catholic Relief Services cosponsor "Help-a-Child" which aids children in India, Thailand, Brazil, and Africa.
- Research an area of the world that is suffering from a current crisis. Create a portfolio of newspaper and magazine stories on this hot spot of trouble.
- Design a poster on the theme of Global Solidarity. Display it in the school hallways.
- Check with your diocesan missionary office for the names of priests, sisters, or lay people who are serving in the foreign missions. Write to one of them and ask how you could help them in their work. As a class, devise some fund-raising activities to help this missionary.
- Contact your diocesan office for migration and refugee service or Catholic Charities. Find out how your class can help sponsor a refugee or immigrant family new to your area.

CHAPTER SUMMARY

- Jesus calls his followers to work for peace. Peace, the tranquility of order, is a gift of Jesus Christ. Jesus the Redeemer, the Prince of Peace, has brought us peace by reconciling us to God through his death on the cross and his glorious resurrection. He has given us two gifts: the gift of his peace and the gift of the Holy Spirit who enables us to work for peace.

- Peace is both a gift from God and a human work. It should be built on truth, justice, freedom, and love. In the famous words of Pope Paul VI, "If you want peace, work for justice." And Pope John Paul II reminded us there is no justice without forgiveness.

- Three principles underlay the Church's vision of peace: the universal common good which respects the rights of others; the right and duty of people everywhere to develop; and the virtue of solidarity which recognizes that we all belong to one another as members of the human family and should care for each other.

- In the Old Testament image, the image of peace was eventually understood as a fruit of God's saving activity and the keeping of the covenant. New Testament images of peace focus on Jesus' proclamation of the coming of God's reign and of his saving deeds and acts that won for us our salvation. Jesus taught the elements of peacemaking: the practice of an all-inclusive love, the living of a nonviolent life, the loving and forgiving of one's enemies.

- Terrorism is a true crime against the human race. Terrorist acts can never be justified. However, in the fight against terrorists, respect must be given to the rule of international law, including a respect for basic human rights. Torture can never be tolerated since it seriously undermines human dignity.

- Through history, the Church has recognized two traditions of dealing with violence: the path of nonviolence and the just-war tradition. Nonviolence combats injustice through peaceful means like dialogue, negotiations, protests, boycotts, civil disobedience, strikes, and the like. Conscientious objectors are those who refuse to participate in war. Pacifists are those who refuse to participate in all wars out of religious conviction. Catholics *must* refuse to cooperate in unjust wars. The Church recognizes the right of people to take the path of nonviolent resistance to evil and not participate in military service. However, such persons must be willing to work for their fellow citizens in some alternative form of service.

- The Church also recognizes the right of legally constituted governments to use force when the common good requires it to protect human dignity and to defend human rights. The just-war tradition has served humanity well by laying out the strict conditions of when governments may participate in a war and of how governments must restrain the damage inflicted by military forces once a war is engaged. These principles allow legitimate authority to use force if the cause is just and a last resort; if comparative justice and proportionality are present; and if the conflict involves a right intention with the clear probability of success. Once war is engaged, civilians must not be directly attacked. Revenge and indiscriminate killing are outlawed. And proportionality requires using the minimum force necessary to obtain military objectives while avoiding undue collateral damage to citizens and property. The decision to fight in a just war must be one of conscience. The Church recognizes military service as a patriotic way of serving one's fellow citizens and a contribution to the maintenance of peace.

- Much global conflict is the result of injustice between the haves and the have-nots. A vision of peacemaking must include an agenda that shows a preferential love for the poor and a commitment to global solidarity. This agenda will work to support and cooperate with an international system, like the United Nations. Such a system will work for peace within and among nations, and it will protect human rights and help promote the universal common good among nations both politically and economically.

- Peace is the fruit of justice. Therefore, a peace agenda must promote human rights within and among nations. Such a defense of human rights must always begin with the right to life. It will take special care to defend the rights of women, children, the victims of religious bigotry, and other vulnerable people.

- Peace is also the fruit of true development. Steps must be taken to rectify the imbalance between the world's rich and the ever-growing numbers of poor people. Rich nations must support the principle of the universal destination of goods, that is, that God intended the goods of the world for the benefit of all, and not just the few. True development of poorer nations could be better achieved with more "no-strings-attached" foreign aid, the rectification of trade relationships, and the relief of the burden of international debt.

- Peace cannot be realized in our lifetime, nor justice done to the poor, unless the world becomes a safer place. Ending the arms race, ceasing the insane arms trade, and outlawing landmines that maim and kill so many innocent people could greatly help the world become a safer place.

- The Austrian peasant Franz Jägerstätter exemplified a person of conscience who stood against an unjust military machine that destroyed human rights.

REVIEW QUESTIONS

1. Define peace.
2. List some virtues of peacemakers.
3. What three elements are necessary in a Christian vision of peacemaking?
4. Briefly discuss the three common causes of war.
5. Discuss four things the Bible teaches about peace.
6. Briefly outline the three levels in the spiral of violence.
7. What are some nonviolent techniques for dealing with conflict?
8. Identify: conscientious objector, pacifist.
9. Cite two historical examples of how nonviolent actions brought about change.
10. Discuss five ways you personally can be a peacemaker.
11. List and describe the seven conditions that must be present to participate in a just war.
12. Discuss three ways the just-war tradition limits the use of force in a war.
13. "It is wrong to fight in a war." "It is wrong not to serve in the military of one's country when asked to do so." How would the Church respond to these two statements?
14. What is meant by the global option for the poor and global solidarity?
15. What role does a strong international system of justice have to play in world peacemaking?
16. Under what conditions would the Church support "forceful humanitarian intervention" into the internal affairs of another nation?
17. Discuss three steps rich nations can take to aid the development of poor nations.
18. How are the arms race and the arms trade an assault on the poor?
19. "If you want peace, work for justice." Explain the meaning of this statement.
20. How does the word development equate with peace?

RESEARCHING ON THE INTERNET

In view of the risks which humanity is facing in our time, all Catholics in every part of the world have a duty to proclaim and embody ever more fully the "Gospel of Peace," and to show that acknowledgment of the full truth of God is the first, indispensable condition for consolidating the truth of peace. God is Love which saves, a loving Father who wants to see his children look upon one another as brothers and sisters, working responsibly to place their various talents at the service of the common good of the human family.

—Pope Benedict XVI
("Message of His Holiness Pope Benedict XVI
for the Celebration of the World Day of Peace," 1 January 2006, No. 11)

1. Report on one of the headlines in the news at one of the following websites or their links:
   United States Catholic Bishops: www.usccb.org/index.shtml (search under "Social Justice Issues")
   Catholic Peace Fellowship: www.catholicpeacefellowship.org
2. Report on the history of the Peace Corps. See: www.peacecorps.gov

---

PRAYER REFLECTION

PRAYER FOR PEACE BY BLESSED POPE JOHN XXIII

Lord Jesus Christ, who are called the Prince of Peace, who are yourself our peace and reconciliation, who so often said, "Peace to you," grant us peace. Make all men and women witnesses of truth, justice, and brotherly love. Banish from their hearts whatever might endanger peace. Enlighten our rulers that they may guarantee and defend the great gift of peace. May all peoples on the earth become as brothers and sisters. May longed for peace blossom forth and reign always over us all. Amen.[15]

NOTES

1. Pope John Paul II, Message of His Holiness Pope John Paul II for the Celebration of the World Day of Peace, 1 January 2002, "No Peace Without Justice, No Justice Without Forgiveness," December 8, 2001.
2. Pope John Paul II, Message of His Holiness Pope John Paul II for the Celebration of the World Day of Peace, 1 January 2002, "No Peace Without Justice, No Justice Without Forgiveness," December 8, 2001.
3. Message of His Holiness Pope John Paul II for the Celebration of the World Day of Peace, 1 January 2004, "An Ever Timely Commitment: Teaching Peace," December 8, 2003.
4. Ibid., §10.
5. Found at Bruderhof Peacemakers' Guide <http://www.peacemakersguide.org/peace/Peacemakers/Thomas_Merton.htm.
6. Thomas Merton's *New Seeds of Contemplation* quoted by The Fellowship of Reconciliation "Peace Quotes."
7. United Nations World Food Programme, "Hunger Facts."

8. National Conference of Catholic Bishops, *Called to Global Solidarity* (Washington, D.C.: United States Catholic Conference, Inc., 1997), p. 4.

9. Pope John Paul II, Message of His Holiness Pope John Paul II for the Celebration of the World Day of Peace, 1 January 2002, "No Peace Without Justice, No Justice Without Forgiveness," December 8, 2001.

10. Pope John Paul II, Message of His Holiness Pope John Paul II for the Celebration of the World Day of Peace, 1 January 2005, "Do Not Be Overcome by Evil But Overcome Evil With Good," December 8, 2004.

11. Kevin Danaher, "A New Approach to the Third World Debt Crisis," Global Exchange.

12. Pope John Paul II, Message of His Holiness Pope John Paul II for the Celebration of the World Day of Peace, 1 January 2005, "Do Not Be Overcome by Evil But Overcome Evil With Good," December 8, 2004.

13. *In Solitary Witness: The Life and Death of Franz Jägerstätter* (Springfield, Illinois: Templegate Publishers, 1964). Revised edition, copyright 1986 by Gordon Zahn.

14. Ibid., pp. 229–230.

15. Found at "What the Church Teaches," *Our Sunday Visitor* <http://www.osv.com/whatthechurchteaches/prayingforpeace/papalprayers.asp>.

CHAPTER OVERVIEW

Work and the Worker
The Catholic tradition views work as an essential way to build a life, not simply a way to "get money."

A Christian View of Work
We are made in God's image and we share in the privilege of helping God in his work of creation.

Rights and Duties of Workers
Each of the three groups—workers, owners (employers), and the government—that make up a nation's economy have certain rights and responsibilities in the area of work.

Work and You: Toil, Job, Career, Vocation
Ideally work can be part of a vocation, a calling from God to do something special for him and his kingdom.

Lech Walesa
Polish labor leader Lech Walesa was instrumental in helping usher in the fall of communism in Europe.

Whatever your work is, put your heart into it as done for the Lord and not for human beings, knowing that the Lord will repay you by making you his heirs. It is Christ the Lord that you are serving.

—Colossians 3:23–24 (NJB)

JUSTICE AND WORK 9

WORK AND THE WORKER

This chapter focuses on **work** and the worker. The Church is concerned about work because work is integral to the life of most adults. Work consumes one third or more of our day and dominates our lifestyle. In 1973 in the United States, the average work week was 40 hours. Today, according to a study by the National Sleep Foundation, the average American employee works 46 hours each week. Additionally, 38 percent of those surveyed replied that they worked more than 50 hours per week.[1] What this means for leisure is very telling. Most other nations in the developed world grant their workers five or more weeks of vacation per year. But in the United States, the average vacation time adds up to only two or two-and-a-half weeks.[2]

Our Catholic tradition sees work not simply as a way to get money for a livelihood, but as an essential way to build a life. The American bishops told us:

Work is a way of supporting our family, realizing our dignity, promoting the common good, and participating in God's creation. This means often doing the ordinary well, making the most of our talents and opportunities, treating others fairly and with dignity, and working with integrity and creativity. (Everyday Christianity: To Hunger and Thirst for Justice, p. 3).

But while there is potential for work to be a positive expression of a person's gifts and talents, there is also the possibility for labor to be abused. Millions of workers in the United States and around the world are abused every day and forced to work long hours in unsafe conditions for extremely low wages. And these workers are not always adults.

The International Labor Organization estimates that 250 million children between the ages of five and fourteen work in developing countries—at least 120 million on a full time basis. Sixty-one percent of these are in Asia, 32 percent in Africa, and 7 percent in Latin America. Most working children in rural areas are found in agriculture; many children work as domestics; urban children work in trade and services, with fewer in manufacturing and construction.[3]

One of the most serious violations of children occurs in India where between 60 million and 115 million children are working, most in agriculture, others picking rags, making bricks, polishing gemstones, rolling cigarettes, packaging firecrackers, working as domestics, and weaving silk saris and carpets. The worst case of child labor on this subcontinent is bonded workers who toil as virtual slaves. In exchange for a loan to their parents, millions of these bonded children earn so little they are never free from debt. In effect

work—Sustained effort with the intent to produce or accomplish something.

they are condemned to lifelong impoverishment and illiteracy and are often crippled by the time they reach adulthood. An eleven-year-old girl, Yeramma, bonded at the age of seven for a loan of the equivalent of $35 U.S., which her parents needed for a hospital bill for her sister, describes her life:

> At 4:00 a.m. I got up and did silk winding. . . . I only went home once a week. I slept in the factory with two or three other children. We prepared the food there and slept in the space between the machines. The owner provided the rice and cut it from our wages. He would deduct the price. We cooked the rice ourselves. We worked twelve hours a day with one hour for rest. If I made a mistake—if I cut the thread—he would beat me. Sometimes [the owner] used vulgar language. Then he would give me more work.[4]

Adults also suffer exploitation. One example occurs in China where the workers in toy factories producing the popular Harry Potter, Monsters Inc., and Barbie toys toil under atrocious conditions. Workers, mostly women, labor for between 15 and 20 hours per day on wages of pennies per hour; forced unpaid overtime results in some workers making only 30 percent of the Chinese national minimum wage. Workers are subjected to unbearable working conditions of 104 degree temperatures and poisonous paint and solvent fumes wafting up from factory floors. Crowded and unsanitary dormitories await the workers for the few hours per day they are not on the job. Sick and pregnant workers are systematically fired. The long hours, sleep deprivation, and lack of time off result in women who are physically drained by the time they reach age thirty-five.[5]

Even American workers suffer. For example, the U.S. meat industry has been criticized by a human rights agency for permitting hazardous working conditions at meat plants and using illegal tactics to suppress employee efforts to report abuses and injuries. A recent 175-page report claimed that meat packers, who hold what is often cited as one of the most dangerous factory jobs in America, face a real danger of losing a limb or their lives because of unsafe work conditions. The report also documented how companies often deny workers' compensation to injured employees, "intimidate and fire workers who try

to organize, and exploit workers' immigrant status in order to keep them quiet about abuses."[6]

Why do these outrageous abuses exist? One reason alone: someone is making vast amounts of money through the exploitation of human beings.

The Church has taken a strong stand to denounce these kinds of horrendous situations involving labor. This chapter explores both positive and negative themes connected with work and asks you to reflect on how God might be calling you to spend your future in the world of work.

WHAT DO YOU PROMISE?

The year 2000 was anticipated worldwide as a turning point in history. Pope John Paul II declared this year to be a jubilee year, a holy year, a special time to remember that we live and work between the Incarnation of Jesus and his Second Coming at the end of time.

Recall that the Old Testament revealed that the Jubilee Year was a special time devoted to Yahweh. During this graced year, the Chosen People honored God as the true owner of creation. In covenant with a loving God, the people were expected to make a special effort to seek just and moral relations with all people. Pious Jews knew that they had to understand the land and its fruits—work, goods, finances, the economy, and everyday life—as part of their way of relating to God.

List and discuss some practical strategies for living justly in the family, school, and workplace.

Which pledge item would you personally find most difficult to keep? Why?

In preparation for this recent jubilee year, the American bishops challenged Catholic lay persons to recommit themselves to a life of charity and justice, to welcome immigrants and to help everyone—especially the "least of these" in our midst. In their *Everyday Christianity: To Hunger and Thirst for Justice* (1998), the bishops invited individuals, families, and parishes to sign a pledge as a concrete way to prepare for the new millennium. This pledge lists ways a person can live justly and lovingly.

Here is the Jubilee Pledge in a slightly rewritten format:

- Pray regularly for greater justice and peace in our world;
- Continue to learn even more about Catholic social teaching and its commitment to protect human life, stand for and by the poor, and care for God's beautiful creation;
- Reach across boundaries of religion, race, ethnicity, gender, and disabling conditions;
- Live justly in my family, school, and workplace;
- Serve those who are poor and vulnerable, sharing my time and talent;
- Give more generously to those in need at home and abroad;
- Advocate public policies that protect human life, promote human dignity, preserve God's creation, and build peace;
- Encourage others to work for greater charity, justice, and peace.

A CHRISTIAN VIEW OF WORK

A Christian theology of work finds its roots in the first two chapters of Genesis. These chapters reveal that we are made in God's image and that we share the privilege of helping God in his work of creation. Work has dignity because we share in God's own activity when we work. Pope John Paul II wrote:

The word of God's revelation is profoundly marked by the fundamental truth that man, created in the image of God, shares by his work in the activity of the creator . . . and continues to develop that activity, and perfects it as he advances further and further in the discovery of the recourses and values contained in the whole of creation (On Human Work, §25).

God invites us to share in his creative activity and also commands us to "Be fertile and multiply; fill the earth and subdue it" (Gn 1:28). By obeying God's command, humans actually realize their dignity as unique creatures who reflect God. In the words of Pope John Paul II:

In carrying out this mandate . . . every human being reflects the very action of the creator of the universe (On Human Work, *§4*).

TWO DIMENSIONS OF WORK: OBJECTIVE AND SUBJECTIVE (CCC, 2459–2461)

Work (labor) is defined as sustained effort with the intent to produce or accomplish something. Work can be manual or intellectual, paid or unpaid, performed by laborers or directed by managers. Farming, mining, and running a business are all examples of work. Being a good parent also takes work and is work. And, as you know all too well, it takes work to be a good student.

All of these activities, and ones like them, involve an *objective* dimension, that is, the product or outcome of our work. The **objective dimension of work** also includes the means we use to accomplish our task. Thus, tools, technology, machinery—as well as the products of research, farming, industry, and the many service-oriented activities—are part of the objective aspect of work.

The *subjective* aspect of work includes the subject, the human person, and his or her involvement in the work. The value of human work, and the basis of its dignity, rests in the person (the **subjective dimension of work**), not in the work being done (the objective aspect).

However true it may be that man is destined for work and called to it, in the first place work is "for man" and not man "for work" (On Human Work, *§6).*

The purpose of work, then, is to fulfill our own humanity and to benefit the humanity of those our work serves.

Think of the work done by an executive secretary. The secretary organizes meetings, types up reports, and screens phone calls, to mention a few tasks. This is the objective part of work. The person doing the work—in this case, the secretary, is the subject of the work. The true value of this work is how it helps the secretary to grow and to develop as a person and how the work done by the secretary benefits others in the organization. Take another example: a pediatrician. The pediatrician's doctoring of children is the objective aspect of the work. The pediatrician is the subject doing the work. The value of the work is tied into whether it enhances or detracts from the subject's dignity as a person and how it enhances or detracts from the dignity of the patients, those the doctor serves. Does it help the person develop as a human being? Does the person participate in God's creative activity, bringing benefit to humanity and order to creation?

The bottom line is this: work exists for human beings; human beings do not exist for work. Any political or economic system that makes the objective element of work its god violates the human person. For example, unbridled capitalism is immoral and contrary to God's plan because it makes profit its god, and it treats workers as mere instruments of production and not as persons with human dignity. Similarly, economic systems like communism that subordinate individual workers and their rights (the subjective dimension) to the work being done (the objective dimension) are likewise immoral.

objective dimension of work–THE PRODUCT OR OUTCOME OF WORK.

subjective dimension of work–THE HUMAN PERSON AND HIS OR HER INVOLVEMENT IN WORK.

As the person is the central focus of work, labor has priority over capital. (*Capital* refers to the natural resources God has given to us to use as well as to all the means of producing and developing them.) Human labor is the more important factor because it involves people and what they do:

*We must emphasize and give prominence to the primacy of man in the production process and the primacy of man over things. Everything contained in the concept of capital in the strict sense is only a collection of things. Man, as the subject of work and independent of the work he does—man alone is a person. This truth has important and decisive consequences (*On Human Work, §12).

A major result of this teaching is that workers and owners depend on each other. Therefore, Pope John Paul II recommended "joint ownership of the means of work, sharing by the workers in the management and/or profits of businesses, so-called shareholding by labor, etc." (*On Human Work,* §14). These recommendations reject the economic extremes of both capitalism and socialism. Extreme capitalism teaches the absolute right to private property. Extreme socialism (like communism) denies that individuals have any right to private property. In contrast, Christian teaching holds that people have the right to private property and that workers have the right to share in profits. However, Christian teaching also warns that private property is not an absolute right and that people come before profits. Everyone has the right to the created goods that God intended for the use of all his children.

POSITIVE DIMENSIONS OF WORK (CCC, 2426–2436)

Work is not an option. The *Catechism of the Catholic Church* teaches that "human work proceeds directly from persons created in the image of God and called to prolong the work of creation by subduing the earth, both with and for one another. Hence work is a duty" (2427). Saint Paul warned, "When we were with you, we instructed you that if anyone was unwilling to work, neither should that one eat" (2 Thes 3:10). It is moral to work; it is wrong if one can work and refuses to do so.

In *Economic Justice for All*, the American bishops stressed the threefold moral significance of work:

1. Work is a fundamental means for people to express and to develop themselves as human beings, unique creatures of God.

2. It is the ordinary way for us to provide for our material needs. This is especially true for heads of families who must feed, clothe, shelter, and educate their children.

3. "Finally, work enables people to contribute to the well-being of the larger community. Work is not only for one's self. It is for one's family, for the nation, and indeed for the benefit of the entire human family" (§97). Pope John Paul II said it this way: "Work serves to add to the heritage of the whole human family, of all the people living in the world" (*On Human Work,* §10).

In brief, work enables us to be and to become human, to provide for ourselves and our families, and to help the rest of society by sharing our gifts.

WORK AS A SHARE IN THE CROSS OF CHRIST

In your life as a student, you have discovered that all work, be it manual or intellectual, involves toil. Work is hard. The toil connected with work marks our journey on earth. In its own way, it announces our coming death. Scripture tells us:

By the sweat of your face shall you get bread to eat,
Until you return to the ground, from which you were taken (Gn 3:19).

However, sweat and toil, when united to the cross of Christ Jesus, can be a way for us to come closer to God. Through the effort of work, we can share in God's saving plan for the world. Work can help us participate in the work of our redemption. It is a way to better our friendship with Jesus and join him in his threefold mission of prophet, priest, and king:

This work of salvation came about through suffering and death on a cross. By enduring the toil of work in union with Christ crucified for us, man in a way collaborates with the Son of God for the redemption of humanity. He shows himself a true disciple of Christ by carrying the cross in his turn every day in the activity that he is called to perform (On Human Work, §27).

As Christians, we carry a small part of Christ's cross when we offer up the toil that is associated with work. However, thanks to our faith in the resurrection of Jesus Christ, through our work, we can find a glimmer of the new life that God has prepared for us.

From the *Catechism of the Catholic Church*:

By enduring the hardship of work in union with Jesus, the carpenter of Nazareth and the one crucified on Calvary, man collaborates in a certain fashion with the Son of God in his redemptive work. He shows himself to be a disciple of Christ by carrying the cross, daily, in the work he is called to accomplish. Work can be a means of sanctification and a way of animating earthly realities with the Spirit of Christ (2427).

JESUS THE WORKER

Jesus did not ignore work. His townsfolk knew him as a craftsman, most probably a carpenter like his foster father Joseph (Mk 6:2–3).

In his public life, Jesus' work was to spread news about the coming of God's reign. He did this work unceasingly by preaching (for example, Lk 4:14–22), teaching and exhorting (as in the Sermon on the Mount, Mt 5–7), and performing miracles (see Mt 8 for examples).

Jesus chose workers to travel alongside him, notably fishermen and even a tax collector.

In his parables on God's reign, Jesus often referred to a variety of human workers including shepherds, farmers, doctors, sowers, householders, servants, stewards, fishermen, merchants, laborers, scholars, and harvesters.

Jesus belonged to the working world and both appreciated and respected human work.

SCRIPTURE LINK

Read the following scripture passages. Answer the questions that follow.

Read Proverbs 6:6–11
1. Whom should we imitate when we work?
2. What will happen to us if we are too lazy?

Read Ecclesiastes 3:22
3. What good advice is given in this passage?

Read Matthew 24:45–51
4. What is the payoff for a vigilant worker?

Read 2 Thessalonians 3:10–12
5. What is the problem in the community that causes Paul's warning?
6. What instruction does he give?

Read John 4:34
7. What is Jesus' true work?

Read John 6:28–29
8. What is the work of Jesus' followers?

Read Matthew 6:25–34. What advice does Jesus give about work?

Read John 13:35. What mark of discipleship is mentioned? What are some practical ways this mark can be translated to the workplace?

JUST WAGE—At minimum, a wage high enough to meet food, clothing, and shelter needs, and to provide for transportation, education, and some form of recreation.

RIGHTS AND DUTIES OF WORKERS

Work is more than a way to make a living; it is a form of continuing participation in God's creation. If the dignity of work is to be protected, then the basic rights of workers must be respected—the right to productive work, to decent and fair wages, to organize and join unions, to private property, and to economic initiative. Respecting these rights promotes an economy that protects human life, defends human rights, and advances the well-being of all.[7]

There are three groups that typically factor in a nation's economy: workers, owners (employers), and the government. Specific rights and duties belong to each of these groups. For example, governments must see to it that laws protect individual freedom and private property. The government also is called to guarantee a stable money supply and efficient public services. It provides the security necessary for workers and business owners to earn their livelihood in honest and efficient ways.

Another task of the state is that of overseeing and directing the exercise of human rights in the economic sector. However, primary responsibility in this area belongs not to the state but to individuals and to the various groups and associations which make up society (CCC, 2431).

For their part, business owners have the right to make a profit for the risks they take in investing their money. These profits guarantee the future of the business which, in turn, creates employment opportunities for workers. However, profits are not supreme. The right to make profits is tempered by the obligation to do so responsibly. For example, in running their enterprises, employers must "consider the good of persons and not only the increase of profits" (CCC, 2432). In addition, businesses must consider that they are "responsible to society for the economic and ecological effects of their operations" (CCC, 2432).

As to the third group, workers, some principal rights follow: Workers have the right to employment, the right to a **just wage**, the right to rest, the right to a safe workplace, the right of association (e.g., labor parties), and, additionally, the right to a system of health care and social security.

THE RIGHT TO EMPLOYMENT

As noted above, everyone has the duty to work. The corresponding right to this duty is the right of *suitable employment for all who are capable of it. The opposite of a just and right situation in this field is unemployment, that is to say, the lack of work for those who are capable of it (On Human Work, §18).*

A job is critically important for two reasons. First, a job helps us earn the material means we need to make a living. This is especially important for parents who are obliged "to provide as far as possible for the physical . . . needs of their children" (CCC, 2252). Second, work helps us achieve human fulfillment. People experience a great loss of personal dignity when they cannot find jobs:

Unemployment almost always wounds its victim's dignity and threatens the equilibrium of his life. Besides the harm done to him personally, it entails many risks for his family (CCC, 2436).

A just society provides jobs for its people. In the words of the American bishops,

Full employment is the foundation of a just economy. The most urgent priority for domestic economic policy is the creation of new jobs with adequate pay and decent working conditions. We must make it possible as a nation for every one who is seeking a job to find employment within a reasonable amount of time. Our emphasis on this goal is based on the conviction that human work has a special dignity and is a key to achieving justice in society (Economic Justice for All, §136).

Because this is so, the bishops recommend government spending, tax, and monetary policies that promote full employment. They also encourage job-training and retraining programs; apprenticeship programs in the private sector supported by business, labor, and governmental agencies; and job-creation programs aimed to help the chronically unemployed and people with special needs. These new jobs should benefit society, for example, by rebuilding the infrastructure of the nation (roads, bridges, parks) or by erecting low-income housing (see *Economic Justice for All*, §156–165).

RIGHT TO A JUST WAGE

Workers have the right to just wages or payment for their work; in turn, they have the duty to provide "an honest day's work for an honest day's pay." Withholding or denying a person a just wage is a grave injustice:

A bread line during the Depression

In every case a just wage is the concrete means of verifying the justice of the whole socioeconomic system and, in any case, of checking that it is functioning justly (On Human Work, §19).

Church teaching, especially in the form of papal encyclicals, has consistently underscored the right of workers to a just wage. But many debate exactly what constitutes a "just" wage. Is a just wage a *living* wage for a single person? What about a *family* wage advocated by Pope John Paul II in *On Human Work*, that is, one that permits only one spouse to work? The pope wrote that wages should be high enough that women with children are not forced to work (*On Human Work*, §19).

In general terms, a just wage is one that will help workers meet their needs, and those of their family, and give them a degree of security. The Second Vatican Council's *The Church in the Modern World* explained it this way:

What job(s) have you held? Describe the employment process.

How can an employer put "people before profits"?

What is a career you are considering? Explain how this career can help to contribute to the well-being of society.

Payment for labor must be such as to furnish a man with the means to cultivate his own material, social, cultural, and spiritual life worthily, and that of his dependents (§67).

It is perhaps easier to describe what is not a just wage than what is a just wage. For example, the United States government would define an unjust wage as one that is below the poverty line for a family of four ($20,000 in 2006). (You can check for current figures at the United States Department of Health and Human Services website.) This is hardly a "living wage." Many people would consider it a mere subsistence wage, and

therefore unjust. In *Rerum Novarum* (*On the Condition of Workers*), Pope Leo XIII wrote

The wage shall not be less than enough to support a worker who is thrifty and upright (§63).

Today, at a minimum, this should include a wage high enough to meet food, clothing, and shelter needs, and to provide for transportation, education, and some form of recreation. This is in line with the thinking of Pope John Paul II, who wrote:

Just remuneration for the work of an adult who is responsible for a family means remuneration which will suffice for establishing and properly maintaining a family and for providing security for its future (On Human Work, *§19*).

The American bishops specify that a just wage also includes benefits like health-care coverage for workers and their dependents, life and disability insurance, a pension plan, and unemployment compensation. Related benefits include healthful working conditions, weekly rest, paid vacations, and emergency leave time, as well as reasonable security against dismissal (*Economic Justice for All*, §103).

Simply because employees agree to a certain wage does not mean it is just (see *CCC*, 2434). This is true because workers are sometimes unable to negotiate a fair wage in the face of profit-taking, downsizing, times of high unemployment, and so forth. Workers may have to settle for an unjust wage just to survive.

In his encyclical *On Christianity and Social Progress*, Pope John XXIII gave some guidance on how to determine what is just:

In determining what constitutes an appropriate wage, the following must necessarily be taken into account: first of all, the contribution of individuals to the economic effort; the economic state of the enterprises within which they work; the requirements of each community, especially as regards overall employment; finally, what concerns the common good of all peoples . . . (§71).

PLANNING A BUDGET

Using the information provided in the section on just wages, work on a budget for a family of four living in your area of the country. Assume the family has two children, three years old and seven years old. How much money would this family need to live on per year with a decent standard of living? What would be a just wage?

Basic Expenses	$ Amount
Rent/Mortgage	
Utilities (electric, gas, water)	
Phone	
Food	
Clothing	
Transportation	
Child Care	
Household (soap, laundry, toiletries, etc.)	
Entertainment	
Insurance (property, life, health)	
Taxes, if any (federal, social security, state, local)	
Monthly total	
Monthly total x 12 (yearly total)	

- Assume a work year of 2000 hours (50 weeks x 40 hours per week). What should be the minimum hourly wage for our family to meet its basic needs?
- What is the actual minimum wage mandated by law for this year?
- Is it possible for one wage earner to support this family on the minimum wage?
- Is it possible for an individual to live on the minimum wage?
- What are some possible remedies for this situation?
- Search and check your figures against the Catholic Campaign for Human Development's Poverty USA website. Click on the "Tour Poverty USA" link.

Why do you attend Mass when you do? Why do you not attend Mass when you don't?

Should employers permit employees to take off from work on holy days for their particular religions? Why or why not?

RIGHT TO REST

The first creation story (Gn 1–2:4) reveals that God rested after the work of creation was complete, sanctifying the seventh day of the week as a holy day. One practical consequence of this divinely appointed "Sabbath rest" is to underscore the right of workers to proper rest. Pope John Paul II taught that

this involves a regular weekly rest comprising at least Sunday and also a longer period of rest, namely the holiday or vacation taken once a year or possibly in several shorter periods during the year (On Human Work, §19).

A key purpose of "Sabbath rest" is to bolster the dignity of workers. Humans are not draft animals. God does not intend us to be slaves to overwork which often leads to physical and psychological breakdown. Pope John Paul II warned of the dangers of consumerism:

All of us experience firsthand the sad effects of this blind submission to pure consumerism: in the first place a crass materialism, and at the same time a radical dissatisfaction, because one quickly learns—unless one is shielded from the flood of publicity and the ceaseless and tempting offers of products—that the more one possesses the more one wants, while deeper aspirations remain unsatisfied and perhaps even stifled *(On Social Concern, §28).*

Rest from work can and should elevate the human spirit by giving people the time on the Lord's day to worship a loving God in humility and thanksgiving for all the gifts bestowed during the previous week. Catholics also have the obligation to participate in Mass on Sunday. Resting from the toil of a job is also a great opportunity to strengthen family life, to spend time with friends, and to cultivate the mind.

THE RIGHT TO A SAFE WORKPLACE

Among the rights that employers must guarantee for their employees is "the right to a working environment and to manufacturing processes which are not harmful to the workers' physical health or to their moral integrity." In addition, workers have a right to health care, "especially in the case of accidents at work" (*On Human Work,* §19).

Many jobs are dangerous, but for a recent year, the Bureau of Labor Statistics listed the following as being the ten most hazardous jobs in America: timber cutters, fishers, pilots, structural metal workers, driver-sales workers, roofers, electrical power installers, farm occupations, construction workers, and truck drivers. Incidentally, note that a pizza deliverer, a job held by many teens, would fall under the driver-sales worker category, the fifth most dangerous job in the country.[8]

Safety standards are in place and laws have been passed to protect the health and safety of workers in thousands of occupations. For example, the Occupational Safety and Health Act (OSHA) has helped to improve working conditions for millions of American workers. Since 1970, it has saved close to 300,000 lives. Despite its success, the AFL-CIO reports that each year:

- More than six million U.S. workers are injured or become sick on the job; 50,000 die from occupational illness; and nearly 6,000 are killed on the job.[9]
- On an average day, 152 workers lose their lives because of workplace injuries and diseases; another 12,877 are injured.
- Immigrant workers suffer a disproportionate amount of workplace injuries, illnesses, and fatalities. This is so because employers hire them at the lowest possible wages to perform the most undesirable and dangerous jobs. These workers are unaware of their legal rights because of language and cultural barriers and receive no training in safety and health. Additionally, workers who do not have immigration status are particularly fearful of speaking out.[10]

A key reason for these unacceptable figures is the lack of adequate personnel to enforce safety laws on the books. Occupational Safety and Health Administration (OSHA) is a small agency. It lacks both the staff and funding to supervise the safety and health of the approximately 100 million workers in the 7.9 million workplaces under its jurisdiction. In a recent year, federal OSHA had less than 900 safety and health inspectors. This means that workplaces can be inspected, on average, once every 106 years.

Other reasons for the lack of job safety include "increased hours of work, intensification of work due to downsizing, increased pace of work and other changes in technologies and work processes. Many of these changes have been associated with repetitive strain injuries, stress, workplace violence and even fatalities."[11]

Regardless of the reasons for unsafe working conditions, the American bishops remind us that "the dignity of workers requires . . . healthful working conditions . . . if workers are to be treated as persons rather than simply as a 'factor of production'" (*Economic Justice for All*, §103).

THE RIGHT OF ASSOCIATION

Recall the social-justice principles of solidarity and subsidiarity. Solidarity reminds us that we are social beings who belong to each other. Subsidiarity holds that grassroots organizations should handle their own problems if possible. Both of these principles support the foundational human *right of association*, one recognized by Pope John XXIII in *Peace on Earth*,

Men are by nature social, and consequently they have the right to meet together and to form associations with their fellows (§23).

Applying the right of association to working people means that workers have the right to form unions to defend and secure other rights due them—like fair wages, decent working conditions, adequate rest, and so forth. The Second Vatican Council affirmed this right:

Among the basic rights of the human person must be counted the right of freely founding labor unions. These unions should be truly able

to represent the workers and to contribute to the proper arrangement of economic life. Another such right is that of taking part freely in the activity of unions without risk of reprisal (The Church in the Modern World, §68).

The American bishops agreed that it is seriously wrong to inflict reprisals on people who join unions:

No one may deny the right to organize without attacking human dignity itself. Therefore, we firmly oppose organized efforts . . . to break existing unions and prevent workers from organizing. . . . We vehemently oppose violations of the freedom to associate, wherever they occur, for they are an intolerable attack on social solidarity (Economic Justice for All, §104-105).

Pope John Paul II observed that unions are vitally important today, especially in industrialized nations, because "they are a mouthpiece for the struggle for social justice" (*On Human Work*, §20). Unions not only help secure worker rights, but they also serve as an outlet for workers to express themselves, "to share in a fully human way in the life of their place of employment" (*On the Hundredth Anniversary of Rerum Novarum*, §15).

As to their duties, unions and their members must

contribute to the well-being of the whole community and should avoid pressing demands whose fulfillment would damage the common good and the rights of more vulnerable members of society (Economic Justice for All, §106).

In the words of Pope John Paul II, a goal of unions is not simply to have more, but to be more, that is, "to realize their humanity more fully in every respect" (*On Human Work*, §20).

Workers also have the right to strike. By definition, a strike is a temporary work stoppage by employees to secure higher pay or better working conditions from employers. Given the "proper conditions and within just limits," strikes are morally acceptable. John Paul II wrote:

Workers should be assured the right to strike, without being subjected to personal penal sanctions for taking part in a strike. While admitting that it is a legitimate means, we must at the same time emphasize that a strike remains, in a sense, an extreme means. It must not be abused; it must not be abused especially for "political" purposes (On Human Work, §20).

An example of an abusive strike would be to shut down the essential services of a community (for example, hospitals), thereby gravely endangering the welfare of humans.

In summary, companies should work with unions to empower workers to feel a sense of ownership in their places of employment. Policies like profit-sharing, employee shareholding, employee participation in determining working conditions, and cooperative company ownership can enhance worker morale, reduce conflict, increase productivity and profits, and ensure job security (see *Economic Justice for All*, §300).

STRIKES: PERMISSIBLE OR NOT?

Recourse to a strike is morally legitimate when it cannot be avoided, or at least when it is necessary to obtain a proportionate benefit. It becomes morally unacceptable when accompanied by violence, or when objectives are included that are not directly linked to working conditions or are contrary to the common good

—CCC, 2435.

You decide: as a last resort to win better wages, or more humane working conditions, would it be permissible for . . .

- a pro basketball team to refuse to play any games until player demands are met?
- air traffic controllers to refuse to do their jobs?
- a police union to instruct its members to stay home?
- teachers to go on a walkout?
- city sanitation workers to refuse to collect rubbish?
- nurses in a hospital to go on strike?
- students to stage a walkout to protest the firing of a popular teacher?

HEALTH CARE: A RIGHT ASSOCIATED WITH WORK

Catholic teaching holds that health care is a basic human right because it is essential to human dignity. The *Catechism of the Catholic Church* puts it this way:

Concern for the health of its citizens requires that society help in the attainment of living-conditions that allow them to grow and reach maturity: food and clothing, housing, health care, basic education, employment, and social assistance (2288).

Yet, for a recent year (2003),

- The number of people without health insurance was 45 million. This is 15.6 percent of the population.[12]
- Another 40 million lack insurance during some part of every year.
- Another 80 million are only partially covered. Most of those who lack health insurance have full time jobs.[13]
- The Institute of Medicine reports that the lack of health insurance causes 18,000 unnecessary deaths in the United States. It also costs the country $65 billion to $130 billion annually.[14]
- Even those who are insured worry about losing their health benefits because of layoffs and cutbacks in health benefits by employers.

Those who are fortunate enough to have health coverage receive it primarily from private insurance, of which more than half is employer-provided. Government-sponsored programs for the aged (Medicare) and the poor and disabled (Medicaid) account for the other two sources of medical coverage in America.

In January of 2004, the Institute of Medicine came out in support of universal health coverage for all citizens. They offered the following guiding principles for working to universal coverage:

- Health care coverage should be universal.
- Health care coverage should be continuous.
- Health care coverage should be affordable to individuals and families.
- The health insurance strategy should be affordable and sustainable for society.
- Health insurance should enhance health and well-being by promoting access to high-quality care that is effective, efficient, safe, timely, patient-centered, and equitable.[15]

Health care costs have far outstripped the rise in inflation because of expensive high-tech equipment, expensive medical treatments for certain diseases, an aging population, an inefficient health-care delivery system, and fraud.

A hotly debated political issue in the last decade or so is how to contain the costs of health care and how to provide universal coverage. Price controls have led to shorter hospital stays and cost-effective treatments that sometimes have harmed patients.

Based on the information in the text, answer the following questions.

Which of the following do you think would be the best health care system?

- Requiring employers to provide health insurance, with the government providing coverage for those not covered in the workplace.
- Requiring individuals to obtain coverage and providing tax credits to help them pay for it.
- Establishing a single-payer system administered by the federal government that would eliminate insurance premiums and enrollment qualifications but require increased taxes.

How would each of these proposals fare under the principles recommended by the Institute of Medicine?

"Health care is a basic need and a fundamental human right." In light of this statement, should our society allow health-care facilities and insurance companies to be profit-makers?

Various rationing plans have been proposed. Health Maintenance Organizations (HMOs) have grown. HMOs have done a generally good job of emphasizing prevention. However, they have been increasingly criticized for limiting the choice of doctors and for implementing cost-reduction strategies that often fail to respond adequately to individual patient needs.

Should the current system be scrapped to move to a "single-payer" system overseen by a governmental agency? One such plan would have a medical board determine prices for particular procedures and drugs. If health care professionals want to charge more than the set limits, the patient would have to pay "out of pocket."

In your opinion, how do a job, profession, and career differ?

What do you think are some possible vocations that God has in mind for you?

WHAT'S IN A NAME?

Note the definition of the following terms as given in *Webster's Encyclopedic Dictionary of the English Language*, revised edition (New York: Gramercy Books, 1996).

Toil: Hard and continuous work; exhausting labor or effort.
Labor: Productive activity, especially for the sake of economic gain.
Work: Exertion or effort directed to produce or accomplish something; labor; toil (54 definitions of this term are given).
Job: Anything a person is expected or obliged to do; duty; responsibility.
Career: An occupation or profession, especially one requiring special training; followed as one's lifework.
Profession: A vocation requiring knowledge of some department of learning or science.
Vocation: A particular occupation, business, or profession; calling.

WORK AND YOU: TOIL, JOB, CAREER, VOCATION

Unless you belong to a very wealthy family or hit a lotto-type jackpot, one day you will have to enter the work world to provide for your material needs. Even if you do not have to work, you will likely want to work. Work provides a chance for you to develop your personality and to grow as a fuller human person. It also helps you contribute to the common good, that is, to make society a better place for everyone. Through our work we share in God's creative activity and help to develop this beautiful world he gave for our benefit.

As a Christian youth, your best preparation for the world of work is to study hard during your high-school years. This is the time in your life to learn and to practice the fundamental skills that you will need to survive and thrive in an increasingly complex society. These are also the years to learn what you are good at and what interests you so you can begin to explore possible careers and professions.

Ideally, your work will not be mere toil or simply a job. One hopes that you will choose a career or profession that matches your interests and abilities. Hopefully you will even see your work as a vocation, a calling from God to do something special for him and his kingdom. Some vocations are religious calls from God in which men and women serve God and the Christian community as priests, sisters, or brothers. Marriage and the single life are also callings from God. These last two vocations especially lend themselves to a variety of occupations through which people can gain a livelihood, fulfill their humanity, and contribute to the common good.

Unfortunately, our contemporary society sometimes neglects to appreciate the important vocation of parenthood, especially of mothers who have the awesome responsibility of bringing forth new life. Full-time mothers are sometimes made to feel that they are less valuable as persons because they are not in the work force. However, the Catholic tradition greatly values the role of mothers and teaches that society needs to respect their irreplaceable contribution. Pope John Paul II wrote:

Experience confirms that there must be a social re-evaluation of the mother's role, of the toil connected with it, and of the need that children have for care, love and affection in order that they may develop into responsible, morally and religiously mature and psychologically stable persons. It will redound to the credit of society to make it possible for a mother—without inhibiting her freedom, without psychological or practical discrimination, and without penalizing her as compared with other women—to devote herself to taking care of her children and educating them in accordance with their needs, which vary with age. Having to abandon these tasks in order to take up paid work outside the home is wrong from the point of view of the good of society and of the family when it contradicts or hinders these primary goals of the mission of a mother (On Human Work, §19).

CHOOSING A CAREER

How many times have you heard, "What do you want to be when you grow up?" This is a good time in your life to begin seriously considering this question and also asking yourself what God might have in mind for you.

In this chapter, we have been looking at the Church's teaching on work and the rights of workers. Have you been thinking about your own future and how you might best use your talents to make a living? What kind of work would you like to do?

Here is something else to consider: Have you ever thought about how the career you will choose will help promote justice? If so, how would you practically implement your plan? How do you begin the process of career selection?

These are all good questions. It is never too early to begin looking into your future. Some ideas to get you started follow:

Pray. As God has a plan for you, you need to stay in touch with him throughout your life. Ask for the guidance of the Holy Spirit to help you know how you are supposed to use your gifts for other people.

Determine your interests and abilities. List what you do well. List what kinds of activities you are interested in (some ideas are provided in the box below).

SKILLS: What I'm good at (e.g., working math problems, mechanical ability, writing, sports, art, music, analyzing complex problems, leading others, listening, helping people with their problems, etc.). In your journal, list six skills you are really good at.

INTERESTS: What enthuses me (e.g., being outdoors, reading, working with my hands, growing things, analyzing movies, tinkering with cars, cooking, socializing with others, playing sports, helping others, teaching others, etc.). In your journal, list six interests that you have.

Research types of jobs that match your skills and interests. Check with the Internet, libraries, career and guidance counselors, family friends, relatives, and neighbors who work in your field of interests.

Gain experience. Search for summer or after-school jobs in your area of interest. Do volunteer work and learn from professionals in the field.

Work on a long-range career goal. Doing so entails finding an occupation that matches your skills and interests, finding out the educational requirements necessary to enter this career, researching some schools or programs that can get you the education you need to enter your chosen career, and mapping out some strategies on how to achieve your goal.

SOME JOB TITLES FROM THE UNITED STATES GOVERNMENT'S OCCUPATIONAL OUTLOOK HANDBOOK

PROFESSIONAL SPECIALTY OCCUPATIONS

- Life scientists (e.g., agricultural scientists, foresters and conservation scientists)
- Lawyers and judges
- Social scientists (e.g., economists, psychologists, urban and regional planners)
- Social and recreation workers (e.g., human service workers, recreation workers, social workers)
- Clergy
- Teachers, librarians, and counselors
- Health diagnosing practitioners (e.g., dentists, physicians)
- Health assessment and treating occupations (e.g., occupational therapists, registered nurses, speech-language pathologists)

SERVICE OCCUPATIONS

- Correctional officers, firefighting occupations, police, detectives
- Health service occupations (like medical and dental assistants, nursing aides, etc.)

These job titles, and many others included in the *Handbook,* seem to be more directly related to careers that promote and defend human dignity and life, protect the environment, defend rights, promote truth, or care for people's physical, psychological, or spiritual needs.

But, in truth, every respectable occupation calls us to be just in our dealings with others and to promote the cause of justice. Whether a person is an architect or engineer, carpenter or steelworker or roofer, sales clerk or insurance broker, manager or typist or secretary, a bus driver or postal clerk, auto repair mechanic or plumber, musician or filmmaker or designer—all workers are called to justice. This involves sharing one's talents, promoting human life, supporting the common good of all, defending the weak in our midst, treating others as equals and defending their rights, acting as good stewards, and so forth.

Visit the U.S. Department of Labor website to investigate careers that might match your interests. Report on the qualifications, typical pay, and job prospects for two careers that might interest you. For further information, check the *Occupational Outlook Handbook,* found at www.bls.gov/oco/home.htm

INVESTIGATING A SERVICE PROFESSION

Choose one of the Professional Specialty Occupations or Service Occupations from the article on page 222 and arrange to shadow a person who works in that field while they are on the job. Write a summary of your experience. Tell whether or not you could see yourself working in that field in the future. Also, interview the person you worked with and record his or her answers to the following questions:

1. How do you see your job as helping others?
2. How do you consider your job a vocation?
3. What is the major ethical issue facing your career? How do you personally deal with it?
4. How are worker rights honored at your place of employment? What are some of the current issues confronting the workers?
5. What is your level of job satisfaction? that of your coworkers?
6. Would you recommend that I pursue this career? Why or why not?

CASE STUDY: CHANGE OF CAREER?

Background:

Carlos, one of the top engineers in Mexico, took a job in the United States to work on the space shuttle program. Soon after, Carlos found out that some of his work would also be applied to the defense industry and the construction of nuclear arms.

Debate:

- What should Carlos do?
- If Carlos quits his job, his family in Mexico will be without their primary salary earner. Should this make a difference in Carlos's decision?
- What kind of positive meaning can be drawn from the decision you chose for Carlos?
- What is the value of Carlos's current job?

LECH WALESA (1943–)
CHAMPION OF WORKERS' RIGHTS

Lech Walesa, born on September 29, 1943, in Popowo, Poland, embodies the virtues of faith, courage, patriotism, and spontaneity. Along with Pope John Paul II and the former Soviet leader Mikhail Gorbachev, Lech Walesa deserves credit for helping to usher in the fall of communism in Europe. This resulted in the end of the Cold War that had threatened world security since the close of World War II.

The son of a carpenter, Walesa was only an average student at his parish school. He received a vocational education and in 1967 began work as an electrician at the huge Lenin Shipyard in Gdansk, Poland. There, in 1970, he witnessed worker riots in which the police killed a number of demonstrators. When protests broke out against the communist government in 1976, Walesa got involved in anti-government union activities. As a result he lost his job at the Lenin Shipyard. He worked sporadically the next four years, fixing electrical machinery at state-run farms.

In the late 1970s, Poland's economy nose dived, fueled by an ever-growing international debt. To save the sinking economy, the communist government imposed wage controls and price increases. This sparked nationwide protests, including an explosive scene at the Lenin Shipyard. There, on August 14, 1980, Lech Walesa returned to his former place of employment and, in a famous scene, climbed over the shipyard fence to join the occupation strike. With his quick wit, down-to-earth speaking style, and attractive personality, Lech emerged as the leader of a strike committee that eventually inspired other factories from various industries to strike. Walesa's leadership led to something unthinkable in a communist country: the recognition of trade unions and the right to strike.

The breath of freedom and respect for worker rights fanned deep solidarity among Polish workers, a movement that led to the *Solidarnosc* (Solidarity) union nationwide. Within months, Solidarity grew to ten million members, a quarter of the Polish populace, with Walesa as its undisputed leader.

For the next sixteen months, Walesa tried to use moderate means to help his union coexist with the dictatorial communist regime, always under the threatening and watchful eye of the Soviet leaders. Unfortunately, the air of freedom proved too heady for the repressive Polish regime. It declared martial law on December 13, 1981, outlawed Solidarity, and arrested its leaders, including Walesa, who was interred for eleven months.

But the movement would not die. Walesa remained its symbol. He was awarded the Nobel Peace Prize in 1983, an act greatly criticized by the Polish government. Walesa sent his wife, Danuta, to Oslo, Norway, to receive the prize on his behalf. He feared that the government would not allow him back into the country if he went himself. President Ronald Reagan praised the choice of Walesa, "It's a victory for those who seek to enlarge the human spirit over those who seek to crush it." In a spirit of generosity, Walesa donated the Nobel Prize's monetary award to a fund the Catholic Church had been trying to set up to help the country's farmers.

With support from the Holy Father and the U.S. government, Walesa served the Solidarity Movement as its underground leader. A man of deep faith, he said that he could not have endured the struggle without his faith, especially in the face of a lucrative bribe the government offered him to give up the struggle for justice and for worker rights. He credited the Blessed Mother who helped him stay the course, strengthening him to endure a constant barrage of governmental harassment tactics waged against him.

Lech Walesa's fidelity and courage paid off. In 1988, Walesa joined yet another important worker's strike in the Gdansk shipyard. A few months later, Walesa and other Solidarity leaders wrested concessions from the Polish authorities that led to semi-free elections. Solidarity triumphed in these elections, resulting in a Solidarity-led government. This remarkable revolution of persistent championing of human rights inspired other communist governments to follow suit, thus ushering in the collapse of the Soviet Empire in 1989 and the subsequent years.

In 1990, in a landslide victory, Lech Walesa won Poland's first direct presidential election. As president, he converted Poland's economy into a free-market system and oversaw Poland's first free parliamentary elections. He narrowly lost his reelection bid in 1995 due, in some measure, to his confrontational style of leadership, his plain speech, and his strong Catholic and pro-life views that alienated some of his fellow citizens.

However, Lech Walesa's position in world history is secure. He was instrumental in leading the strike in the Lenin Shipyard that led to the birth of Solidarity. He stayed the course through persecution to help Solidarity survive martial law. This led eventually to the democratization of Poland, the collapse of communism, and the demise of the Cold War.

Read more about Lech Walesa at these websites:

www.time.com/time/time 100/leaders/profile/ walesa.html

http://nobelprize.org/ peace/laureates/1983/ walesa_bio.html

How did Walesa act on his convictions?

How is your faith important in helping you do the right thing despite adversity?

SOCIAL SECURITY OR SOCIAL INSECURITY?

In recent years, there has been much talk about reforming the Social Security system in the United States to keep it from becoming insolvent in the future—at the time you will become a senior citizen. Many proposals have been discussed and debated.

In their document entitled *A Commitment to All Generations: Social Security and the Common Good*, the American bishops have applied the principles of social justice derived from Catholic teaching to this ongoing discussion. They remind us that to maintain human dignity, the sick, disabled, and elderly in our community have a right to security. Because we live for and with each other, we must all work across generational and economic lines for the sake of the common good, and for the general welfare of the entire human family.

It is true that families and community groups have a role to play. But the principle of subsidiarity also requires that governmental institutions promote the common good and help protect human dignity. Although private pension plans and personal savings help workers and their families be secure against unemployment, sickness, accident, old age, and death, they are often not enough without the help of government-supported social insurance. This is especially true for average- and low-wage earners and their families. And we must always remember that our commitment to justice requires that we first look out for the poor and vulnerable in our midst.[16]

With the above principles in mind, the Catholic Church teaches that the government should participate in an insurance program to protect citizens against illness, disability, unemployment, and old age. The Church urges all Americans to support such a social security system and to work at making it even more fair and solvent by applying the following principles to any reform proposals:

- Any proposed change in Social Security must not put at risk those individuals and families whose resources are already limited.
- The disability and survivors' portions of the Social Security program should remain linked to the retirement portion.
- If the tax structure must be changed, it should be weighted in favor of the poor. The more affluent should shoulder more of the Social Security tax burden.

- There are some glaring inequities toward unmarried women in the current system. These must be fixed.
- To help support the Social Security program, it is only fair for employees from all sectors of the economy (for example, state employees) to come under the umbrella of the Social Security system. This would promote the common good by increasing the number of workers who would contribute to the support of the program.[17]

Research two current Social Security reform proposals offered by various politicians or economists. Judge their value in light of the five criteria outlined by the bishops. Judge especially how well they meet the needs of the poorest in our midst. Then do one of the following:

- Write a letter to a newspaper expressing your views on one of the proposals under consideration.
- Write to a politician voicing your opinion on one of the proposals.

CHAPTER SUMMARY

- Workers have dignity because they are made in God's image and likeness. Workers are the *subjective* aspect of work; what they produce is the *objective* dimension. Work exists for human beings, not the other way around. Therefore, the subjective dimension (humans) always outranks what is accomplished or how it is accomplished (the objective dimension). Any economic or political system that makes profit supreme (like unbridled capitalism), or subordinates the individual to the system (like Marxism), is immoral.
- We have a duty to work if we are able to do so. Through work we express and develop ourselves as human beings, provide for our material needs, and contribute to the well-being of society.
- The toil of work can be redemptive if we join it to the cross of Jesus Christ, our Redeemer. We look to Jesus Christ who worked as a craftsman and spent his public life laboring to spread the gospel. He chose workers to join him and often referred to various kinds of work in his teachings.
- Governments have a duty to protect individual freedom and private property, to guarantee a stable money supply, and to provide efficient public services. Governments must also pass laws that help workers and businesses earn an honest living in an efficient manner.
- Business owners have a right to make profits. However, they must do so responsibly. They must consider the good of persons and take responsibility for the economic and ecological effects of their efforts.
- Workers have the right to employment. Therefore, governments and businesses have a duty to adopt policies that encourage full employment.
- Workers also have a right to a just wage that meets basic needs and allows for transportation, education, and some form of recreation. A just wage is a living wage. Furthermore, society should consider adopting a family wage that would allow a parent to stay home and care for the family's children, a nation's most precious asset. For their part, workers must give "a full day's work for a full day's wages."
- Workers are entitled to reasonable rest and a safe work environment. They also have the right to form unions to serve as a mouthpiece in the struggle for social justice. In extreme situations, workers have the right to strike; however, they may not do so if the common good would be severely and dangerously harmed.
- The Church supports the right to universal health care for all workers and all other people because health care is an absolute necessity in the exercise of the right to life.
- God calls each of us to develop our talents so that we might one day use them to provide for our material needs, to share our gifts with others, and to grow more fully as humans made in God's image. The high-school years are a good time to begin exploring career options. Prayer will also help

a person discern if God might be calling him or her to serve others in some profession that is directly related to the promotion of justice.

- Lech Walesa is an outstanding example of a Catholic worker who exercised his rights and helped bring about the collapse of twentieth century communism. His religious faith and devotion to the Blessed Mother helped him stay the course as he fought for human rights.

REVIEW QUESTIONS

1. Why does work have dignity?
2. What are the two dimensions of work? Which has priority? Why?
3. What does it mean to say that labor has priority over capital? Give some examples of how this principle can be abused.
4. According the American bishops, what is the threefold significance of work?
5. How can the "toil of work" be transformed into spiritual meaning?
6. What are some things we learn from Jesus about work?
7. What are the principal duties of governments concerning work?
8. List and discuss some rights and duties of business owners.
9. What societal duty corresponds to everyone's right to employment?
10. Discuss some factors that go into a just wage.
11. Distinguish between a just wage, a living wage, and a family wage.
12. Explain what you think would be fair to give workers in regard to the right to rest.
13. Why do workers have the right to unionize?
14. Explain when a strike might be justified. Give an example of when it might be unjustified.
15. Why does everyone have the right to health care?
16. List some steps you can take to choose a career.
17. No matter what job you will one day have, you must always be a just worker. What does this mean?
18. Why is Lech Walesa known as a champion of workers' rights?

RESEARCHING ON THE INTERNET

If you are called to be a street sweeper, sweep streets even as Michelangelo painted, or Beethoven composed music, or Shakespeare wrote poetry. Sweep streets so well that all the hosts of heaven and earth will pause to say, "Here lived a great street sweeper who did his job well."

—Martin Luther King, Jr.

1. Report on one of the issues confronting farm workers today at Catholic Migrant Farm Worker Network: www.cmfn.org.
2. Read and report on a labor justice issue at SALT: http://salt.claretianpubs.org/issues/work/index.html.
3. Report on an issue of current concern at Jobs with Justice: www.jwj.org.
4. Record in your journal three key quotes from Catholic teaching on work, found at the Office of Social Justice for the Diocese of Minneapolis-St. Paul: www.osjspm.org/cst/q_work.htm.
5. Read and summarize *Laborem Exercens* (*On Human Work*) at: www.vatican.va/edocs/ENG0217/_INDEX.HTM.
6. Read and report on one of the issues listed on the National Labor Committee home page: www.nlc-net.org/news.
7. Investigate the Bureau of Labor Statistics' website. Report on a topic of interest: www.bls.gov.

PRAYER REFLECTION

Pope Saint Pius X composed this "Prayer to Saint Joseph," the patron saint of workers:

Glorious Saint Joseph, model of all who are devoted to labor, obtain for me the grace to work in the spirit of penance in expiation of my many sins; to work conscientiously by placing love of duty above my inclinations; to gratefully and joyously deem it an honor to employ and to develop by labor the gifts I have received from God, to work methodically, peacefully, and in moderation and patience, without ever shrinking from it through weariness or difficulty to work; above all, with purity of intention and unselfishness, having unceasingly before my eyes death and the account I have to render of time lost, talents unused, good not done, and vain complacency in success, so baneful to the work of God. All for Jesus, all for Mary, all to imitate thee, O patriarch Saint Joseph! This shall be my motto for life and eternity.[18]

NOTES

1. "How Long Is the Average Work Week in the U.S.?" reported at Library Spot.
2. Arthur Frommer, "The Scandal of American Vacation Time," © 2005 Newsweek Budget Travel, Inc.
3. Human Rights Watch, "Children's Rights: Child Labor" <http://www.hrw.org/children/labor.htm> (23 February 2005).
4. Human Rights Watch, *Small Change: Bonded Labor in India's Silk Industry*, January 2003, Vol. 15, No. 2, p. 5.
5. National Labor Committee, "Harry Potter and Monsters Inc. Toys Spell Misery for Chinese Workers," 2 January 2002.
6. Reuters, "Human Rights Group Blasts U.S. Meat Industry," January 25, 2005.
7. United States Conference of Catholic Bishops, *Sharing Catholic Social Teaching: Challenges and Directions* (Washington, D.C.: USCCB, 1998), p. 5.
8. Les Christie, "America's Most Dangerous Jobs," October 13, 2003, *CNN/Money*.
9. AFL-CIO, "Safety and Health at Work" <http://www.aflcio.org/yourjobeconomy/safety/>.
10. AFL-CIO, "Facts about Worker Safety and Health" <http://www.aflcio.org/yourjobeconomy/safety/tools/factsaboutwsh.cfm> (2 February 2005).
11. Ibid.
12. U.S. Department of Commerce, U.S. Census Bureau News, August 24, 2004.
13. Campaign for National Health Program Now.
14. The Associated Press, "Panel Calls for Universal Health Insurance," January 14, 2004, MSNBC.
15. Institute of Medicine of the National Academies, *Insuring America's Health: Principles and Recommendations*, January 14, 2004.
16. Administrative Board of the United States Catholic Conference, *A Commitment to All Generations: Social Security and the Common Good* (Washington, D.C.: United States Catholic Conference, Inc., 1999), pp. 5–8.
17. Ibid., pp. 9–15.
18. Found at Catholic Culture™ website. Original source credited as Francis L. Filas, S.J., *The Family for Families* (Milwaukee, Wisconsin: Bruce Publishing Company, 1947).

CHAPTER OVERVIEW

God's Grandeur Threatened

How we treat the environment is a justice issue that affects everyone.

Our World

We are called to be good stewards of the world and its resources following the model of Jesus, who taught what it means to be a good steward.

The Scope of the Environmental Problem

The earth is a single ecosystem and threats against it have reached crisis proportions.

Church and World Teaching on the Environment

The American bishops' pastoral statement Renewing the Earth offers a synopsis of themes of ecological responsibility. World leaders have also responded to the issue.

Saint Francis of Assisi

Saint Francis embraced all of nature as part of his love for God's family and is the patron saint of ecology.

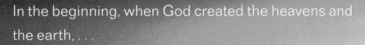

In the beginning, when God created the heavens and
the earth, . . .
God said, "Let the earth bring forth vegetation. . . ."
Then God said, "Let the water teem with an abundance
of living creatures, and on the earth let birds fly
beneath the dome of the sky. . . ."
Then God said: "Let us make man in our image, after
our likeness. Let them have dominion. . . ."
God looked at everything he had made, and he found it
very good.

—Genesis 1:1, 11, 20, 26, 31

JUSTICE AND THE ENVIRONMENT 10

GOD'S GRANDEUR THREATENED

In southern Ireland, there is a small church where every window but one has stained glass depicting Jesus and his saints. When worshipers look through the one plain-glass window they see in the foreground a stunning view of a blue lake with emerald-green islets and in the background a breathtaking range of purple hills. Inscribed under the window is the biblical verse, "The heavens declare the glory of God, and the firmament showeth his handiwork."[1] Yes, we have a beautiful world—"charged with the grandeur of God," in the words of Jesuit poet Gerard Manley Hopkins.

But our world currently faces an ecological crisis:

> Today, the dramatic threat of ecological breakdown is teaching us the extent to which greed and selfishness—both individual and collective—are contrary to the order of creation, an order which is characterized by mutual interdependence (The Ecological Crisis: A Common Responsibility).

The environmental atrocities against our world are too numerous to mention. Consider the following sampling:

- Mexico City, the most populous urban region in the world, suffers from life-threatening air pollution most days of the year. Dust storms plague the city, kicking up dry refuse. The exhaust from millions of cars and thousands of factories spew carbon monoxide, sulfur dioxide, and other contaminants into the atmosphere, making breathing the air for one day the equivalent of smoking one pack of cigarettes. All of these contaminants are intensified twofold because of high elevation. The result of this ecological reality is that air pollution contributes to around 12,000 deaths per year, with children and old people being increasingly treated for respiratory diseases.[2]

- Approximately 50 percent of all hospital beds worldwide are filled with people who have water-born illnesses. Many women in poorest nations spend three hours a day carrying water—using up to 33 percent of their daily energy from their food. Six thousand children die every day from dirty water and poor hygiene. In Bangladesh, 35 million people drink water from arsenic-contaminated wells.[3]

- More than 60 percent of America's coastal rivers and bays are moderately to severely degraded by nutrient runoff. In addition, "paved surfaces have created expressways for oil, grease, and toxic pollutants into coastal waters. Every eight months, nearly 11 million gallons of oil run off our streets and driveways into our waters—the equivalent of the *Exxon Valdez* oil spill."[4]

- No one today doubts the effects of global warming. Global temperatures rose about one degree Fahrenheit in the twentieth century. One of global warming's recent effects is the visible melting of the ice caps, which will contribute to the rise of sea water up to twenty inches by 2050 thus flooding coastal cities, inundating coastal wetlands, and forcing people to flee to higher ground. Already glacial retreat in countries like Bolivia is threatening water supplies, the ability to make hydroelectric power, and tourism.[5]

- Scientists estimate that between 150 and 200 species of life become extinct every day.[6]
- Low-income people and minorities suffer more from environmental contamination than do higher-income communities. Because of the relative powerlessness of poor people in the political sphere, toxic-waste incinerators, chemical plants, and solid-waste dumps are often located in low-income neighborhoods.

How we treat the environment is a justice issue that affects everyone. This chapter offers wise guidance from the Christian tradition on how we should care for the beautiful creation God gave us.

WHAT DO YOU THINK?

According to scientists, three rules apply to the health of our planet:
1. Everything is connected. What we do to one system affects another.
2. Everything goes somewhere. If we take something out of the earth and use it, we must dispose of its byproducts.
3. There is no such thing as a free lunch. Mother Nature will exact a price for our individual and collective selfishness.

God gave us this good earth to use for our own advantage. But he also instructed us to be good stewards, to use it in such a way that it will also benefit future generations.

Here are some statements on the environment. What do you think about them? Check the column that best reflects your own personal view: **SA=strongly agree; A=agree; DK=I don't know what to think; D=disagree; SD=strongly disagree.**

Some Statements to Think About	SA	A	DK	D	SD
1. Jobs and economic development are more important than a clean environment.					
2. There's way too much hoopla over the so-called burning of the rainforests in South America. It's much to do about nothing.					
3. All restaurants should ban smoking. You can't train smoke to stay away from patrons in the non-smoking section.					
4. Giving tax breaks to communities that are willing to have toxic wastes dumped in their backyards is a good way to solve the problem.					
5. Animals and plants have rights—the most basic right is the right to survive extinction.					
6. Let's face it: the Endangered Species Act has really hurt vital industries like logging. It should be modified because human jobs are more important than preserving a species like the spotted owl.					
7. The way to solve the ecological problem is to solve the population explosion, even if this means the government should limit the number of children a couple can have.					

- Would your position change on any of these issues if you were a member of Congress? a businessperson? a parent?
- In your view, what is the biggest threat to ecology in today's world? Why?
- What should the government do to protect the environment?

OUR WORLD (CCC, 295-302; 307; 337-354; 397-405; 410-412; 418)

Contemporary thinkers view our world in different ways. One line of thought focuses on the inherent worth of all living things and stresses that all living species, including humans, are interdependent. However, this model of creation holds that humans are not superior to other living things nor masters of them. Rather, we are simply part of creation and co-dependent on it.

Another ecological theory holds that both non-human and human ecosystems have an equal right to flourish in all their richness and diversity. According to this view, humans are not to be preferred over non-human creatures. In fact, humans are seen as the major offenders against the natural world. The solution to the problem is to decrease human population so humans will not further destroy the non-human world.[7]

These and other modern theories about the environment often criticize Bible-based religions, claiming that these religions hold that humans are God's special creation and superior to non-human creations, and therefore have contributed to the contemporary ecological crisis. This view is not accurate. The Bible reveals that it is *human sinfulness* that has alienated us from God. Sin and alienation have led to the serious abuses which have created our environmental crisis. Some main points of biblical teaching on the environment follow.

Creation is good. A recurring refrain in the book of Genesis is God's declaration that all creation is good, "God looked at everything he had made, and he found it very good" (Gn 1:31). In his wisdom and power, every creation that God made reveals God's goodness. This includes the heavens and the earth, the sun and the moon, the land and the sea, fish and birds, animals and especially human beings. All creation is a gift from God. All creatures are good. They all reveal something about the loving Creator who made them and keeps them in existence.

Humans are God's special creatures. God gave his gift of creation to humans. Humans are the summit of God's creation because God made us in his image and likeness. We are to have dominion over the earth and all of its resources. However, dominion over the earth does not mean exploiting it. When God placed Adam and Eve in the Garden of Eden, he told them "to cultivate and take care of it" (Gn 2:15).

Dominion over creation requires cultivation and care. God alone has sovereignty over creation. Dominion over creation involves cultivation and care and requires humans to preserve "the beauty, diversity, and integrity of nature, as well as . . . fostering its productivity" (*Renewing the Earth*, p. 4). God alone has sovereignty over the earth; we are the earth's stewards. We may not do what we want with God's wonderful gift of the earth to its detriment. As Pope John Paul II wrote:

One cannot use with impunity the different categories of beings, whether living or inanimate—animals, plants, the natural elements—simply as one wishes, according to one's own economic needs. On the contrary, one must take into account the nature of each being and of its mutual connection in an ordered system, which is precisely the cosmos (On Social Concern, §34).

Sin has led humans to abuse the gift of creation. Pride, selfishness, materialism, consumerism, and so forth, have led humanity to rebel against God and act as though God's beautiful creation is ours to do with as we want. These sins flow from the disobedience of our first parents.

Human sin harms the earth. The prophet Hosea wrote that when humans abandon God and act unjustly, then all of nature suffers:

> *Hear the word of the LORD, O people of Israel,*
> *for the LORD has a grievance against the*
> *inhabitants of the land:*
> *There is no fidelity, no mercy,*
> *no knowledge of God in the land.*
> *False swearing, lying, murder, stealing and*
> *adultery!*
> *in their lawlessness, bloodshed follows*
> *bloodshed.*
> *Therefore the land mourns,*
> *and everything that dwells in it languishes:*
> *The beasts of the field, the birds of the air,*
> *and even the fish of the sea perish (Hos 4:1–3).*

Sin leads to a disorder in all of creation. If we are not at peace with God, we cannot be at peace with God's creation.

The prophets warned the Israelites about the truths of nature. For example, they instructed the people to rest the land every seven years, taking care to restore the balance between the land and the people, and to restore God's justice, especially by looking out for the needs of the poor. However, the people were repeatedly unfaithful to the Law. The minority became rich. The rich dispossessed the poor and exhausted the land. The prophets warned of a coming day of judgment. But they also told of a day when humans and nature would be renewed and made whole again by God's Spirit.

Jesus reconciles everything to the Father, including bringing harmony to creation. Christians believe that the death and resurrection of our Lord Jesus Christ brought about our reconciliation with God. Through our Savior, humanity and all of creation are liberated. And through Christ Jesus, the Father reconciled "all things to him, everything in heaven and everything on earth, by making peace through his death on the cross" (Col 1:19–20). Jesus overcame what separates us from God and each other, and he has overcome the hostility between nature and human beings. The gift of his Holy Spirit gives us the power to renew the earth, to serve each other, and to respect the gift of God's good earth and all the creatures in it.

Jesus teaches what it means to be a good steward. When he lived on earth, Jesus showed his closeness to and love of creation. He compared God to a loving shepherd who sought out his lost sheep. Jesus himself is the Good Shepherd. He spoke of the lilies of the field and the birds of the air to teach us to trust a loving God and to stop worrying about material possessions. In his parables, Jesus talked of images like wheat growing, farmers sowing, vineyard workers caring for their vines. All of these images teach us that humans are to be good stewards of God's beautiful creation. And Jesus spoke more directly about stewardship in a parable in Luke's gospel (19:11–17). A rich noble entrusted his fortune to ten of his servants and instructed them to invest it on his behalf. On his return, the noble praised and rewarded those who invested the money and earned him a profit; he punished the servant who buried the money out of fear.

When we apply the meaning of the parable to God's beautiful gift of creation, we are compelled to conclude that we must wisely use and develop creation for the good of all people. We must not hoard our gifts. In another parable on stewardship, Jesus warned:

> *Much will be required of the person entrusted*
> *with much, and still more will be demanded of*
> *the person entrusted with more (Lk 12:48).*

SCRIPTURE LINK

The psalms acknowledge God as Creator. Read the following psalms. Answer the questions that follow.

Read Psalm 8

1. What does this psalm reveal about God's intention?

Read Psalm 104

2. What are your favorite two verses? (Write these verses in your journal.)

Read Psalm 148

3. What is the theme of this psalm?

THE SCOPE OF THE ENVIRONMENTAL PROBLEM

From a historical perspective, concern about the environment is a relatively recent phenomenon. For example, in the nineteenth century, recent American immigrants sent postcards of their new hometown that pictured industrial factories belching dark smoke into the air back home to their relatives. These smokestacks were a point of pride because they showed that the city was prospering economically.

People were willing to accept a certain amount of pollution. They believed that the earth could easily absorb industrial byproducts. It was a small price to pay for economic progress.

In the latter half of the twentieth century, however, the environment has felt the effects of this attitude and practice. Industrialization spread from North America and Europe to many countries around the world. Additionally, the world's population began to increase at unprecedented rates, thereby putting a major strain on nature's limited resources. With industrialization came wealth and disposable income. Items like cars—owned by a majority of employed adults—contributed greatly to the smog problem in many cities throughout the world.

Today, photographs taken from outer space graphically drive home that the earth is a single ecosystem, consisting of a community of animals, plants, microorganisms, and the like. This fragile environment is shared by all humans, regardless of their nationality, language, political or religious beliefs, or ethnic background.

Finally, in recent years, individuals and nations have awakened to the ecological crisis that is confronting our very survival. In the words of Pope John Paul II, we have learned that,

We cannot interfere in one area of the ecosystem without paying due attention both to the consequences of such interference in other areas and to the well-being of future generations (The Ecological Crisis: A Common Responsibility, §6).

This lack of attention is evidenced by the creation of industrial waste, the burning of fossil fuels, unrestricted deforestation, and the use of certain herbicides, coolants, and propellants. These practices have depleted the ozone layer and created a "greenhouse effect" that threatens the survival of all living species on earth.

Pope John Paul II rightly warned that this ecological crisis, fundamentally a moral problem, is due to a profound disrespect for life. Economic interests have too often taken precedence over human dignity. The exploitation of natural resources and the destruction of animal and plant life have contributed immensely to the ecological imbalances we are experiencing today. Without a profound respect for the dignity of the human person and for God's good creation, we will never find our way out of this crisis. The American bishops agree that there is a relationship between the ecology and human beings, stating that a society that will easily dispose of God's good earth will also find disposing of people easy as well. This is why the Church shows so much concern about how what we do to the environment affects the poor. "Caring for God's creation" underscores the important first theme of Catholic social teaching, the "life and dignity of the human person." They reinforce each other.[8]

The following sections provide a short sampling of some of the major areas of concern in the current ecological crisis.

LAND

We need the land to grow food, yet the world's topsoil is subject to waterlogging, salinization, and erosion. Good farm land is turning into desert. Urbanization is also cutting into precious farmlands. The diminishing farmland is a serious problem, but the loss of rainforests presents an especially grave risk for life on earth. These risks are summarized below as reported by the Rainforest Action Network:[9]

- Rainforests comprise 6 percent of the earth's land mass, yet they are home to more than half the plant and animal species on earth.
- One-fourth of the medicines that heal humanity come from plants. Drugs used to treat leukemia, Hodgkin's disease, and other cancers, as well as medicines to treat the heart, hypertension, and arthritis, come from rainforest plants. Yet fewer than 1 percent of tropical species have been examined for their chemical compounds.
- Rainforests are linked to the health of the atmosphere because they hold vast reserves of carbon in their vegetation. When they are burned the carbon is released into the air as carbon dioxide (CO_2), the second largest factor contributing to the greenhouse effect. Deforestation means fewer trees to absorb and neutralize greenhouse gases. A vicious cycle has been created.
- Four-fifths of the nutrients in rainforests exist in the vegetation. Soils are nutrient-poor and quickly become eroded and unproductive when rainforests are cleared.
- Rainforests are being destroyed at a staggering rate. At least 50 million acres a year are lost, exceeding the size of England, Wales, and Scotland combined.

WATER

Without drinkable water, there is no life on earth. It is that simple. Yet, today there is a crisis in the availability of clean water for the world's population. Over one billion people lack access to clean water in developing countries. Both the United Nations and World Health Organization report that 80 percent of diseases in developing nations stem from consumption of and exposure to unsafe water, which kills more than 25,000 people each day.[10]

Industrial pollutants (e.g., heavy metals and hazardous wastes) are a major factor in contaminating the world's water supply. Underground tanks used to store gas or chemicals leak over time and seep into the ground water. The leak of merely one gallon of gasoline, which contains 250 cancer-producing ingredients, can pollute an aquifer and contaminate the water supply of a city of 50,000 people. Pesticides are another major water polluter. They seep into the ground and run off with rain or irrigation, contaminating groundwater and nearby streams and rivers. Excess

GREENHOUSE EFFECT—A phenomenon whereby the earth's atmosphere traps solar radiation.

ECOLOGY—The science that studies the relationship between organisms and their environment.

RAINFOREST—A dense tropical forest with an annual rainfall of at least 100 inches.

organic matter, thermal pollution that depletes oxygen levels near discharge points at factories, and infectious organisms in the drinking water are other major sources of water pollution.

Covering 71 percent of the earth's surface, oceans contain 99 percent of the habitat space on earth. They provide both food and drinkable water in many areas. (The use of desalination plants enables oceans to produce drinkable water.) But oceans are not immune to pollution. Here are some disturbing facts:

- Coral reefs are very beneficial to human life. For example, inhabitants of many coral reefs produce useful chemicals like histamines, hormones, and antibiotics that are used in medicines and medical research. The porous limestone of coral skeletons is used for human bone grafts. Coral reefs also form natural barriers that protect nearby shore-lines from erosion, thus protecting coastal dwellings, agricultural land, and tourist beaches.[11] However, 10 percent of the world's reefs have been completely destroyed. And in the Philippines, where coral reef destruction is the worst, over 70 percent have been destroyed and only 5 percent can be said to be in good condition.[12]
- Based on EPA estimates, in one week a 3,000-passenger cruise ship generates about 210,000 gallons of sewage, 1,000,000 gallons of gray water (shower, sink, and dishwashing water), 37,000 gallons of oily bilge water, more than 8 tons of solid waste, millions of gallons of ballast water containing potential invasive species, and toxic wastes from dry cleaning and photo-processing laboratories.
- Each summer, nutrient pollution creates a dead zone the size of Massachusetts in the Gulf of Mexico.
- More than 13,000 beaches were closed or under pollution advisories in 2001, an increase of 20 percent from the previous year.[13]
- Every year over 300,000 dolphins, porpoises, and whales die an agonizing death because of entanglement in fishing nets.[14]

Air

Air pollution and acid rain are other ongoing problems in today's world. Over 20 percent of the world's population breathes filthy, polluted, unhealthy air. Air pollution causes respiratory diseases, eye irritation, cancer, birth defects, and other ills.

Acid rain is produced as the burning of fossil fuel releases nitrogen and sulfur oxides into the atmosphere, which later fall as acid rain. Pollutants that contaminate the air from Midwest smokestacks drift in clouds to fall as acid rain in large sections of the northeastern United States and southeastern Canada. This rain pollutes lakes, rivers, trees, and vegetation. For example, in the Adirondack Mountains in upstate New York, half the lakes that are 2,000 feet above sea level or more are so acidic that no fish can live in them. Acid rain damages various trees differently, sometimes affecting the size and color of their leaves but also seeping into the ground and affecting the soil quality at the base of trees.

Regarding **global warming**, the United Nations' Intergovernmental Panel on Climate Change projects an average rise in global temperature by 1 to 3.5 degrees Celsius by the year 2100. This projected temperature rise is caused by the greenhouse effect. The greenhouse effect is the accumulation of certain gases in the upper atmosphere, most notably created by the burning of fossil fuels and the production of other gaseous emissions (for example, methane released by livestock). There is increasing evidence that this global warming is in full gear right now, most notably because of the increase of carbon dioxide in the atmosphere, which is responsible for 70 percent of the global warming. "The global surface temperature average for the period 2000–2004 was 0.20 degrees Celsius higher than the average for the 1990s. The rate of change since the mid 1970s, when the latest warming phase began, has been three times that over the past 100 years."[15] The five hottest years on record have taken place since 1997. The year 2005 saw hurricanes like Katrina result in the worst natural disasters to affect the United States in its history.

Global warming is a serious worldwide problem with devastating effects, including:

- increased prevalence of drought leading to wildfires and worldwide crop failure;
- more intense rainstorms causing devastating floods;
- more heat-related deaths (for example, in 2003 a deadly heat wave killed 20,000 Europeans);
- decreased habitats for some animals, causing species die-off, while the range of insects expands, helping to spread virulent tropical diseases.

One of the deadliest effects of global warming is the melting of the polar ice caps. Glaciers are retreating, permafrost is melting, and ice shelves are breaking up at an alarming pace. An important Intergovernmental Panel on Climate Change report projects that sea level will rise between four and 35 inches by 2100. More than a hundred million people throughout the world live within three feet of sea level. If the sea should rise at the high end of the projection, countries like Bangladesh will lose a fifth of their arable lands and cities like New Orleans will be permanently under water. The economic and human costs will be incalculable.[16]

The impact of global warming on the air would be an increase of cloud cover. Scientists are unsure where the extra moisture would go. Hurricanes would probably range farther north and south as a result of the warmer waters.

In the past sixty years the earth's ozone layer has been damaged by the release of ozone-depleting substances, most notably chlorofluorocarbons (CFCs) used in refrigeration and air conditioning, cleaning agents, aerosol spray cans, and foam insulation and packing materials. Located in the stratosphere, ten to thirty miles above the earth, the ozone layer is comprised of a blanket of ozone molecules. This gas shield's primary benefit is to protect life on earth against the deadly ultraviolet rays of the sun. Without the ozone layer, there would be no life on earth.

Although the planet has many ozone holes, the largest two are centered over the South Pole (discovered in 1985) and over the Arctic's North Pole. In August of 2003, the hole over Antarctica was just short of 11 million square miles. But scientists are mildly optimistic because of the 130 nations who signed the Montreal Treaty. This treaty promised to cut down on the emission of ozone-depleting chemicals. However, it will take at least another ten years to see if the atmosphere is indeed on the road to recovery. In the meantime, a major point of contention in the international community is the United States' refusal to sign the Kyoto

GLOBAL WARMING—A TREND CAUSED BY THE GREENHOUSE EFFECT IN WHICH THE WORLD'S AVERAGE TEMPERATURE IS EXPECTED TO RISE 1 TO 3.5 DEGREES CELSIUS BY 2100.

treaty, the goal of which is to curb carbon dioxide emissions.

Ozone depletion has brought many serious health risks, including the following:

- New cataract-induced cases of blindness are increasing each year because of exposure to chronic ultraviolet-B (UV-B) radiation;
- Malignant and non-malignant skin cancers are growing at epidemic proportions worldwide;
- UV-B radiation can suppress the human immune system, leaving the body vulnerable to many bacteria and viruses;

> The average temperature on the West Antarctic Peninsula has increased the following amount since 1950:
> winter: 8.8°F
> annual: 4.5°F[17]

- Through modification in the biological and chemical environments, increased UV-B radiation will reduce productivity among crops, livestock, and the ocean food chain. For example, it is estimated that a 16 percent ozone depletion would kill 5 percent of the phytoplankton (the basis of all food in the seas). This would lead to a loss of about 7 percent of the world's annual fishery output.[18]

SPECIES EXTINCTION

Pollution of air, water, and land have all contributed to what some scientists are calling "the sixth extinction." The last major extinction of earth's species took place 65 million years ago at the end of the Mesozoic Era when the dinosaurs disappeared from the earth. Scientists believe the previous five extinctions were caused by some drastic environmental change, for example, the impact of a comet, volcanic eruption, or some similar disaster. Today, however, the rapid pace of species extinctions are caused by humans, what one scientist has termed the "exterminator species."[19]

Scientists believe there are between ten and thirty million plant and animal species on earth, most of them unidentified. Further, some scientists estimate that as many as 137 species disappear daily, most of them unknown to us, and largely because of human activity. In addition, in a recent year, the World Conservation Union reported that:

- Today's rates of extinction are at least 100 to 1,000 times greater than natural rates found in the fossil record.
- A total of 15,589 known species (7,266 animal species and 8,323 plant and lichen species) are now at risk of extinction.
- One in three amphibians and almost half of all turtles and tortoises are known to be threatened with extinction, along with one in four mammals, one in five sharks and rays, and one in eight birds.

- The numbers of threatened species are increasing across almost all major taxonomic groups.[20]

A pessimistic assessment of these facts tells us that humans are the only species in the history of life on earth that has the power to cause a mass extinction of many other species. On the other hand, we are also the only species that has the God-given ability to responsibly save other species. The United States has passed laws like the Clean Water Act and the Toxic Substances Control Act which are monitored by the EPA (Environmental Protection Agency). Other nations have bonded together through international agencies like the United Nations to sponsor Earth Summit meetings and have entered into agreements to clean up the environment. But much more needs to be done.

ECOLOGICAL CRISIS

Choose an ecological issue to research. Create a 10 to 15 point fact sheet about your issue. Include photos, charts, or other graphic material to illustrate some of your points. Present your findings using an overhead or PowerPoint® presentation. Discuss your findings with your classmates.

Report on one of the following topics. Describe the ecological problem and its origins.

Ecological Issues:
- water pollution
- air pollution
- deforestation
- global warming
- ozone depletion
- dangers in the use of pesticides
- toxic waste disposal
- endangered species

Note who is most affected by the problem and how. Report on how it especially affects the poorest and most vulnerable members of the human family. Give some of the possible short- and long-term consequences for the health of humans and the planet if the problem does not receive immediate attention.

- Do any groups believe the problem is overstated? If so, how?
- What is being done to correct the problem? What more needs to be done?
- What will it cost to correct the problem? What will be the economic impact if nothing is done?

STEWARDSHIP:
WHAT YOU CAN DO

In our daily life there is much we can do protect, nurture, and preserve the gifts of creation. Here are some ideas for good stewardship:

1. SAVE ENERGY. Turn off lights and other electrical appliances when you're not using them. Walk when possible. If you have a car, make sure it is tuned up. Car pool. *What are other things you can do to save energy?*
2. RECYCLE. Recycle paper and plastic products through your local community. Avoid buying plastic containers and styrofoam products. These products don't decompose and cause landfill problems. Cut back on using paper products. Though convenient, paper napkins, towels, plates, and cups can be wasteful. *Name some other recycling ideas.*
3. DON'T LITTER. *What are some opportunities to participate in a school or neighborhood clean-up campaign?*

4. PLANT A VEGETABLE GARDEN. Growing your own food will keep you close to nature, give you a healthy, outdoor hobby, and provide a healthy food source. *Donate some of the produce from your vegetable garden to a local food bank.*

5. DON'T SMOKE OR DO DRUGS. Polluting one's personal environment negatively affects God's greatest creation—you. *What are some ways you personally say "no" to tobacco and drug use?*

6. SIMPLIFY YOUR LIFESTYLE BY CONSUMING LESS. Buy things because you need them, not simply for their status value. Take to heart the words of Saint Elizabeth Ann Seton, "Live simply so that others may simply live." *What are three personal items that you might donate to an agency that helps the poor?*

7. VOLUNTEER YOUR TALENTS. *Join a community group that helps clean the environment or help in some other conservation efforts.*

8. WRITE TO LOCAL POLITICIANS AND ENCOURAGE THEM TO PASS AND ENFORCE LAWS THAT PROTECT THE ENVIRONMENT. *Inform yourself on the positions on the environment taken by your elected officials.*

9. PRAY. At Mass, praise and thank God for his goodness and the beauty of his creation. Pray for children (including the unborn) and for poor people because they are at greatest risk for environmental hazards and suffer the most from environmental destruction. Pray for a spirit of conversion away from consumerism that contributes to ecological waste. *Ask God to teach you how to serve as a responsible steward of his good earth.*

CHURCH AND WORLD TEACHING ON THE ENVIRONMENT (CCC, 2415-2418; 2456-2457)

The American bishops' pastoral statement on the environment, *Renewing the Earth*, discusses the following themes of ecological responsibility and provides a good synopsis of Church teaching on the environment:

1. A God-centered, sacramental world. The entire universe is God's dwelling place. The earth is a small but especially blessed corner of God's wondrous creation. It is our home, a place where people in past ages have met the loving Creator through the natural wonders of mountains, deserts, streams, oceans, and all the other diamonds of natural beauty.

Though urban people are often alienated from the natural rhythms of life, Catholics believe that we live in a sacramental universe. This means that visible and tangible signs like the wonders of creation can reveal God's presence. Therefore, we must both respect and protect the environment so humans can continue to discover and meditate on the mystery of God's greatness and his love for us.

We are to be faithful stewards, caretakers, so we might find fullness of life:

Stewardship implies that we must both care for creation according to standards that are not our own making and at the same time be resourceful in finding ways to make the earth flourish (Renewing the Earth, p. 6).

2. Respect for life. Respect for life and respect for nature are intimately connected. All of God's creatures glorify him. The immense variety of ecosystems and the millions of species God created are part of the divine plan. They all require our respect. Other creatures and the natural world are not just for human use; they also possess an independent value. We must care for them by:

- preserving natural environments;
- protecting endangered species;
- working to make human environments compatible with local ecology;
- using appropriate technology and carefully evaluating new technological breakthroughs as we adopt them (*Renewing the Earth*, p. 7).

3. Planetary common good and solidarity. We live in a global village. We are interdependent. The pollution from one country affects the people in other nations. Very often the worst polluters are the least affected by their thoughtlessness.

The virtue of solidarity commits us to work for the common good, to sacrifice for the sake of others, rather than simply to further our own interests. Pope John Paul II warned:

The ecological crisis reveals the urgent moral need for a new solidarity, especially in relations between the developing nations and those that are highly industrialized. . . . This need presents new opportunities for strengthening cooperative and peaceful relations among states (The Ecological Crisis: A Common Responsibility, §10).

The industrialized and developed nations must recognize that they have helped to create the problem:

Modern society will find no solution to the ecological problem unless it takes a serious look at its lifestyle. In many parts of the world society is given to instant gratification and consumerism while remaining indifferent to the damage which these cause. . . . The seriousness of the ecological issue lays bare the depth of man's moral crisis. . . . Simplicity, moderation and discipline, as well as a spirit of sacrifice, must become a part of everyday life, lest all suffer the negative consequences of the careless habits of a few (The Ecological Crisis: A Common Responsibility, §13).

4. Universal purpose of created things. (See also CCC, 2401–2406.) The Second Vatican Council's *The Church in the Modern World* taught,

God intended the earth with everything contained in it for the use of all human beings and peoples. Thus, under the leadership of justice and in the company of charity, created goods should be in abundance for all in like manner (§69).

The goods of the earth are for the benefit of all. God neither excludes nor favors anyone. Unfortunately, many poor people do not have access to what is needed to live with dignity. Therefore,

we are obligated to work for a just economic system which equitably shares the bounty of the wealth of human enterprise with all peoples (Renewing the Earth, p. 8).

5. Option for the poor. The assault on the environment most often hurts the poor. For example, native peoples die when their forests and grasslands are destroyed. In a nuclear plant accident, as at Chernobyl, the poor and working people suffer the worst contamination. As societies begin to respond to the environmental crisis, the needs of the poor must not be neglected. Nor should the costs of ecological reform be at the expense of working people.

In his message on the environment, Pope John Paul II tells of how rural poverty and unjust land distribution have caused subsistence farming and soil exhaustion. Many farmers clear new land; this leads to unchecked deforestation. Another problem is how poor countries in heavy debt to the rich nations often destroy their natural heritage, and cause grave ecological problems, to create new

DESTRUCTION OF THE RAINFOREST IN MALAYSIA

241

TO BE AND GROW

In his desire to have and to enjoy rather than to be and to grow, man consumes the resources of the earth and his own life in an excessive and disordered way. At the root of the senseless destruction of the natural environment lies an anthropological error, which unfortunately is widespread in our day. Man, who discovers his capacity to transform and in a certain sense create the world through his own work, forgets that this is always based on God's prior and original gift of the things that are. Man thinks that he can take arbitrarily use of the earth, subjecting it without restraint to his will, as though the earth did not have its own requisites and a prior God-given purpose, which man can indeed develop but must not betray. Instead of carrying out his role as a cooperator with God in the work of creation, man sets himself up in place of God and thus ends up provoking a rebellion on the part of nature, which is more tyrannized than governed by him.

—*On the Hundredth Anniversary of Rerum Novarum, §37*

In light of this quote from Pope John Paul II, compose two lists. In one, list ten things that humans do to simply "have and enjoy." Make another list of activities that exemplify what it means "to be and to grow." Share and discuss.

export products to help relieve their debt. These examples are built into the structures of society. Structural injustice also leads to environmental devastation.

6. *Authentic development, consumption, and population.* Many in the rich and developed nations of the world blame overpopulation as the major cause of environmental degradation. The truth is that the biggest factor contributing to environmental destruction is over-consumption by developed nations. A key way to address the population problem in developing countries is sustainable social and economic growth. The American bishops wrote:

Only when an economy distributes resources so as to allow the poor an equitable stake in society and some hope for the future do couples see responsible parenthood as good for their families. In particular, prenatal care; education; good nutrition; and health care for women, children, and families promise to improve family welfare and contribute to stabilizing population (Renewing the Earth, p. 9).

The Church judges the population issue in light of the values of respect for life, just economic and social development, care for the environment, and the right of parents to decide on the number and spacing of births. The Church is against any coercive method of population control:

Respect for nature ought to encourage policies that promote natural family planning and true responsible parenthood (Renewing the Earth, p. 9).

DECLARATION ON HUMAN RIGHTS AND THE ENVIRONMENT

In 1994, human rights and environmental specialists met in Geneva to write the first declaration of principles on human rights and the environment. Listed below are some paraphrased statements from that document.[21]

Statement on Basic Human Rights and the Environment

Basic human rights such as the right to life, health, and culture can only be enjoyed in a healthy and ecologically sound environment.

The right to a secure, healthy, and ecologically sound environment includes:

- freedom from pollution and activities that threaten the environment;
- safe and healthy food and water adequate to our well-being;
- protection and preservation of the air, soil, water, sea-ice, flora and fauna, and the essential processes necessary to maintain biological diversity and ecosystems.

Everyone has the right to:

- be consulted and included in any decisions affecting their environment;
- active and free participation in planning and decision making on the impact of any development that impacts on their environment.

DECLARATION ON HUMAN RIGHTS AND THE ENVIRONMENT *(continued)*

Duties and responsibilities that arise from these rights include all states ensuring the right to a secure, healthy, and ecologically sound environment by:

- banning substances and activities that are harmful to the environment;
- repairing the damage that has already been done to the environment;
- ensuring that our natural resources are distributed fairly;
- reducing wasteful processes of production and patterns of consumption; and
- ensuring that transnational and international corporations respect environmental rights.

CASE STUDY: LANDFILL IN THE NEIGHBORHOOD

Background:

A three-year-old suburban development of homes has a well-placed park, soccer field, and recreation area at its center. Now, the local Environmental Protection Agency reports to the homeowners that the park and field have been built over a toxic waste site.

Debate:

- How should the homeowners respond to this situation?
- What are the dangers of this situation?
- Because of this incident, property values in the development have plummeted. Is there any way for the homeowners to recoup their investment?
- Who is responsible for this situation?

CARING FOR MOTHER EARTH

Do one of the following:

- Photograph some favorite nature scenes. Snap some contrasting pictures of where humanity has ruined the environment or disfigured nature's beautiful face. Create a presentation to depict the contrast between God's beauty and human folly. Write a prayer to conclude your presentation.
- Compose an imaginary monologue with Mother Earth as the speaker. Let her tell humanity what ails her.

SAINT FRANCIS OF ASSISI (1181 OR 1182–1226) PATRON SAINT OF ECOLOGY

In 1979, Pope John Paul II named Saint Francis of Assisi the patron saint of ecology. Next to our Blessed Mother, this joyous, simple, lovable, outgoing man is probably the most popular Christian saint. He has earned the nickname "Troubadour for Christ," and because of his literal interpretation of Mark 10:21—"Go and sell everything you own"—he also is known as "The Little Poor Man."

Francis's mother had him baptized John (Giovanni) after Saint John the Baptist. However, when his absent father Peter Bernadone found out, he changed the baby's name to Francesco ("Frenchmen") to reflect the father's love for France. Peter did not want his son dedicated to religion. His dream for Francis was that he would come to admire his own worldly ways—that of a cloth merchant and lover of France.

During his youth, the charming Francis lived a carefree life of self-indulgence, leading a bunch of other youths in a life of bad habits. He longed to be a noble, and in his own mind achieved some glory when he was imprisoned after a petty war with a neighboring town. After a year in chains, Francis returned to his former life, but longed for even greater glory. He joined in the efforts of a local war, but not a day's ride from Assisi he had a powerful dream in which God revealed to Francis that he was seeking glory in the wrong place. Francis returned home to mocking villagers and to an angry father who felt Francis had wasted money on armor for a battle he would never fight.

Francis turned to prayer and shed tears over his former dissolute life. A turning point came when Francis kissed the hand of a leper, someone whose physical appearance disgusted him. When the leper returned his kiss of peace, Francis felt an indescribable joy. When he began to ride off and turned to wave goodbye to the leper, Francis saw that the leper had disappeared. Francis interpreted this as a test from God.

Francis set off to repair an ancient church at San Damiano, paying for the repairs from the proceeds of some of his father's goods. His father thought his son a madman and dragged Francis before the local bishop to disinherit him. Francis gave back the money and stripped off his father's clothes. He declared that his only father was "Our Father who art in heaven." From that day on, Francis begged for his food, preached, and joyfully sang about God's goodness.

Before long, Francis's own holiness and simple joy in living in union with Christ Jesus attracted companions. Francis instructed his followers to live by the gospel and trust in God's goodness to provide. He wanted his friends to work for the bare necessities and turn to begging only if they had to. He did not want them to own money or possessions because he felt with ownership came the need to have weapons to defend them. Francis desired true freedom and believed you cannot rob from a person who has nothing to steal.

Eventually, in 1210, Pope Innocent II approved his brotherhood—a "mendicant" order which begged for its sustenance as they joyfully proclaimed the gospel. Francis and his brothers treated everyone—rich and poor alike—with respect, honor, and love.

Francis's love embraced all of nature as part of God's family, including all living creatures. The stories about Francis's love for God's creatures are many. In one, Francis preached to the birds and told them to thank God for how he clothed them, for their freedom, and for God's care. The story tells how the birds quieted down when Francis was with them and only flew off when he gave them permission to do so.

Another famous story is about a wolf that had been attacking a town, devouring human beings for food. When the outraged citizens wanted to kill the wolf, Francis spoke to the wolf and ordered him not to kill any more humans. The wolf obeyed and, before long, became a pet who was well fed by the townsfolk.

Francis's mystical vision found God in all things: in sunrises and sunsets, in the smile of a baby, in a sparrow winging its way across an open field, in a gentle babbling brook, in grass growing, in leaves falling. He taught all his followers to praise and thank God for all his creation and all his gifts. His example encourages us to care for and respect God's precious creation.

To finish Francis's story: In his lifetime, his ever-growing order experienced dissension. Some friars argued for a need for more organization. They decided it was impractical for such a large order not to own goods. Francis saw that times were changing and eventually surrendered his leadership role. He and a few followers retired to a pilgrimage at Mount Alvernia where Francis suffered much in his last years.

Francis's profound devotion to the suffering Lord led to his receiving the stigmata, the five wounds of Christ. His austere life had led to blindness and suffering. But toward the end of his life, he composed the beautiful "Canticle of the Sun," a hymn praising God for his awesome creation. Francis died on October 4, 1226, at the age of forty-five.

CHAPTER SUMMARY

- The biblical view of creation holds that creation is good, that all creatures reveal something about our magnificent Creator God, and that creation is a gift of God to us. Because we are made in God's image and likeness, humans are God's special creatures who have been given dominion over the rest of the earth. Dominion, however, does not mean indiscriminate destruction of creation. Rather, it means responsible stewardship that involves both respect and care. Scripture also reveals that sin—prideful attitudes and actions of choosing self over God—has led humanity to abuse God's beautiful gift of creation. An unfortunate consequence of sin is that God's good earth and the creatures in it have been harmed.

- We live in a global village, sharing the precious earth God has given us. Yet, a disturbing ecological crisis is all-too-evident in today's world. The land is polluted with hazardous wastes, beautiful fields are cemented over, rainforests are being cut down at a staggering rate. There is not enough clean water for all the earth's people, especially those in developing countries. Much of the world's fresh water and ocean waters are polluted. This pollution leads to countless human deaths through disease and the decimation of many species of marine life. Acid rain, smog, and polluted air are taking an immense toll on human, animal, and plant life. Especially alarming are global warming and the depletion of the ozone layer. All these environmental crises have already led to what some scientists are calling the "sixth extinction." For example, in the next one hundred years, half the world's species—fish, birds, insects, and mammals—face the real possibility of extinction.

Research and report on Saint Francis of Assisi's life at one or more of these websites:

American Catholic.org: www.americancatholic.org/features/francis/

Catholic Online: www.catholic.org

Capuchin-Franciscan website: www.capuchins.org

Franciscan Friars, Province of the Holy Spirit (article on Francis and nature): www.franciscans.org.au/spirituality/index.html

245

- Catholic social teaching offers principles for environmental ethics. We see the universe as God's dwelling place. God's beautiful creation is a sign of his presence; we can discover God in his magnificent creation. When we fail to treat created reality as a gift, we dishonor our Creator. Respect for nature and respect for life go hand-in-hand. God's creatures have a value independent of their usefulness for humans. We must care for them.

- Our world is a global village in which we are interdependent. We must be concerned with the common good of our globe and unite in solidarity with our neighbors around the world. Christians must especially realize that God intended the goods of this world for the benefit of all people. In our ecological decisions, we must especially be in solidarity with poor people.

- Unrestrained economic growth is not the solution to the ecological crisis. Moderate consumption in the use of material sources, major cutbacks in the over-consumption of developed nations, and thoughtful development in agriculture and industry that benefits people are signs of authentic growth.

- We look to Saint Francis of Assisi as a model of one who lived in harmony with and celebrated God's good creation. He is the patron saint of ecology.

Review Questions

1. Discuss three truths that the Bible reveals about God's good creation.
2. What role do humans play in God's creation?
3. From a biblical point of view, what is the root of our ecological crisis?
4. What does it mean to be a good steward?
5. List some facts that prove we have an ecological crisis. Include these areas:
   a. land
   b. water
   c. air
   d. species extinction
6. Why are global warming and depletion of the ozone layer especially worrisome?
7. List five things you can do to help improve the environment.
8. Discuss four principles of Catholic social teaching that help us arrive at a theology of the ecology.
9. What is meant by the planetary common good?
10. Discuss an example of how the poor really suffer from the assault on the environment.
11. "Over-consumption by the rich nations is at the root of the ecological crisis." Discuss the truth of this statement.
12. List five human rights as they relate to the environment.
13. In what ways is Saint Francis of Assisi the patron saint of ecology?

RESEARCHING ON THE INTERNET

Treat the earth well. It was not given to you by your parents. It was lent to you by your children.

— *an African proverb*

1. Read and summarize Pope John Paul II's message for the 1990 World Day of Peace, "*The Ecological Crisis: A Common Responsibility.*"
2. Visit the Catholic Conservation Center website. Read and report on its introduction to Catholic Environmental Justice. See: http://conservation.catholic.org.
3. Report on a recent article on some aspect of the mass species extinction. Use a search engine to find links to this topic.
4. Report on some aspect of water, sanitation, and health at the World Health Organization's website: www.who.int/water_sanitation_health/en/.
5. Report on an environmental issue of current interest by researching the links on the About.com website: http://environment.about.com.
6. Read more about global warming at the EPA website: http://yosemite.epa.gov/oar/globalwarming.nsf/content/index.html.
7. Report on an article of interest at the Ocean Conservancy website: www.oceanconservancy.org/site/PageServer?pagename=home.
8. Browse a comprehensive list of ecological sites. See: http://pbil.univ_lyon1.fr/ Ecology/Ecology_WWW.html.
9. Explore the World Wildlife Fund's website: www.worldwildlife.org.

PRAYER REFLECTION

Pray these famous words of Saint Francis of Assisi, "Canticle of the Sun."

Most High, all-powerful, good Lord,
Yours are the praises, the glory, the honor, and all blessing.
To You alone, Most High, do they belong,
and no man is worthy to mention Your name.
Praised be You, my Lord, with all your creatures,
especially Sir Brother Sun,
Who is the day and through whom You give us light.
And he is beautiful and radiant with great splendor;
and bears a likeness of You, Most high One.
Praised be You, my Lord, through Sister Moon and the stars, in heaven
You formed them clear and precious and beautiful.
Praised be you, my Lord, through Brother Wind,
and through the air, cloudy and serene, and every kind of weather
through which You give sustenance to Your creatures.
Praised be You, my Lord, through Sister Water,
which is very useful and humble and precious and chaste.
Praised be You, my Lord, through Brother Fire,
through whom You light the night

and he is beautiful and playful and robust and strong.
Praised be You, my Lord, through our Sister Mother Earth,
who sustains and governs us,
and who produces varied fruits with colored flowers and herbs.
Praised be You, my Lord, through those who give pardon for
*   Your love*
and bear infirmity and tribulation.
Blessed are those who endure in peace for by You,
Most High, they shall be crowned.
Praised be You, my Lord, through our Sister Bodily Death,
from whom no living man can escape.
Woe to those who die in mortal sin.
Blessed are those whom death will find in Your most holy will,
for the second death shall do them no harm.
Praise and bless my Lord and give Him thanks
and serve Him with great humility.

Notes

1. Told by Robert Gibbings in Tony Castle's *Quotations for All Occasions* (London, England: Marshall-Pickering, 1989), p. 68. The verse quoted is from Psalm 19:2.
2. International Atomic Energy Agency, "Nuclear Science Helps Mexico City Breathe Easier," January 21, 2005.
3. Dr. Patrick Dixon, "The Future of the Environment" <http://www.globalchange.com/future environment.htm>.
4. Pew Oceans Commission, "America's Oceans in Crisis" <http://www.actionbioscience.org/environment/pew.html>.
5. Charles J. Hanley, "The Big Thaw," *Austin American-Statesman*, January 30, 2005, Section H1, H4.
6. United Nations Environment Programme, "Key Facts on Biodiversity."
7. These and other ecological theories are discussed in Edward Stevens' *Developing Moral Imagination: Case Studies in Practical Morality* (Kansas City: Sheed & Ward, 1997), pp. 214–228.
8. *In the Footsteps of Jesus: Resource Manual on Catholic Social Teaching* (Washington, D.C.: United States Conference of Catholic Bishops, 2004), p. 68.
9. Check the fact sheets found on their website at: www.ran.org.
10. Public Television Service (PBS), NOW, "Leasing the Rain: World Water Facts," July 5, 2002 <http://www.pbs.org/now/science/water2.html>.
11. The Nature Conservancy, Rescue the Reef®, "Coral Reef Facts" <http://nature.org/joinanddonate/rescuereef/resources/>.
12. Ocean World, "Coral Reef Destruction and Conservation" <http://oceanworld.tamu.edu/students/coral/coral5.htm>.
13. These last three studies were reported by the Pew Oceans Commission's major study, *America's Living Oceans: Charting a Course for Sea Change*, May 2003, pp. 4–5.
14. Whale and Dolphin Conservation Society (WDCS), "Clean and Healthy Seas."
15. Tiempo Climate Newswatch, "Global Climate 2004" <http://www.tiempocyberclimate.org/newswatch/report050116.htm>.

16. Many frightening facts on, and convincing evidence about, global warming can be found in the September 2004 issue of *National Geographic*, vol. 206, no. 3, pp. 2–75.

17. Daniel Glick, "The Big Thaw," *National Geographic*, September 2004, vol. 206, no. 3, p. 33.

18. Greenpeace Ozone Crisis, "The Dangers of U-V Radiation for Human Health and the Global Biosphere" <http://archive.greenpeace.org/ozone/>.

19. See Virginia Morrell, "The Sixth Extinction," *National Geographic,* vol. 195, no. 2, February 1999, pp. 42–59. This entire issue of the magazine is dedicated to the fragile web of biodiversity.

20. MSNBC News, "Species Disappearing at an Alarming Rate, Report Says," November 17, 2004.

21. Jane Deren, Marissa Maurer, and Julie Vieira, *Catholic Social Teaching and Human Rights: An Educational Packet* (Washington, D.C.: Center of Concern, 1998), E-5.

APPENDIX:
CATHOLIC HANDBOOK FOR FAITH

A. BELIEFS

APOSTLES' CREED

I believe in God, the Father almighty,
Creator of heaven and earth.

I believe in Jesus Christ, his only son, our Lord.
He was conceived by the power of the Holy
Spirit,
and born of the Virgin Mary.
He suffered under Pontius Pilate,
was crucified, died, and was buried.
He descended into hell.
On the third day he rose again.
He ascended into heaven,
and is seated at the right hand of the Father.
He will come again to judge the living and
the dead.

I believe in the Holy Spirit,
the holy catholic Church,
the communion of saints,
the forgiveness of sins,
the resurrection of the body,
and the life everlasting. Amen.

NICENE CREED

We believe in one God,
the Father, the Almighty,
maker of heaven and earth,
of all that is seen and unseen.
We believe in one Lord, Jesus Christ,
the only Son of God,
eternally begotten of the Father,
God from God, Light from Light,
true God from true God,
begotten, not made, one in Being
with the Father.
Through him all things were made.
For us men and for our salvation
he came down from heaven:
by the power of the Holy Spirit
he was born of the Virgin Mary, and
became man.

For our sake he was crucified under Pontius
Pilate;
he suffered, died, and was buried.
On the third day he rose again in fulfillment of the Scriptures;
he ascended into heaven and is
seated at the right hand of the
Father.
He will come again in glory to judge the
living and the dead,
and his kingdom will have no end.
We believe in the Holy Spirit, the Lord, the
giver of life,
who proceeds from the Father and
the Son.
With the Father and the Son he is wor-
shiped and glorified.
He has spoken through the Prophets.
We believe in one holy catholic and apostolic Church.
We acknowledge one baptism for the forgiveness of sins.
We look for the resurrection of the dead,
and the life of the world to come.
Amen.

GIFTS OF THE HOLY SPIRIT

1. Wisdom
2. Understanding
3. Counsel
4. Fortitude
5. Knowledge
6. Piety
7. Fear of the Lord

FRUITS OF THE HOLY SPIRIT

1. Charity
2. Joy
3. Peace
4. Patience
5. Kindness
6. Goodness
7. Generosity
8. Gentleness
9. Faithfulness
10. Modesty
11. Self-control
12. Chastity

THE SYMBOL OF CHALCEDON

Following therefore the holy Fathers, we unanimously teach to confess one and the same Son, our Lord Jesus Christ, the same perfect in divinity and perfect in humanity, the same truly God and truly man composed of rational soul and body, the same one in being (homoousios) with the Father as to the divinity and one in being with us as to the humanity, like unto us in all things but sin (cf. Heb 4:15). The same was begotten from the Father before the ages as to the divinity and in the later days for us and our salvation was born as to his humanity from Mary the Virgin Mother of God.

We confess that one and the same Lord Jesus Christ, the only-begotten Son, must be acknowledged in two natures, without confusion or change, without division or separation. The distinction between the natures was never abolished by their union but rather the character proper to each of the two natures was preserved as they came together in one person (prosôpon) and one hypostasis. He is not split or divided into two persons, but he is one and the same only-begotten, God the Word, the Lord Jesus Christ, as formerly the prophets and later Jesus Christ himself have taught us about him and as has been handed down to us by the Symbol of the Fathers.

From the General Council of Chalcedon (451)

B. GOD AND JESUS CHRIST

ATTRIBUTES OF GOD

Saint Thomas Aquinas named nine attributes that tell us some things about God's nature. They are:

1. *God is eternal.* He has no beginning and no end. Or, to put it another way, God always was, always is, and always will be.

2. *God is unique.* God is the designer of a one and only world. Even the people he creates are one of a kind.

3. *God is infinite and omnipotent.* This reminds us of a lesson we learned early in life: God sees everything. There are no limits to God. Omnipotence is a word that refers to God's supreme power and authority over all of creation.

4. *God is omnipresent.* God is not limited to space. He is everywhere. You can never be away from God.

5. *God contains all things.* All of creation is under God's care and jurisdiction.

6. *God is immutable.* God does not evolve. God does not change. God is the same God now as he always was and always will be.

7. *God is pure spirit.* Though God has been described with human attributes, God is not a material creation. God's image cannot be made. God is a pure spirit who cannot be divided into parts. God is simple, but complex.

8. *God is alive.* We believe in a living God, a God who acts in the lives of people. Most concretely, he came to this world in the incarnate form of Jesus Christ.

9. *God is holy.* God is pure goodness. God is pure love.

THE HOLY TRINITY

The Trinity is the mystery of one God in three persons—Father, Son, and Holy Spirit. The mystery is impossible for human minds to understand. Some of the Church dogmas, or beliefs, can help:

★ *The Trinity is One.* There are not three Gods, but one God in three persons. Each one of them—Father, Son, and Holy Spirit—is God whole and entire.

★ *The three persons are distinct from one another.* For example, the Father is not the Son, nor is the Son the Holy Spirit. Rather, the Father is Creator, the Son is begotten of the Father, and the Holy Spirit proceeds from the Father and Son.

★ *The divine persons are related to one another.* Though they are related to one another, the three persons have one nature or substance.

Saint John Damascus used two analogies to describe the doctrine of the Blessed Trinity.

Think of the Father as a root,
of the Son as a branch,
and of the Spirit as a fruit,
for the substance of these is one.

The Father is a sun
with the Son as rays
and the Holy Spirit as heat.

Read the *Catechism of the Catholic Church* (232–260) on the Holy Trinity.

FAITH IN ONE GOD

There are several implications for those who love God and believe in him with their entire heart and soul (see *CCC* 222–227):

★ It means knowing God's greatness and majesty.

★ It means living in thanksgiving.

★ It means knowing the unity and dignity of all people.

★ It means making good use of created things.

★ It means trust God in every circumstance.

FAMOUS QUOTATIONS ABOUT JESUS CHRIST

Meekness was the method Jesus used with the Apostles. He put up with their ignorance and roughness and even their infidelity. He treated sinners with a kindness and affection that caused some to be shocked, others to be scandalized, and still others to gain hope in God's mercy. Thus he bade us to be gentle and humble of heart.

Saint John Bosco

Christ with me, Christ before me
Christ behind me, Christ in me,
Christ beneath me, Christ above me,
Christ on my right, Christ on my left,
Christ where I lie, Christ where I sit,
Christ where I arise,
Christ in the heart of everyone who thinks
    of me,
Christ in the mouth of everyone who
    speaks of me,
Christ in every eye that sees me,
Christ in every ear that hears me,
Salvation is of the Lord,
Salvation is of Christ,
May your salvation, Lord be ever
    with us.

from the breastplate of Saint Patrick

Oh, if all were to know how beautiful Jesus is, how amiable he is! They would all die of love.

Saint Gemma Galgani

About Jesus Christ and the Church, I simply know they're just one thing, and we should not complicate the matter.

Saint Joan of Arc

Our Lord does not come down from heaven every day to lie in a golden ciborium. He comes to find another heaven which is infinitely dearer to him—the heaven of our souls.

Saint Thérèse of Lisieux

JUDAISM'S BELIEF IN ONE GOD

Like Catholics, Jews are monotheistic, that is, they believe in one God. Jews believe that God reveals himself in the Torah, through the prophets, in the life of the Jewish people, and through the history of the Jews. The key event of Jewish history is the Exodus, when God freed the Jewish nation from slavery in Egypt. This pivotal event is recounted every year during the seven-day festival known as Passover, celebrated around the time of Easter.

Jews believe that the covenant God established with Abraham and the Sinai covenant require Israel to adore and serve God always, and to observe his Law. In turn, they believe God will remain faithful to them and treat the members of the Jewish nation as special.

Jews believe that God is eternal, almighty, all-knowing, present everywhere, and loving of his creation. In prayer, God is addressed as *Adonai* (Lord). Jews use God's name respectfully and avoid saying the name revealed to Moses—Yahweh—because it is so holy. Jewish faith is summed up in a prayer pious Jews recite every day, the *Shema:*

Hear, O Israel! The LORD is our God, the LORD alone! Therefore, you shall love the LORD, your God, with all your heart, and with all your soul, and with all your strength (Dt 6:4–5).

Jews differ on how God will fulfill his covenant with them, how God's kingdom will be established, and on the nature of the final judgment. For example, some Jews believe the concept of a Messiah refers to an individual person; others think of it in terms of the community of God's people or the development of historical events; still others believe God himself will intervene directly into human history.

The Catholic Church encourages utmost respect for the Jewish faith. For example, at the Second Vatican Council, Church fathers wrote:

This sacred Synod . . . recalls the spiritual bond linking the people of the New Covenant with Abraham's stock. . . .

The Church, therefore, cannot forget that she received the revelation of the Old Testament through the people whom God in his inexpressible mercy deigned to establish the Ancient Covenant. . . .

The Church recalls too that from the Jewish people sprang the apostles, her foundation stones and pillars, as well as most of the early disciples who proclaimed Christ to the world. . . .

The Jews still remain most dear to God because of their fathers, for He does not repent of the gifts He makes nor of the calls He issues (*Declaration on the Relationship of the Church to Non-Christian Religions,* No. 4).

C. SCRIPTURE AND TRADITION

CANON OF THE BIBLE

There are seventy-three books in the canon of the Bible, that is, the official list of books the Church accepts as divinely inspired writings: forty-six Old Testament books and twenty-seven New Testament books. Protestant Bibles do not include seven Old Testament books on its list (1 and 2 Maccabees, Judith, Tobit, Baruch, Sirach, and the Wisdom of Solomon). Why the difference? Catholics rely on the version of the Bible that the earliest Christians used, the *Septuagint.* This was the first Greek translation of the Hebrew Scriptures begun in the third century BC. Protestants, on the other hand, rely on an official list of Hebrew Scriptures compiled in the Holy Land by Jewish scholars at the end of the first century AD. Today, most Protestant Bibles print the disputed books in a separate section at the back of the Bible called the *Apocrypha.*

The twenty-seven books of the New Testament are divided into three categories: the gospels, the letters written to local Christian communities or individuals, and the letters intended for the entire Church. The heart of the New Testament, in fact all of Scripture, is the gospels. The New Testament is central to our knowledge of Jesus Christ. He is the focus of all Scripture.

There are forty-six books in the Old Testament canon. The Old Testament is the foundation for God's self-revelation in Christ. Christians honor the Old Testament as God's word. It contains the writings of prophets and other inspired authors who recorded God's teaching to the Chosen People and his interaction in their history. For example, the Old Testament recounts how God delivered the Jews from Egypt (the Exodus), led them to the Promised Land, formed them into a nation under his care, and taught them in knowledge and worship.

The stories, prayers, sacred histories, and other writings of the Old Testament reveal what God is like and tell much about human nature, too. In brief, the Chosen People sinned repeatedly by turning their backs on their loving God; they were weak and easily tempted away from God. Yahweh, on the other hand, *always* remained faithful. He promised to send a Messiah to humanity.

Listed below are the categories and books of the Old Testament and the New Testament:

THE OLD TESTAMENT

The Pentateuch

Genesis	Gn
Exodus	Ex
Leviticus	Lv
Numbers	Nm
Deuteronomy	Dt

The Historical Books

Joshua	Jos
Judges	Jgs
Ruth	Ru
1 Samuel	1 Sm
2 Samuel	2 Sm
1 Kings	1 Kgs
2 Kings	2 Kgs
1 Chronicles	1 Chr
2 Chronicles	2 Chr
Ezra	Ezr
Nehemiah	Neh
Tobit	Tb
Judith	Jdt
Esther	Est
1 Maccabees	1 Mc
2 Maccabees	2 Mc

The Wisdom Books

Job	Jb
Psalms	Ps(s)
Proverbs	Prv
Ecclesiastes	Eccl
Song of Songs	Sg
Wisdom	Wis
Sirach	Sir

The Prophetic Books

Isaiah	Is
Jeremiah	Jer
Lamentations	Lam
Baruch	Bar
Ezekiel	Ez
Daniel	Dn
Hosea	Hos
Joel	Jl
Amos	Am
Obadiah	Ob
Jonah	Jon
Micah	Mi
Nahum	Na
Habakkuk	Hb
Zephaniah	Zep
Haggai	Hg

| Zechariah | Zec |
| Malachi | Mal |

THE NEW TESTAMENT

The Gospels

Matthew	Mt
Mark	Mk
Luke	Lk
John	Jn
Acts of the Apostles	Acts

The New Testament Letters

Romans	Rom
1 Corinthians	1 Cor
2 Corinthians	2 Cor
Galatians	Gal
Ephesians	Eph
Philippians	Phil
Colossians	Col
1 Thessalonians	1 Thes
2 Thessalonians	2 Thes
1 Timothy	1 Tm
2 Timothy	2 Tm
Titus	Ti
Philemon	Phlm
Hebrews	Heb

The Catholic Letters

James	Jas
1 Peter	1 Pt
2 Peter	2 Pt
1 John	1 Jn
2 John	2 Jn
3 John	3 Jn
Jude	Jude
Revelation	Rv

HOW TO LOCATE A SCRIPTURE PASSAGE

Example: 2 Tm 3:16–17

1. *Determine the name of the book.*
   The abbreviation "2 Tm" stands for the second book of Timothy.

2. *Determine whether the book is in the Old Testament or New Testament.*
   The second book of Timothy is one of the Catholic letters in the New Testament.

3. *Locate the chapter where the passage occurs.*
   The first number before the colon—"3"—indicates the chapter. Chapters in the Bible are set off by the larger numbers that divide a book.

4. *Locate the verses of the passage.*
   The numbers after the colon indicate the verses referred to. In this case, verses 16 and 17 of chapter 3.

5. *Read the passage.*
   For example: "All Scripture is inspired by God and is useful for teaching, for refutation, for correction, and for training in righteousness, so that one who belongs to God may be competent, equipped for every good work."

TIMELINE OF CHURCH HISTORY

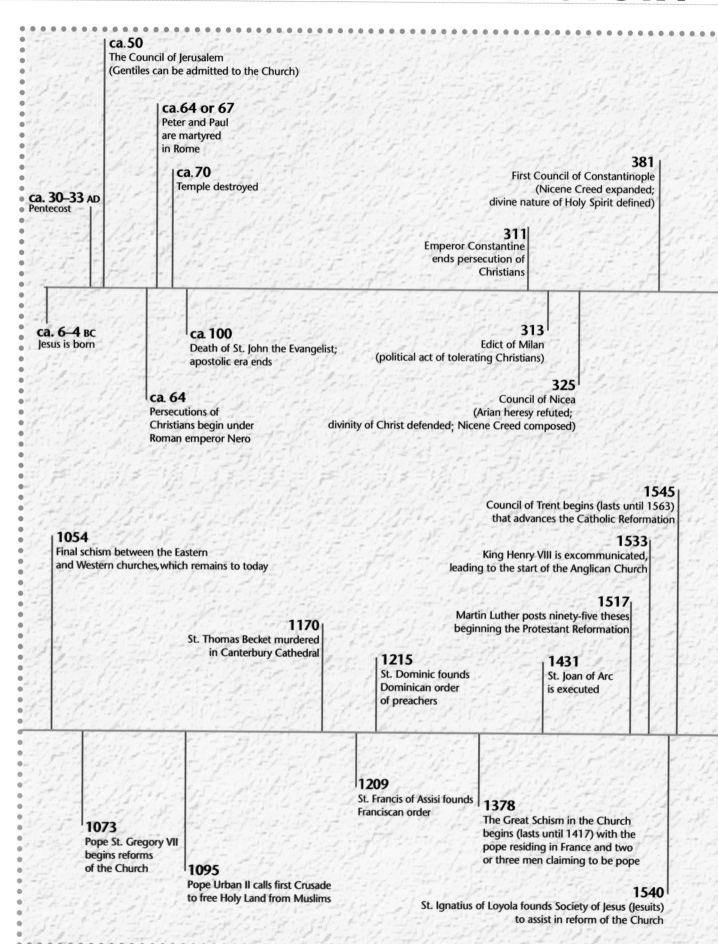

ca.50
The Council of Jerusalem
(Gentiles can be admitted to the Church)

ca.64 or 67
Peter and Paul
are martyred
in Rome

ca.70
Temple destroyed

381
First Council of Constantinople
(Nicene Creed expanded;
divine nature of Holy Spirit defined)

ca. 30–33 AD
Pentecost

311
Emperor Constantine
ends persecution of
Christians

ca. 6–4 BC
Jesus is born

ca.100
Death of St. John the Evangelist;
apostolic era ends

313
Edict of Milan
(political act of tolerating Christians)

ca. 64
Persecutions of
Christians begin under
Roman emperor Nero

325
Council of Nicea
(Arian heresy refuted;
divinity of Christ defended; Nicene Creed composed)

1545
Council of Trent begins (lasts until 1563)
that advances the Catholic Reformation

1054
Final schism between the Eastern
and Western churches, which remains to today

1533
King Henry VIII is excommunicated,
leading to the start of the Anglican Church

1517
Martin Luther posts ninety-five theses
beginning the Protestant Reformation

1170
St. Thomas Becket murdered
in Canterbury Cathedral

1215
St. Dominic founds
Dominican order
of preachers

1431
St. Joan of Arc
is executed

1209
St. Francis of Assisi founds
Franciscan order

1378
The Great Schism in the Church
begins (lasts until 1417) with the
pope residing in France and two
or three men claiming to be pope

1073
Pope St. Gregory VII
begins reforms
of the Church

1095
Pope Urban II calls first Crusade
to free Holy Land from Muslims

1540
St. Ignatius of Loyola founds Society of Jesus (Jesuits)
to assist in reform of the Church

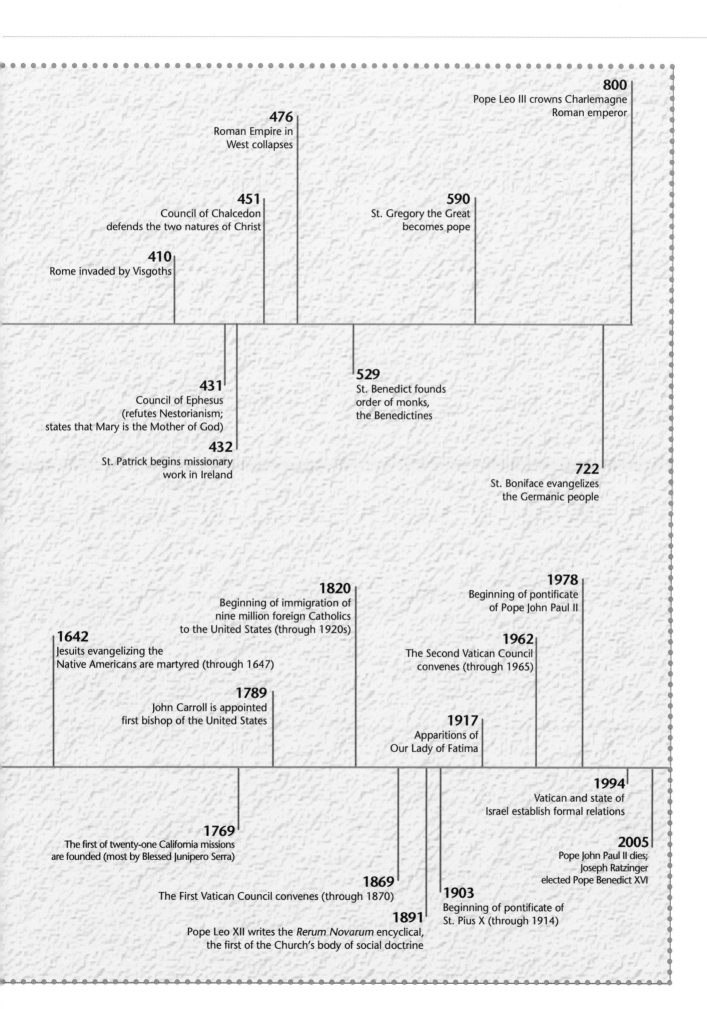

800
Pope Leo III crowns Charlemagne
Roman emperor

476
Roman Empire in
West collapses

451
Council of Chalcedon
defends the two natures of Christ

590
St. Gregory the Great
becomes pope

410
Rome invaded by Visgoths

431
Council of Ephesus
(refutes Nestorianism;
states that Mary is the Mother of God)

529
St. Benedict founds
order of monks,
the Benedictines

432
St. Patrick begins missionary
work in Ireland

722
St. Boniface evangelizes
the Germanic people

1820
Beginning of immigration of
nine million foreign Catholics
to the United States (through 1920s)

1978
Beginning of pontificate
of Pope John Paul II

1642
Jesuits evangelizing the
Native Americans are martyred (through 1647)

1962
The Second Vatican Council
convenes (through 1965)

1789
John Carroll is appointed
first bishop of the United States

1917
Apparitions of
Our Lady of Fatima

1994
Vatican and state of
Israel establish formal relations

1769
The first of twenty-one California missions
are founded (most by Blessed Junipero Serra)

2005
Pope John Paul II dies;
Joseph Ratzinger
elected Pope Benedict XVI

1869
The First Vatican Council convenes (through 1870)

1903
Beginning of pontificate of
St. Pius X (through 1914)

1891
Pope Leo XII writes the *Rerum Novarum* encyclical,
the first of the Church's body of social doctrine

D. CHURCH

MARKS OF THE CHURCH

1. *The Church is one.* The Church remains one because of its source: the unity in the Trinity of the Father, Son, and Spirit in one God. The Church's unity can never be broken and lost because this foundation is itself unbreakable.

2. *The Church is holy.* The Church is holy because Jesus, the founder of the Church, is holy and he joined the Church to himself as his body and gave the Church the gift of the Holy Spirit. Together, Christ and the Church make up the "whole Christ" (*Christus totus* in Latin).

3. *The Church is catholic.* The Church is catholic ("universal" or "for everyone") in two ways. First, it is catholic because Christ is present in the Church in the fullness of his body, with the fullness of the means of salvation, the fullness of faith, sacraments, and the ordained ministry that comes from the Apostles. The Church is also catholic because it takes its message of salvation to all people.

4. *The Church is apostolic.* The Church's apostolic mission comes from Jesus: "Go, therefore, and make disciples of all nations" (Mt 28:19). The Church remains apostolic because it still teaches the same things the apostles taught. Also, the Church is led by leaders who are successors to the apostles and who help to guide us until Jesus returns.

THE POPE

The bishop of Rome has carried the title "pope" since the ninth century. Pope means "papa" or "father." Saint Peter was the first bishop of Rome and, hence, the first pope. He was commissioned directly by Jesus:

> And so I say to you, you are Peter, and upon this rock I will build my church, and the gates of the netherworld shall not prevail against it. I will give you the keys to the kingdom of heaven. Whatever you bind on earth shall be bound in heaven; and whatever you loose on earth shall be loosed in heaven (Mt 16:18–19).

Because Peter was the first bishop of Rome, the succeeding bishops of Rome have had primacy in the Church. The entire succession of popes since Saint Peter can be traced directly to the apostle.

The pope is in communion with the bishops of the world as part of the Magisterium, which is the Church's teaching authority. The pope can also define doctrine in faith or morals for the Church. When he does so, he is infallible and cannot be in error.

The pope is elected by the College of Cardinals by a two-thirds majority vote in secret balloting. Cardinals under the age of eighty are eligible to vote. If the necessary majority is not achieved, the ballots are burned in a small stove inside the council chambers along with straw that makes dark smoke. The sign of dark smoke announces to the crowds waiting outside Saint Peter's Basilica that a new pope has not been chosen. When a new pope has been voted in with the necessary majority, the ballots are burned without the straw, producing white smoke signifying the election of a pope.

RECENT POPES

Since 1900 and through the pontificate of Pope Benedict XVI, there were ten Popes. Pope John Paul II was the first non-Italian pope since Dutchman Pope Adrian VI (1522–1523). The popes since the twentieth century through Pope Benedict XVI with their original names, place of origin, and years as pope:

★ Pope Leo XIII (Giocchino Pecci): Carpineto, Italy, February 20, 1878–July 20, 1903.

★ Pope Saint Pius X (Giuseppe Sarto): Riese, Italy, August 4, 1903–August 20, 1914.

(continued on page 260)

THE APOSTLES AND THEIR EMBLEMS

 SAINT ANDREW

Tradition holds that Andrew was crucified on a bent cross, called a *saltire*.

 SAINT BARTHOLOMEW

Bartholomew was flayed alive before being crucified. He was then beheaded.

 SAINT JAMES THE GREATER

James the Greater, the brother of John, was beheaded by Herod Agrippa. It is the only death of an apostle mentioned in Scripture (Acts 12:2). The shell indicates James's missionary work by sea in Spain. The sword is of martyrdom.

 SAINT JAMES THE LESS

James the Less is traditionally known as the first bishop of Jerusalem. The saw for his emblem is connected with the tradition of his body being sawed into pieces after he was pushed from the pinnacle of the Temple.

 SAINT JOHN THE EVANGELIST

John was the first bishop of Ephesus. He is the only apostle believed to have died a natural death, in spite of many attempts to murder him by his enemies. One attempt included his miraculous survival of drinking a poisoned drink.

 SAINT JUDE

Some traditions have Jude and Saint Peter martyred together. It is thought that he traveled throughout the Roman Empire with Peter.

 SAINT MATTHEW

Matthew's shield depicts three purses reflecting his original occupation as tax collector.

 SAINT MATTHIAS

Matthias was the apostle chosen by lot to replace Judas. Tradition holds that Matthias was stoned to death and then beheaded with an ax.

 SAINT PETER

Simon Peter was the brother of Andrew. The first bishop of Rome, Peter was crucified under Nero, asking to be hung upside down because he felt unworthy to die as Jesus did. The keys represent Jesus' giving to Peter the keys to the kingdom of heaven.

 SAINT PHILIP

Philip may have been bound to a cross and stoned to death. The two loaves of bread at the side of the cross refer to Philip's comment to Jesus about the possibility of feeding the multitudes of people (Jn 6:7).

 SAINT SIMON

The book with fish depicts Simon as a "fisher of men" who preached the gospel. He was also known as Simon the Zealot.

 SAINT THOMAS

Thomas is thought to have been a missionary in India, where he is thought to have built a church. Hence, the carpenter's square. He may have died by arrows and stones. It is then thought that he had a lance run through his body.

* Pope Benedict XV (Giacomo della Chiesa): Genoa, Italy, September 3, 1914–January 22, 1922.

* Pope Pius XI (Achille Ratti): Desio, Italy, February 6, 1922–February 10, 1939.

* Pope Pius XII (Eugenio Pacelli): Rome, Italy, March 2, 1939–October 9, 1958.

* Pope John XXIII (Angelo Giuseppe Roncalli), Sotto il Monte, Italy, October 28, 1958–June 3, 1963.

* Pope Paul VI (Giovanni Battista Montini): Concessio, Italy, June 21, 1963–August 6, 1978.

* Pope John Paul I (Albino Luciani): Forno di Canale, Italy, August 26, 1978–September 28, 1978.

* Pope John Paul II (Karol Wojtyla): Wadowice, Poland, October 16, 1978–April 2, 2005.

* Pope Benedict XVI (Joseph Ratzinger): Marktl am Inn, Germany, April 19, 2005–present.

FATHERS OF THE CHURCH

Church Fathers, or Fathers of the Church, is a traditional title that was given to theologians of the first eight centuries whose teachings made a lasting mark on the Church. The Church Fathers developed a significant amount of doctrine which has great authority in the Church. The Church Fathers are named as either Latin Fathers (West) or Greek Fathers (East). Among the greatest Fathers of the Church are:

Latin Fathers	Greek Fathers
St. Ambrose	St. John Chrysostom
St. Augustine	St. Basil the Great
St. Jerome	St. Gregory of Nazianzen
St. Gregory the Great	St. Athanasius

Pope Benedict XVI

DOCTORS OF THE CHURCH

The Doctors of the Church are men and women honored by the Church for their writings, preaching, and holiness. Originally the Doctors of the Church were considered to be Church Fathers Augustine, Ambrose, Jerome, and Gregory the Great, but others were added over the centuries. Saint Teresa of Avila was the first woman Doctor (1970). Saint Catherine of Siena was named a Doctor of the Church the same year. The list of Doctors of the Church:

NAME	LIFE SPAN	DESIGNATION
St. Athanasius	296–373	1568 by Pius V
St. Ephraem the Syrian	306–373	1920 by Benedict XV
St. Hilary of Poitiers	315–367	1851 by Pius IX
St. Cyril of Jerusalem	315–386	1882 by Leo XIII
St. Gregory of Nazianzus	325–389	1568 by Pius V
St. Basil the Great	329–379	1568 by Pius V
St. Ambrose	339–397	1295 by Boniface VIII
St. John Chrysostom	347–407	1568 by Pius V
St. Jerome	347–419	1295 by Boniface XIII
St. Augustine	354–430	1295 by Boniface XIII
St. Cyril of Alexandria	376–444	1882 by Leo XIII
St. Peter Chrysologous	400–450	1729 by Benedict XIII
St. Leo the Great	400–461	1754 by Benedict XIV
St. Gregory the Great	540–604	1295 by Boniface XIII
St. Isidore of Seville	560–636	1722 by Innocent XIII
St. John of Damascus	645–749	1890 by Leo XIII
St. Bede the Venerable	672–735	1899 by Leo XIII
St. Peter Damian	1007–1072	1828 by Leo XII
St. Anselm	1033–1109	1720 by Clement XI
St. Bernard of Clairvaux	1090–1153	1830 by Pius VIII
St. Anthony of Padua	1195–1231	1946 by Pius XII
St. Albert the Great	1206–1280	1931 by Pius XI
St. Bonaventure	1221–1274	1588 by Sixtus V
St. Thomas Aquinas	1226–1274	1567 by Pius V
St. Catherine of Siena	1347–1380	1970 by Paul VI
St. Teresa of Avila	1515–1582	1970 by Paul VI
St. Peter Canisius	1521–1597	1925 by Pius XI
St. John of the Cross	1542–1591	1926 by Pius XI
St. Robert Bellarmine	1542–1621	1931 by Pius XI
St. Lawrence of Brindisi	1559–1619	1959 by John XXIII
St. Francis de Sales	1567–1622	1871 by Pius IX
St. Alphonsus Ligouri	1696–1787	1871 by Pius IX
St. Thérèse of Lisieux	1873–1897	1997 by John Paul II

ECUMENICAL COUNCILS

An ecumenical council is a worldwide assembly of bishops under direction of the pope. There have been twenty-one ecumenical councils, the most recent being the Second Vatican Council (1962–1965). A complete list of the Church's ecumenical councils with the years each met:

Nicaea I	325
Constantinople I	381
Ephesus	431
Chalcedon	451
Constantinople II	553

Constantinople III	680
Nicaea II	787
Constantiople IV	869–870
Lateran I	1123
Lateran II	1139
Lateran III	1179
Lateran IV	1215
Lyons I	1245
Lyons II	1274
Vienne	1311–1312
Constance	1414–1418
Florence	1431–1445
Lateran V	1512–1517
Trent	1545–1563
Vatican Council I	1869–1870
Vatican Council II	1962–1965

E. MORALITY

The Ten Commandments

The Ten Commandments are a main source for Christian morality. The Ten Commandments were revealed by God to Moses. Jesus, himself, acknowledged them. He told the rich young man, "If you wish to enter into the life, keep the commandments" (Mt 19:17). Since the time of Saint Augustine (fourth century) the Ten Commandments have been used as a source for teaching baptismal candidates.

I. I, the Lord am your God: you shall not have other gods besides me.

II. You shall not take the name of the Lord, your God, in vain.

III. Remember to keep holy the Sabbath day.

IV. Honor your father and your mother.

V. You shall not kill.

VI. You shall not commit adultery.

VII. You shall not steal.

VIII. You shall not bear false witness against your neighbor.

IX. You shall not covet your neighbor's wife.

X. You shall not covet your neighbor's goods.

The Beatitudes

The word *beatitude* means "happiness." Jesus preached the Beatitudes in his Sermon on the Mount. They are:

Blessed are the poor in spirit, for theirs is the kingdom of God.

Blessed are they who mourn, for they will be comforted.

Blessed are the meek, for they will inherit the land.

Blessed are they who hunger and thirst for righteousness, for they will be satisfied.

Blessed are the merciful, for they will be shown mercy.

Blessed are the clean of heart, for they will see God.

Blessed are the peacemakers, for they will be called children of God.

Blessed are they who are persecuted for the sake of righteousness, for theirs is the kingdom of heaven.

Cardinal Virtues

Virtues—habits that help in leading a moral life—that are acquired by human effort are known as moral or human virtues. Four of these are called the cardinal virtues because they form the hinge that connects all the others. They are:

★ Prudence   ★ Fortitude

★ Justice   ★ Temperance

Theological Virtues

The theological virtues are the foundation for moral life. They are related directly to God.

★ Faith   ★ Hope   ★ Love

CORPORAL (BODILY) WORKS OF MERCY

★ Feed the hungry.
★ Give drink to the thirsty.
★ Clothe the naked.
★ Visit the imprisoned.
★ Shelter the homeless.
★ Visit the sick.
★ Bury the dead.

SPIRITUAL WORKS OF MERCY

★ Counsel the doubtful.
★ Instruct the ignorant.
★ Admonish sinners.
★ Comfort the afflicted.
★ Forgive offenses.
★ Bear wrongs patiently.
★ Pray for the living and the dead.

PRECEPTS OF THE CHURCH

1. You shall attend Mass on Sundays and on holy days of obligation and rest from servile labor.
2. You shall confess your sins once a year.
3. You shall receive the sacrament of Eucharist at least during the Easter season.
4. You shall observe the days of fasting and abstinence established by the Church.
5. You shall help to provide for the needs of the Church.

CATHOLIC SOCIAL TEACHING: MAJOR THEMES

The 1998 document *Sharing Catholic Social Teaching: Challenges and Directions—Reflections of the U.S. Catholic Bishops* highlighted seven principles of the Church's social teaching. They are:

1. Life and dignity of the human person
2. Call to family, community, and participation
3. Rights and responsibilities
4. Option for the poor and vulnerable
5. The dignity of work and the rights of workers
6. Solidarity
7. Care for God's creation

SIN

Sin is an offense against God.

Mortal sin is the most serious kind of sin. Mortal sin destroys or kills a person's relationship with God. To be a mortal sin, three conditions must exist:

★ The moral object must be of grave or serious matter. Grave matter is specified in the Ten Commandments (e.g., do not kill, do not commit adultery, do not steal, etc.).

★ The person must have full knowledge of the gravity of the sinful action.

★ The person must completely consent to the action. It must be a personal choice.

Venial sin is less serious sin. Examples of venial sins are petty jealousy, disobedience, and "borrowing" a small amount of money from a parent without the intention of repaying it. Venial sins, when unrepented, can lead a person to commit mortal sins.

Vices are bad habits linked to sins. The seven capital vices are pride, avarice, envy, wrath, lust, gluttony, and sloth.

F. LITURGY & SACRAMENTS

CHURCH YEAR

The cycle of seasons and feasts that Catholics celebrate is called the Church Year or Liturgical Year. The Church Year is divided into six main parts: Advent, Christmas, Lent, Triduum, Easter, and Ordinary Time.

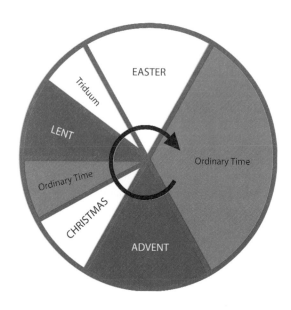

HOLY DAYS OF OBLIGATION IN THE UNITED STATES

★ Immaculate Conception of Mary
December 8

★ Christmas
December 25

★ Solemnity of Mary, Mother of God
January 1

★ Ascension of the Lord
Forty days after Easter

★ Assumption of Mary
August 15

★ All Saints Day
November 1

THE SEVEN SACRAMENTS

1. Baptism
2. Confirmation
3. Eucharist
4. Penance and Reconciliation
5. Anointing of the Sick
6. Holy Orders
7. Matrimony

HOW TO GO TO CONFESSION

1. Spend some time examining your conscience. Consider your actions and attitudes in each area of your life (e.g., faith, family, school/work, social life, relationships). Ask yourself, "Is this area of my life pleasing to God? What needs to be reconciled with God? with others? with myself?"

2. Sincerely tell God that you are sorry for your sins. Ask God for forgiveness and for the grace you will need to change what needs changing in your life. Promise God that you will try to live according to his will for you.

3. Approach the area for confession. Wait an appropriate distance until it is your turn.

4. Make the Sign of the Cross with the priest. He may say: "May God, who has enlightened every heart, help you to know your sins and trust his mercy." You reply: "Amen."

5. Confess your sins to the priest. Simply and directly talk to him about the areas of sinfulness in your life that need God's healing touch.

6. The priest will ask you to pray an act of contrition. Pray an Act of Contrition you have committed to memory. Or, say something in your own words, like: "Dear God, I am sorry for my sins. I ask for your forgiveness and I promise to do better in the future."

7. The priest will talk to you about your life, encourage you to be more faithful to God in the future, and help you decide what to do to make up for your sins—your penance.

8. The priest will then extend his hands over your head and pray the Church's official prayer of absolution:

   God, the Father of mercies, through the death and resurrection of his Son, has reconciled the world to himself and sent the Holy Spirit among us for the forgiveness of sins; through the ministry of the Church may God give you pardon and peace, and I absolve you from your sins in the name of the Father, and of the Son, and of the Holy Spirit.

   You respond: "Amen."

9. The priest will wish you peace. Thank him and leave.

10. Go to a quiet place in the church and pray your prayer of penance. Then spend some time quietly thanking God for the gift of forgiveness.

ORDER OF MASS

There are two main parts of the Mass, the Liturgy of the Word and the Liturgy of the Eucharist. The complete order of Mass:

The Introductory Rites

The Entrance
Greeting of the Altar and of the
   People Gathered
The Act of Penitence
The Kyrie Eleison
The Gloria
The Collect (Opening Prayer)

The Liturgy of the Word

Silence
The Biblical Readings (the reading of the Gospel is the high point of the Liturgy of the Word)
The Responsorial Psalm
The Homily

The Profession of Faith (Creed)
The Prayer of the Faithful

The Liturgy of the Eucharist

The Preparation of the Gifts
The Prayer over the Offerings
The Eucharistic Prayer
The Communion Rite
The Lord's Prayer
The Rite of Peace
The Fraction (Breaking of the Bread)
Communion
Prayer after Communion

The Concluding Rites

COMMUNION REGULATIONS

To receive Holy Communion properly, a person must be in the state of grace (free from mortal sin), have the right intention (only for the purpose of pleasing God), and observe the Communion fast.

The fast means that a person may not eat anything or drink any liquid (other than water) one hour before the reception of Communion. There are exceptions made to this fast only for the sick and aged.

THREE DEGREES OF THE SACRAMENT OF ORDERS

There are three degrees of the sacrament of Holy Orders: the ministries of bishop, priest, and deacon.

The bishop receives the fullness of the sacrament of Orders. He is the successor to the apostles. When he celebrates the sacraments, the bishop is given the grace to act in the person of Christ who is the head of the body of the Church.

Priests are ordained as co-workers of the bishop. They too are configured to Christ so that they may act in his person during the sacraments of Eucharist, Baptism, and the Anointing of the Sick. They may bless marriages in the name of Christ and, under the authority of the bishop, share in Christ's ministry of forgiveness in the sacrament of Penance and Reconciliation.

Deacons are ordained for service and are configured to Christ the servant. Deacons are ordained to help and serve the priests and bishops in their work. While bishops and priests are configured to Christ to act as the head of Christ's body, deacons are configured to Christ in order to serve as he served. Deacons may baptize, preach the Gospel and homily, and bless marriages.

SACRAMENTALS

"Sacramentals are prayers and sometimes actions or things which resemble the sacraments and signify spiritual effects which are obtained through the intercession of the Church. Sacramentals do not confer grace the way the sacraments do, but by the Church's prayer, they prepare us to receive grace and dispose us to cooperate with it" (CCC, 1670). Examples of sacramentals include:

★ *Actions* (blessings; genuflections; the Sign of the Cross; church processions)
★ *Objects* (candles; holy water; statues and icons; blessed ashes; blessed palms; rosaries; relics; incense; vestments; scapulars, church building; religious medals)
★ *Places* (the Holy Land, Rome, Fatima, Lourdes, and other places of pilgrimage; chapels; retreat centers)
★ *Prayers* (short prayers we say throughout the day; grace before meals)
★ *Sacred Time* (holy days; feast days; special days of prayer, fasting, and abstinence)

G. MARY AND THE SAINTS

MOTHER OF GOD

Mary, the mother of Jesus, is the closest human to cooperate with her Son's work of redemption. For this reason, the Church holds her in a special place. Of her many titles, the most significant is that she is the Mother of God.

The Church teaches several truths about Mary.

First, she was conceived immaculately. This means from the very first moment of her existence she was without sin and "full of grace." This belief is called the Immaculate Conception. The feast of the Immaculate Conception is celebrated on December 8.

Second, Mary was ever-virgin. She was a virgin before, in, and after the birth of Jesus. As his mother, she cared for him in infancy and raised him to adulthood with the help of her husband, Joseph. She witnessed Jesus' preaching and ministry, was at the foot of his cross at his crucifixion, and present with the apostles as they awaited the coming of the Holy Spirit at Pentecost.

Third, at the time of her death, Mary was assumed body and soul into heaven. This dogma was proclaimed as a matter of faith by Pope Pius XII in 1950. The feast of the Assumption is celebrated on August 15.

The Church has always been devoted to the Blessed Virgin. This devotion is different than that given to God—Father, Son, and Holy Spirit. Rather, the Church is devoted to Mary as her first disciple, the Queen of all Saints, and her own Mother. Quoting the fathers of the Second Vatican Council:

> In the meantime the Mother of Jesus, in the glory which she possesses in body and soul in heaven, is the image and the beginning of the Church as it is to be perfected in the world to come. Likewise she shines forth on earth, until the day of the Lord shall come, a sign of certain hope and comfort to the pilgrim People of God (*Lumen Gentium*, 68).

MARIAN FEASTS THROUGHOUT THE YEAR

January 1	Solemnity of Mary, Mother of God
March 25	Annunciation of the Lord
May 31	Visitation
August 15	Assumption
August 22	Queenship of Mary
September 8	Birth of Mary
September 15	Our Lady of Sorrows
October 7	Our Lady of the Rosary

November 21	Presentation of Mary
December 8	Immaculate Conception
December 12	Our Lady of Guadalupe

CANONIZATION OF SAINTS

Saints are those who are in glory with God in heaven. *Canonization* refers to a solemn declaration by the Pope that a person who either died a martyr or who lived an exemplary Christian life is in heaven and may be honored and imitated by all Christians. The canonization process first involves a process of beatification that includes a thorough investigation of the person's life and certification of miracles that can be attributed to the candidate's intercession.

The first official canonization of the universal Church on record was Saint Ulrich of Augsburg by Pope John XV in 993.

Some non-Catholics criticize Catholics for "praying to saints." Catholics *honor* saints for their holy lives but we do not pray to them as if they were God. We ask the saints to pray with us and for us as part of the Church in glory. We can ask them to do this because we know that their lives have been spent in close communion with God. We also ask the saints for their friendship so that we can follow the example they have left for us.

PATRON SAINTS

A patron is a saint who is designated for places (nations, regions, dioceses) or organizations. Many saints have also become patrons of jobs, professional groups, and intercessors for special needs. Listed below are patron saints for several nations and some special patrons:

Patrons of Places

Americas	Our Lady of Guadalupe, St. Rose of Lima
Argentina	Our Lady of Lujan
Australia	Our Lady Help of Christians
Canada	St. Joseph, St. Anne
China	St. Joseph
England	St. George
Finland	St. Henry
France	Our Lady of the Assumption, St. Joan of Arc, St. Thérèse of Lisieux
Germany	St. Boniface
India	Our Lady of the Assumption
Ireland	St. Patrick, St. Brigid, St. Columba
Italy	St. Francis of Assisi, St. Catherine of Siena
Japan	St. Peter
Mexico	Our Lady of Guadalupe
New Zealand	Our Lady Help of Christians
Poland	St. Casmir, St. Stanislaus, Our Lady of Czestochowa
Russia	St. Andrew, St. Nicholas of Myra, St. Thérèse of Lisieux
Scotland	St. Andrew, St. Columba
Spain	St. James, St. Teresa of Avila
United States	Immaculate Conception

Special Patrons

Accountants	St. Matthew
Actors	St. Genesius
Animals	St. Francis of Assisi
Athletes	St. Sebastian
Beggars	St. Martin of Tours
Boy Scouts	St. George
Dentists	St. Apollonia
Farmers	St. Isidore
Grocers	St. Michael
Journalists	St. Francis de Sales
Maids	St. Zita
Motorcyclists	Our Lady of Grace
Painters	St. Luke
Pawnbrokers	St. Nicholas
Police Officers	St. Michael

Politicians	St. Thomas More
Priests	St. John Vianney
Scientists	St. Albert
Skaters	St. Lydwina of Schiedam
Tailors	St. Homobonus
Teachers	St. Gregory the Great, St. John Baptist de la Salle
Wine Merchants	St. Amand

H. DEVOTIONS

THE MYSTERIES OF THE ROSARY

Joyful Mysteries

1. The Annunciation
2. The Visitation
3. The Nativity
4. The Presentation in the Temple
5. The Finding of Jesus in the Temple

Mysteries of Light

1. Jesus' Baptism in the Jordan River
2. Jesus' Self-manifestation at the Wedding of Cana
3. The Proclamation of the Kingdom of God and Jesus' Call to Conversion
4. The Transfiguration
5. The Institution of the Eucharist at the Last Supper

Sorrowful Mysteries

1. The Agony in the Garden
2. The Scourging at the Pillar
3. The Crowning with Thorns
4. The Carrying of the Cross
5. The Crucifixion

Glorious Mysteries

1. The Resurrection
2. The Ascension
3. The Descent of the Holy Spirit
4. The Assumption of Mary
5. The Crowning of Mary as the Queen of Heaven and Earth

HOW TO PRAY THE ROSARY

Opening

1. Begin on the crucifix and pray the Apostles' Creed.
2. On the first bead, pray the Our Father.
3. On the next three beads, pray the Hail Mary. (Some people meditate on the virtues of faith, hope, and charity on these beads.)
4. On the fifth bead, pray the Glory Be.

The Body

Each decade (set of ten beads) is organized as follows:

1. On the larger bead that comes before each set of ten, announce the mystery to be prayed (see above) and pray one Our Father.
2. On each of the ten smaller beads, pray one Hail Mary while meditating on the mystery.
3. Pray one Glory Be at the end of the decade. (There is no bead for the Glory Be.)

Conclusion

Pray the following prayer at the end of the rosary:

Hail, Holy Queen

Hail, holy Queen, Mother of Mercy,
our life, our sweetness, and our hope.
To thee do we cry,
poor banished children of Eve.
To thee do we send up our sighs,
mourning and weeping in this valley
of tears.
Turn then, most gracious advocate,
thine eyes of mercy toward us;
and after this our exile,
show unto us the blessed fruit of thy
womb, Jesus.
O clement, O loving, O sweet Virgin
Mary.
Pray for us, O holy Mother of God,
that we may be made worthy of the
promises of Christ.
Amen.

STATIONS OF THE CROSS

The stations of the cross is a devotion and also a sacramental. (A sacramental is a sacred object, blessing, or devotion.) The stations of the cross are individual pictures or symbols hung on the interior walls of most Catholic churches depicting fourteen steps along Jesus' way of the cross. Praying the stations means meditating on each of the following scenes:

1. Jesus is condemned to death.
2. Jesus takes up his cross.
3. Jesus falls the first time.
4. Jesus meets his mother.
5. Simon of Cyrene helps Jesus carry his cross.
6. Veronica wipes the face of Jesus.
7. Jesus falls the second time.
8. Jesus consoles the women of Jerusalem.
9. Jesus falls the third time.
10. Jesus is stripped of his garments.
11. Jesus is nailed to the cross.
12. Jesus dies on the cross.
13. Jesus is taken down from the cross.
14. Jesus is laid in the tomb.

Some churches also include a fifteenth station, the resurrection of the Lord.

NOVENAS

The novena consists of the recitation of certain prayers over a period of nine days. The symbolism of nine days refers to the time Mary and the apostles spent in prayer between Jesus' ascension into heaven and Pentecost.

Many novenas are dedicated to Mary or to a saint with the faith and hope that she or he will intercede for the one making the novena. Novenas to Saint Jude, Saint Anthony, Our Lady of Perpetual Help, and Our Lady of Lourdes remain popular in the Church today.

LITURGY OF THE HOURS

The Liturgy of the Hours is part of the official, public prayer of the Church. Along with the celebration of the sacraments, the recitation of the Liturgy of the Hours, or Divine Office (office means "duty" or "obligation"), allows for constant praise and thanksgiving to God throughout the day and night.

The Liturgy of the Hours consists of five major divisions:

1. An hour of readings
2. Morning praises
3. Midday prayers
4. Vespers (evening prayers)
5. Compline (a short night prayer)

Scriptural prayer, especially the psalms, is at the heart of the Liturgy of the Hours. Each day follows a separate pattern of prayer with themes closely tied in with the liturgical year and feasts of the saints.

THE DIVINE PRAISES

These praises are traditionally recited after the benediction of the Blessed Sacrament.

Blessed be God.
Blessed be his holy name.
Blessed be Jesus Christ, true God and true man.
Blessed be the name of Jesus.
Blessed be his most Sacred Heart.
Blessed be his most Precious Blood.
Blessed be Jesus in the most holy sacrament of the altar.
Blessed be the Holy Spirit, the Paraclete.
Blessed be the great Mother of God, Mary most holy.
Blessed be her holy and Immaculate Conception.
Blessed be her glorious Assumption.
Blessed be the name of Mary, Virgin and Mother.
Blessed be Saint Joseph, her most chaste spouse.
Blessed be God in his angels and his saints.

I. PRAYERS

SIGN OF THE CROSS

In the name of the Father,
and of the Son,
and of the Holy Spirit. Amen.

OUR FATHER

Our Father
who art in heaven,
hallowed be thy name.
Thy kingdom come;
thy will be done on earth as it is in
heaven.
Give us this day our daily bread
and forgive us our trespasses
as we forgive those who trespass
against us.
And lead us not into temptation,
but deliver us from evil.
Amen.

GLORY BE

Glory be to the Father
and to the Son
and to the Holy Spirit,
as it was in the beginning,
is now,
and ever shall be,
world without end. Amen.

HAIL MARY

Hail Mary, full of grace,
the Lord is with thee.
Blessed art thou among women
and blessed is the fruit of thy womb,
Jesus.
Holy Mary, Mother of God,
pray for us sinners now
and at the hour of our death. Amen.

MEMORARE

Remember, O most gracious Virgin
Mary,
that never was it known
that anyone who fled to your protection,
implored your help,
or sought your intercession was left
unaided.
Inspired by this confidence,
I fly unto you,
O virgin of virgins, my mother,
To you I come, before you I stand,
sinful and sorrowful.
O Mother of the word incarnate,
despise not my petitions,
but in your mercy hear and answer
me. Amen.

HAIL, HOLY QUEEN

Hail, holy Queen, Mother of Mercy,
our life, our sweetness and our hope!
To you do we cry,
poor banished children of Eve;
to you do we send up our sighs,
mourning and weeping in this valley
of tears.
Turn then, O most gracious advocate,
your eyes of mercy toward us,
and after this exile,
show us the blessed fruit of your
womb, Jesus.
O clement, O loving, O sweet Virgin Mary.
V. Pray for us, O holy mother of God.
R. that we may be made worthy of the promises of Christ. Amen.

THE ANGELUS

V. The angel spoke God's message to Mary.

R. And she conceived by the Holy Spirit.

Hail Mary . . .

V. Behold the handmaid of the Lord.

R. May it be done unto me according to your word.

Hail Mary . . .

V. And the Word was made flesh.

R. And dwelled among us.

Hail Mary . . .

V. Pray for us, O holy mother of God.

R. That we may be made worthy of the promises of Christ.

Let us pray: We beseech you, O Lord, to pour out your grace into our hearts. By the message of an angel we have learned of the incarnation of Christ, your son; lead us by his passion and cross, to the glory of the resurrection. Through the same Christ our Lord. Amen.

REGINA CAELI

Queen of heaven, rejoice, alleluia. The Son you merited to bear, alleluia, has risen as he said, alleluia. Pray to God for us, alleluia.

V. Rejoice and be glad, O Virgin Mary, alleluia.

R. For the Lord has truly risen, alleluia.

Let us pray.

God of life, you have given joy to the world by the resurrection of your son, our Lord Jesus Christ. Through the prayers of his mother, the Virgin Mary, bring us to the happiness of eternal life. We ask this through Christ our Lord. Amen.

GRACE AT MEALS

Before Meals

Bless us, O Lord, and these your gifts, which we are about to receive from your bounty, through Christ our Lord. Amen.

After Meals

We give you thanks, almighty God, for these and all the gifts which we have received from your goodness through Christ our Lord. Amen.

GUARDIAN ANGEL PRAYER

Angel of God, my guardian dear, to whom God's love entrust me here, ever this day be at my side, to light and guard, to rule and guide. Amen.

PRAYER FOR THE FAITHFUL DEPARTED

Eternal rest grant unto them, O Lord.

R: And let perpetual light shine upon them. May their souls and the souls of all faithful departed, through the mercy of God, rest in peace.

R: Amen.

MORNING OFFERING

O Jesus, through the immaculate heart of Mary, I offer you my prayers, works, joys, and sufferings of this day in union with the holy sacrifice of the Mass throughout the world. I offer them for all the intentions of your Sacred Heart: the salvation of souls, reparation for sin, the reunion of all Christians. I offer them for the intentions of our bishops and all members of the apostleship of prayer and in particular for those recommended by your Holy Father this month. Amen.

ACT OF FAITH

O God,
I firmly believe all the truths that you
have revealed
and that you teach us through your
Church,
for you are truth itself
and can neither deceive nor be
deceived.
Amen.

ACT OF HOPE

O God,
I hope with complete trust that you
will give me,
through the merits of Jesus Christ, all
necessary grace in this world
and everlasting life in the world to
come,
for this is what you have promised
and you always keep your promises.
Amen.

ACT OF LOVE

O my God, I love you above all things, with
my whole heart and soul, because you are
all good and worthy of all my love. I love my
neighbor as myself for the love of you. I forgive all who have injured me, and I ask pardon of all whom I have injured. Amen.

PRAYER FOR PEACE
(SAINT FRANCIS OF ASSISI)

Lord, make me an instrument of your
peace.
Where there is hatred, let me sow
love;
where there is injury, pardon;
where there is doubt, faith;
where there is despair, hope;
where there is darkness, light;
where there is sadness, joy.
O Divine Master,
grant that I may not seek so much to
be consoled as to console;
to be understood, as to understand,
to be loved, as to love.
For it is in giving that we receive,
it is in pardoning that we are par-
doned,
and it is in dying that we are born to
eternal life.

GLOSSARY

Abba—An Aramaic term of endearment that means "papa" or "dada." Jesus taught us that God is a loving and compassionate Father (Abba) whom we can and should approach with faith and trust.

abortion—The deliberate killing of unborn human life by means of medical or surgical procedures. Direct abortion is seriously wrong because it is an unjustified attack on innocent human life.

affirmative action—The policy and programs established to correct past discrimination in educational and employment opportunities directed against women, blacks, and members of other minorities.

ageism—Prejudice exhibited against the elderly because of their age.

anti-Semitism—Prejudice manifested in word or deed against people of Jewish origin.

apartheid—The long-term policy in South Africa of strict racial segregation and economic and political discrimination against nonwhites.

cardinal virtues—"Hinge" virtues that enable us to live moral lives. Prudence is right reason in action, good common sense to discern the good and the ways to achieve it. Fortitude is the courage to persist in doing the good. Temperance regulates our sensual appetites. Justice enables us to render to God and each person what is their due.

The Catholic Worker—The newspaper and movement founded by Dorothy Day and Peter Maurin to make public the social teaching of the Church

Chicano—A person of Mexican American heritage.

common good—The sum of the spiritual, material, and social conditions needed for a person to achieve full human dignity.

commutative justice—Calls for fairness in exchanges between individuals and private groups.

conscientious objector—A person who refuses to participate in a war out of reasons of conscience either because a given war is unjust or because of religious convictions against all war.

consistent ethic of life—The viewpoint of Catholic social teaching that calls for the respect of all human life, especially the most defenseless in our midst, a "seamless garment" of protection, womb to tomb.

covenant—An open-ended contract of love between God and his people. It involves promises and the duty to be faithful to the promises.

dignity—The quality or state of being worthy, honored, or esteemed. Humans possess dignity because we are made in God's image and likeness, endowed with a spiritual soul. Therefore, we are valuable, worthy of honor and esteem, simply because we are so precious in God's eyes.

distributive justice—Sees to the just distribution of the goods of creation that God intends for all to use and share.

ecology—The science that studies the relationship between organisms and their environment.

encyclical—A pastoral papal letter sent to the whole Church, and sometimes to all people, on some important aspect of Church teaching.

euthanasia—"An act or omission which of itself and by intention causes death, with the purpose of eliminating all suffering" (The Gospel of Life, §65). Euthanasia is a violation of the fifth commandment which forbids killing; it can never be justified.

free will—"The power, rooted in reason and will, . . . to perform deliberate actions on one's own responsibility" [CCC, 1731].

global warming—A trend caused by the greenhouse effect in which the world's average temperature is expected to rise 1 to 3.5 degrees Celsius by 2100.

globalization—"The process whereby the world's goods, communications, and peoples are more fully integrated, accessible, and interdependent" (Strangers No Longer, p. 51).

greenhouse effect—A phenomenon whereby the earth's atmosphere traps solar radiation.

immigrant—A person who leaves one country to take up permanent residence in another country. (An "undocumented" immigrant is in a country without the permission of that country's government.)

just wage—At minimum, a wage high enough to meet food, clothing, and shelter needs, and to provide for transportation, education, and some form of recreation.

just-war tradition—A set of principles developed through the centuries by the Church that clearly outlines when a nation may ethically participate in a war. It also sets clear limits on armed force once a war is engaged.

legal justice—Regulates citizens' obligations to the larger society and government.

migrant—One who moves within one's country or between nations, often in search of work.

natural law—God's plan written into the way He made things. The light of understanding infused in us by God, whereby we understand what must be done and what must be avoided.

objective dimension of work—The product or outcome of work.

original sin—The state or condition of sin into which all generations of people are born since the time of Adam and Eve's turning away from God.

pacifist—Someone who opposes all war as a means of settling disputes.

Peace on Earth (Pacem in Terris)—An important social justice encyclical written by Pope John XXIII in 1963 that lists important human rights.

pornography—The depiction of sexual acts or nudity with the purpose of gratifying lustful desires. Pornography violates the privacy of the human body and debases human dignity by turning people into objects to be used rather than persons to be respected.

poverty—From a Latin word paupertas, it literally translates as pauper, or poor.

preferential option for the poor—A preferential love for the poor that allows one to see things from the perspective of the poor and powerless and to assess lifestyle, policies, and social institutions in terms of their impact on the poor. This choice for the poor follows the example of Jesus who sided with those most in need.

prejudice—An unsubstantiated or preformed judgment about an individual or group.

principle of proportionality—The rule that requires the damage inflicted and the costs incurred in a war (or a particular action in a war) to be commensurate with the good expected.

racism—"Awareness of the biologically determined superiority of one's own race or ethnic group with respect to others" (The Church and Racism, §2).

rainforest—A dense tropical forest with an annual rainfall of at least 100 inches.

refugee—A person who leaves his or her country and is unwilling to return because of fear of religious, racial, ethnic, political, or some other form of persecution.

Rerum Novarum—The seminal social justice encyclical written by Pope Leo XIII in 1891 to address economic and other injustices plaguing the late-19th century world. It began the Church's social teaching in the modern era.

rights—Claims we can make on each other and on society to guarantee attaining certain basic minimum conditions to live a truly human life.

scapegoating—Blaming an individual or group for something that the individual or group is not responsible for. Blaming another person or group for societal problems because of that person's group identity.

sexism—The wrong opinion that one sex is superior to the other by the very nature of things, leading typically to prejudice against women.

social justice doctrine—The body of Church doctrine that applies Jesus' gospel to our life together, that is, to society, its institutions, and its economic and political structures.

social justice—Applies the gospel of Jesus Christ to society's structures, systems, and laws so people's rights are guaranteed. Also known as contributive justice, it ensures that persons have a fair say in social, economic, and political institutions, thus fulfilling their duty to give back to the larger community.

society—"A group of persons bound together organically by a principle of unity that goes beyond each one of them" (CCC, 1880).

solidarity—The virtue of social charity, friendship, and responsible sharing whereby we recognize our interdependence on others and that we are all brothers and sisters of one family under a loving Father.

stereotype—An oversimplified generalization.

subjective dimension of work—The human person and his or her involvement in work.

subsidiarity—The principle of Catholic social teaching that holds that a higher unit of society should not do what a lower unit can do as well (or better).

theological virtues—God-given powers that direct us to our loving, Triune God. Faith enables us to believe all that God has revealed, or His Church proposes for belief, because He is truth itself. Hope empowers us to trust in God's promises. Charity enables us to love God above all things and our neighbor as ourselves out of love of God.

virtue—"Firm attitudes, stable dispositions, and habitual perfections of the intellect and will that govern our actions, order our passions, and guide our conduct according to reason and faith" (CCC, 1804).

work—Sustained effort with the intent to produce or accomplish something.

INDEX

A

Abba, 16, 18
Abortion, 77–83
Abraham, 35
Adoption, 80–81
Affirmative action, 125–26, 129
African Americans, 126–29
Ageism, 110
Always Our Children, 105–106
Ambrose, Saint, 38
Anti-Semitism, 113–14
Apartheid, 128
Apostles, 259
Aquinas, Thomas, Saint, 31, 89–90
Aristotle, 16
Augustine of Hippo, Saint, 16, 38; and euthanasia, 87

B

Beatitudes, 36–37, 262
Bernardin, Joseph, 94
Bible, 253–255; and justice, 35–38; on peace 179–80; and poverty, 151–53
Bread for the World Institute, 157
Brothers and Sisters to Us, 126–31, 138

C

Capital punishment, 89–92
Cardinal virtues, 31, 262. *See also individual virtues*
Castro, Fidel, 132
Catholic Campaign for Human Development, 164
Catholic Charities, 39, 164
Catholic Relief Services, 61, 62, 164
Catholic social teaching, 263; on justice, 38–43; principles of, 13–15

Catholic Worker, The, 166–67
Challenge of Peace, The, 176, 186-187, 190, 192–93
Charity, 32
Charter of the Rights of the Family, 67-68
Chavez, Cesar, 45
Chesterson, G. K., 16
Chicanos, 130–31
Children, exploitation of, 204–205
Christians: and feeding the hungry, 155-156; and peace, 175–79; and service to others, 160-162
Christifideles Laici, 18
Chrysostom, John, Saint, 160
Church: history of, 256–62; marks of, 258
Church in the Modern World, The: and abortion, 77–78; and creation, 243; and discrimination, 111–12; and hunger, 154; and just wage, 211–12; and justice, 33; and peace, 176, 187-188, 196; and society, 56; and solidarity, 60; and unions, 216
Civil rights laws, 58
Common good, 13; elements of, 15, 59-63; promotion of, 60; and respect, 60
Community, 14
Conscientious objector, 183
Consumerism, 150
Covenant, 35
Creation: and ecological crisis, 230–31, 234–40; and ecology, 234–35; and stewardship of, 239–43
Crime, 89–92

D

Day, Dorothy, 166–67

Death: and compassion, 87; culture of, 77–78
Death penalty. *See* Capital punishment
Declaration of Euthanasia, 87
Devotions, 268–69
Didache, 79
Dignity: definition of, 12; human, 13–14; of work, 15
Discrimination, 109–12
Donne, John, 55
Drexel, Katherine, Saint, 139

E

Ecological crisis, 230–31; Christian response to, 240–43; scope of, 234–39
Ecological Crisis, The, 230, 234, 241
Ecology, 232–34
Economic Justice for All: and peace, 192–96; and poverty, 62, 151, 160–162, 164; and social justice, 34; and society, 57; and work, 208, 211, 212, 215, 216
Economy, 160–62
Ecumenical councils, 261-62
Employment, right to, 210–11
Encyclical, definition of, 20
Environment. *See* Ecological Crisis
Equality, 15
Eucharist, 11, 159
Euthanasia, 76, 85–88, 110
Evangelization in the Modern World, 60
Everyday Christianity, 204, 206
Extinction, 238-39

F

Faith, 32
Family, 14, 67–68
Forgiveness: and abortion,

81–82; and peace, 191
Fortitude, 31
Francis of Assisi, Saint, 38, 244–245, 247–249
Frederick the Great, 16
Free will, 10, 17

G

Gandhi, Mohandas, 102, 183
Global warming, 234, 235, 236–37
Globalization, 46
God: attributes of, 251; and justice, 35; love of, 18, 37, 152-53
Gospel of Life, The, 75; and abortion, 78–79, 80, 82; and ageism, 110; and capital punishment, 89, 90; and dignity, 65, 94–95; and euthanasia, 85, 87–88; and Jesus, 18
Government: and common good, 59–60; and culture of death, 76, 78, 80; just, 57; responsibilities of, 65–66, 156; role of, 57
Greenhouse effect, 234, 235, 236–37

H

Haile, Berard, 135
Harvest of Justice, The, 176–77, 178, 185, 192–96
Health care, 217–218
Heilbroner, Robert, 146
Hinge virtues. *See* Cardinal virtues
Hippocratic oath, 78
Hispanic Americans, 130–33
Holy Spirit, 251-252
Homosexuality, 105–106
Hope, 32
Humans: and compassion, 18; dignity of, 13–14, 76–92; and ecological crisis, 234–39, and ecology,

232–33, 240–43; and Jesus, 18–19; and love, 19; made in God's image, 16–17, 56; responsibilities of, 65–66; rights of, 20–23; social nature of, 55–56; view of, 16–19
Hunger, 154–59; causes of, 155; and the Eucharist, 159; and government responsibilities, 155–156; response to 155–56

I

Ignatius of Loyola, Saint, prayer of, 51
Immigrant, 46–47
Immigration, 46–48, 130–32, 215
Inalienable rights. *See* Rights, types of
Industrialization, and ecological crisis, 234
Inviolable right. *See* Rights, types of
Irenaeus, Saint, 19

J

Jägerstätter, Franz, 197
Jefferson, Thomas, 78
Jesus, 251–53; and being human, 18–19; and capital punishment, 89; and ecological crisis, 233; and example to serve, 37–38; as God's new covenant, 36; and hunger, 159; and justice, 36; and love, 36–37, 102; parables of, 37, 152–53; and the poor, 62, 151, 152; and racism, 137; and work, 209
John XXIII, 20, 26, 212, 215
John Paul II: and abortion, 77–78; and ageism, 110; on being created in God's image, 18; on

consumerism, 150; and ecological crisis, 232, 234, 236, 243; and human rights, 22; and hunger, 156; and jubilee year, 205–206; and peace, 175, 177, 189, 191–92, 195; on solidarity, 15, 61; and work, 206–11, 214, 219
Jubilee year, 151, 205–206
Judaism, 253
Just wage, 163, 210, 211–12
Just war. *See* War
Justice: and the Bible, 35–38; Catholic social teaching on, 38–43; as essential, 41; types of, 33–34; as a virtue, 32–34
Justice in the World, 41
Justification, 37

K

King, Martin Luther, Jr., 32, 127, 183

L

de Las Casas, Bartolome, 135
Leo XIII, 11, 40, 212
Life: dignity of, 76, 94–96; and abortion, 77–82; and capital punishment, 89–92; and ecological crisis, 234, 240–41; and euthanasia, 85–88; and stem cell research, 83–85; right to, 77
Lincoln, Abraham, 174
Liturgy, and sacraments, 264–66
Love, 18, 132; of God, 18, 37, 152; and Jesus, 36–37, 102

M

Malnutrition, 10, 154
de Marillac, Louise, Saint, 39
Marx, Karl, 40
Marxism, 40

Mary, 38, 266–67, 268, 269, 270, 271
Mercy, works of, 160–61
Merton, Thomas, 190
Migrant, 47
Molla, Gianna Beretta, Saint, 93–94
Moses, 35–36
Mother Teresa, 24–25

N

Native Americans, 134–36
Natural law, 20, 64–65
New Testament: and justice, 36–38; and the poor, 152–53

O

Old Testament: and justice, 35–36; and the poor, 151–52
On Christianity and Social Progress, 56
On Human Work, 206–09, 210–14, 219
On Reconstructing the Social Order, 34, 57
On Social Concern, 15, 41; and consumerism, 150; and ecological crisis, 232; and peace, 194, 196; and solidarity, 61
On the Hundredth Anniversary of "Rerum Novarum": and family, 67; and peace, 177, 191, 192, 195; and rights, 22; and solidarity, 156; and work, 216
Oppenheim, James, 16
Original sin, 10

P

Pacem in Terris. See Peace on Earth
Pacifism, 183, 187–88

Papacy, 258, 260. *See also individual names*
Parks, Rosa, 127–28
Pastoral Constitution on the Church in the Modern World, 59
Paul, Saint: and peacemaking, 176; and racism, 137; and work, 208
de Paul, Vincent, Saint, 38-39
Paul III, 135
Paul VI, 175
Peace, 174, 190–96; and Christians, 175–79; and forgiveness, 191; and Scripture, 179–80; and violence, 181–84; and war, 185–89
Peace on Earth, 20, 26
Pius XI: on charity and justice, 34; on subsidiarity, 57
Pollution. *See* Ecological Crisis
Pope. *See individual names*
Population, 234, 242
Pornography, 22–23
Poverty: and Bible, 151–53; and child labor, 204–205; Christian response to, 160–62; and consumerism, 63; and ecological crisis, 241–42; and education, 163; elimination of, 162–65; and just wage, 211–12; materialism, 148–49; and peace, 191–92, 194–95; scourge of, 146; types of, 147–49
Prayer: examples of, 270–72; and peacemaking, 177
Preferential option for the poor, 15, 60, 62–63, 160–62
Prejudice, 103–107, 108–18. *See also* Racism
Pro life, 79–83
Property, 208
Prophets, 36
Prudence, 31

Q

Quarles, Francis, 16

R

Racism, 124, 137–38; against African Americans, 126–29; against Hispanic Americans, 130–33; against Native Americans, 134–36; institutional, 125–26. *See also* Prejudice
Rainforest, 235
Red Cross, 61
Refugee, 47
Religion, freedom of, 68
Renewing the Earth, 232, 240–42
Rerum Novarum, 40, 212
Respect, 60
Rest, 204, 214
Revelation: and creation, 230, 240; and natural law, 64
Rights: definition of, 14; of humans, 20–22; types of, 20; of workers, 15
Right to die, 88
Right to life, 14, 20
Roe v. Wade, 10, 78

S

Sabbath. *See* Rest
Sabbatical year, 151
Sacraments, 11; and liturgy, 264–66
Safety, 214–15
Saints, 267–68
Second Vatican Council, 40, 59; and abortion, 77–78; on hunger, 154
Segregation, 127, 134
Sermon on the Mount, 36–37
Seton, Elizabeth Ann, Saint, 39

Sex, 80–81

Sexism. *See* Discrimination

Shakespeare, William, 16

Sharing Catholic Social Teaching, 13–15

Sin, 265; and abortion, 79; and ecological crisis, 232–33; and prejudice, 105, 116–17

Slavery, 127

Social justice: Catholic teaching on, 11; doctrine of, 12; key documents on, 42–43

Social Security, 223–24

Society: responsibilities of, 65–66; rules for, 56; types of, 56

Solidarity, 15, 60–61; call to, 47; and hunger, 156; and personal action, 61

Stations of the Cross, 269

Statement on Capital Punishment, 90, 91

Stem cell research, 83–85

Stereotype, 105–107

Stewardship, 15, 239–243

Story of a Soul, 69

Strangers No Longer, 48

Strikes, 216

Subsidiarity, 15, 156; principles of, 57–59

Suffering, 85–86

T

Teresa of Avila, Saint, 12

Temperance, 31

Ten Commandments, 36, 64, 262

Terrorism, 188–89, 193–94

Theological virtues, 32, 264. *See also individual virtues*

Thérèse of Lisieux Saint, 69–70

Tradition, 253–57

Trinity, 12, 251–53

U

Unions, 215–16

United Nations, 192–93

Universal rights. *See* Rights, types of

Urban VIII, 135

V

Vanier, Jean, 118

Violence, 10; and capital punishment, 91; and peace, 181–84; and prejudice, 112–13

Virtues: cardinal, 31, 262; and peace making, 177; theological, 32, 262; types of, 31–32. *See also individual virtues*

W

Walesa, Lech, 222–23

War, 185–89; causes of, 178–79; and weapons, 195–96

Weisel, Elie, 77

Welcoming the Stranger Among Us, 47

Welfare, 163, 165

Wheel of justice, 13–15

Work, 204–206, 218–21; Christian view of, 206–209; good, 263; and health care, 217–18; and just wage, 163, 211–12; right to, 210–11; and safety, 214–15; and unions, 215–16

Workers: exploitation of, 204–205; and health care, 217–18; rights of, 15, 210–18, 222–23

World Hunger—A Challenge for All, 154, 157

SCRIPTURE INDEX

GENESIS

1:1	229
1—2:4	214
1:11, 20	229
1:26–27	115, 193
1:26–28	16
1:28	206
1:31	229, 232
2:15	232
2:15—3:24	17
2:18	17, 55
3:19	209

EXODUS

| 3:7–8 | 36 |

LEVITICUS

| 26:11–12 | 179 |

PSALMS

| 8:2 | 9 |
| 8:4–7 | 9 |

PROVERBS

| 22:22–23 | 152 |

ISAIAH

| 1:15–17 | 36 |
| 2:2,4 | 180 |

HOSEA

| 4:1–3 | 233 |

AMOS

| 5:24 | 35 |
| 8:4, 10 | 151–52 |

MICAH

| 6:8 | 29, 36 |

ZECHARIAH

| 7:9–10 | 151 |

MATTHEW

4:4	147
5:1–12	36
5:3	148
5:3–10	180
5:9	173, 175
5:21–26	115
5:38–39	89
5:43–48	115
6:1–18	191
6:7–15	115
6:12	193
6:24	153
7:12	101, 115, 153
8:20	152
10:42–44	37
18:21–22	89
20:1–16	37
22:38–39	36
25	15
25:31–40	115
25:31–46	37
25:35–36	63
25:40	19, 60
25:41–43	153
25:45–46	153
26:52	89, 180

MARK

| 6:30–44 | 152 |
| 7:21–23 | 115 |

LUKE

4:18–19	18, 36, 151
6:27	115
6:35–36	177
7:11–17	152
8:3	152
10:29–37	37
10:30–37	153
12:15	153
12:16–21	153
12:33–34	153
12:48	233
15:1–2	115
16:19–31	153
19:11–17	233
23:34	89

JOHN

3:16	18
6:1–13	152
6:35	159
15:9–13	115
15:12	36
15:14–17	115
15:17	32

17:20–21	56
19:23	94
19:23–24	152

Acts
| 2:44–47 | 38 |
| 17:26–29 | 115 |

Romans
1:10,16	53
2:14–15	64
12:2	176

1 Corinthians
| 11:18–34 | 38 |
| 13:2 | 32 |

2 Corinthians
| 8:1–15 | 38 |

Galatians
| 3:28 | 101, 137 |

Philippians
| 2:6–8 | 152 |

Colossians
1:15	18
1:19–20	233
3:23–24	203

2 Thessalonians
| 3:10 | 208 |

Hebrews
| 1:3 | 18 |

James
| 2:15–17 | 145 |
| 3:18 | 175 |

1 John
| 4:8 | 111 |

CATECHISM OF THE CATHOLIC CHURCH INDEX

295–302	232	2297	189
307	232	2302–2317	181
337–354	232	2304	175
397–405	232	2305	176
410–412	232	2307–2309	185
418	232	2312–2314	185
595–598	114	2314–2317	187
1397	161	2317	191
1700–1715	16	2318–2320	77
1731	10, 17	2321	89
1747	79	2322–2323	77
1803	31	2324–2325	85
1803–1845	31	2327–2328	185
1804	31	2327–2330	181
1806	31	2330	185
1807	33	2331–2350	77
1808	31	2354	22
1809	31	2357–2359	105
1814	32	2358	106
1817	32	2393–2395	77
1878–1896	55	2401–2406	241
1880	56	2402–2406	160
1913–1923	65	2411–2412	33
1928	32	2415–2418	240
1929–1938	16	2419–2425	38
1934–1948	111	2423	12
1939–1942	60	2426–2430	162
1941	192	2426–2436	208
1943	55	2427	208, 211
1943–1945	16	2431	210
1948	60	2432	210
1954–1960	64	2435	216
1978–1979	64	2436	211
2196	137	2437–2442	190
2201–2213	67	2443–2448	160
2207	67	2446	160
2234–2236	67	2447	160
2235–2246	65	2450–2454	160
2252	210	2456–2457	240
2255–2256	65	2458–2462	160
2258	77	2459–2461	207
2263–2267	89	2462–2464	160
2267	90	2493	106
2270–2275	77	2596	19
2276	87	2822	137
2276–2283	85		
2288	217		

PHOTO CREDITS

ASSOCIATED PRESS
Page 45, 113, 127, 128, 156, 178, 183, 185, 187, 188, 192, 193, 2239, 205, 222 © *Associated Press*

BRIAN ATKINSON/GLOBAL AWARE
Page 62 © *Brian Atkinson*

CORBIS
Page 10, 11, 21, 38, 40, 46, 54, 57, 58, 65, 78, 86, 91, 103, 109, 123, 139, 149, 152, 177, 181, 191, 211, 241 © *Corbis*

DESIGN PICS
Page 60, 61, 67

THE IMAGE WORKS
Page 102, 174 © *The Image Works Archives*

SKJOLD PHOTOGRAPHS
Page 47 © *Skjold Photography*

THOMAS MERTON CENTER
Page 190. *Photograph of Thomas Merton by John Lyons. Used with permission of the Merton Legacy Trust and the Thomas Merton Center at Bellarmine University.*

PICTUREQUEST
Page 9, 31, 48, 53, 63, 75, 83, 150, 173, 186, 195

VEER
Page 23